Managerial Economics and Operations Research
THIRD EDITION

Managerial Economics
and
Operations Research

Techniques, Applications, Cases

THIRD EDITION

EDITED BY

Edwin Mansfield

UNIVERSITY OF PENNSYLVANIA

W·W·NORTON & COMPANY·INC·*NEW YORK*

Copyright © 1975, 1970, 1966 by W. W. Norton & Company, Inc.
Library of Congress Cataloging in Publication Data
Mansfield, Edwin, ed.
Managerial economics and operations research.
Includes bibliographical references.
1. Managerial economics—Addresses, essays, lectures.
2. Operations research—Addresses, essays, lectures.
I. Title.
HD58.5.M36   1975   658'.001'84   74-11192
ISBN 0-393-05536-1
ISBN 0-393-09297-6 (pbk.)
ALL RIGHTS RESERVED
Published simultaneously in Canada
by George J. McLeod Limited, Toronto
PRINTED IN THE UNITED STATES OF AMERICA

1 2 3 4 5 6 7 8 9 0

To Charity L.

A GREAT WOMAN AND A GREAT HORSE

Contents

Preface

The postwar period has witnessed exciting and important developments in economics and related disciplines, with the invention or adaptation of new techniques and concepts for solving major managerial problems of business firms, government agencies, and other organizations. In the process of extending economic analysis to meet the need for greater precision in the management of the business enterprise, a new field, managerial economics, has emerged. Managerial economics draws upon economic analysis for such concepts as cost, demand, profit, and competition. It attempts to bridge the gap between the purely analytical problems that intrigue many economic theorists and the problems of policy that management must face. It now offers powerful tools and approaches for managerial policy-making.

In recent years, another new field—operations research or management science—has been opened up. Its boundaries are not easy to define. According to one definition, operations research involves "the use of systematic quantitative analysis to aid in the making of management decisions." [1] Emphasis is placed on a scientific approach to decision-making, with considerable reliance on advanced mathematical techniques and a computer-based technology. First used on a sustained and significant scale in connection with military activities during World War II, operations research has spread rapidly throughout American industry, and is now a very important managerial tool.

This book provides an elementary description of important facets of managerial economics, as well as relevant aspects of operations research. Aimed primarily at students of economics

1. Charles Hitch, "Economics and Military Operations Research," *Review of Economics and Statistics,* August 1958, p. 200.

xiii

and business administration with modest training in mathematics, it provides a general introduction to the nature, purpose, and potential usefulness of various concepts and techniques in managerial economics (and operations research) without going far into their technical details. Much published material is available for the advanced student with some mathematical sophistication, but little is available for the beginner. Hopefully, this book will help to fill the gap.

The papers in Part One explore the nature of the decision-making process. The papers in Part Two deal mainly with costs and production, while those in Part Three are concerned with profits, demand, and pricing. Part Four takes up capital budgeting and investment, and Part Five deals with business and economic forecasting. In Part Six, linear programming and related techniques are examined in theory and in practice; in Part Seven the focus shifts to decision theory and scheduling techniques. Part Eight deals with game theory, inventory policy, and queuing analysis. The role played by the computer in modern management is considered in Part Nine. Part Ten deals with the use of economics in solving important problems in the public sector of the economy.

In this third edition, I have tried to alter the book's contents in the light of the reactions of the many instructors who have used the book in their courses. The length of the book has been increased considerably, with the result that much more attention is devoted to the detailed application of the techniques of managerial economics to the real-life problems of business firms and of the public sector of the economy. Also, some of the older articles have been removed, new ones have been added, and some have been reprinted in expanded form. About 30 percent of this edition is new. Once again, I want to thank the many teachers and students who have given me (and the book) the benefit of their comments and suggestions.

E. M.

Part One

The Decision-making Process

SINCE managerial economics and operations research deal with decision making, we begin by considering the nature of the decision-making process as it presently exists in most industrial organizations. Alfred P. Sloan describes some of his experiences as a top executive of General Motors and concludes that the great difference in decision-making between today and yesterday "is what might be referred to as the necessity of the scientific approach, the diminution of operation by hunches; this affects men, tools, and methods." Herbert Simon then discusses the various phases of the decision-making process, which he characterizes as: finding occasions for making a decision, finding possible courses of action, and choosing among courses of action.

In the next article, Eugene Grant points out that many managerial decisions are made improperly because the decision-maker fails to reason clearly about the costs and benefits of alternative courses of action. To arrive at a realistic cost figure for decision-making, it is necessary to define the alternatives clearly; otherwise some costs that are common to both alternatives may influence the choice. Grant notes two important corollaries of this: average and marginal costs should not be confused, and "sunk costs are sunk." The concluding paper in this part is Parkinson's Law. This famous, and amusing, law is based on the proposition that "work expands so as to fill the time available for its completion." Although Parkinson is writing about the British bureaucracy, his observations also provide interesting insights into the decision-making process and the growth of bureaucracies in large industrial organizations.

Industrial Decision-making:
Old Style and New

ALFRED P. SLOAN

One of America's leading industrialists,
Alfred P. Sloan was president of General
Motors from 1923 to 1937 and chairman of
its board of directors from 1937 to 1956.
This short piece is taken from his book,
Adventures of a White-Collar Worker.

[When I was vice-president of General Motors and Mr. Durant was president,] I was constantly amazed by his daring way of making decisions. My business experience had convinced me facts are precious things, to be eagerly sought and treated with respect. But Mr. Durant would proceed on a course of action guided solely, as far as I could tell, by some intuitive flash of brilliance. He never felt obliged to make an engineering hunt for facts. Yet at times he was astoundingly correct in his judgments.

One legend concerning him goes back to 1912, when a gathering of automobile manufacturers pooled guesses on the next year's production, each man dropping his slip of paper into a derby hat. That year 378,000 cars had been made. Mr. Durant guessed that in the next year they would manufacture half a million cars.

The others gasped. They said, "People can't buy that many

cars. Our industry will be ruined by such overproduction before
it really gets started."

Mr. Durant mildly rebuked them, saying, "Gentlemen, you
don't realize the purchasing power of the American people. I
look forward to the time we'll make and sell one million cars a
year."

Those men thought he was being fantastic. Actually, his vision
was clear. In 1929 the industry was to make, and sell, 5,621,000
automobiles. However, this example of Mr. Durant's vision does
not alter the fact that many costly errors would have been
avoided had his practice been to base decisions on a comprehensive analysis of all facts and circumstances. He was invariably optimistic. It was easy to be optimistic, though, if you had
been in a position to observe the booming growth of Detroit,
Flint, and other places where cars were being made; and Durant
had seen all of it.* * *

Although I had important responsibilities under Mr. Durant,
our methods of approaching operating problems were entirely
different. But I liked him even when I disagreed with him.
Durant's integrity? Unblemished. Work? He was a prodigious
worker. Devotion to General Motors? Why, it was his baby!
He would have made any sacrifice for it, and he did make for
it almost the ultimate sacrifice. But the question constantly in
my mind was whether the potential industrial force under the
General Motors emblem could be realized by the same boldness
and daring that had been needed to enlist the units of that force.
General Motors had become too big to be a one-man show. It
was already far too complicated. The future required something
more than an individual's genius. In any company I would be
the first to say that William C. Durant was a genius. But General Motors justified the most competent executive group that
could possibly be brought together.

In bringing General Motors into existence, Mr. Durant had
operated as a dictator. But such an institution could not grow
into a successful organization under a dictatorship. Dictatorship
is the most effective way of administration, provided the dictator
knows the complete answers to all questions. But he never does
and never will. That is why dictatorships eventually fail. If

General Motors were to capitalize its wonderful opportunity, it would have to be guided by an organization of intellects. A great industrial organization requires the best of many minds.* * *

After forty years of experience in American industry, I would say that my concept of the management scheme of a great industrial organization, simply expressed, is to divide it into as many parts as consistently can be done, place in charge of each part the most capable executive that can be found, develop a system of coordination so that each part may strengthen and support each other part; thus not only welding all parts together in the common interests of a joint enterprise, but importantly developing ability and initiative through the instrumentalities of responsibility and ambition—developing men and giving them an opportunity to exercise their talents, both in their own interests as well as in that of the business.

To formalize this scheme, I worked out what we speak of in industry as an organization chart. It shows how the business functions from the standpoint of the relationship of the different units, one to another, as well as the authority delegated to the executives, also in relation to one another. I grouped together those operations which had a common relationship, and I placed over each such group for coordinating purposes what I termed a Group Executive. These group executives were the only ones that reported to me. Then I developed a General Staff similar in name and purpose to what exists in the army. The general staff was on a functional basis: engineering, distribution, legal, financial affairs, and so on. Each of these functions was presided over by a vice-president, the purpose being twofold: first, to perform those functions that could be done more effectively by one activity in the interests of the whole; and second, to coordinate the functional activities of the different operating units as well as to promote their effectiveness. In the General Motors scheme, for instance, the vice-president in charge of sales is a coordinating executive. He has a staff at his command. His contribution is in developing better and more advanced policies of distribution technique through research and in other ways.

He cooperates with the sales departments of the different operating units. But he has no direct authority over their operations; that exists exclusively in the chief executive of the operation itself.

There is no need of repeating the story of how Chevrolet grew and grew, until it gained world leadership among the motorcars in the low-priced field, and how it has successfully maintained that leadership.

As I proudly make that observation there comes into my mind a rather interesting incident.

At the time Mr. du Pont became president, someone had the idea of having a survey made of the General Motors properties, with recommendations as to what might be done in the way of a reconstruction program. The job was entrusted to a firm of consulting engineers of high standing. The most illuminating recommendation was that the whole Chevrolet operation should be liquidated. There was no chance to make it a profitable business. We could not hope to compete. I was much upset because I feared the prestige of the authors might overcome our arguments to the contrary. So I went to Mr. du Pont and told him what we thought we might accomplish if we built a good product and sold it aggressively. We urged upon him the fact that many more people always could buy low-priced cars than Cadillacs and even Buicks. That it was an insult to say we could not compete with anyone. It was a case of ability and hard work. He listened most patiently, and finally said, "Forget the report. We will go ahead and see what we can do." Mr. du Pont was always that way. He had the courage of his convictions. Facts were the only things that counted. So Chevrolet was saved and General Motors avoided what would have been a catastrophe.

The great difference in managerial technique between the industry of today as compared with that of yesterday is what might be referred to as the necessity of the scientific approach, the elimination of operation by hunches; this affects men, tools and methods. Many associate the word scientific with physics. But it means much more than that. Scientific management means a constant search for the facts, the true actualities, and their intelligent, unprejudiced analysis. Thus, and in no other way, policies and their administration are determined. I keep saying to the General Motors organization that we are prepared to spend any proper amount of money to get the facts. Only by increased knowledge can we progress, perhaps I had better say survive. That is really research, but few realize that research can and should be just as effectively used in all functional branches of industry as in physics. Research into the problem of distribution, for instance, has paid General Motors big dividends. Again it is the scientific approach. I keep mentioning it because it seems to me the willingness and ability to apply such methods might well determine the extent of success of any enterprise, and the larger the enterprise, the more vital it becomes. I had thought much about all this as an executive working under Mr. Durant; hence it was natural, as chief executive of the corporation, that I should turn to that type of managerial approach. The answer would be found in the facts.

The Decision-making Process

HERBERT A. SIMON

Herbert A. Simon is Associate Dean of the Graduate School of Industrial Administration at Carnegie Institute of Technology. The following paper comes from his book, The New Science of Managerial Decision Making, *published in 1960.*

Decision making comprises three principal phases: finding occasions for making a decision; finding possible courses of action; and choosing among courses of action. These three activities account for quite different fractions of the time budgets of executives. The fractions vary greatly from one organization level to another and from one executive to another, but we can make some generalizations about them even from casual observation. Executives spend a large fraction of their time surveying the economic, technical, political, and social environment to identify new conditions that call for new actions. They probably spend an even larger fraction of their time, individually or with their associates, seeking to invent, design, and develop possible courses of action for handling situations where a decision is needed. They spend a small fraction of their time in choosing among alternative actions already developed to meet an identified problem and already analysed for their consequences. The three fractions, added together, account for most of what executives do.[1]

1. The way in which these activities take shape within an organization is described in some detail in James G. March and Herbert A. Simon, *Organizations* (New York: John Wiley & Sons, Inc., 1958), chapters 6 and 7.

8

The first phase of the decision-making process—searching the environment for conditions calling for decision—I shall call *intelligence* activity (borrowing the military meaning of intelligence). The second phase—inventing, developing, and analysing possible courses of action—I shall call *design* activity. The third phase—selecting a particular course of action from those available—I shall call *choice* activity.

Let me illustrate these three phases of decision. In the past five years, many companies have reorganized their accounting and other data processing activities in order to make use of large electronic computers. How has this come about? Computers first became available commercially in the early 1950s. Although, in some vague and general sense, company managements were aware that computers existed, few managements had investigated their possible applications with any thoroughness before about 1955. For most companies, the use of computers required no decision before that time because it hadn't been placed on the agenda.[2]

The intelligence activity preceding the introduction of computers tended to come about in one of two ways. Some companies—for example, in the aircraft and atomic energy industries—were burdened with enormously complex computations for engineering design. Because efficiency in computation was a constant problem, and because the design departments were staffed with engineers who could understand, at least in general, the technology of computers, awareness of computers and their potentialities came early to these companies. After computers were already in extensive use for design calculations, businesses with a large number-processing load—insurance companies, accounting departments in large firms, banks—discovered these new devices and began to consider seriously their introduction.

Once it was recognized that computers might have a place in modern business, a major design task had to be carried out in each company before they could be introduced. It is now a commonplace that payrolls can be prepared by computers. Programs in both the general and computer senses for doing this are relatively

2. Richard M. Cyert, Herbert A. Simon, and Donald B. Trow, "Observation of a Business Decision," *Journal of Business*, Vol. 29 (1956), pp. 237-248.

easy to design in any given situation.[3] To develop the first computer programs for preparing payroll, however, was a major research and development project. Few companies having carried their investigations of computers to the point where they had definite plans for their use, failed to install them. Commitment to the new course of action took place gradually as the intelligence and design phases of the decision were going on. The final choice was, in many instances, almost *pro forma*.

Generally speaking, intelligence activity precedes design, and design activity precedes choice. The cycle of phases is, however, far more complex than this sequence suggests. Each phase in making a particular decision is itself a complex decision-making process. The design phase, for example, may call for new intelligence activities; problems at any given level generate subproblems that, in turn, have their intelligence, design, and choice phases, and so on. There are wheels within wheels within wheels. Nevertheless, the three large phases are often clearly discernible as the organizational decision process unfolds. They are closely related to the stages in problem solving first described by John Dewey:

What is the problem?
What are the alternatives?
Which alternative is best?[4]

3. For a good discussion on the use of the computer for such purposes, see Robert H. Gregory and Richard L. Van Horn, *Automatic Data-Processing Systems* (San Francisco: Wadsworth Publishing Company, Inc., 1960).

4. John Dewey, *How We Think* (New York: D. C. Heath & Company, 1910), chapter 8.

The Comparison of Alternatives

EUGENE L. GRANT AND
W. GRANT IRESON

Eugene Grant is Professor of Economics of Engineering at Stanford University. In 1960 he, together with W. Grant Ireson, wrote Principles of Engineering Economy, *from which this article is taken.*

The conduct of a business enterprise requires a successive series of business decisions—decisions between possible alternatives with reference to the future. These decisions are of all degrees of importance, varying from trivial matters to matters of major policy. Some of them are made by intuitive judgments or "hunches" without any conscious attempt to express the alternatives to be compared in commensurable terms, or perhaps even to see clearly what these alternatives really are. Others, however, involve choices between definite alternatives which have been made commensurable by reducing them to terms of money and time. There is much evidence that many of these latter decisions, based on conscious economy studies involving estimates of expected costs (and possibly of revenues) are incorrectly made because of the failure of the estimator to reason clearly about the *differences* between alternatives which involve common elements.

WHAT IS THE "COST" OF AN AUTOMOBILE TRIP?

To illustrate the type of error that may occur if alternatives are not clearly defined, let us consider a familiar and relatively simple situation. Suppose it is desired to estimate the cost of a 600-mile automobile trip.

Bill Jones, who has agreed to "share the cost" of such a proposed trip to be taken in the car of his friend Tom Smith, may calculate merely the expected out-of-pocket expense for gasoline. If Smith's car makes 15 miles to the gallon, and gasoline costs 25 cents per gallon, this is 1⅔ cents per mile. He therefore concludes that the trip will cost $10.

Tom Smith, on the other hand, may estimate all of the costs associated with the ownership and operation of his automobile over its expected life in his service, in order to find an average cost per mile. His car has a first cost of $2,000; he expects to drive it 10,000 miles per year for four years; at the end of this time he hopes to realize $1,000 from its sale. His estimates of total cost might be as follows:

1. Gasoline (40,000 miles at 1⅔¢ per mile)	$ 667
2. Oil and grease	163
3. Tires	150
4. Repairs and maintenance	600
5. Insurance	400
6. Storage (48 months at $5 per month)	240
7. License fees and property taxes	120
8. Total depreciation in 4 years ($2,000-$1,000)	1,000
9. Interest on investment in car	260
(This is based on average interest at 4% per annum.)	———
	$3,600

Divided among 40,000 miles of travel, this is an average cost of 9 cents per mile. At this rate a 600-mile trip appears to cost $54.

The Concept of Cost Must Be Related to Specific Alternatives if It Is to Be a Reliable Guide to Decisions · The second of these two figures for the cost of a given service is 540 percent of the first one. At first glance it would appear that one or the other of the two figures must be wide of its mark. However, a more critical consideration will disclose that the simple question "What is its cost?" with reference to a particular service does not define any mark for the estimator to shoot at.

To use a cost figure as a basis for a decision, it is necessary to have clearly in mind the alternatives between which it is desired to decide. Otherwise, certain costs which, after a clear definition of alternatives, would be recognized as common to both, may be given weight in influencing the choice. It is dangerous to base conclusions on average costs without regard to the specific alternatives which it is intended to compare. The fact that widely differing cost figures may be required for different decisions about a given service may be illustrated by examining some of the different pairs of alternatives which might arise relative to the service of a given automobile.

A Situation in Which It Is Necessary to Estimate Total Cost of Ownership and Operation · If Tom Smith did not own an automobile, and wanted to decide whether or not to purchase one, he might set up the following alternatives for comparison:

Alternative A. Buy a $2,000 car and operate it approximately 10,-000 miles per year for the next four years.

Alternative B. Do not buy a car. Use some others means of transportation as railway, street car, bus, taxicab, his friends' automobiles, and his own legs for part of the contemplated mileage and do without the rest.

If these are the alternatives, all of the items included in his estimate of $3,600 for four years' service are disbursements[1] which will take place if Alternative A is selected, and which will not take place if Alternative B is selected. Thus, the unit cost of 9 cents per mile is relevant to Smith's decision whether or not to own a car. The total cost (which in this case is more important than the average cost per unit of service) of $3,600 should be compared with the costs associated with Alternative B. The higher cost of A, if any, should then be judged in the light of differences which are not reducible to money terms, and in the light of Smith's prospective ability to pay this higher cost.

A Situation in Which It Is Necessary to Estimate the Increment Cost of an Added Service · On the other hand, if Smith has

1. That is, they are all disbursements with the possible exception of interest which might in some cases be a disbursement and in others an income given up—an opportunity foregone.

already purchased an automobile and intends to continue to own and operate it, but is undecided about the annual mileage he will drive, the kinds of alternatives to be compared are quite different. In order to determine the effect on cost of driving extra miles, he might set up two alternatives differing only in annual mileage:

Alternative A. Continue to own the car, driving it 12,500 miles per year for four years before disposing of it.
Alternative B. Continue to own the car, driving it 10,000 miles per year for four years before disposing of it.

In comparing these alternatives, it is necessary to consider the various elements of total cost of ownership which have already been listed, item by item, and estimate the effect on each of a total increase of 10,000 miles in the mileage driven over the life of the car.

Item 1, gasoline, and item 2, oil and grease, may be expected to increase at least in proportion to the increase in mileage. It is likely that the increase would be somewhat more than in direct proportion, because of the tendency of the rate of consumption of fuel and lubricants to increase after a car has been driven a good many miles. Perhaps if the car had averaged 15 miles per gallon in its first 40,000 miles, it might average only 14.3 miles per gallon in the following 10,000 miles. In general, item 3, tires, may be expected to increase in proportion to driving mileage; the actual effect of any proposed increase in mileage will depend on whether it requires the purchase of tires and tubes during the extended period of service. Item 4, repairs and maintenance, will doubtless tend to increase somewhat more than in direct proportion to mileage.

On the other hand item 5, insurance, item 6, storage, and item 7, license fees and property taxes, will be unchanged by an increase in mileage driven in any given time. Because the second-hand price of automobiles seems to depend almost entirely on age and not on miles driven, it is probable that the estimated realizable value after four years will be affected very little, if at all, by an increase of 25 percent in total mileage. If this is the case, neither item 8, total depreciation, nor item 9, interest, will be changed by the contemplated increase in mileage.

Smith might make his estimate of the extra costs associated

with increasing his total expected mileage from 40,000 to 50,000 somewhat as follows:

1.	Gasoline (10,000 miles at 1¾¢ per mile)	$175
2.	Oil and grease	50
3.	Tires	50
4.	Repairs and maintenance	225
		$500

If this estimate is correct, so that an increase of 10,000 miles would increase total costs by $500, then the average cost for each increased mile of travel is 5 cents. This unit increment cost might then be applied to the mileage of any proposed trip, in order to get an idea of how the proposed trip will affect automobile costs in the long run. If this is done for a proposed 600-mile trip, the conclusion will be that this trip ultimately will be responsible for $30 of extra expense.[2]

It will be noted that although this estimated unit increment cost of 5 cents per mile is much less than the estimated 9 cents per mile for ownership and operation over the life of the automobile, it is three times the 1¾ cents per mile estimate that Bill Jones made for the out-of-pocket expense of a short trip. The difference between the 5-cent and the 9-cent figures lies in those costs that are "fixed" by the decision to buy and to continue to own and operate the car, and which are, therefore, independent of its miles of operation. On the other hand, the difference between the 1¾-cent and the 5-cent figures is the difference between short-run and long-run viewpoints. It may well be true that the only out-of-pocket expenses of a 600-mile trip will be for gasoline; nevertheless, the long-run effect of increasing the number of miles of

2. Incidentally, it may be noted that the question of what, in equity, Bill Jones ought to pay when he rides in Tom Smith's car "sharing the cost" of a trip is a question of social conduct which cannot be answered by an economy study. All an economy study can do is to disclose the expected differences between alternatives. Thus, if Tom is making the trip in any event, an economy study might indicate that the least he could afford to accept from Bill without loss would be nothing at all; this is the difference between the alternatives: (*a*) make the trip, taking Bill along, and (*b*) make the trip, leaving Bill behind. On the other hand, if he is making the trip entirely for Bill's convenience, his estimates would appear to indicate that the least he could afford to take for a 600-mile trip is $30; here the alternatives are: (*a*) make the trip with Bill and (*b*) do not make the trip at all.

operation of an automobile will be to increase the expenditures for lubricants, tires, and repairs.

A Situation in Which It is Necessary to Estimate the Costs of Continuing a Machine in Service · If Smith purchases an automobile, and then has misgivings as to whether or not he can afford to continue to own and operate it, the alternatives which present themselves to him are still different, and different cost figures from any we have yet discussed will be required as a basis for his decision. Suppose he sets up the following alternatives for comparison:

Alternative A. Continue to own the car, driving it 10,000 miles per year for four years.

Alternative B. Immediately dispose of the car for the best price obtainable, thereafter using other means of transportation.

In considering the difference between these two alternatives, it is necessary to recognize that the $2,000 purchase price of the car has already been spent, no matter which alternative is chosen. The important question here is not the past outlay for the car, but rather the "best price obtainable" for it if Alternative B is selected.

If Smith's decision had been made, say, in 1947, when it was possible to sell certain makes of new cars in a so-called used car market at several hundred dollars more than the purchase price, this best price obtainable might have been $2,500. If so, Smith's question would obviously have been whether or not he could afford to continue to own an automobile that he could sell for $2,500. On the other hand, if his decision is to be made under the more normal conditions where the resale price of a new automobile is substantially below its purchase price, even though the car may have been driven only a few miles, the best price obtainable might possibly be $1,700. Under these circumstances, Smith's question is whether or not he can afford to continue to own an automobile that he could sell for $1,700. The $300 difference between the $2,000 purchase price and the $1,700 resale price is gone whether he keeps the car or disposes of it at once.

The principles underlying financial calculations to determine whether or not to continue to own a given asset enter into a wide variety of engineering economy studies. . . . At this point it is sufficient to note that there is a substantial difference in principle between a decision whether or not to acquire an asset and a decision whether or not to continue to own and operate that asset once it is acquired. To guide the latter type of decision intelligently, attention must be focused on the net realizable value of the machine (that is, on the prospective net receipts from its sale if it should be disposed of). Once an asset has been purchased, its purchase price has been paid regardless of whether it is continued in service or disposed of at once. This past investment may be thought of as a "sunk cost" that, generally speaking, has no relevance in decisions for the future.

COMPARING ALTERNATIVES IN BUSINESS SITUATIONS

These examples from the familiar situation of automobile ownership have illustrated the necessity for recognizing definite alternatives to be compared before using cost as a basis for decisions. No doubt the different kinds of relevant "costs" which should be considered in automobile ownership and operation are recognized in their qualitative aspects by many automobile owners. However, even in these relatively simple situations which have been discussed, it will be noted that in order to express differences quantitatively we were obliged to make assumptions which, in order to be definite, were somewhat arbitrary. For instance, in order to estimate increment costs per mile of operation, we found it necessary to assume two definite total mileages, and to assume that the four-year period of ownership would be unchanged by a change in the total miles of operation.

In industry, the circumstances in which comparisons are made are likely to be more involved. The machines and structures which are the subjects of engineering economy studies are generally parts of a complex plant, and this complexity may create difficulties in differentiating the effects of alternatives. As has been stated, industrialists are often misled as to the costs which are relevant to particular decisions by failure to define alternatives clearly. In industrial situations, even more than in the automobile cost illustration, it is necessary to make definite assumptions in order to have a basis for decisions.

Irreducible Data in Comparing Alternatives · In the case of the alternatives involving Tom Smith's decision whether or not to purchase a car, we noted briefly that there would be certain advantages and certain hazards incident to the ownership of an automobile which could not be reduced to money terms, but which, nevertheless, would have considerable influence on Smith's choice.

This is characteristic of many economy studies. Although the reduction of units which would otherwise be incommensurable (for example, tons of coal, pounds of structural steel, barrels of cement, gallons of oil, kilowatt-hours of electric energy, hours of skilled machinists' labor, hours of common labor) to terms of money and time is essential to all business decisions which are not made entirely on "hunch," some differences between alternatives will generally remain which cannot be reduced to money terms. In an economy study, it is as much a part of the estimator's duty to note these irreducibles as it is to predict the money receipts and disbursements at various dates. The final decision must give weight to the irreducible differences, as well as to the money differences.

Differences Between Alternatives Are in the Future · If it is recognized that only those matters which are different as between two alternatives are relevant to their comparison, it should be obvious that everything that has happened in the past is irrelevant, except as it may help in the prediction of the future. Whatever has already happened is past and gone, regardless of which of two future alternatives is selected. This implies, among other things, that apportionments against future times of expenditures already past should not be included in economy studies. It also implies that economy studies are based on forecasts, and that their conclusions are dependent on predictions of future events, predictions which are either conscious forecasts or implied ones.

The Limitations of Accounting as a Basis for Estimates in Economy Studies · Generally speaking, the accounts of an enterprise constitute the source of information which has the greatest potential value in making estimates for economy studies. Nevertheless, the uncritical use of accounting figures is responsible for many errors in such estimates. There are a number of important differences between the point of view of accounting and that which should be taken in an economy study.

Accounting involves a recording of past receipts and expenditures. It deals only with what happened regarding policies actually followed and is not concerned with alternatives that might have been followed; it is concerned more with average costs than with differences in cost. It involves apportionment of past costs against future periods of time, and apportionment of joint costs between various services or products. It does not involve consideration of the time value of money.

Engineering economy, on the other hand, always involves alternatives; it deals with prospective differences between future alternatives. It is concerned with differences between costs rather than apportionments of costs. It does involve consideration of the time value of money.

Parkinson's Law

C. NORTHCOTE PARKINSON

C. Northcote Parkinson is Raffles Professor of History at the University of Singapore. This article first appeared in the Economist *in November 1955.*

It is a commonplace observation that work expands so as to fill the time available for its completion. Thus, an elderly lady of leisure can spend an entire day in writing and dispatching a postcard to her niece at Bognor Regis. An hour will be spent in finding the postcard, another in hunting for spectacles, half-an-hour in a search for the address, an hour and a quarter in composition, and twenty minutes in deciding whether or not to take an umbrella when going to the pillar-box in the next street. The total effort which would occupy a busy man for three minutes all told may in this fashion leave another person prostrate after a day of doubt, anxiety and toil.

Granted that work (and especially paper work) is thus elastic in its demands on time, it is manifest that there need be little or no relationship between the work to be done and the size of the staff to which it may be assigned. Before the discovery of a new scientific law—herewith presented to the public for the first time, and to be called Parkinson's Law[1]—there has, however, been insufficient recognition of the implication of this fact in the field of public administration. Politicians and taxpayers have assumed

1. Why? Why not?—Editor.

(with occasional phases of doubt) that a rising total in the number of civil servants must reflect a growing volume of work to be done. Cynics, in questioning this belief, have imagined that the multiplication of officials must have left some of them idle or all of them able to work for shorter hours. But this is a matter in which faith and doubt seem equally misplaced. The fact is that the number of the officials and the quantity of the work to be done are not related to each other at all. The rise in the total of those employed is governed by Parkinson's Law, and would be much the same whether the volume of the work were to increase, diminish or even disappear. The importance of Parkinson's Law lies in the fact that it is a law of growth based upon an analysis of the factors by which the growth is controlled.

The validity of this recently discovered law must rely mainly on statistical proofs, which will follow. Of more interest to the general reader is the explanation of the factors that underlie the general tendency to which this law gives definition. Omitting technicalities (which are numerous) we may distinguish, at the outset, two motive forces. They can be represented for the present purpose by two almost axiomatic statements, thus:

Factor I. An official wants to multiply subordinates, not rivals; and

Factor II. Officials make work for each other. We must now examine these motive forces in turn.

THE LAW OF MULTIPLICATION OF SUBORDINATES

To comprehend Factor I, we must picture a civil servant called A who finds himself overworked. Whether this overwork is real or imaginary is immaterial; but we should observe, in passing, that A's sensation (or illusion) might easily result from his own decreasing energy—a normal symptom of middle-age. For this real or imagined overwork there are, broadly speaking, three possible remedies:

(1) He may resign.
(2) He may ask to halve the work with a colleague called B.
(3) He may demand the assistance of two subordinates to be called C and D.

There is probably no instance in civil service history of A choosing any but the third alternative. By resignation he would lose his pension rights. By having *B* appointed, on his own level in the hierarchy, he would merely bring in a rival for promotion to *W*'s vacancy when *W* (at long last) retires. So *A* would rather have *C* and *D*, junior men, below him. They will add to his consequence; and, by dividing the work into two categories, as between *C* and *D*, he will have the merit of being the only man who comprehends them both.

It is essential to realize, at this point, that *C* and *D* are, as it were, inseparable. To appoint *C* alone would have been impossible. Why? Because *C*, if by himself, would divide the work with *A* and so assume almost the equal status which has been refused in the first instance to *B*; a status the more emphasized if *C* is *A*'s only possible successor. Subordinates must thus number two or more, each being kept in order by fear of the other's promotion. When *C* complains in turn of being overworked (as he certainly will) *A* will, with the concurrence of *C*, advise the appointment of two assistants to help *C*. But he can then avert internal friction only by advising the appointment of two more assistants to help *D*, whose position is much the same. With this recruitment of *E*, *F*, *G* and *H*, the promotion of *A* is now practically certain.

THE LAW OF MULTIPLICATION OF WORK

Seven officials are now doing what one did before. This is where Factor II comes into operation. For these seven make so much work for each other that all are fully occupied and *A* is actually working harder than ever. An incoming document may well come before each of them in turn. Official *E* decides that it falls within the province of *F*, who places a draft reply before *C*, who amends it drastically before consulting *D*, who asks *G* to deal with it. But *G* goes on leave at this point, handing the file over to *H*, who drafts a minute, which is signed by *D* and returned to *C*, who revises his draft accordingly and lays the new version before *A*.

What does *A* do? He would have every excuse for signing the thing unread, for he has many other matters on his mind. Knowing now that he is to succeed *W* next year, he has to decide whether *C* or *D* should succeed to his own office. He had to agree to *G* going on leave, although not yet strictly entitled to it. He is worried whether *H* should not have gone instead, for reasons of health. He has looked pale recently—partly but not solely because of his domestic troubles. Then there is the business of *F*'s special increment of salary for the period of the conference, and *E*'s application for transfer to the Ministry of Pensions. *A* has heard that *D* is in love with a married typist and that *G* and *F* are no longer on speaking terms—no one seems to know why. So *A* might be tempted to sign *C*'s draft and have done with it.

But *A* is a conscientious man. Beset as he is with problems created by his colleagues for themselves and for him—created by the mere fact of these officials' existence—he is not the man to shirk his duty. He reads through the draft with care, deletes the fussy paragraphs added by *C* and *H* and restores the thing back to the form preferred in the first instance by the able (if quarrelsome) *F*. He corrects the English—none of these young men can write grammatically—and finally produces the same reply he would have written if officials *C* to *H* had never been born. Far more people have taken far longer to produce the same result. No one has been idle. All have done their best. And it is late in the evening before *A* finally quits his office and begins the return journey to Ealing. The last of the office lights are being turned off in the gathering dusk which marks the end of another day's administrative toil. Among the last to leave, *A* reflects, with bowed shoulders and a wry smile, that late hours, like grey hairs, are among the penalties of success.

THE SCIENTIFIC PROOFS

From this description of the factors at work the student of political science will recognize that administrators are more or less bound to multiply. Nothing has yet been said, however, about the period of time likely to elapse between the date of *A*'s appointment and the date from which we can calculate the pensionable service of *H*. Vast masses of statistical evidence have been collected and it is from a study of this data that Parkinson's Law has been deduced. Space will not allow of detailed analysis, but research began in the British Navy Estimates.

These were chosen because the Admiralty's responsibilities are more easily measurable than those of (say) the Board of Trade. The accompanying table is derived from Admiralty statistics for 1914 and 1928. The criticism voiced at the time centered on the comparison between the sharp fall in numbers of those available for fighting and the sharp rise in those available only for administration, the creation, it was said, of "a magnificent Navy on land." But that comparison is not to the present purpose. What we have to note is that the 2,000 Admiralty officials of 1914 had become the 3,569 of 1928; and that this growth was unrelated to any possible increase in their work. The Navy during that period had diminished, in point of fact, by a third in men and two-thirds in ships. Nor, from 1922 onwards, was its strength even expected to increase, for its total of ships (unlike its total of officials) was limited by the Washington Naval Agreement of that year. Yet in these circumstances we had a 78.45 percent increase in Admiralty officials over a period of fourteen years; an average increase of 5.6 percent a year on the earlier total. In fact, as we shall see, the rate of increase was not as regular as that. All we have to consider, at this stage, is the percentage rise over a given period.

ADMIRALTY STATISTICS

	1914	1928	Percentage increase or decrease
Capital ships in commission	62	20	−67.74
Officers and men in Royal Navy	146,000	100,000	−31.50
Dockyard workers	57,000	62,439	+ 9.54
Dockyard officials and clerks	3,249	4,558	+40.28
Admiralty officials	2,000	3,569	+78.45

Can this rise in the total number of civil servants be accounted for except on the assumption that such a total must always rise by a law governing its growth? It might be urged, at this point, that the period under discussion was one of rapid development in naval technique. The use of the flying machine was no longer confined to the eccentric. Submarines were tolerated if not approved. Engineer officers were beginning to be regarded as almost human. In so revolutionary an age we might expect the storekeepers would have more elaborate inventories to compile. We might not wonder to see more draughtsmen on the payroll, more designers, more technicians and scientists. But these, the dockyard officials, increased only by 40 percent in number, while the men of Whitehall increased by nearly 80 percent. For every new foreman or electrical engineer at Portsmouth there had to be two or more clerks at Charing Cross. From this we might be tempted to conclude, provisionally, that the rate of increase in administrative staff is likely to be double that of the technical staff at a time when the actually useful strength (in this case, of seamen) is being reduced by 31.5 percent. It has been proved, however, statistically, that this last percentage is irrelevant. *The Officials would have multiplied at the same rate had there been no actual seamen at all.*

It would be interesting to follow the further progress by which the 8,118 Admiralty staff of 1935 came to number 33,788 by 1954. But the staff of the Colonial Office affords a better field of study during a period of Imperial decline. The relevant statistics are set down below. Before showing what the rate of increase is, we must observe that the extent of this department's responsibilities was far from constant during these twenty years. The colonial territories were not much altered in area or population between 1935 and 1939. They were considerably diminished by 1943, certain areas being in enemy hands. They were increased again in 1947, but have since then shrunk steadily from year to year as successive colonies achieve self-government.

COLONIAL OFFICE OFFICIALS

1935	1939	1943	1947	1954
372	450	817	1,139	1,661

It would be rational, prior to the discovery of Parkinson's Law, to suppose that these changes in the scope of Empire would be reflected in the size of its central administration. But a glance at the figures shows that the staff totals represent automatic stages in an inevitable increase. And this increase, while related to that observed in other departments, has nothing to do with the size— or even the existence—of the Empire. What are the percentages of increase? We must ignore, for this purpose, the rapid increase in staff which accompanied the diminution of responsibility during World War II. We should note rather the peacetime rates of increase over 5.24 percent between 1935 and 1939, and 6.55 percent between 1947 and 1954. This gives an average increase of 5.89 percent each year, a percentage markedly similar to that already found in the Admiralty staff increase between 1914 and 1928.

Further and detailed statistical analysis of departmental staffs would be inappropriate in such an article as this. It is hoped, however, to reach a tentative conclusion regarding the time likely to elapse between a given official's first appointment and the later appointment of his two or more assistants. Dealing with the problem of pure staff accumulation, all the researches so far completed point to an average increase of about 5¾ percent per year. This fact established, it now becomes possible to state Parkinson's Law in mathematical form, thus:

In any public administrative department not actually at war the staff increase may be expected to follow this formula:

$$x = \frac{2k^m + p}{n}$$

where k is the number of staff seeking promotion through the appointment of subordinates; p represents the difference between the ages of appointment and retirement; m is the number of man-hours devoted to answering minutes within the department; and n is the number of effective units being administered. Then x will be the number of new staff required each year.

Mathematicians will, of course, realize that to find the percentage increase they must multiply x by 100 and divide by the total of the previous year, thus:

$$\frac{100\,(2k^m + p)}{yn}\,\%$$

where y represents the total original staff. And this figure will invariably prove to be between 5.17 percent and 6.56 percent, irrespective of any variation in the amount of work (if any) to be done.

The discovery of this formula and of the general principles upon which it is based has, of course, no emotive value. No attempt has been made to inquire whether departments ought to grow in size. Those who hold that this growth is essential to gain full employment are fully entitled to their opinion. Those who doubt the stability of an economy based upon reading each other's minutes are equally entitled to theirs. Parkinson's Law is a purely scientific discovery, inapplicable except in theory to the politics of the day. It is not the business of the botanist to eradicate the weeds. Enough for him if he can tell us just how fast they grow.

Part Two

Cost and Production

MANAGERIAL economics is concerned with the application of economic concepts and economic analysis to the problems of formulating rational managerial decisions. The essays in Part Two describe some of these basic economic concepts and techniques and illustrate how they can be useful to the manager. Although the concepts are elementary, they often turn out to be important in pointing up fundamental ways of viewing problems and in showing the way to well-reasoned conclusions.

The papers in Part Two deal with costs and production. Neil E. Harlan, Charles J. Christenson, and Richard F. Vancil, like Eugene Grant in Part One, are concerned with the proper measurement of the costs of alternative courses of action. Using a hypothetical case, they describe the different cost concepts used by accountants and economists, and conclude that the economist's notion of opportunity cost is more appropriate for decision-making than the accountant's notion of acquisition cost. The second selection, an article from *Business Week*, describes how Continental Air Lines has used marginal analysis to increase its profits. This is a well-known case study of managerial economics at work.

In the next paper, Leslie Cookenboo shows how the economist's concepts of production functions and cost functions can be estimated in the case of crude oil pipe lines. These concepts are central to managerial economics, and it is important that the student get some feel for how they can be applied in real-life cases. The editor and Harold H. Wein describe in the last essay how the relationship between output and cost can be used to control cost and performance. This is a case study of the application of cost functions to the operating problems of the railroad industry.

Cost Analysis

NEIL E. HARLAN,
CHARLES J. CHRISTENSON,
AND RICHARD F. VANCIL

Neil Harlan is Professor of Business Administration at Harvard University. In 1962 he, together with Charles Christenson and Richard Vancil, wrote Managerial Economics, *from which the following article is taken.*

Why is cost analysis so important in making business decisions? The answer lies in the objectives of the business enterprise and in the way its accomplishments are measured in our economy.

In a narrow, simplified sense it might be said that business administration consists of the twin tasks of (1) allocating resources among alternative uses and (2) supervising the activities of people to insure that the resources are efficiently utilized toward achieving the assigned goals. While there is nothing wrong with this definition as a theoretical concept, it glosses over the uncertainties of the complex world of business. Business administration is an art. While there have been rapid advances in scientific, professional management during the last half-century, successful business administration still requires an intangible ability best described as *skill*.

The success of a commercial enterprise in allocating its resources effectively is usually measured by the profit it earns, and

31

a primary goal of most firms is, therefore, to earn a profit, either the maximum possible profit or a satisfactory profit consistent with other goals of the firm. But what is profit? Both the accountant and the economist use this word to mean the difference between the revenues earned from the sale of goods and services and the costs incurred in earning these revenues. Yet, despite this agreement on the basic concept of profit, the accountant and the economist would generally disagree if each were asked to measure the profit of a particular business enterprise.

The disagreement would arise primarily because of a difference between the accounting concept and the economic concept of cost, Even here, however, there is an element of agreement: both the accountant and the economist consider cost as a measurement in monetary terms of the resources consumed by the firm in producing its revenue. The accountant usually measures the *acquisition cost* of these resources, in the sense of the money amount which the firm had to pay when it initially acquired the resources. The economist, in contrast, thinks in terms of the *opportunity cost* of the resources. The opportunity cost of devoting a resource to a particular use is the return that the resource could earn in its best alternative use. The economist's concept of cost, therefore, involves an explicit recognition of the problem of choice faced by the businessman in the utilization of resources.

Opportunity cost may be either greater or less than acquisition cost. Suppose, for example, that a firm is considering the production of an item which would require the use of material on hand for which $100 was originally paid; the acquisition cost, then, is $100. If the material could currently be sold on the market for $125, however, its opportunity cost must be $125, since the use of the material requires the firm to forego the opportunity of receiving $125. If, on the other hand, the material currently has no market value nor any alternative use, its opportunity cost is zero.

The businessman lives with both these concepts of cost. For decision-making purposes, the economist's concept of opportunity cost is the relevant one, since a rational decision must involve the comparison of alternative courses of action. The accountant's role as a "scorekeeper" for outside investors is also important to the businessman. Moreover, accounting records are often a primary source of information for decision-making purposes.

Types of Resources · The basic resource of business is money, or perhaps more precisely, the power that money has in our society to command the primary resources, the labor provided by men and the materials provided by nature. Money by itself is powerless, however, without a manager or entrepreneur to decide how to put it to work. Even then, capital does not become productive until it is exchanged for more tangible resources than imagination: labor, raw materials, and combinations of labor and materials in the form of products manufactured by other business. In the "raw" state, as money, the wise utilization of resources is difficult; it becomes even more difficult once the money resource has been exchanged for a wide variety of heterogeneous resources, each with a specialized productive capability.

An operating business possesses a variety of resources in addition to money: a building which is adaptable to a greater or lesser variety of uses, equipment which can be used to produce a range of products with varying degrees of efficiency, and employees whose productive skills may embrace a broad spectrum. At first glance, the problem of allocating physical resources might not seem vastly different from that of allocating money. All of these resources have been purchased with money, and their values can be measured in monetary terms. Why, then, did Henry J. Kaiser, a man with adequate capital resources and a reputation as an efficient shipbuilder during World War II, fail in his attempt to establish a new line of passenger cars in the late 1940's? It is not an easy task to convert raw capital into an efficient combination of productive resources. And the converse is also true: It is very difficult to measure the value of an existing set of productive resources in monetary terms.

In the "long run," money is the basic business resource. But business decisions are made in the short run, and money, the best available common denominator for all resources, is an imperfect yardstick. At the core of the broad problem of resource allocation, therefore, is the problem of measurement. Actually, the measurement problem can usefully be broken into two parts for purposes of analysis: (1) what types of resources will be required in order to carry out each course of action being considered? and (2) what is the value (or cost) of the combination of resources required for each alternative?

Classification of Problems · As a practical matter, businessmen rarely refer to their problems as problems in resource allocation. Rather, they say, "I've got a make-or-buy problem," or a "capital expenditure problem," or a "lease-or-buy problem," or a "pricing problem," and so forth. This "specific problem" orientation is not necessarily due to a failure to recognize the resource allocation characteristic of the problem, it is simply an attempt to find a practical way to begin the analysis that will eventually lead to a decision.

Dividing business decisions into problem categories has two advantages:

1. From his prior experience with similar problems in the past, the businessman may have observed the kinds of resources that typically are involved in the evaluation of alternatives, and may be familiar with some of the most common problems in measuring the cost of the resources required. Categorizing the problem facilitates making maximum use of this experience.

2. Some types of problems may be best resolved using analytical techniques that have been developed specifically for that class of problems. Identifying the type of problem thus serves also to identify the techniques which may aid in the solution.

There is a danger, too, in the classification of business problems: the danger of a closed mind that can only follow familiar decision patterns used in the past rather than searching imaginatively for new and better ways to grapple with the problems of today and tomorrow.

FORMULATING THE PROBLEM

In order to illustrate some of the most common problems of cost analysis, let us examine the decision process in a simple example. The Webber Company manufactures industrial equipment in a small plant with fifty employees. A recent increase in orders has taxed the one-shift capacity of the plant, and management can see that the company will fail to meet its delivery schedules unless some action is taken. What should be done?

The first step in analyzing this problem, and the most important step by far, is to determine the alternative courses of action that might solve the problem. The list is longer than one might first suppose. There are three main types of actions which might be taken: restricting the quantity sold to the present capacity of the plant; increasing the plant capacity on a permanent or semipermanent basis; or increasing capacity on a temporary basis. Under each of these broad headings, further actions can be identified, as the list below demonstrates.

1. Restricting the quantity sold by:
   (a) Refusing to accept orders in excess of present plant capacity.
   (b) Accepting all orders and apologizing to customers when deliveries are late.
   (c) Raising prices enough to reduce volume of orders down to present plant capacity.
2. Increasing plant capacity by:
   (a) Building an addition to the present plant.
   (b) Operating the present plant on two shifts.
3. Providing temporary capacity by:
   (a) Using overtime.
   (b) Buying some components from another manufacturer rather than making them.

This initial stage of formulating the problem is vital to wise decision making. It is a waste of time to do a careful analysis of three alternatives and to select the best of the three if a fourth course of action which is far better is completely overlooked. Analysis is no substitute for imagination. A few extra minutes devoted exclusively to the preparation of an exhaustive list of alternatives will nearly always be time well spent.

So that the exhaustive list does not become exhausting, the next (and sometimes simultaneous) step in problem formulation is to select those alternatives that merit further investigation. Several alternatives on Webber Company's list may be eliminated in this screening process. Items 1(a) and 1(c) would have the effect of reducing the demands placed on the factory. If the company had long-run growth in sales volume as one of its objectives, these two actions might be rejected as incompatible with the goal. Even if the company's only goal were "maximization of long-run profits" (as we will usually assume, in the absence of a specific statement of goals), alternative 1(a) is not acceptable if the additional product could be produced profitably. The profit effect of raising prices is more difficult to assess. Let us simply assume that we are interested in determining the best course of action at the present price in order to compare it with the results obtainable at a higher price.

Alternative 1(b) might appear attractive as a method of accepting the available orders without incurring additional production costs. Evaluation of this alternative should, however, recognize that it involves the consumption of an intangible business resource, customer "goodwill." Depending upon competition and normal trade practices in Webber's industry, it may be that stretching out of delivery schedules is the best solution to the problem. In most industries, however, this practice might be a costly one, and we will eliminate it from further consideration here.

The remaining four alternatives are ways to provide increased production in order to meet the increased demand. It is difficult to reject any of these solutions based only on a cursory analysis. It may be useful, however, to realize that there are major differences in type and magnitude of the resources required for each course of action. Expanding the plant or adding a second shift will cause significant changes in Webber's fixed costs as well as in its productive capacity. Even a second shift is a semipermanent action that involves hiring new supervisors as well as laborers, and may require a heavy expenditure of the vital *management* resource. Neither of these two actions would be wise unless Webber's management believed that the increase in demand was a relatively permanent one.

As a temporary solution to their problem, therefore, Webber's management might decide to narrow their analysis to a choice between alternatives 3(a) and 3(b), the use of overtime in the plant or the purchase of some components from outside vendors. The selection of either of these solutions can easily be changed in the future, and a few months from now management may be in a better position to assess the permanence of the current spurt in demand.

The final stage in formulating the problem is now at hand. How shall we evaluate the alternatives that we have decided to examine? What is the criterion on which we shall make our decision? A careful restatement of the problem at this point may help us to see the best way to point our subsequent analysis. It is little help at this point to say that we have a problem in resource allocation. It may be of more use to define the problem as "fulfilling our production requirements while minimizing the consumption of our resources." The businessman would say simply, "Which parts, if any, would it be cheaper to buy outside?"

In situations such as this where the decision has no revenue implications (we have already decided to accept all orders and deliver them on time), the best course of action is the one that costs the least. Realizing that we are equating "cost" with "resource consumption," therefore, we may say that our decision rule will be to choose the "least cost" alternative, and may then turn our attention to measuring the cost of pursuing each course of action.

RELEVANT COSTS

Before we can begin a detailed analysis, we need a more precise statement of the alternatives. For this purpose, we will assume that the anticipated capacity problem will arise only in the machining department of the Webber Company. Normally this department does the machining of all the component parts in the Webber product. Most of the parts are produced in small lots and require specialized skills not possessed by many outside vendors. Two parts, however, are produced in rather large quantities and the machining operations on them are routine. Clearly these parts are the best candidates for outside purchase. If they were purchased outside, the machining department would have no trouble making all the remaining components on schedule.

Having identified the alternatives, we must next determine the resources required to execute them. According to engineering estimates, the production of one unit of Part A requires raw materials costing $3.00 and a half hour of the time of a machine operator, while the production of one unit of Part B requires $8.00 of raw materials and one hour of operator time. The purchasing agent, after checking with several vendors, informs us that the Smithy Corporation, a reliable source, will deliver Part A for $4.50 each and Part B for $11.50 each.

The next step is to determine the cost of the resources required.

Earlier we referred to the different cost concepts used by accountants and economists and we argued that the economist's notion of opportunity cost is more appropriate for decision making than the accountant's notion of acquisition cost. Accounting records provide a useful source of cost data, however, and so we will begin by presenting the costs of the alternatives to the Webber Company as its accountants might prepare them; then we will indicate how these accounting costs must be analyzed and modified to reflect opportunity costs.

Accounting Costs · After being supplied with the list of resources required as given above, the accounting department of the Webber Company provides the following schedule of manufacturing costs:

	Cost per Unit	
	Part A	Part B
Prime Cost:		
Raw materials	$3.00	$ 8.00
Direct labor @ $2.00/hour	1.00	2.00
Total prime costs	$4.00	$10.00
Factory overhead @ 100% of labor	1.00	2.00
Normal manufacturing cost	$5.00	$12.00
Overtime premium @ 50% of labor	0.50	1.00
Overtime manufacturing cost	$5.50	$13.00

The accounting department explains its calculations as follows. The purchase of raw materials is, of course, a direct out-of-pocket cost. The machine operators are paid $2.00 per hour and this rate is applied to the time requirements to arrive at the direct labor cost. The total of raw materials and direct labor costs, representing the cost of resources directly consumed in the manufacture of the parts, is called *prime cost.*

Production of the parts would also require the use of certain common resources of the company: plant, equipment, supervision, and the like. The acquisition costs of these resources, called *overhead costs,* allocated to the machining department are given in Exhibit 1. Since total allocated overhead costs are equal to total direct labor costs, a charge of 100 percent of direct labor is made to cover these overhead costs. Finally, if work were done on overtime, an additional cost of 50 percent of direct labor would be incurred for overtime premium pay.

EXHIBIT 1

WEBBER COMPANY

MONTHLY BUDGET FOR MACHINING DEPARTMENT

Direct labor (2,000 hours @ $2.00)		$4,000
Overhead: Indirect labor—materials handling		$ 300
Department foreman		400
Payroll taxes, vacation and holiday pay, pension contributions, and other fringe benefits		900
Heat, light, and power		250
Shop supplies		150
Depreciation of machinery		800
Repairs and maintenance—machinery		600
Allocated share of plant-wide costs (superintendent, building depreciation and maintenance, property taxes and insurance, watchman, etc.)		600
Total overhead		$4,000

If we look at accounting costs, therefore, both parts are apparently cheaper to buy from Smithy than to produce in our own plant—even ignoring the premium paid for overtime work! But we must take a closer look at the behavior of manufacturing costs.

Another classification of manufacturing costs often used by accountants is into *direct costs* and *fixed costs*. This classification is a little closer to the economist's way of thinking about costs. Direct costs include those which vary at least approximately in proportion to the quantity of production. Prime costs are usually direct costs, but not all direct costs are prime costs: some overhead costs may also vary with production. Analysis of the overhead costs listed in Exhibit 1, for example, might reveal the following facts about the behavior of overhead costs under two circumstances: (*a*) at present volume if one man is laid off and parts are purchased outside; (*b*) at the anticipated increased volume, if overtime is used.

1. *Indirect Labor.* One man is employed as a materials handler in the department. If a machinist were laid off there would be no saving in the wages paid to this man; he would just be a little less busy. If the department worked overtime, however, the materials handling function would have to be performed by someone, either the machinist himself (thereby lowering his productive efficiency) or by the materials handler also working overtime.

2. *Department Foreman.* This cost probably would not vary with either a small decrease or small increase in production. The

machining work to be performed on overtime might not require
the presence of a supervisor; if it did, the overtime paid to the
supervisor would be relevant.

3. *Payroll Taxes, etc.* These costs amount to nearly 20 percent
of Webber's expenses for labor and supervision. If a man were
laid off, the entire 20 percent might be saved. There would be
some increase in these costs on overtime, but the workers would
not get more holidays or longer vacations. The variable portion,
using overtime, might be 10 percent of the labor cost.

4. *Heat, Light, Power, and Shop Supplies.* These costs are
difficult to analyze. There might be an insignificant saving in
power if one machine were shut down. On overtime, additional
power and light would be required.

5. *Depreciation.* This cost is not a cash expenditure but a pro
rata portion of the original cost of the equipment. This cost, caused
simply by the passage of time, will not be changed by management's
decision to either lay off a man or use overtime.

6. *Repairs and Maintenance.* This expense is made up of two
components: routine, preventive maintenance and the repair of
breakdowns. The former is the larger expense, and might be
reduced somewhat if one machine were shut down completely. The
latter probably bears some relationship to the volume of work put
through the equipment and would vary for either a decrease or
increase in production.

7. *Allocated Plant Costs.* These overhead costs occur at the
next higher level in the company, and would not change as a result
of a minor change in production volume in the department.

We may now recapitulate the results of our analysis. Direct
labor seems to be a useful measure of volume in this department
because each man operates one machine and costs that vary in
relation to machine utilization will also vary with labor costs.
In Exhibit 2, therefore, we have computed the direct overhead
cost for each of the two circumstances mentioned above (laying
off one man or using overtime).

How variable are overhead costs? The preceding analysis
illustrates how difficult it is to answer that question in a practical
way. It seems safe to say that overhead is not completely variable,
as might be inferred from the accountant's allocation mechanism.
Saving $1.00 in labor cost will not save $1.00 in overhead in the
machining department. But any further general statement about
overhead variability is useless. For decision-making purposes,
the most useful answer is one based on an analysis of the specific
cost items in the specific situation in which a specific decision is

EXHIBIT 2

WEBBER COMPANY

OVERHEAD COST ANALYSIS

Overhead Item	Monthly budget cost		Variable cost as a % of direct labor cost changes if	
	Amount	% of direct labor	one man laid off	overtime used
Indirect labor—materials handler	$ 300	7.5%	...	7.5%
Department foreman	400	10.0	...	...
Payroll taxes, etc.............	900	22.5 *	19.1%	10.8
Heat, light, and power........	250	6.2	1.0	2.0
Shop supplies	150	3.8	...	...
Depreciation of machinery	800	20.0	...	...
Repairs and maintenance......	600	15.0	12.0	5.0
Allocated plant costs.........	600	15.0	...	...
Total	$4,000	100.0%	32.1%	25.3%

* Stated as a percentage of total departmental payroll, this cost is $\dfrac{900}{4,700}$ = 19.1%. On overtime, it is estimated here that direct payroll taxes would be 10% of wage costs, but would also apply to the materials handler (10% of 7.5%).

to be made. Fortunately, it is possible to gain skill in this kind of analysis, with a concomitant reduction in the analytical time required. This is a skill worth developing, because reliance on rules of thumb or general cost variability classifications is a poor, and sometimes dangerous, substitute for such skill.

Opportunity Costs · The accountant measures the cost of resources consumed in terms of the outlay originally made to acquire them. The economist, in contrast, measures their cost in relation to alternative opportunities for their employment. Let us see how these two concepts differ in the Webber Company example.

On some costs, the accountant and the economist would agree. This would probably be true, for example, of the cost of buying the parts from the Smithy Corporation or the cost of the raw materials if the parts are manufactured. In these cases, the foregone opportunity is to refrain from buying the parts or the raw material, so that the opportunity cost and the acquisition cost would be identical.

It might seem, in fact, that opportunity cost is identical with the accounting concept of direct cost. While there is a close relationship between opportunity cost and direct cost and while they are often identical, there are important differences which must be borne in mind.

We can illustrate this point using the direct labor cost in the company example. The company employs eleven machinists in the machining department; approximately 2,000 hours of production labor are available each month. Before the company's anticipated sales volume increase, tnese men spent about 1,550 hours per month on machining the special, low-volume parts and used the balance of their time, as available, to turn out Parts A and B. Forgetting for the moment about the increase in volume, how would you decide whether or not to have Parts A and B made by Smithy? Are the labor costs true opportunity costs? The answer depends on what action Webber's management would take if the parts were purchased outside. A total of 450 labor hours could be saved. Would two and one-half machinists be laid off? Such action might mean reducing the range of skills now available in an eleven-man force, and might cause morale problems for the man working a short week. If, in fact, only one man would be laid off, then we should not say that the entire labor cost used in producing the parts is an opportunity cost of the parts. The relevant cost in this situation is the *total* amount of money that will be spent for labor under each course of action. If labor costs $2.00 per hour, the cost would be $4,000 if both parts are manufactured inside, and about $3,660 if one man is laid off and some parts were purchased. Although Webber's accountant would say that $900 is spent each month on machining labor for Parts A and B, the *opportunity cost* of that labor is only $340. The other $560 is spent primarily to maintain a balanced labor force with the necessary variety of skills—skills that may be a vital resource in Webber's overall success.

On the other hand, now that the demand for Webber's product is expected to increase, what is the relevant labor cost in deciding whether to use overtime to meet the requirements? With a 10 percent increase in demand, 1,705 hours per month are needed for low-volume parts and 495 hours of machining are needed for Parts A and B. Hiring a twelfth man might provide most of the 200 extra hours needed, but there is no room in the plant for another machine. If overtime is used, the additional labor will cost $3.00 per hour, or $600. This cost is relevant to the decision because its expenditure depends upon the course of action management selects.

Even in the relatively simple case of direct labor, therefore, opportunity cost is not necessarily identical with direct cost. In the example just considered, opportunity cost was less than direct cost, but the reverse could also be true, as we will demonstrate shortly. While the acquisition cost of fixed resources (i.e., accounting fixed overhead) is neither a direct cost nor an opportunity cost, there may be an opportunity cost associated with employing these facilities in one use rather than in an alternative. This opportunity cost is relevant in making decisions regarding the use of the fixed resources although it is not an acquisition cost.

Opportunity cost, then, depends upon the context of a particular decision whereas direct cost does not. The two concepts are similar enough to create both an advantage and a danger: an advantage in that direct cost can often be used to estimate opportunity cost, a danger in that this process can be carried farther than appropriate.

COMPARISON OF ALTERNATIVES

After the problem has been formulated and the relevant costs determined, the next step in the analysis of a decision problem is to recapitulate the results of our analysis to determine which alternative is least costly. If the problem has been formulated properly and the cost analysis done systematically, this ranking task is a simple one. Illustrative calculations for the Webber Company's make-or-buy decisions are shown in Exhibits 3 and 4.

Exhibit 3 is an evaluation of the alternatives that faced Webber under its "normal" demand conditions, i.e., before the anticipated increase in demand. As a result of our analysis, the most promising alternatives have now been more sharply defined. Only one man would be laid off if any parts were purchased outside, eliminating 170 labor hours per month. If this were done, Webber would then have to buy outside either 340 units of A or 170 units of B. In terms of total costs, the best alternative is to continue to manufacture all our requirements inside. The only difficult cost calculation is the overhead cost. If all parts were made inside, the labor and overhead budgets would be unchanged at $4,000 each per month. If one man were laid off, labor cost would decline by $340 and the overhead budget would fall by 32.1 percent of that amount (Exhibit 2).

An alternative analysis in Exhibit 3 arrives at the same conclusion in terms of opportunity costs. According to the cost accountant's statement on page 31, the "normal" cost of one unit of Part A was $5.00. We have seen that this figure is not useful

EXHIBIT 3

WEBBER COMPANY

MAKE-OR-BUY ANALYSIS

CONDITION NO. 1: NORMAL DEMAND

	Make 500 units of A and 200 of B	Lay off one machinist and	
		Buy 340 units of A	Buy 170 units of B
Raw material costs:			
Part A	$ 1,500	$ 480	$ 1,500
Part B	1,600	1,600	240
Purchased parts	...	1,530	1,955
Direct labor	4,000	3,660	3,660
Overhead costs	4,000	3,891	3,891
	$11,100	$11,161	$11,246

ALTERNATIVE ANALYSIS

	Opportunity cost of manufacturing	
	Part A	Part B
Raw material costs	$ 3.00	$ 8.00
Direct labor—one man	1.00	2.00
Overhead at 32.1% of labor	0.32	0.64
Total opportunity cost	$ 4.32	$ 10.64
Purchase price	4.50	11.50
Saving due to manufacturing	$ 0.18	$ 0.86
Number of units produced in 170 hours	340	170
Total savings	$61.00	$146.00

for decision-making purposes; we are interested in the opportunity cost of manufacturing Part A. To measure opportunity cost, we must answer the question, "What costs (resources) will be saved if the parts are purchased outside?" For Part A, we will save $3.00 of raw material for each unit, the labor cost of one man divided by the units he could produce, and approximately 32 percent in overhead costs related to labor. What costs (resources) will be required to achieve those savings? Part A must be purchased at a price of $4.50 each. The savings are less than the additional cost, indicating that outside purchase is not the cheapest course of action. It is no coincidence that the total saving due to manufacturing is equal to the difference in the total costs of the alternatives as computed in the upper part of Exhibit 3.

Exhibit 4 is a similar set of calculations after a 10 percent increase in demand. The overhead cost increase of $138 was computed in two stages as follows: Variable overhead was estimated as 25.3 percent of labor in Exhibit 2, and this percentage was applied to the $400 straight time cost of the added labor. In addition, indirect labor and payroll taxes (18.3 percent of labor) would vary as a function of cost (not time), so that percentage was applied to the $200 of overtime premium pay. The best alternative is to buy 400 units per month of Part A rather than to use overtime.

We have said that most decision problems are basically problems in resource allocation. Cost analysis is used to solve these problems because money is the best common denominator for resources, and because money is the basic "scarce resource" which the business would like to utilize in an optimal fashion. In the Webber Company's overtime decision it is useful to conceive of the problem somewhat differently. The company has 2,000 hours of machining capacity available, and our analysis in Exhibit 3 has shown that this capacity should not be reduced. As demand increases, Webber's real question is, "How should the 2,000 hours be allocated among the available jobs?" The special, low-volume parts are of first priority, and require 1,705 of the available hours. The remaining 295 hours should be used in such a way as to maximize their value to Webber.

EXHIBIT 4

WEBBER COMPANY

MAKE-OR-BUY ANALYSIS

CONDITION NO. 2: INCREASED DEMAND

	Use 200 hours of overtime; make 550 units of A and 200 units of B	Use no overtime and buy 400 units of A	buy 200 units of B
Raw material costs:			
Part A	$ 1,650	$ 450	$ 1,650
Part B	1,760	1,760	160
Purchased parts	...	1,800	2,300
Direct labor—straight time.........	4,400	4,000	4,000
Overhead costs	4,000	4,000	4,000
Overtime premium	200	....	....
Overhead costs applied to premium pay	138	....	....
Total cost	$12,148	$12,010	$12,110

ALTERNATIVE ANALYSIS

	Opportunity cost of manufacturing	
	Part A	Part B
Raw material costs.........................	$ 3.00	$ 8.00
Direct labor—200 hours....................	1.00	2.00
Overhead at 25.3% of labor................	0.25	0.51
Overtime premium	0.50	1.00
Overhead at 18.3% of premium..............	0.09	0.18
Total opportunity cost.................	$ 4.84	$11.69
Purchase price	4.50	11.50
Saving due to purchase...................	$ 0.34	$ 0.19
Number of units produced in 200 hours........	400	200
Total savings from purchase............	$138.00	$38.00

In Exhibit 5 we have computed the contribution per labor hour that would be earned by using the available hours to manufacture Part A or Part B. Labor and its related overhead costs are ignored in this calculation since these costs will not change as a result of our decision. They are part of the fixed resources we desire to allocate optimally. We will spend a total of $4,000 for labor and $4,000 for overhead; our decision is to determine *how* to use this capacity. Additional cash resources are required only

EXHIBIT 5

WEBBER COMPANY

CALCULATION OF CONTRIBUTION PER LABOR HOUR

Hours available:

Total	2,000
Required for low-volume, special parts	1,705
Available for Parts A or B	295

	Part A	Part B
Purchase price per unit	$ 4.50	$11.50
Raw material cost per unit	3.00	8.00
Materials savings per unit	$ 1.50	$ 3.50
Number of units produced per labor hour	2	1
Contribution per labor hour	$ 3.00	$ 3.50
Cost of adding additional labor hours:		
Labor per hour $2.00		
Overhead at 25.3% 0.51		
Overtime premium per hour ... 1.00		
Overhead at 18.3% of premium .. 0.18		
Total cost $3.69	3.69	3.69
Excess cost per hour of making rather than buying	$ 0.69	$ 0.19
Total excess cost for 200 hours	$138.00	$38.00

for materials. For every unit of Part A manufactured we will pay only $3.00 for materials rather than $4.50 for the completed part, a saving of $1.50 per unit or $3.00 per labor hour. Manufacturing Part B is even more attractive because we will save $3.50 per labor hour. In order to get maximum value from our scarce resource (capacity), we should manufacture all of our requirements of Part B before we use any of the capacity to manufacture Part A.

Next, we must decide whether it would be worthwhile to buy additional capacity by using overtime. The cost of adding capacity is $3.69 per hour (Exhibit 5). Since this cost exceeds the contribution earned by the labor hours, the use of overtime is not warranted. The last calculation on Exhibit 5 is proof that this method of analysis is consistent with the two methods shown in Exhibit 4.

Optimal allocation of scarce resources is a primary task of the businessman. The Webber Company example is a simple illustration of what is involved in this task.

An Airline Takes the Marginal Route

BUSINESS WEEK

This article is from Business Week, *April 20,1963.*

Continental Air Lines, Inc. filled only half the available seats on its Boeing 707 jet flights in 1962, a record some fifteen percentage points worse than the national average.

By eliminating just a few runs—less than 5 percent—Continental could have raised its average load considerably. Some of its flights frequently carry as few as thirty passengers on the 120-seat plane. But the improved load factor would have meant reduced profits.

For Continental bolsters its corporate profits by deliberately running extra flights that aren't expected to do more than return their out-of-pocket costs—plus a little profit. Such marginal flights are an integral part of the over-all operating philosophy that has brought small, Denver-based Continental—tenth among the eleven trunk carriers—through the bumpy postwar period with only one loss year.

This philosophy leans heavily on marginal analysis. And the line leans heavily on Chris F. Whelan, vice-president in charge of economic planning, to translate marginalism into hard, dollars-and-cents decisions.

Getting management to accept and apply the marginal concept probably is the chief contribution any economist can make to his company. Put most simply, marginalists maintain that a company should undertake any activity that adds more to revenues than it does to costs—and not limit itself to those activities whose returns equal average or "fully allocated" costs.

The approach, of course, can be applied to virtually any business, not just to air transportation. It can be used in consumer finance, for instance, where the question may be whether to make more loans—including more bad loans—if this will increase net profit. Similarly, in advertising, the decision may rest on how much extra business a dollar's worth of additional advertising will bring in, rather than pegging the advertising budget to a percentage of sales—and, in insurance, where setting high interest rates to discourage policy loans may actually damage profits by causing policyholders to borrow elsewhere.

Whelan finds all such cases wholly analogous to his run of problems, where he seeks to keep his company's eye trained on the big objective: net profit.

Last summer, Whelan politely chewed out a group of operational researchers at an international conference in Rome for being incomprehensible. "You have failed to educate the users of your talents to the potential you offer," he said. "Your studies, analyses, and reports are couched in tables that sales, operations, and maintenance personnel cannot comprehend."

Whelan's work is a concrete example of the truth in a crack by Prof. Sidney Alexander of MIT—formerly economist for Columbia Broadcasting System—that the economist who understands marginal analysis has a "full-time job in undoing the work of the accountant." This is so, Alexander holds, because the practices of accountants—and of most businesses—are permeated with cost allocation directed at average, rather than marginal, costs.

In any complex business, there's likely to be a big difference between the costs of each company activity as it's carried on the accounting books and the marginal or "true" costs that can determine whether or not the activity should be undertaken.

The difficulty comes in applying the simple "textbook" marginal concept to specific decisions. If the economist is unwilling to make some bold simplifications, the job of determining "true" marginal costs may be highly complex, time-wasting, and too expensive. But even a rough application of marginal principles may come closer to the right answer for business decision-makers than an analysis based on precise average-cost data.

Proving that this is so demands economists who can break the crust of corporate habits and show concretely why the typical manager's response—that nobody ever made a profit without meeting all costs—is misleading and can reduce profits. To be sure, the whole business cannot make a profit unless average costs are met; but covering average costs should not determine whether any particular activity should be undertaken. For this would unduly restrict corporate decisions and cause managements to forego opportunities for extra gains.

Management overhead at Continental is pared to the bone, so Whelan often is thrown such diverse problems as soothing a ruffled city council or planning the specifications for the plane the line will want to fly in 1970. But the biggest slice of his time goes to schedule planning—and it is here that the marginal concept comes most sharply into focus.

Whelan's approach is this: He considers that the bulk of his scheduled flights have to return at least their fully allocated costs. Overhead, depreciation, insurance are very real expenses and must be covered. The out-of-pocket approach comes into play, says Whelan, only after the line's basic schedule has been set.

"Then you go a step farther," he says, and see if adding more flights will contribute to the corporate net. Similarly, if he's thinking of dropping a flight with a disappointing record, he puts it under the marginal microscope: "If your revenues are going to be more than your out-of-pocket costs, you should keep the flight on."

By "out-of-pocket costs" Whelan means just that: the actual dollars that Continental has to pay out to run a flight. He gets the figure not by applying hypothetical equations but by circulating a proposed schedule to every operating department concerned and finding out just what extra expenses it will entail. If a ground crew already on duty can service the plane, the flight isn't charged a penny of their salary expense. There may even be some costs eliminated in running the flight; they won't need men to roll the plane to a hangar, for instance, if it flies on to another stop.

Most of these extra flights, of course, are run at off-beat hours, mainly late at night. At times, though, Continental discovers that the hours aren't so unpopular after all. A pair of night coach flights on the Houston–San Antonio–El Paso–Phoenix–Los Angeles leg, added on a marginal basis, have turned out to be so successful that they are now more than covering fully allocated costs.

In conclusion, here is the relevant marginal analysis in a nutshell:

Problem: Shall Continental run an extra daily flight from City X to City Y?

The facts: Fully-allocated costs of this flight. $4,500

           Out-of-pocket costs of this flight. $2,000

           Flight should gross. $3,100

Decision: Run the flight. It will add $1,100 to net profit—because it will add $3,100 to revenues and only $2,000 to costs. Overhead and other costs, totaling $2,500 ($4,500 minus $2,000), would be incurred whether the flight is run or not. Therefore, fully-allocated or "average" costs of $4,500 are not relevant to this business decision. It's the out-of-pocket or "marginal" costs that count.

Production Functions and Cost Functions: A Case Study

LESLIE COOKENBOO

Leslie Cookenboo is Senior Economics Adviser in the Corporate Planning Department of the Exxon Corporation. This piece comes from his book, Crude Oil Pipe Lines and Competition in the Oil Industry, *published by the Harvard University Press.*

This paper is concerned with a discussion of long-, short-, and intermediate-run costs of operating crude oil pipe lines. For the benefit of the reader not conversant with economic jargon, it might be well to begin with a description of the three cost categories. First, it is necessary to distinguish between the various types of costs that may be considered under any of these three categories. "Total" cost (be it long-, short-, or intermediate-run) is the total expenditure necessary for producing a given output. "Average" cost is the cost per unit of producing a given output; it is equal to total cost divided by output. For example, if the total expenditure for an output of 100 units is $1,000, then total cost is $1,000 and average cost (per-unit cost) is $10 per unit ($1,000 divided by 100 units). "Marginal" cost is the change in total cost associated with changes in output. If 100 units cost

$1,000 and 101 units cost $1,008, then "marginal" cost is $8 (the change in total cost divided by the change in output). "Fixed" and "variable" costs are simply parts of total (or average) cost. Fixed costs are those incurred even when no output is produced, for example, interest on the money borrowed to buy machinery, pay taxes, and so forth. Variable costs (out-of-pocket costs) are expenditures that would not be necessary were no output produced, for example, expenditures for labor and raw materials. Total cost is equal to the sum of total fixed cost and total variable cost. Average cost is equal to the sum of average fixed cost and average variable cost.

A "short-run" cost curve shows the cost of producing various outputs with a given amount of fixed capital equipment. In other words, it is the cost curve for a given size of plant, the output of which can be changed simply by using more or less labor and raw materials. Changes in short-run costs with changes in output represent changes in expenditures for items of variable cost *only;* no extra machinery or other capital equipment is needed to increase output.

A long-run cost curve (also called a "planning" curve) is an "envelope" of all possible short-run curves. It shows the least possible expenditure for producing any output. That is, it takes into account all individual plant cost curves in order to determine which plant can produce each output for the least amount possible (relative to all other plants). This is illustrated in Figure 1.

This diagram shows per-unit cost plotted against output (the short-run cost curves) for each of six possible plants (A–F) that might be used to produce some products. The long-run average cost curve is the envelope of these short-run curves (the heavy, wavy line). (If there were an infinite number of plants possible, then the long-run curve would be continuous, not wavy.) It shows the least possible expenditure for any given output in the range of outputs under consideration. Output Q_0 might be produced with either plant A, B, C, D, E, or F. However, D's short-run cost curve lies beneath all the others at Q_0; therefore its cost is the least possible for producing Q_0, and it may be said to be the "optimum" plant for producing that output. In the range of outputs where its cost curve lies beneath all others, its short-run cost is equal to long-run cost. A long-run cost

Cost per Unit

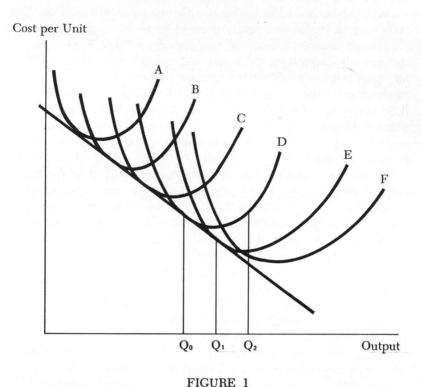

FIGURE 1

LONG- AND SHORT-RUN AVERAGE COST CURVES

curve such as that in Figure 1 is called a "planning" curve because it shows the least amount that could be spent to produce
various outputs if a firm had the option of choosing from several
sizes of plants. Such a long-run cost curve would be of value
when building a new plant or when contemplating entering an
industry. Once a plant is built, it is the short-run curve for this
plant which shows what the firm would spend in order to produce various outputs.

Note the paradox in Figure 1 that D is *not* the optimum plant
for the output at which it itself is most efficient (Q_1). Its most
efficient output is the output which it produces at the least possible cost per unit that *it* is capable of achieving. In Figure 1,

plant E could produce D's optimum output (Q_1) more cheaply than could D; hence E is the optimum plant at D's optimum output. It is a question of optimum *plant* relative to all *other* plants, versus optimum *output* for a *given* plant (without consideration of others) once that plant is built. Because of this paradox, any plant in Figure 1, say D, would be built originally to produce an output less than its own optimum output. Hence, it could subsequently increase its output, should it so desire, and thereby achieve a lower per-unit cost. Indeed, it could increase its output to Q_2 before average costs became higher than they were at the design output. It might be asked why a firm would ever consider producing Q_2 with D when E and F can produce it for less. If the need for Q_2 had been foreseen before any plant was built, then plant E would probably have been built. However, if the original output desired was Q_0, the correct choice would have been D. A subsequent expansion to Q_2 could then be made with plant D. This would be done instead of building a new plant if the cash costs of operating plant D at Q_2 were less than the total costs of operating plant F at Q_2.

One other "paradox" should be pointed out in Figure 1. Note that the short-run average costs decrease and then rise, even though the long-run cost curve falls throughout the range of outputs. Consequently a U-shaped short-run average cost curve may occur for each plant while long-run average costs decline continuously.

In the range of outputs where long-run average costs decrease (in this case throughout the range), there are said to be "economies of scale." That is, by producing larger amounts conglomerately in larger plants, it is possible to achieve lower per-unit costs, better known as "mass-production economies." If the long-run average cost curve declines throughout the range of outputs, then no plant can achieve the least possible (long-run) cost of producing the product, unless there is some size of plant, say F, which is the largest possible for one reason or another. However, something approaching the least possible long-run cost can be had with the large plants, for example, E and F in Figure 1, since the average cost curve declines more and more slowly as output rises. From the point of view of both society and the firm, plants in an industry having costs such as those shown in Figure 1 should be as large as possible in order to achieve as low average costs as possible—apart from any political or sociological disadvantages of large business.

In the case of pipe lines it is also necessary to utilize the concept of "intermediate-run" costs. If the curves labeled A–F in Figure 1 were the basis of a planning curve for pipe lines, they would be called not "short-run," but "intermediate-run" pipe-line cost curves, each representing a given line size carrying various "throughputs." (Pipe-line output is called "throughput"—the volume of liquid carried per unit of time.) In some industries the output of individual plants can be expanded above the original output simply by adding more labor or raw materials; these may be described with short-run cost curves. However, in the case of pipe lines, throughput can be increased above the designed capacity only by the addition of more capital equipment (pumping stations), along with extra labor and fuel. Short-run cost curves which allow for a fixed amount of capital equipment are "reversible." That is, when output is decreased (by laying off workers and buying smaller amounts of raw materials), the short-run curve shows the appropriate cost for the lower output. On the other hand, intermediate-run cost curves which include costs of varying amounts of capital equipment are not reversible. If pipe line D (again referring to Figure 1, this time as a series of intermediate-run curves) were built for throughput Q_0, then the costs of carrying throughput less than Q_0 in line D would *not* be shown by the curve labeled D; these costs would be higher for all throughputs less than Q_0. Why? The curve D would be based, for planning purposes, on the proper (minimum possible) number of pumping stations for each throughput. It takes more stations of a given size to push larger throughputs through a given size pipe. Consequently, the number of stations built on line D for throughput Q_0 would be larger than needed for lesser throughputs. If throughput is cut below Q_0, the number of stations cannot be cut (as could the number of workers in some other industry), since stations represent fixed capital investments—investments which incur costs even if the stations are not needed. In short, too many pumping stations would be present for any lower throughput; consequently there would be higher average costs than if the line had been designed for the lower throughput with the minimum number of stations required for that throughput. Hence, the necessity of the hybrid term "intermediate-run" in the pipe-line case. In this case the long-run curve is the envelope of the intermediate-run curves, not of the short-run curves.

With this digression into the principles of economics in mind, it is possible to proceed with the discussion of pipe-line costs. The costs computed for this study were determined primarily by the method of engineering estimation, not by the use of actual historical costs. Where engineering estimation is feasible for cost studies it should be used, since actual costs may be subject to any number of erratic variations arising from construction or operating conditions unique to particular cases. In the case of the majority of the cost items, the process of computation involved a physical determination of the amount of equipment or services required, followed by the pricing of this amount from current price quotations furnished by suppliers and/or pipe-line companies. In some cases where particular items did not readily lend themselves to a priori engineering estimation, it was necessary to use historical costs. One example of this is the construction materials cost of pumphouses, for which actual costs obtained from a pipe-line company were used as the basis of computation. This particular item also illustrates the dangers of using historical costs. The stations were built in a period of unusually bad weather; hence the labor costs were much higher than would be the case normally. The materials costs were usable, but the labor costs had to be estimated from other sources. The notable exceptions where actual costs were used as the principal basis for computation include costs of surveying the right-of-way, mainline valves, office operation, site improvement at stations, and the pipe-line communications system. Since the details of this cost study are reported elsewhere,[1] it will not be necessary to engage here in an extended discussion of such problems as optimum operating pressure, safety factor, wall thickness of pipe, centrifugal versus reciprocating pumps, diesel engines versus electric motors, and so forth. However, it is necessary to discuss in summary form certain points about pipe-line

1. See L. Cookenboo, Jr., "Costs of Operating Crude Oil Pipe Lines," *Rice Institute Pamphlet*, April 1954, pp. 35–113.

technology and the results of the cost study, since this information is all-important for the subsequent discussion.

PRODUCTION FUNCTION

In order to determine costs by engineering estimation, it is necessary to compute an "engineering production function" relating the factors of production (the goods and services used to produce a product) and output. Such a function shows the possible combinations of the factors of production which can be used to produce various levels of output.

A basic choice between two "factors of production" exists in the determination of the optimum line diameter for carrying any particular throughput. A given size of line may be used for several different throughputs by applying different amounts of power (hydraulic horsepower) to the oil carried—the more horsepower, the more throughput (but less than proportionately more). Conversely, any given throughput can be achieved by the use of several possible sizes of lines with the proper amount of horsepower applied. There are, in short, variable physical proportions of these two basic factors of production, line diameter and horsepower, which may be used to develop any given throughput. As a result, the management of a pipe-line company is forced to choose between several sizes of line when planning to develop a given throughput. Furthermore, the long-run cost of carrying crude oil might vary with throughput, as did the long-run costs in Figure 1. Larger throughputs might cost less or more per barrel. Managements, then, not only have the option of several sizes of line for each throughput, they also may have the option of choosing throughputs having different costs per barrel. Other things being equal, a pipe-line company planning to build a line should select the cheapest combination of line diameter and horsepower for the throughput which can be carried at the least cost per barrel.

A production function relating line diameter, horsepower, and throughput can be derived for crude oil pipe lines. Indeed, many such functions could be derived, depending of the density and viscosity of the oil carried, the wall thickness of pipe used, and so forth. However, for the purposes of this monograph one function will suffice. The only differences among the cost curves derived from different functions are in absolute dollars per barrel-mile for each throughput, not in the relative positions of the intermediate-run cost curves for each line. The latter is the important point for public policy considerations. A crude oil trunk pipe-line production function is shown in Chart 1. This

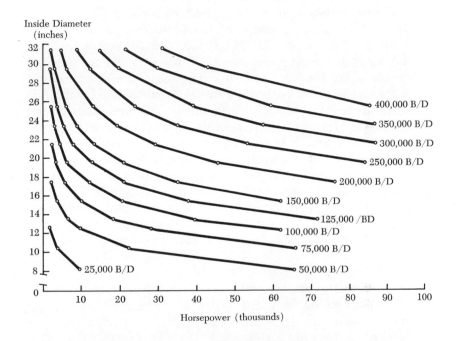

Inside Diameter (inches)

Horsepower (thousands)

CHART 1

PRODUCTION FUNCTION FOR CRUDE OIL TRUNK PIPE LINES:
LINE DIAMETER VERSUS HORSEPOWER VERSUS
THROUGHPUT—1,000-MILE LINES *

* Assumptions: 60 SUS, 34° A.P.I. Crude; no influence of gravity on flow; 5 percent terrain variation (equalized up and down hill); ¼-in. pipe throughout.

chart assumes a more or less typical Mid-Continent (60 SUS viscosity, 34° A.P.I. gravity) crude, ¼-inch pipe throughout the lines, lines 1,000 miles in length with a 5 percent terrain variation (giving 1,050 miles of pipe), and no net gravity flow in the line (there may be hills as long as there are offsetting valleys). The production function covers throughputs of 25, 50, 75, 100, 125, 200, 250, 300, 350, and 400 thousand barrels per day; this encompasses the range of throughputs for crude oil trunk lines which have yet been built. The curves in the chart show the amounts of horsepower required for the several line sizes which might be used for a given throughput; each curve applies to one of the throughputs listed. The line sizes used are 8⅝, 10¾, 12¾, 14, 16, 18, 20, 22, 24, 26, 30, and 32 inches (outside diameter) all having ¼-inch walls. This covers all line sizes used for recent crude trunk lines. (Standard line pipe is only available in these sizes in the 8–32-inch range.) It will be noted that this is in reality a three-dimensional function, with line diameter and horsepower on a plane and with the throughput axis rising perpendicularly to this plane. The production function was computed by the use of a hydraulic formula for computing required horsepowers for various volumes of liquid flow in pipes of the sizes just noted, with appropriate constants for oil of the type used. This formula, simplified, is:

$$T^{2.735} = (H)\ (D^{4.735}) \div (0.01046),$$

where,

T = Throughput,
H = Horsepower, and
D = Inside diameter of pipe.

Chart 2 shows vertical cross sections of the production function drawn perpendicular to the line-diameter axis. These are intermediate-run physical productivity curves which show the amount of horsepower that must be used with any given line size for various throughputs. They are analogous to traditional physical productivity curves of economic theory. Such a physical productivity curve in the textbooks might show the amount of wheat that can be produced from an acre of land by the use of varying numbers of workers, where line diameter is equivalent to the fixed factor (land) and horsepower is more or less equivalent to the variable factor (labor). These curves are not, however, precisely equivalent to the traditional physical productivity curves, since the horsepower factor includes some capital equipment. When it is necessary to expand output over the designed capacity

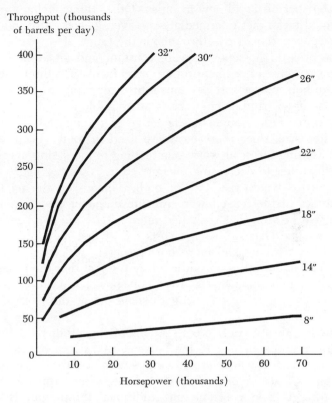

CHART 2

VERTICAL CROSS SECTION OF PRODUCTION FUNCTION:
HORSEPOWER VERSUS THROUGHPUT—LINE DIAMETER
HELD CONSTANT

of the line, it is necessary to add more capital equipment as well as more labor. When throughput is decreased below the designed capacity, unnecessary capital equipment exists—equipment on which fixed costs are incurred. Hence, as was noted above, the designation "intermediate-run" instead of short-run.

It will be observed that these productivity curves exhibit decreasing returns (marginal and average) throughout the range of throughputs. That is, there is a less than proportionate increase in throughput for a given increase in horsepower in a particular size of line. This is a physical phenomenon deriving from the characteristics of liquid flow in pipes. Other things being equal, this would mean that intermediate-run average costs attributable to horsepower should rise throughout the range of throughputs. (If the price of horsepower were constant and an addition to horsepower gave a less than proportionate increase in throughput, then the horsepower cost per barrel of throughput would rise.)

On the other hand, average costs attributable to line diameter will perforce fall throughout the range of throughputs for any given line size, since these costs are fixed in total. There are, then, offsetting forces at work, one tending to increasing average costs, the other to decreasing average costs. Whether aggregate average costs would rise, fall, or both, depends on the relative magnitudes of the horsepower and line diameter costs. In this case it will be seen that U-shaped intermediate-run average cost curves result. That is, average costs fall at first, but then level off and rise as more and more horsepower is added to a given line. (The initial fall is accentuated by the fact that the price of horsepower falls somewhat as total horsepower used on a given line increases, thereby offsetting to some extent the decreasing physical returns.)

Chart 3 shows vertical cross sections of the production function drawn perpendicular to the horsepower axis, as opposed to those in Chart 2 which are drawn perpendicular to the line-diameter axis. These cross sections indicate what happens when horsepower is held constant and additional throughput is obtained by the use of more line-diameter (a long-run movement over the production function surface that is possible only when planning the line, not after the line is built). It will be observed that these curves exhibit *increasing* physical returns (average and marginal) to scale. This means that the same amount of horsepower applied in a large-diameter line as in a small-diameter line will give a more than proportionate increase in throughput. In other words, there is more throughput per horsepower in a large line than in a small one. Since this relationship is the basic reason for the shape of the long-run cost curve, and is therefore the basis for the public policy conclusions which may be drawn from the long-run curve, it will be well to examine the physical reason for these increasing returns.

The increasing returns are attributable to the fact that there is less friction incurred per barrel of oil carried in a large-diam-

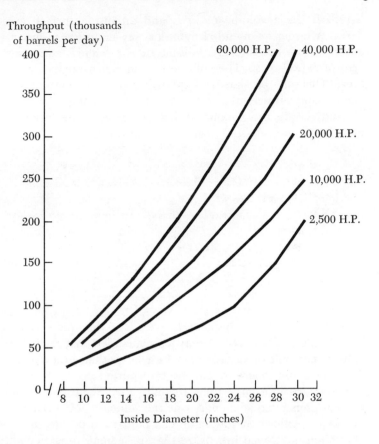

CHART 3

VERTICAL CROSS SECTION OF PRODUCTION FUNCTION:
LINE DIAMETER VERSUS THROUGHPUT FOR
SELECTED HORSEPOWERS

eter pipe than in a small-diameter pipe. Friction is created by only that part of the oil which touches the inside surface of the pipe. Hence it is the amount of surface area per barrel of oil carried that determines the amount of friction per barrel of oil carried. Solid geometry tells us that there is less surface area per unit of volume in a large-diameter cylinder (in this case the line pipe) of a given length than in a small-diameter cylinder of the same length. An open-ended cylinder of inside radius r and length L has a volume of $\pi r^2 L$ and an inside surface area of $2\pi r L$. A larger open-ended cylinder, say of inside radius $r + x$, and the same length, has a volume of $\pi (r + x)^2 L$ and a surface area of $2\pi (r + x)L$. The volume increases more than the surface area. This may be shown as follows (where V_1 and A_1 are the volume and surface area of the smaller open-ended cylinder and V_2 and A_2 are the volume and area of the larger open-ended cylinder):

$$V_1 = \pi r^2 L$$
$$V_2 = \pi (r + x)^2 L = \pi (r^2 + 2xr + x^2)L = \pi r^2 L + 2\pi xrL + \pi x^2 L$$
$$\Delta V = V_2 - V_1 = 2\pi xrL + x^2 \pi L$$
$$A_1 = 2\pi r L$$
$$A_2 = 2\pi (r + x)L = 2\pi r L + 2\pi xL$$
$$\Delta A = A_2 - A_1 = 2\pi xL.$$
Since $2\pi xrL + x^2 \pi L > 2\pi xL,$
$$\Delta V > \Delta A.$$

The volume increased by $(2\pi xrL + x^2 \pi L)$, while the surface area increased only by $2\pi xL$. It may be concluded that there is more volume per unit of surface area in a large than in a small pipe. This means that more oil can be transported per unit of surface area touched in a large than a small pipe. Since the amount of friction generated depends on the amount of surface area touched, it follows that more oil can be carried per given amount of friction developed in a large than in a small pipe. Therefore, the horsepower required to overcome a given amount of friction will propel more oil per day through a large pipe than through a small pipe. In short, because of the volume-area relationship it is possible to develop more throughput per horsepower applied in large pipes than in small ones. (It is interesting to note that the volume-area relationship is responsible for many other important technical economies of scale in industry, for example, economies of large tanks, heat containment, and so forth.) [2]

2. See H. B. Chenerey, *Engineering Bases of Economic Analysis* (unpublished doctoral thesis deposited in Widener Library, 1950), pp. 140–141, and E. A. Robinson, *Structure of Competitive Industry* (London, 1935), p. 29.

Chart 4 indicates the physical returns to scale characteristic of pipe-line operation. It will be remembered that there are decreasing physical returns as more horsepower is added to a given line, but that there are increasing physical returns from using larger lines with a given amount of horsepower. Which of these

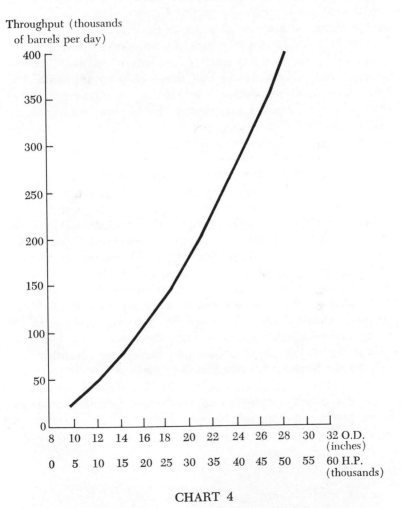

Throughput (thousands of barrels per day)

CHART 4

PHYSICAL RETURNS TO SCALE. VERTICAL CROSS SECTION OF PRODUCTION FUNCTION THROUGH ORIGIN (45° ANGLE)

counteracting tendencies predominates in long-run movements where throughput is increased or decreased by varying the amounts of both factors used? In other words, are there increasing or decreasing returns to scale (to larger size) from carrying larger amounts of oil in the same facilities? This is shown physically by the shape of vertical cross sections of the production function drawn through the origin. Chart 4 shows such a cross section drawn at a 45° angle through the origin of the function. This section indicates the returns to scale when throughput is increased by increasing the use of horsepower and line diameter in equal proportions. (Note that this is only an approximation, since the production function is only realistic at certain points, not over its whole surface; consequently, the 45° line would only by chance intersect each throughput at a point where an available line size exists.) The curve exhibits increasing (average and marginal) returns to scale throughout the range of throughputs. In other words, if the amounts of horsepower and line diameter used are increased in equal proportions, then there would be a more than proportionate increase in throughput. This indicates that on an a priori basis it would be expected that long-run decreasing average costs would characterize pipe-line operation. Only if the price of one or both of the factors should increase sufficiently with the amount of the factor used to offset the increasing returns, would the long-run cost curve turn up. Actually, the price of horsepower decreases somewhat with the amount used, and the price of line diameter does not fluctuate sufficiently with the amount used to offset the physical relationship.

Lest the reader object to drawing these general conclusions only on the basis of an example where expansion is by increased utilization of the factors in equal proportions, it should be pointed out that this is a "homogeneous" production function. Homogeneous production functions exhibit the same type of returns to scale on all parts of the surface. The function used reduces to:

$$T^{2.735} = (H)(D^{4.735})(C), \quad \text{or}$$
$$T = (H^{\frac{1}{2.735}})(D^{\frac{4.735}{2.735}})(C) = (H^{.37})(D^{1.73})(C).$$

[C is a constant.] This is a function of the form,

$$T = H^m D^n C.$$

Such a function is homogeneous if $(m + n)$ is a constant, as it is in this case, where $(m + n) = 2.1$. This also indicates that there are marked increasing returns to scale, since the function is of order 2 (constant returns to scale are implied from a function having an order of one).

The discussion of the technological relationships peculiar to pipe-line transportation of oil may now be summarized. A basic physical relationship may be deduced for the purpose of computing pipe-line costs. This relationship shows that there will be markedly increasing long-run physical returns to scale if larger and larger throughputs are carried. In the intermediate run, physical returns decrease. It follows, assuming that factor prices are more or less constant with the amount of the factor used, that there will be long-run decreasing costs (economies of scale) for pipe-line operation. Intermediate-run costs might rise, fall, or both—since the increasing average costs attributable to horsepower are counteracted by fixed costs attributed to line diameter. Under such conditions, U-shaped curves are feasible. These cost conclusions are based solely on the physical relationships discussed and are independent of the cost determination to be considered next. The conclusions would be invalidated only if the price of one or both of the factors rose sufficiently with increases in the amount of the factor used to offset the increasing physical returns to scale. This is not the case. (This may also be predicted to a considerable extent apart from actual cost determination, since the amounts of the most important single cost items included in each factor are proportional to the amounts of the factors used.)

COSTS

Pipe-line costs may be divided into three basic categories: (1) those variant with line diameter; (2) those variant with horsepower; (3) those variant only with throughput or length of line (a relatively small part of total cost). Since there is a choice for any given throughput among several possible combinations of line diameter and horsepower (as is shown in the production function in Chart 1), in order to be able to compute a long-run cost curve it is necessary to determine which of several possible combinations is least expensive for any throughput. This is done for each throughput by determining the total cost of each possible combination, on, say, an annual basis. That combination whose total cost is least for a given throughput is the optimum combination for that throughput. Note that it is only the costs of line diameter and horsepower which must be so manipulated, since the other costs are irrelevant to the choice of the optimum combination of these two. The other costs are, of course, incurred and cannot be ignored; but they do not influence the choice of the proper size line for a given throughput.

Annual total intermediate-run costs are shown in Chart 5;

Millions of 1952 Dollars

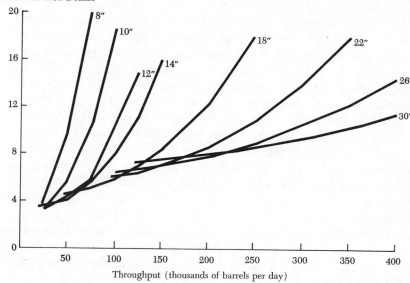

Throughput (thousands of barrels per day)

CHART 5

ANNUAL TOTAL COSTS OF OPERATING CRUDE OIL
TRUNK PIPE LINES

Source: L. Cookenboo, Jr., "Costs of Operating Crude Oil Pipe Lines," *Rice Institute Pamphlet,* April 1954, pp. 106–107 (Table 19).

these are derived by plotting annual total cost against throughput for each line diameter covered in the study. The shaded envelope of the intermediate-run cost curves is the long-run total cost curve. Chart 6 shows intermediate-run costs per barrel per 1,000

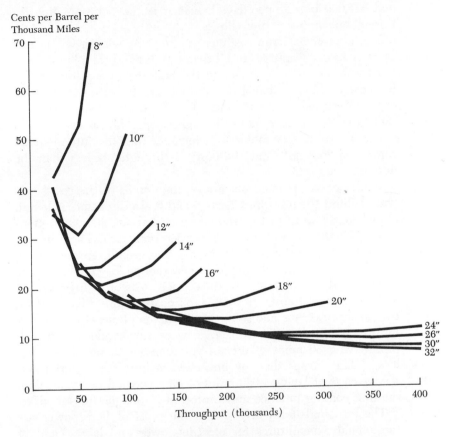

CHART 6

<small>Costs per Barrel of Operating Crude Oil
Trunk Pipe Lines</small>

Source: L. Cookenboo, Jr., "Costs of Operating Crude Oil Pipe Lines," *Rice Institute Pamphlet,* April 1954, pp. 106–107 (Table 19).

miles (that is, average costs). This is a chart analogous to Figure 1 above. Its envelope is the long-run average cost curve. In the range of throughputs where the average cost curve of a given line size lies below all other average cost curves, that line is the optimum line for the throughputs covered. For example, the 30-inch line lies beneath all others between about 225,000 and 325,000 barrels per day; hence, it is the optimum line for throughputs between those limits.

The intermediate-run cost curves also show what it would cost to carry larger quantities of oil than the design throughput if stations were added subsequent to the building of the line. (Pipe lines cannot be operated at throughputs greater than the designed capacity without the additions of more stations, since the design capacity would require the highest operating pressures permitted by the safety factor.) Remember that the intermediate-run curve does *not* show the costs of throughputs less than the design throughput.

While, as was pointed out above, the details of the cost study lying behind the totals in Charts 5 and 6 are discussed at length elsewhere,[3] a word or two should be said about the assumptions involved in the engineering-type cost determination. The principal items involved in the cost of line diameter are all represented by initial outlays made during the construction of the line. The most important line costs are the service costs of laying the line, and the material costs of steel, pipe coating, line block valves, corrosion protection, and so forth. The assumptions of the characteristics of the lines, listed above, were 1,000 miles of ¼-inch pipe having 50 miles of terrain variation (with no net gravity flow). This means that the line costs include the material and service costs of laying 1,050 miles of pipe (coated in accord with the best coating practice and protected by magnesium anodes).

The principal items involved in the costs of horsepower are the annual expenditures for electric power and labor (and of less importance, maintenance) to operate the pumping stations. This category also includes the initial cost of the stations; this represents the most difficult, time-consuming part of a pipe-line cost computation (even though station costs are not too important in relation to total costs). The stations used on the pipe lines described in Charts 5 and 6 are semiautomatic, equipped with centrifugal pumps and electric motors. Stations pumping over 100,000 barrels per day are equipped with three full-size pumps and motors (one motor per pump) which together deliver the capacity throughput, and one half-size pump and motor. This provides flexibility of operation which would otherwise be

3. Cookenboo, "Costs of Operating Crude Oil Pipe Lines," pp. 35–113.

unattainable with constant speed electric motors. (With, as they say, 3½ pumps, seven stages of operation are possible: no pumps, ½ pump, 1½, 2, 2½, and 3 for capacity.) Stations pumping less than 100,000 barrels per day utilize two full-size pumps and one half-size pump. Each station utilizes in-an-out piping to permit the bypassing of any one pump without shutting down the whole station. The labor force required for such semi-automatic stations is two men per shift (regardless of the level of operation), unless the stations are very large; none used in this study was large enough to require extra operators. (In a semi-automatic pumping station the principal tasks of the operators are to watch the controls, shut off motor-operated valves when necessary, and maintain the equipment.)

The principal costs involved in the "other" category are the initial costs of (1) tankage (the lines in this study have 12.5 days' supply (of storage capacity along the line), (2) surveying the right-of-way, (3) damages to terrain crossed, and (4) a communications system (here assumed to be a 12-channel microwave system). It should be noted that while these costs vary either with throughput or with length of line, they are *proportional* to either throughput or length of line as the case may be. There are no significant per-barrel costs of a pipe line which change with length. The only such costs are those of a central office force; these are inconsequential in relation to total. Hence, it is possible to state that costs per barrel-mile for a 1,000-mile trunk line are representative of costs per barrel-mile of any trunk line (those, say, 75 or 100 miles in length and longer).

It will be observed in Chart 6 that there are economies of scale (decreasing long-run average costs) throughout the range of throughputs covered. The analysis was only carried through 32-inch lines and 400,000 barrels per day. However, if larger lines could be had at a constant price per ton of steel (the only price per unit of material likely to change with larger amounts than those used), then the long-run average cost curve would fall even farther. On the other hand, pipe much larger than 34 or 36 inches might well require the creation of special pipe-making facilities and, consequently, might command a higher price per ton than the pipe sizes used in this study. In this case, the long-run average cost curve might turn up near, say, 500,000 barrels per day.

In any event, the rate of decrease of the average cost curve has declined appreciably by the time a throughput of 400,000 barrels per day is reached. Consequently, the cost per barrel of carrying a throughput of 400,000 barrels per day is probably close to the minimum that can be achieved with present pipe-making facilities.

It may also be noted from Chart 6, especially in the case of the large-diameter lines, that throughput can be expanded appreciably over the design throughput before higher per-barrel costs than the original costs are incurred. (For a while, of course, there would actually be a decline in per-barrel costs.) For example, a 24-inch line built for 200,000 barrels per day could, if necessary, later be used for 300,000 barrels per day (after adding the required number of stations) without incurring increased costs per barrel.

Short-run cost curves could be computed for any of the possible combinations of line diameter and horsepower shown in Chart 1 —since each line would have a different short-run cost curve for each throughput it might carry. Building seven stations on an 18-inch line would yield one short-run curve. Building ten stations on an 18-inch line would yield another short-run curve. Building seven stations on a 20-inch line would yield yet another short-run curve—ad infinitum. To avoid the labor involved in computing short-run costs for every combination of line diameter and horsepower covered in the study (75 in all), two were computed: one for an 18-inch line carrying 100,000 barrels per day, another for a 30-inch line carrying 300,000 barrels per day. The relative positions of short- and intermediate-run curves would be the same for any other combinations of line diameter and horsepower. These short-run average cost curves are shown in Chart 7.

Observe that short-run average costs are always higher than intermediate-run average costs for throughputs less than the designed throughput (the short-run curve does not exist for higher throughputs, since pipe lines cannot be operated over the designed capacity without violating the safety factor). The significance of this is that a line built to carry 250,000 barrels per day will incur higher costs than necessary if it consistently carries 200,000 barrels per day. If it had been designed for 200,000

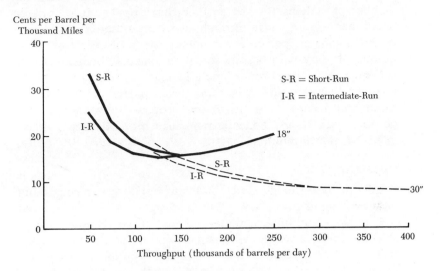

Cents per Barrel per
Thousand Miles

Throughput (thousands of barrels per day)

CHART 7

SHORT-RUN AVERAGE COSTS OF TRANSPORTING CRUDE OIL IN
TRUNK LINES

Note: Eighteen-in. line designed for 150,000 barrels per day. Thirty-in.
line designed for 300,000 barrels per day.

barrels per day, then the intermediate-run cost for 200,000 barrels per day would be the cost incurred. This figure is less than the short-run cost of 200,000 barrels per day on a line with a capacity of 250,000 barrels per day.

This may be made clear by discussing briefly the process of computation of short-run costs. The only significant cost of a pipe line that is not fixed once the line is built is the cost of electric power. If the line is run below capacity, as many workers are still needed; and, of course, the same number of stations and the same amount of pipe exists. The only significant saving is in power costs. In order to compute short-run costs one simply subtracts the cost of the appropriate amount of electric power which is saved when throughput is cut to various levels from the intermediate-run cost at the designed output. This figure must be higher than intermediate-run costs of lesser throughputs because these costs are computed upon the basis of the proper (smaller) number of stations for the smaller throughputs. It should be noted that a given cut in throughput means a more than proportionate saving in power requirements, since electric power requirements vary with horsepower requirements. Remember that it takes a more than proportionate increase in horsepower to get a given increase in throughput; conversely, a decrease in throughput means a more than proportionate decrease in horsepower required—and hence a more than proportionate decrease in electric power required.

SUMMARY

Intermediate-, long-, and short-run costs for carrying crude oil were computed.

The long- and intermediate-run cost curves computed in a study of the engineering estimation type are of the same shape that would be predicted from the physical production functions for pipe-line transportation of crude (with no consideration of costs). The physical production function is homogeneous of order 2; under these conditions there will be marked economies of scale unless factor prices rise sharply with the amount of the factor used. This is not the case in the range of throughputs and line sizes covered.

The long-run average cost curve falls throughout the range of throughputs covered (see Chart 6), and it would continue to fall indefinitely if larger pipe could be obtained without paying a premium price. However, the rate of decline of long-run costs per barrel has slowed considerably by the time a throughput of 400,000 barrels per day is reached. Intermediate-run curves are U-shaped, but throughput can be increased appreciably over the designed level without increased per-barrel costs—especially ·in the case of large-diameter lines where the "U" is rather flat over wide ranges of throughputs.

Short-run costs are always greater than intermediate-run costs for a given line size. The only significant variable cost in pipe-line operation is the cost of power (or fuel).

It may be concluded from these cost curves that the economies of scale characteristic of the operation of pipe lines require that oil must be carried conglomerately in as large quantities as is possible in large-diameter line. This gives the least transportation costs obtainable—the optimum situation from the point of view of both the firm and society. Furthermore, pipe lines should not be run at throughputs appreciably below capacity; otherwise higher (short-run) costs per barrel will be incurred than need be. Finally, the capacity of a large line can be expanded appreciably without increasing average costs; indeed, *decreased* average costs can be obtained with moderate expansions.

Cost Functions and Cost Control

EDWIN MANSFIELD AND
HAROLD H. WEIN

Edwin Mansfield is Professor of Economics at the Wharton School of the University of Pennsylvania. Harold H. Wein is Professor of Management at Michigan State University. This paper is taken from their article in Applied Statistics *in 1958.*

THERE have been numerous studies where the relationship between cost and output has been estimated for manufacturing plants. These studies fall generally into two categories. In the first category, the chief purpose of the work has been to accumulate evidence concerning various cost curves that occupy an important place in economics. In the second category, the work has been done primarily with a view toward the direct usefulness of the relationship of cost and output to industrial managers. This paper falls into the second category.

We give an illustration here of how such a relationship may be used to formulate a simple control chart for costs, a topic which should be of interest to many applied statisticians and industrial managers. The problem of controlling performance and costs is important in almost every sector of industry and trade. Our data, and hence our specific results, pertain to the American railroad industry, but the statistical techniques that are used may be applicable to other industries as well.

Freight yards differ greatly in size, layout, and type, but they have certain physical characteristics and functions in common.

Physical Characteristics · All yards contain sets of tracts. In large yards they are generally of three types: receiving tracks where incoming freight cars are stored, classification tracks where cars are switched, and outbound tracks where cars that were situated on a classification track are stored until a locomotive hauls them away as a train.

Functions · Freight yards switch cars. That is, they sort incoming cars by putting them on the appropriate classification tracks, and in this way they break up incoming trains to form new trains. Most yards also deliver and pick up cars. Engines are assigned to deliver cars to industrial sidings and other yards and to pick them up there. Finally, many yards bill and inspect freight cars and perform such ancillary services as maintenance, repair, and storage.

The importance of freight yards to a railroad is illustrated by the fact that about one-third of its total operating costs may arise in these yards. In view of this, it is clearly important that proper control be maintained over the performance of the yards. However, this problem of maintaining adequate control is made difficult by their number and their distribution over a large area. (For example, in the railroad we studied, about 200 freight yards are scattered along approximately 12,000 miles of track.) It is virtually impossible for any team of managers to have each day a reasonably complete knowledge of what happened at each yard. They must examine selected data concerning the performance of the yards during the day, and from these data they must somehow evaluate a yard's performance. In evaluating performance, one piece of information that is used is the costs incurred in the yard during the day.

At present, the data and techniques used by most railroads do not seem well suited for their purpose. Judging by the opinions of the railroad management with which we worked, their purpose is to detect those days when the costs at a yard are unusually high for the output produced and those series of days when the costs are repeatedly higher than would be expected. Detection of either of these would result in an inquiry concerning the causes of the apparent deterioration of yard performance. In addition, the management is interested in detecting days when costs are unusually low or when they are repeatedly lower than would be expected. In this case there would also be an inquiry, but the intention would be to encourage the responsible factors rather than to remedy them.

In this paper we discuss a control chart based on the relationship between cost and output that may be useful for these purposes. Before discussing the chart, it seems worthwhile to describe the measures of freight-yard output and costs that are used. The two most important services performed at a yard are switching and delivery; and it seems reasonable to use the number of "cuts" switched and the number of cars delivered during a particular period as a measure of output. A "cut" is a group of cars that rolls as a unit on to the same classification track; it is often used as a measure of switching output. The number of cars delivered includes both the cars delivered to sidings and other yards and those that are picked up. This output measure is not ideal, one difficulty being that it conceals considerable heterogeneity. For example, two groups of cars may be delivered but one may be hauled a greater distance than the other. Some of this heterogeneity could be eliminated by further refinements in the output measure, but the extra complexity with regard to data collection and computation might result in a loss of feasibility.

The costs used here include all money costs incurred in the yard except fixed charges, repair costs, maintenance and storage costs, and vacation costs. Only money costs are included; the costs that may be imputed to car delay are not taken into account. Fixed charges are excluded, but some of the included costs are essentially fixed in the very short run.

THE CONTROL CHART

The control chart contains the deviation of actual cost from the cost that would be expected on the basis of the average relationship between cost and output. These deviations are used to detect days when costs are suspiciously high or low. The model that underlies the chart is as follows: for a particular yard, the expected cost on the i'th day (C_i) is assumed to be a linear function of the number of cuts switched on the i'th day (S_i) and the number of cars delivered on the i'th day (D_i).

When the railroad management refer to unusually high or low costs, it seems clear that they mean costs that are unusual if the cost-output relationship and the effects of numerous small disturbances remain at their previous, satisfactory levels. That is, they are interested in detecting those C_i that are unusually high or low if the average relationship between cost and output is unchanged. Similarly, when they refer to a sequence of days when costs are higher or lower than would be expected, it seems clear that they mean a run of the C_i that is unlikely if this relationship is unchanged.

If the model is adequate and if the average relationship between cost and output is known, it is a simple matter to set up a control chart that will aid the management. Each day, the deviation of actual cost from the cost that would be expected on the basis of this relationship can be plotted on a chart that has two sets of control limits. The outer control limits can be set so that, if this relationship remains the same, the probability that a point lies outside them is small. The inner control limits can be set so that, if this relationship remains the same, the probability that two consecutive points lie outside them (in one direction) is small. When a point lies outside the outer limits or a pair of points lies outside the inner limits, there is evidence that the relationship may have changed and that an inquiry should be made.

SETTING UP THE CHART

A control chart was set up at a freight yard located at Toledo, Ohio. This yard constitutes one of the largest and most important links in the railroad we studied. The chief types of freight that pass through the yard are livestock, perishables, coal, and automobiles. Table 1 shows the number of cars switched,

TABLE 1

OUTPUT, COST, AND EMPLOYMENT, FREIGHT
YARD, TOLEDO, 7 DAYS
(*Taken from records of cooperating railroad*)

Item	Fri.	Sat.	Sun.	Mon.	Tues.	Wed.	Thurs.
Number of cuts switched	869	792	762	586	669	732	659
Number of cars switched	2534	2303	2521	1849	2090	2114	1979
Number of cars delivered *	1015	1003	820	548	877	706	1038
Number of crews used	45	45	40	38	46	46	46
Number of engine hours	372	369	329	309	385	381	386
Money costs ($)	7523	7464	6932	6550	7606	7757	7701

* Includes number of cars picked up.

the number of cuts switched, the number of cars delivered, the number of crews employed, the number of engine hours used, and the costs at the yard, for a sample one-week period.

The first step in setting up the chart was to gather historical data concerning cost and output. Data similar to those in Table 1 were collected for sixty-one days, and the average relationship between cost and output was estimated. The resulting relationship was

(1) $$C_i = 4{,}914 + 0.42S_i + 2.44D_i$$

The second step was to test some of the assumptions underlying the chart. Some of these tests are quite similar to those used in quality control to determine if the process is "in control." Taken together, the results of these tests did not cast any great suspicion on the assumptions underlying the chart. Indeed, the results seemed to be quite compatible with these assumptions.

The third step was to draw the inner and outer control limits on the chart. The outer control limits were set at ± $804, and the inner control limits were set at ± $410. These limits (designated by ICL and OCL) are included in Figure 1. If there were no errors in the assumptions, the probability would be 0.05

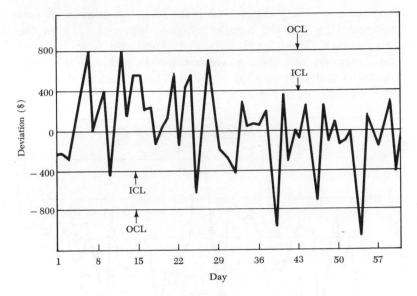

FIGURE 1

DEVIATION OF ACTUAL COST FROM EXPECTED COST BASED ON
AVERAGE RELATIONSHIP BETWEEN COST AND OUTPUT:
FREIGHT YARD, 61 DAYS
Source: records of cooperating railroad.

that a point would lie outside the outer limits if the relationship remained fixed. Similarly, the probability would be about 0.03 that two consecutive points would lie outside the same inner control limit.

After setting the control limits, an attempt was made to determine if any assignable cause could be found for the days that were "out of control." None could be found, and it was assumed that they were due to "chance." The number of such days was almost precisely what one would expect on a chance basis.

PERFORMANCE OF THE CHART

This section describes the performance of the chart during a six-week period that was several months subsequent to the time when the chart was set up. The results apply to the freight yard described above. On each day during the period data were collected concerning the money costs (C), the number of cuts switched (S), and the number of cars delivered (D) on the previous day. Then the deviation of actual cost from expected cost based on the average relationship in equation (1) was computed and plotted on the chart.[1] The deviations that were plotted are shown in Figure 2.

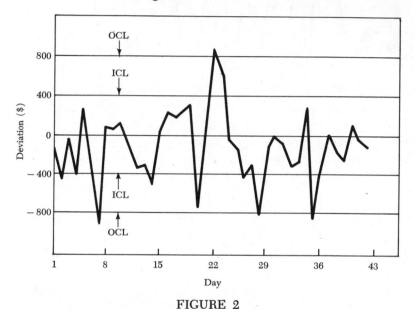

FIGURE 2

CONTROL CHART FOR COSTS: FREIGHT YARD, 42 DAYS
Source: records of cooperating railroad.

During the six-week period, four days seemed to be out of control, and in every case there seemed to be an assignable cause. One of these days was Labor Day. The exceptionally high costs on Labor Day can be attributed to the punitive wage-rates that were paid because it was a holiday. On the other days that were out of control (all of them Sundays) the exceptionally low costs can be attributed in part to the following circumstances: (1) Cars delivered to other yards constituted a large proportion of all cars delivered, and since such cars are rela-

1. Actually, the relationship was recomputed as more and more data became available.

tively easy to deliver, costs were depressed. (2) More efficient methods were used to handle incoming cars. (3) Some work ordinarily performed by the yard was done by another yard; hence costs were reduced somewhat.

The basic data were collected by railroad employees and the points on the chart were computed by officials of the railroad. From their evaluation of the performance of the yard it appeared that the chart provided a reasonably faithful picture of the level of performance. Moreover, the chart stimulated some inquiries that indicated where improvements in yard performance might be made.

To increase further the usefulness of the chart, it appeared that cars delivered to other yards might be separated in the output measure from cars delivered to industrial sidings. In this way an important factor (and in some ways an extraneous one) responsible in part for the low deviations on Sundays would be taken into account. No finality can be claimed for the results, but it appeared that the chart would be useful to the management in controlling yard costs.

Part Three

Profits, Demand, and Pricing

FIRMS must constantly be concerned with profits, demand, and pricing, the topics of Part Three. Thus, it behooves anyone interested in managerial economics to study these topics carefully. In the opening article, Joel Dean contrasts accounting and economic concepts of profit. Focusing on the meaning of depreciation, the treatment of capital gains, and the valuation of assets, he concludes that, for purposes of managerial decision-making, a profit statement based on economic concepts is more useful than one based on the conventions of fiscal accounting. His paper is followed by one taken from *Fortune* which describes the break-even chart, the diagram that projects a firm's revenues and costs at various levels of sales. To illustrate its use, two hypothetical cases are taken up.

The next three papers are concerned with demand and pricing. One of the first things a firm must consider in pricing its product is the price elasticity of demand. The editor's paper discusses the nature and determinants of this elasticity and describes why it is of major importance. Joel Dean's paper suggests various ways in which the firm can estimate the price elasticity of demand, using controlled experiments, consumer questionnaires, engineering estimates, and correlation analyses. He describes in some detail a study of this sort done for a large New York department store.

A case study of the estimation of the price and income elasticities of demand for one of the nation's most important products is contained in the next article, which is a report of a Senate subcommittee on the demand for automobiles. Following this case study, A. D. H. Kaplan, Joel B. Dirlam, and Robert F. Lanzillotti show how a firm's pricing policy is influenced by the character of its product—the type of demand to which it caters, its physical attributes, production requirements, amenability to differentiation, and stage of maturity.

The Measurement of Profits

JOEL DEAN

Joel Dean is Professor of Business Economics
at Columbia University's Graduate School of
Business. This paper is taken from the
Accounting Review.

Profits must be measured differently for different purposes,
and the kind of measurement that is needed for many executive
decisions is not provided by the conventional income statement.
The Bureau of Internal Revenue, the stockholders, and the banks,
all want special kinds of information, and generally have custom-
made income statements designed to fit their requirements. Management also has peculiar demands to make of income analysis in
reaching executive decisions; and the profit statement used by
executives to run a business generally conforms more closely to
the concepts of economic analysis than to the conventions of fiscal
reporting. Many executives are unhappy about the kind of income statement produced by conventional accounting methods
and feel that decision-making could be raised to a more sophisticated plane by relating income statements more closely to management's purposes.

This article attempts to examine from the managerial standpoint the major issues of profit measurement on which economists and accountants have generally taken different positions.
Their most important points of difference center on: (1) the meaning of depreciation; (2) the treatment of capital gains and losses,

and perhaps most important in these times (3) the price level basis for valuation of assets (i.e., current vs. historical costs).

DEPRECIATION

Treatment of depreciation is an important instance of this basic conflict. Only in the last fifty years has depreciation been a generally accepted charge against income. As businessmen came to realize that some provision must be made for the future replacement of equipment, some kind of depreciation reserve accounting was needed. The accountants' insistence that the reserve be related to the original cost rather than to the cost of replacement—which is usually quite different—gives depreciation accounting full economic usefulness only under the simplest hypothetical conditions of stable prices and foreseeable obsolescence.

The objective of depreciation in accounting is to allocate the total cost of equipment to production during the period in which it will be used. The effect is to insure that revenues equal to original cost are not distributed as dividends, but are rather put back into assets, such as more equipment or cash. Whether the amount that is thus put out of reach of dividends will actually be enough for replacement is not considered part of this accounting problem. Replacement is viewed by accountants as having no bearing on measurement of profits.

For economists, there are two distinct kinds of depreciation charge. The first is the opportunity cost of equipment, that is, the most profitable alternative use of it that is foregone by putting it to its present use. The alternative involved in using the asset for one year may be viewed as selling it at the beginning instead of the end of the year. The opportunity cost could then be measured by the fall in value of the equipment during the year. This shrinkage in disposal value, which measures the capital-wastage from postponing its disposal for one year, produces a depreciation cost estimate which is quite different from straight-line depreciation for an individual year. For example, it is common to charge as annual depreciation one-fifth of an automobile's original cost. Yet the decline in disposal value during the first year is normally nearer to 40 percent than to 20 percent of original cost. Inherently it has no relation to cost; disposal value rose during some postwar years, producing negative depreciation costs from an economic viewpoint.

The opportunity-cost of depreciation depends upon the nature of the alternative. The alternative may be to keep the equipment idle and save it for later years. Or there may be no alternative uses in other places or times, and thus no real cost of using it in its present function. A hydroelectric dam is perhaps an illustration of this kind of specialized and immobile sunk investment. The economic cost of using the equipment for one year, in any case, has nothing to do with original cost and nothing to do with eventual disposal of the equipment—the two important factors in accounting depreciation.

The second kind of depreciation cost is the exhaustion of a year's worth of limited valuable life. In the case of the dam, where there is no opportunity cost, the future useful life (which measures its unique value to the going concern) is nevertheless continually running out. To preserve owner's capital, enough of the dam's gross earnings must be saved and reinvested to shift capital out of the dam into equally profitable ventures, perhaps a replacement dam. The amount of this kind of economic depreciation is not determined by the historical cost of the equipment. It is better measured by replacement value of equipment that will produce comparable earnings. This kind of depreciation is not a cost; the cost was incurred when capital was originally frozen into the plant. Rather, it is an act of saving, and the amount to charge each year is a financial problem related to past, present, and future patterns of gross earnings, as well as to price level expectations.

Both of these economic concepts of depreciation are important to management. The first, opportunity cost, is needed for operating problems of profit-making, the second, replacement of eroded earnings ability, is needed for financial problems of preserving and administering capital. For neither, however, does original cost play any role in estimates.

TREATMENT OF CAPITAL GAINS AND LOSSES

Capital gains and losses, or "windfalls," as they are often called, may be defined loosely as unanticipated changes in the value of property relative to other real goods. That is, a windfall reflects a change in someone's anticipation of the property's earning power. Fluctuations in stock market prices are almost all of this nature.

"Property" should be interpreted broadly here to include executive ability, organizational structure, brand names, and market connections. All the assets that comprise the value of the firm are vulnerable to windfall changes. For instance, the value of cash deteriorates in inflation; accounts receivable are hit by defaults not allowed for in bad debt reserves; inventory is subject to fire, flood, price drops, and substitute competition; the value of plant facilities is slashed when competitors install new, cost-cutting equipment; and patent protection can be made worthless by a court decision. The list of possibilities is endless.

These are capital losses, which, in a progressive society, are probably larger on balance than capital gains. Many of these risks can be diluted by insurance-type charges, such as surplus reserve appropriations or high depreciation rates. And when conservative managements actually over-insure, the excess eventually appears as capital gains.

A sound accounting policy to follow concerning windfalls is to avoid recording them until they turn into cash by a purchase or sale of assets, since it is never clear until then *exactly* how large they are in dollar terms. Occasionally major write-downs are made when value has apparently been wiped out; but the chastening experience of 1929–1932 has virtually eliminated the practice of write-ups beyond original cost.

How the windfall is reported in financial statements is not a matter of interest to economists (as long as they are explained). They are concerned with the future, not the past. The important thing is that gains and losses usually can be foreseen for some time before they are realized in cash. A fact-minded management must have some sort of balance sheet, if only an estimated one that realizes surprises long before they have become exact enough to be acceptable to accountants. For example, if prices are to be determined with the objective of producing a "reasonable" rate of return on the valuation of investment, they should reflect projectable windfalls even though not yet cashed. Otherwise, a target rate of return based on an historically "factual," but nevertheless fictitious capital value, may lead to later and unpleasant surprises from the resulting price policies.

CURRENT VS. HISTORICAL COSTS

In measuring income, accountants typically state costs in terms of the price level at the time of the purchase, by recording the historical outlay, rather than in terms of the current price level. Various reasons for this have been advanced by accountants: (1) because historical costs produce more accurate measurement of income; (2) because historical costs are less debatable (more objective) than the calculation of present replacement value; (3) because the function of the accountant is to record history whether or not history has relevance for future business or economic problems, but presumably in the hope that it has.

Arguments on historical cost accounting have been going on for decades, but never was the debate more vigorous than during the 1941–1948 inflation. This was an extremely turbulent time: business was scrambling to fill postwar demand and was jockeying for new market positions; there was a rush to get new products on the market; capital expenditures were being made at a tremendous rate. The situation was rich with windfall gains and losses, resulting from the violent changes in demand, supply, and price structure. Management needed the best kind of information to keep track of conditions and to plan astutely. Inflation carried prices to nearly double their level of ten years before; a general revision of ideas was called for on the value of a dollar and the meaning of the older assets on the books. One of the significant by-products of inflation was a bitter controversy among accountants, lawyers, economists, and politicians on the truth or fiction of accounting practice in such a period. The argument was a cross-hatch of speculations on legal and moral obligations to investors, tax liabilities, established accounting traditions, future price levels, and political convenience. Out of the controversy came income statements with a rash of special reserves and footnote explanations, and some extraordinary depreciation treatments.

The implied assumption of most depreciation policies was that we would eventually get back to prewar prices. This assumption seemed quite unreal and irrelevant to most economists, and it was clear that published income statements had only begun to recognize the basic change in the purchasing power of the dollar. With prices on a new high plateau, depreciation charges in terms of prewar prices were carrying only about half the load of financing postwar replacements, and it was almost impossible to determine what part of the capital investment boom was really adding to the nation's productive capacity.

Statistics of corporate earnings were probably gross overstatements of economic earnings, although the amount of the distortion was difficult to estimate. In a period of inflation, cost of living goes up for corporations as well as for persons. The cost of refilling inventories, replacing worn equipment, and expanding capacity all go up. Yet accounting procedures generally fail to take adequate account of these increases. When inventories and depreciation are charged at original costs, rather than at the higher replacement cost, inventory and plant are revalued as they are turned over. Orthodox accounting vigilantly keeps ordinary revaluations from getting into the profit and loss account—by treating them as surplus adjustments. But when revaluations find their way into the accounts indirectly, by the process of turnover of assets during inflation, they *do* get into the earnings account. These revaluation profits are treated as ordinary business income and cannot in the books be distinguished from other income. Hence, accounting profit overstates real business income, not only during an inflation but for some time after prices have reached stability. It is clearly not enough to deflate the reported income figure by dividing money profits by some cost-of-living index after the manner in which real wages are found. Profits are a residual in a calculation that uses dollars of many different dates—today's cash dollars, last year's inventory dollars, and equipment dollars of many years of prosperity and depression. To measure real profits, all these assets must be stated in dollars of the same purchasing power. This is an elaborate operation, and the desirable data on prices, products, and dates are usually hard to estimate. With some expediting assumptions, however, usable approximations can be made.

A Note on Break-even Charts

Fortune MAGAZINE

This article appeared in the February 1949
issue of Fortune.

Essentially, the break-even chart is a graphic presentation of the relationship between revenue and expense, projected for all levels of sales. There is nothing complicated or novel about such a chart. Progressive managements have used this or similar visual aids for years. The break-even chart is no substitute for either detailed accountancy or management judgment.

The basic chart (Chart 1) was developed some forty years ago by Professor Walter Rautenstrauch of the Industrial Engineering Department of Columbia University. It is the great granddaddy of the many sales-profit charts in use today, and is, in some respects, superior to them. The 45-degree sales line makes it possible to plot the break-even points for any number of years or months on a single chart, and to compare charts for different companies, products, etc. A prerequisite to the construction of this or any other break-even chart, however, is a knowledge of which business expenses are constant and which are variable with changes in volume. Once that is known a total-expense line can be drawn for all levels of sales. Few firms customarily break down their costs in this manner, however. Take, for example, the remuneration paid a salesman. Normal accountancy would probably lump his commissions, salary, and bonus together as sales expense. Actually, however, his commission is a variable

CHART 1 FINDING XYZ COMPANY'S BREAK-EVEN POINT

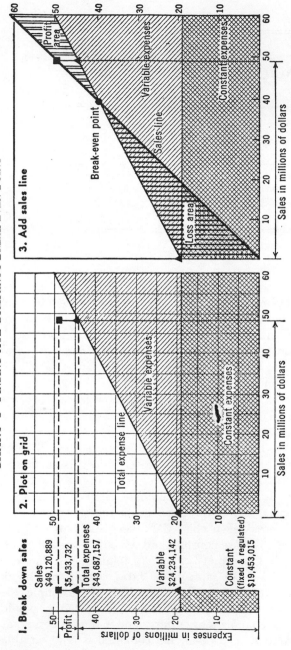

The construction of a break-even chart involves three simple steps. Step 1: Expenses that vary directly with volume (materials, sales commissions, etc.) are segregated from constant expenses (real-estate taxes, depreciation, interest, etc.). Step 2: The total expense line is then plotted on a grid with identical horizontal and vertical dollar scales. Step 3: A sales line is superimposed on this grid forming a 45-degree angle with both scales. That this method of plotting the break-even point is accurate is attested by the fact that the computed break-even volume for the company above (an actual firm) was $38.4 million.

CHART 2

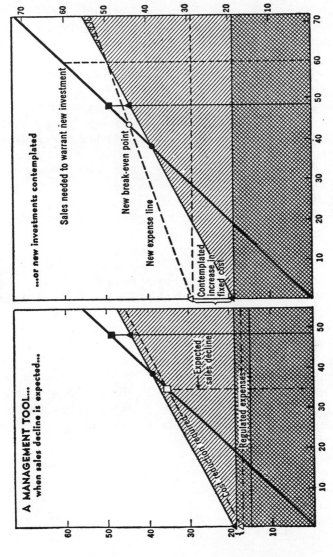

The hypothetical cases above illustrate two of the many ways a break-even chart can be used in management planning. If sales decline $15 million (left) a $4-million loss will result unless costs are cut. If, on the other hand, an investment is contemplated that will increase constant expense by $10 million (right) it can be seen that sales of $60 million are needed to justify the new expense structure.

expense, his salary a constant expense, and his bonus a regulated expense; i.e., although constant in that it is not directly related to sales, it is nevertheless subject to management discretion. The trick of constructing an accurate break-even chart, then, is largely dependent upon proper cost analysis, but that is equally true when the break-even point is computed.

The break-even chart is like a household tape measure. It has many practical uses and yet does not pretend to be microscopically accurate. The total-expense line, for example, is simply a straight line drawn from fixed costs at volume zero through total cost at current volume. No attempt is made at curvilinear refinement because cost figures are themselves mere approximations. Nor can valid deductions be drawn from a break-even chart at volumes widely different from that on which the chart is based. It is important to remember that the chart represents expense at a given moment and under given conditions and that any change in price, wages, et al., will alter the sales-expense relationship. If these limitations are borne in mind, however, the break-even chart can be used to analyze and control costs and to estimate profits under a variety of assumptions.

In Chart 2, the effect of a sales decline or of an additional capital outlay are considered. A decline in sales of $15 million would obviously put the firm into the red unless regulatable expenses (research, promotion, the president's salary, etc.) were cut $4 million. In the other case it is assumed that a contemplated investment will increase constant cost by $10 million but will reduce variable expenses. The chart quickly shows at what volume the new investment becomes profitable. Although these charts are for an entire company, break-even charts can also be constructed for individual departments, plants, products, or even salesmen.

The Importance of the Price Elasticity of Demand

EDWIN MANSFIELD

Edwin Mansfield is Professor of Economics at the Wharton School, University of Pennsylvania. This article was written for the present volume.

The price elasticity of demand is the percentage change in the quantity demanded that results from a 1 percent increase in price. A sharp distinction should be made between an industry's elasticity and a particular firm's elasticity. Whereas the former gauges the sensitivity of total industry demand to industry-wide changes in price, the latter shows the sensitivity of demand for a particular firm's product to changes in its price, the price set by other firms in the industry being held constant. A firm's elasticity depends heavily on the similarity of its product to that of competitors. For instance, a Gulf station is likely to lose a considerable share of its market to a neighboring Esso station whose price is half a cent a gallon less.

The price elasticity of demand is of great importance to the firm. When costs are increasing, it is tempting for the firm to pass on the increases by raising the price to the consumer. If demand for the product is relatively inelastic,[1] this action may succeed.

1. Demand at a particular price is said to be inelastic if the price elasticity is less than one in absolute value. In this case, total revenue decreases with decreases in price.

97

However, when there are many substitutes and demand is quite elastic,[2] increasing prices may lead to a reduction in total revenues rather than an increase. The result may be lower rather than higher profits. Similarly, businessmen are sometimes surprised by a lack of success of price reductions, this merely being a reflection of the fact that demand is relatively inelastic.

Most businessmen intuitively are aware of the elasticity of demand of the goods they make, although they may not have a detailed, precise estimate. Nonetheless, some firms tend to be conservative and underestimate the elasticity of demand. For example, classical phonograph records were high-priced luxury items for a long time. In 1938, Columbia cut the price per record from $2 to $1, and the response was overwhelming. To the surprise of much of the industry, total expenditure on classical records rose greatly, the price elasticity of demand being relatively large.

Using techniques like those described in "Estimating the Price Elasticity of Demand," it is possible to estimate the price elasticity of demand for a particular product. Some of the results are shown in Table 1. As would be expected, the price elasticity of demand for basic foodstuffs is relatively low. For sugar, potatoes, hay, and wheat, it is less than 0.5 percent in absolute value. That is, a 1 percent increase in the price of these products will result in less than a 0.5 percent decrease in the quantity consumed. On the other hand, the demand for millinery is quite elastic, a 1 percent increase in price leading to a 3 percent decrease in quantity consumed.

One of the most important factors influencing the price elasticity of demand is the availability of substitutes. If a product is faced with extremely close substitutes, its demand will be very elastic. For example, take the case of the Gulf and Esso dealers cited above. Their products, location, and services are so similar that a very small differential in price will result in a considerable shift in sales. On the other hand, in the case of basic foodstuffs such close substitutes do not exist, the result being that the price elasticity of demand is much lower.

2. Demand at a particular price is said to be elastic if the price elasticity is greater than one in absolute value, in which case total revenue increases with decreases in price.

TABLE 1

ESTIMATED PRICE ELASTICITIES OF DEMAND FOR SELECTED
COMMODITIES, UNITED STATES

Product	Price elasticity
beef	—0.92
millinery	—3.00
gasoline	—0.52
sugar	—0.31
corn	—0.49
cotton	—0.12
hay	—0.43
wheat	—0.08
potatoes	—0.31
oats	—0.56
barley	—0.39
buckwheat	—0.99

Source: H. Schultz, *Theory and Measurement of Demand* (Chicago: University of Chicago Press, 1938), and M. Spencer and L. Siegelman, *Managerial Economics* (Homewood, Ill.: Richard D. Irwin, 1959).

Finally, to illustrate very briefly the sorts of studies that have been made of the price elasticity of demand, consider a study of the fare structure of the New York subway and its effect on passenger travel. Table 2 gives forecasts of demand and revenues

TABLE 2

ALTERNATIVE ESTIMATES OF DEMAND CURVE FOR SUBWAY
SERVICE

(passengers and revenues in millions per year)

Fare (cents)	Case A Passengers	Case A Revenues	Case B Passengers	Case B Revenues	Case C Passengers	Case C Revenues	Case D Passengers	Case D Revenues
5	1945	$97.2	1945	$97.2	1945	$97.2	1945	$97.2
10	1683	168.3	1683	168.3	1683	168.3	1683	168.3
15	1421	213.2	1458	218.7	1530	229.5	1547	232.0
20	1159	231.8	1262	252.4	1421	284.2	1457	291.5
25	897	224.2	1092	273.0	1347	336.8	1390	348.2
30	635	190.5	945	283.5	1278	383.4	1340	402.0

Source: W. S. Vickrey, *The Revision of the Rapid Transit Fare Structure of the City of New York* (Technical Monograph No. 3, Finance Project, Mayor's Committee on Management Survey of the City of New York), p. 87.

based on various fare levels. In Case *A*, quantity demanded was a linear function of price, i.e.,

$$q = a - bp$$

where q is quantity demanded and p is price. In Case *B*,

$$\log q = a - bp.$$

In Case *C*,

$$q = a - b \log p.$$

And in Case *D*,

$$\log q = a - b \log p.$$

The author concludes that Case *B* probably represents the most reasonable case. We are not concerned here with the methods used to derive such estimates or with the factors that prompted him to choose Case *B* over the others. Methods of estimation are discussed in the subsequent paper. For present purposes, the important thing is the relevance of the information provided in Table 2 to decisions that must be made by the firm. Table 2 shows that the demand for this product is inelastic—and the extent to which it is inelastic. In determining its price policy, the New York Transit Authority would do well to recognize this fact. Although price reductions for some items, like Columbia's records, may be profitable, in this case they will reduce both revenues and profits.

Estimating the Price Elasticity
of Demand

JOEL DEAN

*Joel Dean is Professor of Business Economics
at Columbia University's Graduate School of
Business. This article comes from his book,*
Managerial Economics, *published in 1960.*

CONTROLLED EXPERIMENTS

The most promising method of estimating short-run price
elasticity for the product of an individual firm is usually by
controlled experiments. The essence of this method is to vary
separately certain determinants of demand which can be manipulated, e.g., prices, advertising, packaging, and try to conduct the
experiment so that other market conditions either remain fairly
constant or can be allowed for. Geographic differentiation is one
way to manipulate prices or marketing strategy, comparing sales
in separate localities, and usually reversing the arrangement as
a check to eliminate the effects of other factors. Or prices and
promotion can be manipulated through time in the same market,
although this is usually less informative.

The Parker Pen Co. conducted a price experiment recently to
determine whether they should raise the price of Quink, which
was then selling at a loss to the company and at little profit to
the dealer. The increase in price from 15¢ to 25¢ was tested in
four cities. Results indicated such low elasticity of demand that

the sales loss was more than offset by the added profit margin. After the price was advanced, experimentation was continued in cooperation with fifty dealers. In some stores the old package priced at 15¢ was placed next to a package marked "New Quink, 25¢." Two out of five customers bought the 25¢ package. In other stores Quink was placed on display beside competitive inks priced at 15¢ and at 10¢. In order to test specifically cross-elasticity of demand Quink was sold at 15¢ for two weeks, then at 25¢ for another two weeks. At the higher price there was a slight decline of Quink sales in relation to sales of two competitive inks. Consumer panel reports indicated that volume declined at first and then began to rise both absolutely and relative to competitors. Several competitors followed the price advance of Parker, which is the largest ink manufacturer.

Another example of field tests of competitive cross-elasticity is the Simmons Mattress experiment. Identical mattresses, some bearing the Simmons brand and others an unknown brand, were offered for sale, first at the same prices and then at various price-spreads, to determine the effect on sales. With parity prices the Simmons brand outsold the other fifteen to one; with a five dollar premium, sales were eight to one; and with a 25 percent premium, sales were equal. A parallel experiment with Cannon towels produced similar results.

Field testing of prices is sometimes used in connection with the introduction of new products. Thus, a manufacturer of duplicating supplies introduced a new product in two supposedly comparable geographic areas at different prices. The indicated demand elasticity was less than unity so the product was priced at the higher level. A similar case is that of a large food manufacturer who was faced with the problem of setting the price for frozen orange juice when it was first introduced. He experimented with three different prices in different cities. All three prices were below the then parity level of fresh oranges. Sales did not appear to differ significantly among the three price levels.

To cite another example, a new type of roll-around shopping cart which collapses into an eminently portable form was developed recently. Experimental probing for the right price included an effort to sell it house-to-house for $4.98. But it wouldn't go. Simultaneously, a large Chicago department store was supplied with a lot to be offered at $3.98. At this price and through this channel the shopping carts sold well. Efforts to pare the costs enough to make it profitable to sell at this price through department stores were unsuccessful, however, so the product had to be withdrawn from the market.

For products that are normally sold by mail order, opportunities for experimental analysis of demand are rich. Price, promotion, and even product design, can be varied among keyed mailings, chosen as successive samples of the same prospect population. Several years ago a mail-order house sent out a batch of catalogs in which the price of one item varied from $1.88 to $1.99 and then observed the relation of sales to the range of prices to find the price elasticity.

A new product that is not to be permanently sold by mail can be experimentally offered by direct mail at different prices to carefully controlled and geographically separated sectors of a mailing list. By analyzing the actual order response to each of the series of prices, some conception of demand elasticity can be obtained. This approach may be viewed as a variant of the prospect questionnaire method, but it avoids the difficulty of bridging the gap between declaration of intention and actual purchasing action. It has limitations both in the difficulty of getting satisfactory comparability of the market sectors and in the failure to duplicate the actual purchasing environment.

There are serious problems in determining demand schedules by controlled experiments. Such experiments are expensive, hazardous and time-consuming. In planning the study it is not always clear just what conditions should be held constant. Moreover, it is difficult, costly, and dangerous to set up a pricing experiment that will include all the effects of a price change that you want to measure, and exclude all the effects of other factors that you don't want. It is hard to reflect realistically the reaction of rivals to the price change. And dealers' responses are often atypical since they are privy to the experiment. The temporary impact of a local price raid may be all that is measured, whereas the problem concerns the effect of full-scale and more permanent price reductions. For example, the great responsiveness of sales to price-cuts in the Macy experiment conducted by Whitman (discussed below) probably measures stocking-up to take advantage of a short-lived opportunity and also reflects lags by competitors in meeting Macy's prices. Sufficient reaction time to feel the full effect of price is seldom possible before other conditions change significantly. Thus, the results often have limited generality, since they are tied to the particular conditions of the experiment.

Pricing experiments are costly and hazardous. They run risks of unfavorable side-reactions of dealers, consumers, and competitors. Nonetheless, this method deserves wider use than it has had, and constitutes one of the most promising implements for demand analysis in current markets.

CONSUMER QUESTIONNAIRES

Personal interviews and written questionnaires are widely used to probe the buying motives, intentions and habits of customers and prospects. They are sometimes helpful (in the absence of better measurements) in guessing at the sensitivity of demand to price. Little confidence can be placed in answers to questions that ask consumers what they think they would pay, or how much they would buy if prices were lower, or if price-spreads over competitors and substitutes were different. This kind of frontal attack on the intricate psychological problem of buyers' intentions and actions is still a highly dubious method of analysis, even when the market consists of a few large industrial customers. Not until the psychometric techniques of depth interviewing have advanced far beyond their present status can much be expected from such direct probing.

But collateral information obtained from such interviews can brace up a guess at price sensitivity. For example, interviews revealed that most buyers of a branded baby food chose it on their doctor's recommendation, and that most were quite ignorant about substitutes and about prices. This knowledge, together with other information, led the manufacturer to guess that demand for his product was quite inelastic.

Occasionally questionnaire research can indicate the outer limits of price. For example, an automatic timer developed for photographers was never commercialized because questionnaires indicated that the lowest profitable price was far above what most photographers *said* they would pay. But in general such research is a frail foundation for pricing decisions.

ENGINEERING ESTIMATES

For producers' goods, it is sometimes possible to guess at the effect of price upon the sales of a capital good by making engineering estimates of the cost savings and other benefits that can be produced by the product for a sample of prospects. By applying some standard of capital earnings, e.g., a three-year crude pay-out, it is possible to translate estimates of savings into demand for equipment.

The cost savings of customers will vary because prospects differ in size, wage rate, efficiency of displaced equipment, and other such conditions. To estimate the way these divergent conditions affect the quantity of equipment that will be purchased, a sample of prospects that is representative of various strata of customer size, wage rates, equipment efficiency, etc., is selected. From estimates of the cost savings and the number of prospects in each category, the sample results can be blown up to yield a projected schedule of equipment sales at various prices. Estimates of the cost savings of new equipment types can be supplemented and verified by test installations in major prospect categories.

The most difficult practical problems usually arise not in estimating the cost savings in a particular situation, but in translating these savings into a demand schedule that reflects a composite of all situations. Comprehensive knowledge of the operations of a buying industry are required for the equipment, both to determine the appropriate conversion factors for capitalizing cost savings and to select the sample and blow it up.[1]

1. This approach concentrates on obsolescence replacement, since it is here that pricing affects engineering feasibility. Cultural lags of ignorance, uncertainty, and speculation contaminate this relationship. Buying equipment on the basis of its prospective earnings on capital is unfortunately not yet sufficiently common to be the sole basis for analysis of demand. The age, distribution, and the status of depreciation reserves of existing equipment, though they should be irrelevant, may properly enter into forecasts of the rate of displacement of obsolete machinery.

CORRELATION ANALYSIS

Often, information on price elasticity can be found by applying a correlation technique to historical records of prices and sales. The important problem in this method is to design a function that can sift out the price relations from data that show the composite effect of all sales determinants.

Correlation analysis of price elasticity has been applied most extensively to demand for agricultural products, notably by Henry Schultz. Using very simple relationships[2] Schultz found fairly high correlations of price and consumption for most farm products[3] over periods of about fifteen years.

Farm products have economic characteristics that make them particularly susceptible to this kind of analysis: they are homogeneous and staple, so that their demand curves change very slowly over the years; they are sold in highly competitive markets, where prices are flexibly adjusted to demand and supply; supply varies widely from year to year, but annual production, once under way, is hard to control by producers. Wide swings in supply plus highly stable demand can in these conditions be assumed to produce a series of prices that, when plotted against consumption, trace out the shape of the demand curve.

These are far different pricing conditions from those prevailing in manufacturing industry, where prices are a combination of rigid, official quotations and undercover concessions, where products are rarely comparable, and where current demand is more closely matched by current production. Nevertheless, in some industries, price data for this kind of analysis is produced inadvertently. Price wars, regional differences in competitive

2. For instance, he used functions in the forms
$$x = a + by + ct$$
$$x = Ay^m e^{nt}$$
where x is per capita consumption, y is the deflated price, and t is time, while a,b,c,A,m,n, and e are constants. In another form of analysis, price and consumption were used not in absolute terms but as deviations from a long-term trend; time was omitted as an explicit variable. Another variant of the analysis was a correlation of year-to-year changes in price with corresponding changes in consumption, a method first used by Henry Moore (*Economic Cycles: Their Law and Cause*, New York, 1914).

3. An important exception was wheat, for which price behavior was largely governed by a world market rather than a national one.

and substitute price spreads, and the distortion of relative prices caused by inflation create research opportunities that are too often neglected. Statistical analysis of such price experience can sometimes provide usable knowledge about how prices and price spreads affect both the company's market share and the industry's battle with substitutes. A state sales tax on soft drinks recently created data inadvertently that demonstrated a high price elasticity for one bottling company. This company found that a one cent per bottle tax could not be added to the wholesale price without cutting volume enough to lower total revenue. Differences in state taxes on gasoline, together with geographical differences in laid-down cost, have furnished oil companies with data for making correlation analyses of the relationships between price and volume.

When a product's price is rigid, changes in substitutes' prices shift the relative price of the product and give data on price elasticity. For example, in studying the price elasticity of policy-loans made by an insurance company, it was found that the policy-loan rate stayed constant while competing lenders reduced their rates. Thus the relative price of policy-loans was rising in a way that was measurable and could be related to changes in loan volume, both absolutely and relative to competitors' volume.

PRICE ELASTICITY—AN ILLUSTRATIVE STUDY

One of the best studies of the short-run relation of price to sales was done for Macy's department store by R. H. Whitman.[4] In several respects this is an ideal field for such research: (1) prices are an important sales factor—they are featured in advertising, and customers shop between stores; (2) prices are unusually flexible—seasonal patterns and style cycles make careful price administration a must for managing large inventories profitably; (3) there is substantial and regular competition among stores, but with some leeway for price policy; (4) there is keen competition between substitute products on the same counter, which presents the raw material for well controlled experiments.

4. "Demand Functions for Merchandise at Retail," *Studies in Mathematical Economics and Econometrics* (Chicago: University of Chicago Press, 1942), pp. 208-221.

Whitman was thus able to sidestep some of the obstacles discussed earlier in the chapter. For instance, he used a very short time period (two and one-half months), which stabilized consumer income, but which nevertheless saw many price changes. He analyzed only staple products in order to obviate the style cycles problem. He assumed that when Macy's changed its price the pattern of reactions of other stores during the analysis period would be repeated under similar conditions in the future. These simplifying circumstances neutralized the effect of several independent variables that must be used in most demand situations, and permitted him to use simple correlation of price and quantity sold to find price elasticity.

Whitman created his data by systematically manipulating price over a wide range during a short period. Parallel experiments were performed for a number of staples.

When correlation analysis is worked out in its mathematical (least-squares) form, the first step is to set up an algebraic function to express the relation. There is usually room for judgment in deciding on the best form to use. In choosing his demand equation, Whitman rejected the common form, $q = a + bp$ and used instead $q = Ap^a$. ($q =$ quantity sold; $p =$ price; A, a, and b are constants.)[5]

CHART 1

ALTERNATIVE FORMS OF DEMAND FUNCTION

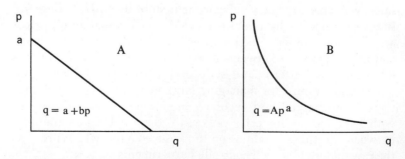

5. Exponential functions of this type are used in logarithmic form for correlation analysis:

$$\log q = \log A + a \log p.$$

An important feature of the hyperbolic demand curve is its constant elasticity: regardless of the level of price, the ratio of a small fixed percent change in price to the resulting percent change in quantity sold is constant. This ratio is equal to the constant a, which is the price elasticity of demand, and which is negative. For example, if a is -5, a drop in price of 1 percent will increase sales by 5 percent and revenue by 4 percent. In the simplest case, where $a = -1$, sales vary inversely with price just enough to keep total revenue constant for all values of p.

In the straight-line demand curve, on the other hand, a \$1 change in price will produce a constant absolute change in quantity sold regardless of the level of price. In this case there is a price which gives a maximum revenue, namely $a/2$.

Whether the hyperbola is more realistic is not clear *a priori:* there is certainly a price where none at all can be sold, and the amount that can be given away is also finite. But for the relevant range of actual prices, Whitman found it a better fit to the facts than a straight line.

The price elasticities that resulted from this analysis told a significant story and were surprisingly reliable in a statistical sense. Chart 1 presents the demand schedule for one product, showing a price elasticity of about -6 (with a standard error of .78) and a correlation coefficient of $-.89$, which indicates a close relation between sales and prices. Other commodities showed comparable price elasticities and correlations. Moreover, by comparing results for the same calendar months in two successive years, Whitman found that the change during the year was relatively slight compared to the margin of probable error.

These price elasticities are relatively high, and mean that sales are sensitive to prices for these products. For these products, price is a powerful weapon in competition—probably too powerful to be used freely. Low elasticity, in contrast, shows products where price competition is too ineffective to be important, compared to the returns from advertising.

Whitman also ran a multiple correlation analysis to find the relation of sales to prices of other products, using as independent variables both the product's price and an index of competing

Joel Dean

CHART 2

DEPARTMENT STORE DEMAND FUNCTION

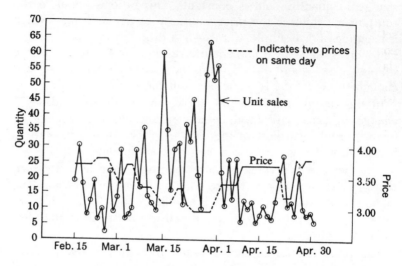

(Source: R. H. Whitman, "Demand Functions for Merchandise at Retail,"
Studies in Mathematical Economics and Econometrics, Chicago, University
of Chicago Press, 1942, pp. 210, 214.)

CHART 3

DEPARTMENT STORE PRICES AND SALES. ORIGINAL DATA

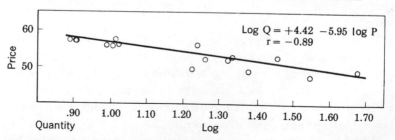

(Source: R. H. Whitman, "Demand Functions for Merchandise at Retail,"
Studies in Mathematical Economics and Econometrics, Chicago, University
of Chicago Press, 1942, pp. 210, 214.)

products.[6] The closeness of fit for this equation was not impressively high, but the analysis did contribute some information on cross elasticity of demand, which for different products ranged from 1.4 to 16.2.

As we indicated above, this analysis had a rather ideal short-run setting, which is unattainable for most products. It is much more common for prices to change from year to year than from day to day, and for reaction patterns to be much slower. Nevertheless, it is highly probable that there are other areas where it can be useful.

6. The equation took the form: $Q = Ap^a P^b$.

The Price Elasticity of Demand for Automobiles

SENATE SUBCOMMITTEE ON ANTITRUST AND MONOPOLY

This selection is from a report published in 1958 by the Senate Subcommittee on Antitrust and Monopoly.

Durable goods, such as automobiles, have certain characteristics not present in perishable goods which must be taken into account in any analysis of the elasticity of demand. Consumers, at least in the abstract, do not buy commodities for the purpose of just having them around. They buy them for the satisfaction or utility which these commodities will give them. An article of food yields utility only in the eating and disappears in the process, whereas an automobile yields utility over many years. Thus, there is a significant difference between the demand for food and the demand for new automobiles. Price, income, etc. affect the demand for the flow of satisfaction which the commodity yields and not the new purchases of the commodity itself. In the case of food, the correspondence of the flow of satisfaction and new purchases can be made easily, since the act of obtaining utility from a unit of food results in its destruction. But in the case of automobiles no such correspondence can be made. A consumer can obtain a flow of satisfaction or utility by buying a new car, by buying a used car, or by simply holding on to the car he already owns. Though new-car purchases cannot be equated directly with the factors which influence demand, the ownership of automobiles can be so equated, but ownership must be taken in a very special sense. . . .

Automobiles are distinguished from other commodities, both perishable and durable, in the magnitude of expenditure involved. No other commodity except a house requires such a large initial outlay relative to the typical consumer's income or his accumulated savings. Because of the size of the expenditure, and because consumers may have previously committed substantial portions of their incomes, it may not be possible for a consumer to increase his level of ownership as rapidly as he might like to, as a result of a change in income or price. Moreover, most consumers have relatively small savings. Thus even if, because of lower prices or higher incomes, they wish to maintain a higher level of ownership, they cannot do so unless credit is readily available at favorable terms. However, easy credit terms cannot significantly affect new purchases when price has risen or income has fallen and ownership is therefore declining. A consumer does not usually need credit to hold on to his old car. . . .

Six major studies have been made of the elasticity of demand for automobiles which utilize historical data; they are those of: (1) P. de Wolff, (2) M. J. Farrell, (3) C. F. Roos and V. von Szeliski, (4) L. J. Atkinson, (5) G. C. Chow, and (6) D. B. Suits. Neither Mr. de Wolff's study nor Mr. Farrell's study lends itself to easy interpretation in terms of the price elasticity of demand for new cars. Chow and Suits testified before the subcommittee and their testimony will be discussed later. The studies by Roos and Von Szeliski and Atkinson are based entirely on pre-World War II data, and are briefly summarized here.

In 1939 General Motors Corp. published Roos and Von Szeliski's now classic study of automobile demand. Their study is long and quite complicated; however, they have provided a summary which is quoted in full:

From the demand standpoint, the outstanding characteristic of passenger automobiles and other durable goods is their durability. In consequence, consumption of these goods is dissociated from purchase and ordinarily extends five to fifteen years beyond the date of acquisition. Consumers' car stocks thus take a prominent part in determining new-car purchases. The demand situation is quite unlike that for perishable goods, in which the part played by consumers' stocks is negligible. Additions to consumers' stocks of automobiles, or new-owner sales, depend chiefly on the difference between the actual car stock and the maximum stock or ownership level attainable under current conditions of income, price, operating costs, and car life.

The concept of a variable maximum ownership level is of primary importance in the automobile industry because when car ownership is near the level of maximum ownership and a decrease in national income occurs, the effect is to make the market suddenly saturated. A consequence is the elimination of new-owner sales, and even the forcing of liquidation of part of the consumers' car stock. It is found by statistical analysis that a 1-percent increase in supernumerary income (national income less direct taxes and necessary living cost) would raise the maximum ownership level by about 0.4 percent. Income changes also affect replacement sales, and a 1-percent increase in supernumerary income would increase replacement sales by about 1.2 percent. The overall effect of income on total new-car sales, new owners as well as replacement, appears to be that a 1-percent change in income causes a 2.5-percent change in sales. When consumer car stocks approach the maximum ownership level and the quality of these stocks is high, new-car sales can be drastically lowered by moderate declines in income.

The influence of price on replacement sales is such that with each 1-percent increase in price, replacement sales tend to decrease by 0.74 percent (without allowance for possible correlation of price with operating costs). The overall effect of price on combined new owners and replacement sales (after allowance for intercorrelation of price with operating costs) appears to be that a 1-percent decrease in price increases sales by between 1 and 2 prcent, depending upon the degree of saturation of the market. A figure of 1.5 can be accepted as a fair average value of the elasticity of demand with respect to price under current conditions.

Automobile sales can be explained with an average error of 4.17 percent for the period 1919–37 with the above factors and without taking into account such factors as changes in financing plans, dealers' used-car stocks, highway carrying capacity and style.

In an article on durable-goods demand published in April 1952, L. Jay Atkinson presents a brief statistical study of the demand for new passenger cars. He obtained a price elasticity of −1.4 and an income elasticity of +2.5. All the studies discussed in this chapter, with the exception of Atkinson's, rest, more or less, on the foundation that ownership is considered as basic, and new purchases are derived from ownership. His analysis relates new private passenger-car registration per 1,000 households to four variables: (1) real disposable income per household in 1939 dollars, (2) percentage of current to preceding year real disposable income in 1939 dollars, (3) ratio of average retail price of new automobiles to the BLS Consumer Price Index, and (4) average scrappage age. For the period 1925–40, Atkinson's analysis explains 98 percent of the variation in new-car purchases. Predictions based on his analysis for recent years in the postwar period are reasonably accurate, as can be seen below:

TABLE 1

New Car Registrations in the United States, Actual and Computed by Formula of Atkinson [1]

Year	Actual (millions)	Computed (millions)	Percentage difference
1955	7.2	6.3	−13
1956	6.0	6.5	+8
1957	6.0	6.0	0

[1] Calculations made by the subcommittee staff.

THE STATISTICAL INVESTIGATIONS OF CHOW AND SUITS

The studies of Dr. Gregory C. Chow, of the Massachusetts Institute of Technology, and Dr. Daniel B. Suits, of the University of Michigan, have been singled out for more detailed discussion, principally on the grounds that they are the two most recent analyses and the only studies incorporating post-World War II data.

Professor Chow finds the price elasticity for new-car sales to be − 1.2 and the income elasticity to be + 3.0. These elasticities are derived from the elasticities between ownership and price and income:

To understand the mechanism governing sales of automobiles, first of all, we have to understand the mechanism governing automobile ownership.

People buy automobiles because they want to use automobiles, and their wants are satisfied not only by the new cars that they have just bought, but by the total number of automobiles in existence. So that

the demand for automobile services actually is a demand for automobile ownership rather than the demand for purchase.
The demand for purchase is derived from the demand for automobile ownership.

In obtaining his figure for total car ownership, Chow adjusts for age in the following manner:

. . . the measure of automobile ownership really depends on how much the new car is worth as compared with the used cars, and I have observed the relative prices of automobiles of different age groups at one point in time.

I have found that, historically, approximately 25 percent is depreciated in a year, roughly speaking, so that if we count a new car as 1 unit, we will count a one-year-old car as one 0.75 unit, and a two-year-old car as 75 percent of 75 percent, or something like a half unit. . . .

In his analysis, which covers the period 1920–41 and 1948–53, Chow relates ownership per capita in this sense to the average price of all cars, new and used, deflated by a general price index, real disposable income per capita, and the ownership of automobiles the preceding year. He thus takes account of four of the major factors affecting the demand for any commodity: its price, the general price level, consumer income, and population. The way in which Chow has allowed for delays in adjustment assumes that such delays are the same, no matter in which direction the adjustment takes place. As indicated above, there are strong reasons for believing that the delays are less marked in a downward direction.

In describing his results on the income and price elasticities of the demand for ownership, Chow said:

I have estimated that for every percent increase in per capita income, automobile ownership would be increased by 1½ percent.
How about the effect on price? I have also estimated that for every percent increase in price, there will be [a] 0.6 percent drop in automobile ownership; it would decrease people's desire of ownership by 0.6 percent.

Since he assumes that the ownership level depreciates at the rate of 25 percent a year, the elasticities for new-car sales would be 4 times the ownership elasticities, or 2.4 for price and 6 for income. However, for the reasons described earlier (principally other commitments and transactions costs), he assumes that consumers do not fully adjust their level of ownership to changed prices and incomes within a one-year period. He testified:

The responses of 6 percent to a 1-percent change in income and 2.4 percent to a 1-percent change in price would result if the consumers adjusted their car ownership to the desired [or equilibrium] level at once. But they do not. Time elapses between decision and the act of purchasing. But more important is the cost involved in making a transaction. No one will change his car to a better one the moment his income increases, and to a cheaper one the moment his income drops. If he does that, he will be spending quite a bit of his time and money with the automobile dealers. I have found that about half of the desired change in ownership is achieved in one year. This means that a 1-percent change in income, while raising the desired ownership by 1.5 percent to be achieved in due course, will raise actual ownership only by 0.75 percent in the current year. Therefore, the percentage response in sales within one year to a 1-percent rise in income during that year will be only 3 percent, and not 6. Similarly, the response of sales to price will only be 1.2 percent, and not 2.4.

This, of course, assumes that delays in adjustment are symmetrical with respect to the direction of adjustment. In a memorandum inserted in the record, Dr. John M. Blair, chief economist of the subcommittee, pointed out that although there are grounds for supposing that delays do exist in both upward and downward adjustments in ownership, there are convincing reasons for believing that these delays are asymmetrical, i.e., that the rates of adjustment differ for upward and downward adjustments. The factor of other commitments is not operative in downward adjustments, while transactions cost is operative to a lesser degree in downward than in upward adjustments. The subcommittee staff did not have the time or the resources necessary to assess the full effects of this possible modification of Chow's results. However, it was possible to make a comparison between the results obtained by Chow's method in which it is assumed that only half of the adjustment is made in one year and those secured by an alternative method in which the extreme assumption is made that no delay occurs when new-car purchases are declining. Chow's elasticities of −0.6 and +1.5 for ownership with respect to price and income constituted the underlying basis of the calculations.

Since 1921 there have been nine year-to-year downturns in new-car purchases. The downturns in 1923–24 and 1953–54 were relatively minor, amounting to less than 10 percent, and were accordingly omitted. For each of the downturns, percentage change in price and in income were computed. On the basis of these changes, the percentage changes in new-car purchases were computed by two methods:

(a) A price elasticity of −1.2 and an income elasticity of +3.0 were applied to the percentage changes in price and income, respectively. The resulting percentage changes were then summed to obtain the calculated value of the percentage change in new-car purchases. The result is carried under the column labeled "Predicted by Chow's method" in the table.

(b) When the direction of price change was upward, an elasticity of −2.4 was applied; when it was downward, an elasticity of −1.2 was applied. When the direction of the income change was downward, an elasticity of +6.0 was applied; when it was upward, an elasticity of +3.0 was applied. The price and income effects were summed and the result is carried in the last column of the table, labeled "Predicted by alternative method."

TABLE 2

PER CAPITA NEW-CAR PURCHASES, ACTUAL PERCENTAGE CHANGES, AND PREDICTED BY 2 METHODS

Years	Actual change (percent)	Predicted by Chow's method (percent)	Predicted by alternative method (percent)
1926–27	−23.6	−5.2	−16.7
1929–30	−35.0	−3.5	−28.4
1930–31	−28.8	−28.6	−72.5
1931–32	−42.7	−48.0	−96.6
1937–38	−44.6	−55.7	−100.0
1950–51	−21.4	−6.9	−13.8
1951–52	−19.2	−3.3	−10.5
1955–56	−18.4	+1.9	+.4
1957–58 [1]	−29.8	−14.9	−29.8

[1] The 1957–58 estimates were derived by assuming new-car purchases in 1958 of 4,200,000, a decline in real disposable income per capita of 3.4 percent and a price increase of 3.9 percent in real terms.

Of the nine downturns, the alternative method yielded better results in six, though in one, 1955–56, both were in error as to the direction of change. The only downturns in which Chow's method, per se, proved superior were those of 1930–31, 1931–32, and 1937–38. Each of these was a year of extremely depressed economic activity. A possible explanation for the better results yielded by Chow's method for these years, might be that in a period of extreme depression the ownership of automobiles, defined in Chow's terms, would be reduced to relatively low levels. This means that only the hard-core users of transportation services from privately owned automobiles were effectively in the market for cars. Consequently, the basic ownership elasticities of demand must have been lower than the −0.6 price elasticity and the +1.5 income elasticity which Chow obtained over the long-run period of 1921–53. In those years of deep depression Chow offsets his too-high elasticities for ownership with his downward adjustment for new-car purchases. Under the alternative method the overstatement in the elasticity of ownership is not offset, and consequently the decline in car sales during such years is overstated.

There is thus a reasonable basis for assuming that the experience of the deep depression years was atypical (except for downswings of comparable severity), and that the evidence supports the hypothesis that adjustments to changes in price and income are asymmetrical, with the downward adjustments in stock and purchases taking place more rapidly than upward adjustments. The showing for 1957–58 rather strikingly confirms this view. The inference would be that in periods of economic decline (except at the bottom of a severe depression) the elasticities arrived at by Professor Chow are conservative.

His elasticities as well as those of the other students of the problem are conservative for still another reason: they ignore the so-called secondary effects on income of price-induced changes in production—effects which cannot be measured. As was pointed out in the subcommittee's report on steel:

The automobile workers who lose their jobs because of a price-induced reduction in automobile output lose their ability to purchase cars, as do the workers who would have been employed in making the steel that would have gone into those cars, and so on. Since the production of automobiles is a vast industry, this secondary effect cannot be disregarded.

Dr. Suits' investigation concerns new purchases entirely, although the framework of his analysis does include elements which allow new-car purchases to depend indirectly on ownership. Suits' formulation is basically the same as Chow's, except that population is excluded entirely, some measure of credit terms is introduced, and ownership is treated in absolute numbers rather than in age-comparable units. His analysis covers the period 1929 through 1956, omitting the years 1942–48.

In view of the similarity in the formulation of Suits and Chow it is rather surprising that their statistical results turned out to be so different. Suits obtained a price elasticity of −0.6 and an income elasticity of +4.2 for new-car purchases. Thus his price elasticity is only half of that which Chow obtained and his income elasticity is nearly 40 percent greater. The difference appears to be due largely to two factors: (a) the use of different price series and (b) a statistical procedure employed by Suits which has the effect of causing his analysis to ignore the 30 to 40 percent of all cars not sold on credit. With respect to the former, Suits did not use the BLS retail price index for new automobiles, nor did he, as Chow did, use newspaper advertisements. Instead, Suits constructed his own index by multiplying the BLS wholesale index of new car prices by a retailers' margin factor. Suits described his procedure and the rationale behind it to the subcommittee as follows:

This price index is essentially a markup of the passenger and automobile part of the BLS wholesale price index which is somewhat more inclusive than the consumer price index component—this marked up by an estimate of the gross margin of automobile dealers.

I think I can explain the matter this way: When a dealer sells a car he receives in payment cash or a credit instrument of cash equivalent, and ordinarily, a used car of some value. This used car is then sold and again cash or credit instruments are obtained and generally another used car. This continues down until the cars of course are scrapped out at the bottom.

The sum total of this operation is the way in which the dealer receives his payment for the new car.

So that essentially what I have done is take the ratio of the average value of a new passenger automobile at wholesale, to the average receipts per new car sold of automobile dealers, *receipts of both payments for new and used cars alike.*

Obviously, the price which is relevant to an analysis of the demand for new cars is the price of new cars, not the price of all cars, and certainly not the margins on used cars. Moreover, it matters not at all how an automobile dealer receives the price of a new car; the important factor is the price of a new car, what he gets and what the buyer pays, and the margins on used cars can surely not be relevant to the purchaser of a new car. The whole question thus revolves around how good the price series constructed by Suits is for his purpose. A comparison of this series with the BLS retail price index for new cars raises a number of questions. A memorandum inserted in the record, prepared by Dr. Browne of the subcommittee staff, shows (1) that one of the important series used by Suits is based primarily on the BLS retail price index for new passenger cars; (2) that this same series includes, during certain periods, expenditures on numerous items, such as house trailers, not relevant to the determination of the margins of dealers on new cars; (3) that the BLS wholesale price index which enters Suits' calculation is considered by the Bureau of Labor Statistics itself to be less reliable than the retail price index; and (4) that the BLS series and Suits' series move in different directions in several crucial periods such as 1955. In view of the fact that Suits bases his analysis on year-to-year changes, this last point is especially important.

Thus, Suits does not free himself from the supposed shortcoming of the BLS retail price series, but in the course of his attempt to do so he introduces possibly extensive errors into his price series.

With respect to the second factor, Suits' use of data on average contract duration is unusual. Instead of using average contract duration as a separate variable in his analysis designed to explain year-to-year changes in new-car purchases, Suits divides real retail price by it and uses only the ratio of the two, i.e., he computes what he calls the "real monthly payment" and never introduces contract duration and price as separate variables. In the postwar period only some 50 to 70 percent of all new automobiles purchased have been purchased on credit. Thus, to imply as Suits does that a variable representing the monthly payment for a new automobile is the only effective "price" variable is somewhat misleading because not all purchases of new cars are made on time. Retail price and contract duration should exert separable and possibly different effects on new-car demand.

In order to test whether Suits' procedures had the effect of reducing the price elasticity of demand (which would tend to explain the difference between his elasticities and those of Chow), the subcommittee staff made a statistical analysis which was identical to that made by Suits, except in two respects: (1) The BLS index of retail prices of new automobiles divided by the BLS Consumer Price Index was substituted for Suits' own price series; and (2) average contract duration, as measured by Suits, was treated as a separate variable, i.e., price was not divided by average contract duration, but average contract duration was included in the analysis as a separate variable. The results of this analysis were as follows: The price elasticity of demand obtained was —1.2, identical with that which Professor Chow presented to the subcommittee. The income elasticity obtained was +3.9, which compares to the 3.0 of Chow. The elasticity of new purchases with respect to average contract duration was found to be —0.7. It is thus apparent that Suits' use of a questionable price series and his division of price by contract duration had the effect of reducing the price elasticity which he obtained.

SUMMARY COMPARISON OF STATISTICAL FINDINGS

The investigation of the quantitative effect of price and income upon new-automobile purchases is a complex and difficult subject, about which much more needs to be known. However, there is a substantial measure of agreement among the various authorities, as can be seen below:

TABLE 3

SUMMARY COMPARISON OF SEVERAL STUDIES OF
AUTOMOBILE DEMAND

Study	Elasticity of new purchases with respect to—	
	Price	Income
Suits:		
1. As presented	−0.6	+4.2
2. As reworked by the subcommittee staff	−1.2	+3.9
Chow [1]	−1.2	+3.0
Roos and von Szeliski	−1.5	+2.5
Atkinson [1]	−1.4	+2.5

[1] Per capita basis.

Except for Suits' original analysis, the results presented in the table show price elasticities ranging between −1.2 and −1.5 and income elasticities ranging between +2.5 and +3.9. Because of the considerations which have been described above, a price elasticity of −1.2 appears to be a minimum estimate.

Pricing and the Character of the Product

A. D. H. KAPLAN, JOEL B. DIRLAM, AND ROBERT F. LANZILLOTTI

A. D. H. Kaplan is a senior economist at the Brookings Institution. Together with Joel Dirlam and Robert Lanzillotti, he wrote Pricing in Big Business *from which the following paper is taken.*

The character of the product—the type of demand to which it caters, as well as its physical attributes, production requirements, amenability to differentiation, and stage of maturity—sets boundaries to the pricing discretion of the company, big or little. When interpreting the role of product characteristics, however, the possibility that reaction may run both ways must be kept in mind. These characteristics are not fixed or unadjustable. They themselves may be affected by price. But the basic concern at this point is with pricing policies that seem to be imposed by the nature of the product, rather than vice versa.

With a product like fresh meat, perishable and subject to unpredictable output and shipments of the primary commodity, even a firm of the importance of Swift & Company has a limited opportunity to bend wholesale prices to company policy. A durable product with controlled raw material output, and production based on orders, better lends itself to fairly stable price quotations, as in steel or crude oil. Copper, on the contrary, with its volatile price behavior points up the effect on the manageability of prices of a widely diffused raw material supply and a world market. Limitations on the transportability of the product (transportation cost in relation to product value) may give locational advantage in pricing even when there are business giants in the industry.

New products, with varying degrees of marketable uniqueness, provide opportunities for pricing discretion not generally available in standardized goods. Large companies whose resources are concentrated in established standard products are aware of the general unprofitability of price wars when confronted with similarly large and resourceful competitors; hence they keep in step with the competition on price and depend on such factors as favorable location, or availability of adequate supplies and satisfactory service to customers, for their competitive strength at the going price. In the use of these devices, however, product features (*e.g.*, vulnerability to substitution) may determine how successful a stable price policy can be, even for the large and resourceful company.

New Products and Matured Products · The natural frame of reference for pricing a new product is the price range of existing substitutes. For example, it was recognized that nylon was capable of penetrating the markets of a variety of textile fibers. The problem of effectively introducing this new fiber resolved itself through a compromise between pricing for the widest possible use and pricing for the more limited, but in the long run, more sustainable and profitable quality market. In cellophane, the same company reached more aggressively for more extensive market penetration without undermining the profit potential. Apparently, the cost elasticity of volume output and the price elasticity of growing demand were sufficiently high to permit a more rapid rate of expansion than was possible in nylon. The introduction of a major consumer appliance, for which demand is as yet an expectation rather than a reality, has entailed elaborate market research to select a price niche that will permit the inclusion of features required for optimum acceptance. In the pricing of a major piece of farm machinery such as the cotton picker, the decision settles on a middle ground between the estimated maximum economic value as a replacement for hand labor and a sufficiently low price to give assurance of widespread adoption. Prices determined in this manner may well limit the components that can be selected for incorporation in the assembled product; automobiles and other consumer durables considered earlier were cases in point. With the accumulation of know-how and the lowering of costs, subsequent pricing turns on whether the product can readily be imitated, whether the prestige acquired in its pioneering can be prolonged through improvement and product differentiation, or whether lower cost reflected in lower price will open up a highly profitable volume increase.

An established standard product, be it a metal, flour, or heavy chemical, does not entail such conscious balancing of alternative possibilities to fix its price levels. The price may start from a fairly well-recognized cost base, but the profit is a residual reflecting the current willingness or ability of the market to keep the capacity employed. Large firms with heavy investments in established areas of primary production have constantly feared that price changes will lead to hazards of unpredictable magnitude. This fear has often been justified in the past—witness the gyrations of price with accompanying demand fluctuations in copper, lead, or zinc; and even with price leadership, boom and depression fluctuations in steel prices have not been unknown. There is in consequence an undercurrent of antipathy in the firms interviewed to policies that would disturb the pattern of stable and infrequently changing prices. The instability of copper prices is certainy not due to lack of desire on the part of Kennecott and other primary producers to keep firm the price of their metal. The volatility issues rather from the fickleness of a world market, in which fluctuation is accentuated by extremes of overflow or scarcity in the supply of copper scrap.

At least until the Second World War, Alcoa supplied and priced aluminum in the United States with some regard to the fact that it had to penetrate the markets of copper and other metals as well as some non-metallic products. Its technical development in a capital-intensive form with integrated production and standardization of finished products now tends to assert itself; so that while product promotion remains vigorous, pricing in the basic aluminum lines is showing resemblances to steel's pattern of base prices and extras.

The type of use to which a product is put also has a bearing on the importance attached to price variations. The stable pricing of containers carried by American Can and Continental Can has met with little resistance by their customers, and this is not solely because of the duopoly leadership in can manufacture; it is largely due to the fact that what the final user is buying is not the container but the contents. Similarly, flexible packaging materials, aluminum fabrications, special electrical equipment items, and industrial gases permit the manufacturer a minimum of concern with price competition because these are products sold as part—an incidental part—of the larger end product in which the cost of the contributing item is not a prime consideration.

Cost Structure · Production and cost characteristics of the main product play a primary role in conditioning pricing policies. The overriding importance of certain materials in the total cost structure, as in the case of tin plate for can manufacture; the leanness of the ore, and the consequent magnitude of the mining operations of Kennecott Copper; the relatively small runs and large number of items, as in the case of Alcoa's fabricated operations; and of course the high proportion of indirect cost in basic steel production—all these distinctive features are transmuted into pricing policy. U. S. Steel seeks to avoid cutthroat price competition, and evolves a fair return philosophy. Alcoa finds a standard cost system unusable for many items. Kennecott, when prices drop, has to pile up inventory and await more settled prices; it looks with favor on stabilized prices. American Can, and perhaps even the oil companies, in the long run, become transmission belts for passing material and labor costs on to consumers with an inelastic demand. Thus a large part of price policy may be the response to the cost pattern inherent to the product.

Part Four

Capital Budgeting and Investment

To SOLVE most investment and capital budgeting problems, it is necessary to reduce funds received or spent at different points in time to comparable terms. Because a firm can realize a positive return from the investment of its funds, a dollar now is worth more than a dollar later. Pearson Hunt, Charles Williams, and Gordon Donaldson provide the solutions to various investment problems and show how to compute an investment's rate of return.

In a paper which is now a classic in this field, Joel Dean discusses various ways of measuring the economic worth of investment proposals. He evaluates the three most commonly used yardsticks of investment worth—degree of necessity, payback period, and rate of return—and concludes that rate of return is the best. After discussing some of the mistakes that are made in estimating the rate of return, he describes and illustrates the use of the discounted-cash-flow method of computing economic worth, a method which he regards as "demonstrably superior to existing alternatives in accuracy, realism, relevance, and sensitivity."

The next article, by David Hertz, describes risk analysis, a technique that is commonly employed in industry today. As Hertz emphasizes, the "discipline of thinking through the uncertainties of the problem will in itself help to ensure improvement in making investment choices. For to understand uncertainty and risk is to understand the key business problem—and the key business opportunity." This paper too is a classic in the field.

In the final article in this part of the book, Burton Malkiel describes and comments on various approaches to stock-market investing. He provides an informal and amusing account of the "firm-foundation theory" and the "castle-in-the-air theory," and goes on to describe "the growth-stock and new-issue craze of the 1959–61 period, the conglomerate boom of the mid-1960's, and the performance cult of the late 1960's." In view of the enormous attention devoted to the stock market, this article should be of widespread interest.

Time Adjustments of Flows of Funds

Pearson Hunt,
Charles M. Williams, and
Gordon Donaldson

Pearson Hunt is Professor of Business Administration at Harvard University. In 1961, together with Charles Williams and Gordon Donaldson, he published Basic Business Finance *from which this paper is taken.*

Many decisions involve in some way a comparison of the usefulness of receiving or paying funds at one time rather than another, and we need a means of evaluating the effect of the time span involved. The procedure of *time adjustment* provides a consistent and accurate means for the needed evaluation.

One basic assumption must be made before application of the mathematical procedure, which involves nothing more than compound interest. We assume that a firm always can find some way to invest funds to produce some net gain, or *rate of return*. The rate may be very low, as when funds are temporarily placed in short-term treasury bills, or it may be as high as the gain from some new product greatly in demand. In fact, if a firm does not act to obtain some return from the use of its funds, we speak of the *opportunity cost*, which is the loss of revenue because an opportunity was not taken. Therefore, since there can always be earnings from the investment of funds, we can say as a general rule that whenever a business has a choice of the time when it will obtain certain funds, the rule should be "the sooner, the better."

The first step to an understanding of time adjustment is to relate the amounts involved to one another along a scale of time. The time is divided into periods (e.g., days, months, years), and a particular point in time is selected as the starting point from which the effect of compound interest on the funds will be regarded. This time is named the *focal date*. Periods later than this date are designated by the plus sign, periods earlier by the minus sign, and the focal date is designated by zero. To the mathematician, it is unimportant what actual time is chosen as the focal date. The financial analyst can choose any date, past or present, most convenient for his purposes. In fact, for many problems of financial planning, it is convenient to have the focal date in the future, usually the date at which a specific sum will be received or paid, or at which a certain periodic flow of funds will terminate.

It is necessary to calculate the changing values of flows of funds as they occur both before and after the focal date. We first turn to *compounding*, that is, the subsequent growth in the value of funds initially invested at the focal date, because this process is one with which most readers will be familiar from such well-advertised operations as savings accounts on which interest is compounded. We shall then turn to *discounting*, which looks in the other direction from the focal date along the time scale.

COMPOUNDING

There are three quantities necessary for the calculation:

1. *The rate of return.* In the following exposition, to show the effects of different rates, we shall use two that are well within the range of business experience.
2. *The amount of funds in question.* It is convenient to use the sum of $1.00 to develop the formulas, since if one knows how the values of this sum are affected by time, one can compute the values of any other sum by simple multiplication.
3. *The length of time from the focal date.* This may be measured in days, weeks, etc., so that for the sake of generality,

one refers to the *period* rather than to some specific unit of time. One warning is necessary here. The rate of return used must be stated consistently with the actual length of the time period. Thus, 6 percent per year becomes 0.5 percent per month, and so on.

The growing amount that will be found at later times from an investment of $1.00 at the focal date is referred to as the *compound amount* (of a single sum). Interest is computed on the original sum and then added to the original sum at the end of the first period. The new and larger principal is then the base for the interest calculation in the second period, and so on. Jumping over the detailed mathematics, we can turn to any set of tables for business computations, among which we shall find values for the compound amount of a single sum invested at a given time. See Table 1 for a portion of such a table.

DISCOUNTING

The process of compounding discloses how the value of an investment made at the focal date grows in later time. We now turn to *discounting,* a process which looks at times preceding the focal date and answers the question: How much must be invested before the focal date to produce a desired sum at the time of the focal date?

The answers to such questions are determined by using the reciprocals of the values in the table of compound amounts, for the reasons exemplified in the following instance. Take four periods and 4 percent. Table 1 shows that if $1.00 is compounded

TABLE 1

COMPOUND AMOUNT OF $1.00

Periods	Rate 4%	Rate. 10%
0	1.000	1.000
+1	1.040	1.100
+2	1.082	1.210
+3	1.125	1.331
+4	1.170	1.464
+5	1.217	1.611

for this time and rate, it will increase to $1.17. To have only $1.00 at the end of four periods of compounding, we obviously need to invest less than $1.00. The calculation is:

$$\frac{1.000}{1.170} = \frac{x}{1.000}$$

$$x = 0.855$$

The number so produced is known as the *present value* (at the selected time and rate) which will produce $1.00 at the focal date. The term *discounted value* is also used, although less frequently.

Since present values are often used in financial calculations, a table of present values is provided in most books on finance. For convenience, we reproduce a portion of such a table in Table 2.

Having shown how to evaluate a sum both before the focal date (by discounting) and after the focal date (by compounding), we are in a position to picture the changing value of the sum of $1.00 at the time of the focal date over a time scale. This is presented graphically in Chart 1, where the figures from Tables 1 and 2 are used.

The basic relationships to be observed are simple but very important:

1. The value of a sum invested at any time grows as time passes.
2. The necessary investment to produce a future sum decreases as the time to produce it is increased.
3. Both these effects are magnified as the rate of return increases.

TABLE 2

PRESENT VALUE OF $1.00

Periods	Rate 4%	Rate 10%
0	1.000	1.000
−1	0.962	0.909
−2	0.925	0.826
−3	0.889	0.751
−4	0.855	0.683
−5	0.822	0.621

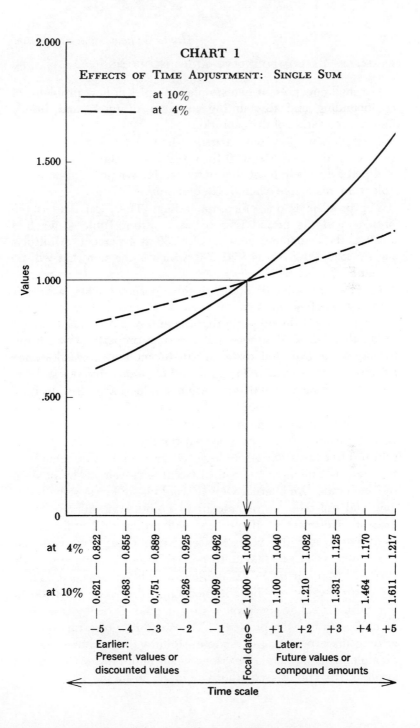

CHART 1

EFFECTS OF TIME ADJUSTMENT: SINGLE SUM

———————— at 10%
— — — — at 4%

EXAMPLES OF COMPOUNDING AND DISCOUNTING

We shall now present two simple examples of how problems of compounding and discounting arise in business, and briefly indicate the nature of their solution.

Example 1. A firm with a major debt maturity at the end of two years sets aside $500,000 for investment in tax-exempt bonds at 4 percent to help meet the maturity. How much will be available from this source when the debt matures?

The problem is one of compounding. The focal date is the present, and the period is two years. From Table 1, we find 1.082 as the compound amount of $1.00 at 4 percent. Multiplying by $500,000 gives us $541,000, which is the sum that will be on hand.

Example 2. A factor often given importance when a firm is deciding whether to own or lease land and buildings is the residual value of the property that the firm would own if it bought rather than leased. Suppose that a certain property, now costing $1 million, is expected to be worth $2 million after allowance for taxes on the capital gain at the end of twenty-five years. How much importance should this terminal value have on a decision now?

The problem is one of discounting. The concept of opportunity cost also enters. Let us assume that the firm averages 10 percent return (after taxes) on assets invested in the business. One way to obtain $2 million at the end of twenty-five years is by holding the real estate. An alternative way would be to invest some funds now and use them at 10 percent to produce $2 million. What present investment at 10 percent will produce $2 million at a focal date twenty-five years hence? From Table 2 we find that the present value of $1.00 at 10 percent after twenty-five periods is 0.092. Multiplying by $2 million, we obtain $184,000. Thus, the desired value can be obtained either by using $184,000 in the business, allowing profits to compound, or by spending $1 million to buy the property. The possibility of error in over-valuing the expectation of remote capital gains is shown by this example. It is particularly serious when high rates of return are available from funds used otherwise in the business.

FINDING THE RATE OF RETURN

There is another use to which tables of present values are often put in financial work. Given values at two dates, one is sometimes required to find the rate of return that will produce a desired change in value. Using the figures from Example 2 above, the problem can be stated as follows: At what rate of return will $1 million grow to $2 million in twenty-five years?

The focal date is the end of the twenty-five-year period, when the present value table expects $1.00 to be paid. Converting the data from the actual case therefore requires division of the initial and terminal value by $2 million:

$$\frac{2,000,000}{2,000,000} = 1.000$$

and

$$\frac{1,000,000}{2,000,000} = 0.500.$$

The question has become: At what rate of discount will 0.50 become 1.00 at the end of twenty-five periods?

Looking at a table of present values for twenty-five periods, we find:

> Rate 2% 0.610
> Rate 4% 0.375

By the process of interpolation, we find the answer, which is 2.9 percent (much lower—and therefore less desirable—than the use of funds to produce 10 percent).

ANNUITIES

Our explanation of the effects of time on the value of funds has so far dealt only with single sums. That is, we have confined ourselves to watching the growth in value of a single in-

$$
\begin{array}{ll}
1.\; 2\% = 0.610 & 2\% = 0.610 \\
 4\% = 0.375 & x = 0.500 \qquad \dfrac{110}{235}\,(2\%) = x = 0.9\% \\
\hline
 2\% = 0.235 & \overline{0.110}
\end{array}
$$

vestment, once it is made. We now turn to what is perhaps more frequently experienced in business, namely, the receipt or payment of a series of sums periodically over a stated number of time periods. Examples are rent and the flow of funds attached to a tax shield arising from depreciation.

There is much similarity between the mathematics already used and that which is necessary for *annuities*, as this type of periodic payment is termed by mathematicians. The focal date, however, takes on a new meaning, which the conventions of financial mathematics make even more complex. If one is looking into periods following the focal date, that date is the beginning of the first period of the annuity. In this case the applicable value at the focal date is zero, for the first payment of the annuity will take place only at the end of the first time period. If one is looking at times which are earlier than the focal date, however, the focal date is defined as the end of the last period, just after the moment of the final payment of the annuity. Again, the value is zero.

We shall introduce the annuity tables in the same order as before; that is, we first look ahead in time to consider the *compound amount* of an annuity, and then back to consider the *present value* of an annuity.

Compounding · Any annuity can be separated into a series of single payments and evaluated by the table of compound interest already described.

Suppose $1.00 is to be received at the end of each period, and that each $1.00 is to be invested at compound interest. How much will be the amount of the annuity a specified number of periods after the focal date? Let us take 4 percent and five years. The answer can be built up from Table 1, of compound amount, as follows:

$1.00 received at time +1 at 4% for 4 years becomes $1.170
1.00 received at time +2 at 4% for 3 years becomes 1.125
1.00 received at time +3 at 4% for 2 years becomes 1.082
1.00 received at time +4 at 4% for 1 year becomes 1.040
1.00 received at time +5 at 4% for 0 year becomes 1.000

Total Value, Amount of Annuity $5.417

From this example, we can see that a table of the desired values for annuities can be obtained by accumulating values from compound interest tables. See Table 3 for a brief portion of such a table.

TABLE 3

AMOUNT OF ANNUITY OF $1.00 PER PERIOD

Periods	Rate 4%	Rate 10%
0	0	0
+1	1.000	1.000
+2	2.040	2.100
+3	3.122	3.310
+4	4.246	4.641
+5	5.416*	6.105

* The difference between this figure and 5.417, the amount of annuity given above, is due to rounding.

The question answered by such a table is: How much will the periodic receipt of $1.00 grow if all payments are held at compound interest at a specified rate and for a specified number of periods? In business terms, we are dealing with an annuity that is to be received.

Discounting · We now look at an annuity that is being paid out by the business, asking the question: How much must be invested in period $-n$ at the specified rate to permit the payment of an annuity of $1.00 per period, leaving nothing at the focal date? As before, this can be broken down into separate payments, which can be evaluated from the table of the present value of single sums. Let us take 4 percent and five years once more. Table 2 can be used.

> At the beginning of period -5:
> it takes 0.822 to produce $1.00 in 5 years,
> it takes 0.855 to produce $1.00 in 4 years,
> it takes 0.889 to produce $1.00 in 3 years,
> it takes 0.925 to produce $1.00 in 2 years,
> it takes 0.962 to produce $1.00 in 1 year.
> Total 4.453, Value of Annuity at Period -5

This example shows how the desired present values of annuities can be obtained by accumulating values from the table of the present values of a single sum. Such a table is included in most books on finance. For convenience, we reproduce a portion in Table 4.

TABLE 4

PRESENT VALUE OF $1.00 RECEIVED PERIODICALLY FOR n PERIODS

Periods	Rate 4%	Rate 10%
0	0	0
−1	0.962	0.909
−2	1.886	1.736
−3	2.775	2.487
−4	3.630	3.170
−5	4.452*	3.791

* The difference between this figure and 4.453, the value of the annuity given above, is due to rounding.

When we were dealing with the changing values of a single sum over time, we ended our explanation with a diagram. A similar one, Chart 2, can be presented for annuities, although the situation is more complex. The reader will note, in studying the charted annuities, that the values get larger as one proceeds in either direction from the focal date. This is because of the periodic payments of $1.00 that are involved. The reader will also note here, as in the more simple case, that changing the rate of return has considerable influence on the values, especially as time becomes more remote. In each instance the higher the rate, the greater the advantage to the user of the funds. That is, if 10 percent is applied, an annuity will cost less, or produce more, than if a lower rate were applied.

Before we leave the subject of the present values of annuities, we shall describe in another way the operation of the investment of $4.452 at 4 percent to permit paying $1.00 per year for five ·years. This will not add to the theoretical structure, but it will picture the process in a way that is more useful in financial thinking.

At the beginning of year −5, invest $4.452.
At the end of year −5, take interest of $0.178, and withdraw $0.822.
At the beginning of year −4, remainder invested becomes $3.630.

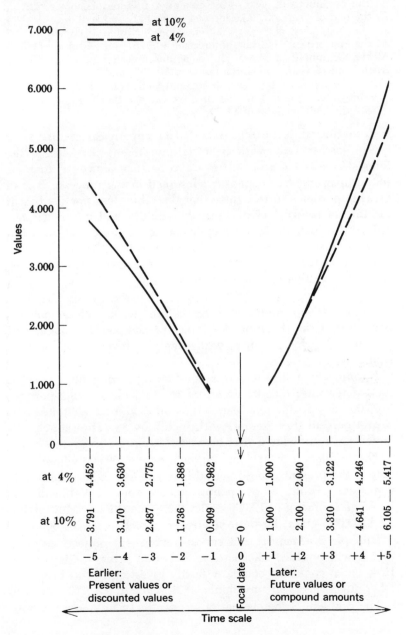

CHART 2

Effects of Time Adjustment: Annuity

At the end of year −4, take interest of $0.145, and withdraw $0.855.
At the beginning of year −3, remainder invested becomes $2.775.
At the end of year −3, take interest of $0.111, and withdraw $0.889.
At the beginning of year −2, remainder invested becomes $1.886.
At the end of year −2, take interest of $0.075, and withdraw $0.925.
At the beginning of year −1, remainder invested becomes $0.961.
At the end of year −1, take interest of $0.038, and withdraw $0.962.
There is a difference between $0.962 and $0.961, because of the use of
abbreviated tables. Ignoring this, we can see that the annuity ends
with the final payment of $1.00.

From this table, it can be seen that a company can receive $1.00
a year for five years with an initial investment of $4.452, if the
interest rate is 4 percent. It can also be seen, however, that the
initial investment of capital is consumed in the process. It is of
great importance to recognize that the table does *not* say that if
the rate of return is 4 percent, the annuity will go on without
reducing principal. If the principal is to be preserved, its with-
drawals must not be consumed, but invested elsewhere. Also,
if 4 percent is to continue to be obtained from the use of funds,
the new investment opportunities must yield this rate.

Examples Using Annuities · As before, we conclude our explanation of the derivation of tables of compound amount and
present value for annuities with examples taken from business
situations.

Example 1. A firm which is considering setting up a pension
fund determines that it can afford to set aside for this purpose
$100,000 a year for ten years. It is advised that a trustee can
earn 4 percent (tax exempt) with such moneys. How much will
have been accumulated after ten years?

The problem is to evaluate an annuity of $100,000 whose focal
date is the present, whose period is ten years, and whose rate is
4 percent. Tables of compound amount (not available in this
book) give a factor of 12.006 under these conditions. Multiplying
by $100,000 gives the desired answer, which is $1,200,600.

Example 2. Analysis of a certain investment project indicates
that it will produce $50,000 a year, before taxes, for ten years.
How much could the company justify investing in this project if
other investments are available at 4 percent? At 10 percent?

The problem is the evaluation as of now of an annuity whose

focal date is ten years from the present. We find the present value factor for ten periods to be 8.111 for 4 percent, and 6.145 for 10 percent. Multiplying by $50,000, we find $405,550 for 4 percent and $307,250 for 10 percent. These are the sums that could be invested at the specified rates to produce $50,000 a year for ten years.

Example 3. Taking the figures as developed in Example 2, assume that the firm finds that $350,000 is required as an investment to establish the project. Since this number is more than the present value at 10 percent, the firm should not undertake the project if it has other opportunities on which 10 percent can be earned. The firm should, however, consider the project an excellent one if the alternative opportunities are offering 4 percent return.

Finding the Rate of Return · One last step in the use of present value tables will be illustrated here. Given the periodic amount of an annuity and the original investment, what is the rate of return? Using the figures from Example 3, above, what rate of return will produce a ten-year annuity of $50,000 from the investment of $350,000?

The focal date is the end of the ten-year period, when the last payment will be received. The present value table is based on annuities of $1.00 per period, so the figures in the actual case must be converted by dividing through by $50,000:

$$\frac{50,000}{50,000} = 1.000$$

and

$$\frac{350,000}{50,000} = 7.000.$$

Looking at the table of present values of an annuity for ten periods, we find:

Rate 6%. 7.360
Rate 8%. 6.710

By interpolation, the answer can be computed. It is 7.1 percent.

Measuring the Productivity of Capital

Joel Dean

Joel Dean is Professor of Business Economics at Columbia University's Graduate School of Business. This article comes from the Har-vard Business Review of January 1954.

The president of one of our largest oil companies, who was pushing through a program of drastic decentralization of management, stated recently that the last thing he would delegate would be decisions about capital expenditures. This is understandable because capital-expenditure decisions form the framework for a company's future development and are a major determinant of efficiency and competitive power. The wisdom of these corporate investment decisions, therefore, has a profound effect upon a company's future earnings and growth.

From the standpoint of the stockholder and of the consumer, capital expenditures are the principal bulwark against the seemingly endless progression of wage increases. From the standpoint of labor, capital expenditures are the basic economic source of future wage advances since they embody the creative forward strides of advancing technology. Finally, capital expenditures, both by their aggregate size and by their cyclical timing, have a great deal to do with the character of the economy as a whole, and thus with the government's role in maintaining stability.

MANAGEMENT PROGRAM

Farsighted judgment is an essential requisite for wise decisions about capital expenditures. But such judgment, to be sound, must be based on analysis of all the facts, many of them extremely technical and complex. In particular, top management needs an objective means of measuring the economic worth of individual investment proposals in order to have a realistic basis for choosing among them and selecting those which will mean the most to the company's long-run prosperity. The basic measure of economic worth is the productivity of capital, which means its power to produce profits. The purpose of this article is to suggest better ways of making that measurement.

Unfortunately, the problem of managing capital expenditure has not generally been attacked with the kind of thorough and objective analysis that has paid such big dividends in other management areas. I have made a study of the capital-expenditure methods of some fifty large companies. These are all well-managed companies so far as production, engineering, and marketing methods are concerned, and I have a great deal of admiration for their executives. But on capital expenditures they show widespread failure to measure the investment worth of individual proposals directly, lack of defensible objective standards of an acceptable investment, and distorted dedication to procedures and paper work, with inadequate understanding of the economic content of the concepts used. In other words, when it comes to capital expenditures, they are still forced to play by ear to a distressing extent.

The development of an effective system for managing capital expenditures requires a complex combination of disciplines: (*a*) application of economic theory at several vital points; (*b*) knowledge of financial mathematics, which most of us acquired in our apprenticeship days but have inevitably forgotten long since; (*c*) economic forecasting; (*d*) techniques for projecting the amount and timing of outlays and receipts; and (*e*) techniques of control through comparison of actualities with projections. Top management clearly needs technical help. No executive, even if he had the time to analyze each capital proposal personally, could be expected to have all the necessary disciplines at his command; they can only be gathered together in a team of specialists.

This article concentrates on the measurement of the economic worth of individual investment proposals. But we must remember that, though this is likely to be the critical element, it is only one of many components in a well-rounded program of capital management.

ARE PROFITS CONTROLLING?

As we turn, now, to the phase of capital-expenditure management that is our main concern here—measurement of capital productivity—we must face an underlying question: To what degree are investment decisions actually controlled by profit considerations?

Concern with capital productivity of course implies that the company's goal is profits. But actually in many cases money making is a secondary objective. Often the primary goal is strategic—to maintain or increase the company's share of the market, to achieve growth in sales volume or number of employees, or simply to build reputation and status. Often capital expenditures capture and embody this kind of motivation in the form of corporate monuments made "just to become the kind of company we want to be." I am thinking of welfare and prestige investments like gymnasiums, country clubs, and palatial offices.

A corporation is not single-minded. It is composed of groups and individuals whose interests conflict. The concept of management as arbiter among employees, customers, and stockholders can lead to capital-expenditure policies and commitments that stray from the directional beam of capital productivity. Not that this is necessarily wrong. But, at least, when a company does let such goals as welfare or prestige govern, it ought to know the cost of such a policy. The only way to find out this cost is to determine the profitability of capital projects and see how much profit is being passed up in order to build such corporate monuments. The cost of prestige, then, is the amount of earnings foregone by departing from a pattern of investment ruthlessly directed at profit maximization.

Even where money making does dominate, the theory that a company tries to maximize its profits needs some qualification. Much more prevalent is what can be described as the doctrine of *adequate profits.* Of course, when profits performance or outlook is inadequate, the stockholder's power does come into play and capital expenditures are likely to be oriented toward profit maximization. But so long as the company is making adequate profits, the drive to have all capital expenditures selected on the basis of profit maximization is blunted.

Thus, I am well aware that making maximum profits is often not the sole or even the dominant goal in managing capital expenditures. But that does not lessen the importance of being able to measure the productivity of capital (i.e., its power to produce profits). Moreover, my viewpoint here remains that of the missionary rather than the anthropologist. As in other applications of managerial economics, the objective is to help executives improve policies, not simply to report practice (or malpractice).

YARDSTICKS OF INVESTMENT WORTH

The heart of good capital-expenditure management, then, is the measurement of the investment worth of individual proposals. But in order to measure how good a project is, we must have the right kind of yardstick. Just what should a good yardstick do?

The productivity of capital can be indicated in several ways, but the central requirement of a good yardstick is that it should measure what the proposed outlay will do to earnings, and do this in a way that permits realistic comparison of one investment proposal with another. What we seek is a measuring rod which will help decide, for example, whether a $5,000 project that will earn $2,000 a year for three years is more attractive than a $60,000 project that will earn $10,000 a year for ten years.

A good yardstick of investment worth should summarize in a single figure all the information that is relevant to the decision whether or not to make the particular investment, and none that is irrelevant. It should be applicable to all types of proposals and should permit appraisal in terms of a single set of standards. Also, it should provide an index that is relatively simple to compute; once the basic data on the proposal have been assembled, the operating people should be able to measure the project's worth easily and without any need to explain how they do it.

Finally, the yardstick should permit simple adjustments to allow for ranges of uncertainty in the earnings estimates, since one of the facts to be taken into account is man's inability to see very far into the future with any great precision.

How do the three most commonly used yardsticks—(a) degree of necessity, (b) payback period, and (c) rate of return—stack up against those criteria?

Degree of Necessity · The degree of urgency of the proposed project—that is, the extent to which it cannot be postponed to later years—is one kind of yardstick for assigning priority to investment proposals. For example, a railroad might put a power crane replacement proposal ahead of a repair shop modernization request because the old crane had broken down and something had to be done about it immediately, whereas the repair shop project could wait.

Degree of necessity has a place in the capital budgeting scheme. Some investments must be made to meet requirements imposed by a government agency. Grade-crossing eliminations for railroads, sanitary facilities in food-processing plants, and mandatory smoke-control installations are examples. Other investments clearly must be made if the company is to remain in business, e.g., replacement of a washed-out section of a railroad's main line. In these cases the alternative is such that its adoption would have a catastrophic effect on the firm's profits. Projects of this nature seldom bulk large in a company's over-all capital-expenditure program.

A serious defect of degree of urgency is that it fails to measure the capital productivity of a proposal—that is, the effect it will have on the company's earnings. A plant-modernization project may be highly postponable; but if it can produce annual savings which will yield 30 percent on the added capital tied up, it is to be preferred to a less postponable but less profitable project. Or, replacement of a shop destroyed by fire may seem completely unpostponable, whereas actually the company might find its over-all profits enhanced by subcontracting the operations formerly performed in the destroyed facilities.

Moreover, the degree of urgency is not a measurable quantity. Proposed projects cannot be assembled and arranged in a single priority ladder; acceptance standards cannot be set up to choose wisely among projects submitted on a necessity basis.

The most serious result of accepting or rejecting proposals primarily on the basis of how urgent they seem to be is that the capital budgeting program is likely to degenerate into a contest of personalities. The biggest share of the capital-expenditure money will go to the division heads who are the most eloquent or most persistent in presenting their requests, rather than to those who have taken the time and effort necessary to make an objective appraisal of the project's economic worth. The result is that all projects come up for review in an atmosphere of haste and emergency, with full scope allowed for the arts of persuasion and exhortation. Not only will projects whose economic desirability is dubious be pushed through to acceptance, but also a large proportion of investments that would yield big savings and high profits may be put off almost indefinitely.

Payback Period · The yardstick of payback period—that is, the number of years required for the earnings on the project to pay back the original outlay with no allowance for capital wastage— is unquestionably the most widely used measure of investment worth. Payback is superior to postponability since it takes into consideration the projected gross earnings, and it does have certain uses in capital-expenditure management:

Payback can serve as a coarse screen to pick out high-profit projects that are so clearly desirable as to require no refined rate-of-return estimates and to reject quickly those projects which show such poor promise that they do not merit thorough economic analysis. In addition, it may be adequate as a measure of investment worth for companies with a high outside cost of capital and severely limited internal cash-generating ability in comparison with the volume of highly profitable internal investment opportunities. If a shortage of funds forces the company to accept only proposals which promise a payback period after taxes of two years or less, the use of a more refined measure might not affect the list of accepted projects.

It also can be useful for appraising risky investments where the rate of capital wastage is particularly hard to predict. Since payback weights near-year earnings heavily and distant earnings not at all, it contains a sort of built-in hedge against the possibility of a short economic life.

For most corporations, however, payback is an inadequate measure of investment worth. It is a cash concept, designed to answer the single question of how soon the cash outlay can be returned to the company's treasury. As such it fails in three important respects to provide a satisfactory yardstick for appraising all the profit-producing investments of a firm:

1. Payback tends to overweight the importance of liquidity as a goal of the capital-expenditure program. No firm can ignore needed liquidity. But most can achieve it by means that are more direct and less costly than sacrificing profits by allowing payback to govern the selection of capital projects.

2. It ignores capital wastage. By confining analysis to the project's gross earnings (before depreciation) it takes no cognizance of its probable economic life.

3. It fails to consider the earnings of a project after the initial outlay has been paid back. By concentrating on liquidity, it ignores the vital matter of what the life pattern of the earnings will be. Up to the end of the payback period the company has just got its bait back. How much longer the earnings will last is what determines the profitability of the investment. A three-year payback project may yield a 30 percent return on average investment if it has a long life, but only 12 percent if its life is four years, and no return at all if just three years.

In short, because payback does not measure or reflect all the dimensions of profitability which are relevant to capital expenditure decisions, it is neither inclusive enough nor sensitive enough to be used as the company's over-all measure of investment worth.

Rate of Return · Measurement of the economic worth of an investment proposal by means of rate of return relates the project's anticipated earnings to the amount of funds which will be tied up during the investment life of the facility. Rate of return embodies the concept of *net* earnings after allowing for capital wastage. Neither degree of necessity nor payback period uses this concept, since payback is measured in terms of gross earnings, and urgency does not consider earnings at all.

Rate of return has its shortcomings. A sound rate-of-return

system is more complex than most of the methods of rationing a corporation's capital that are in current use. It costs more to install and put into operation. Also it may run into obstacles because it is unfamiliar and possibly because it will block privileged channels from access to capital funds.

But such limitations should not be decisive. Good management of capital expenditures is too vital to be blocked by ignorance, caution, or smugness. Overcoming the old organization's natural resistance to learning new tricks and training it in a new pattern of thought about capital expenditures is a one-shot affair. Once the system is installed, very little effort and cost are needed to keep it going.

The positive superiorities of a rate-of-return measure of investment worth are imposing. It takes account of the full lifetime of a capital-expenditure proposal. Two projects, each of which shows a three-year payback, may differ greatly in the length of time for which they will produce earnings for the company. Take this experience which one company had:

Certain refinery equipment that showed a three-year payback actually became obsolete and was replaced in less than three years. This project's rate of return, therefore, was less than zero, despite what appeared to be a very satisfactory payback. In contrast, a pipeline that had the same three-year payback kept on earning (and promises to continue for twenty years more). Clearly its rate of return was much higher.

Capital wastage—that is, the gradual loss of the economic value of the facility over a period of time—is of vital importance in the appraisal of an investment proposal. Capital productivity should be measured by earnings over the whole life of the investment, even though estimates of the distant future may be subject to wide margins of error.

Because rate of return considers the full life of an investment proposal, correct comparisons of the degree of value of projects can be made. Proposals can therefore be arranged in a ladder of priority even where they seem to be of the same degree of urgency or to have the same payback period. Moreover, the fact that the projects themselves may differ widely in their characteristics does not impede the comparison. New-product investments can thus be compared with cost-reducing projects; or a proposal this year can be compared with one which will not be ready until next year.

Better standards of rejection are made possible by rate of return. A company's combined cost of capital—say, 15 percent—can be used to determine the proper rate of cutoff on the capital-demand ladder just discussed; i.e., the minimum acceptable profitability of a proposal. This not only provides an objective, defensible basis for acceptance or rejection; it also aids top management in delegating authority by providing sound bench marks for personnel down the line to use in killing off the worst propositions before they have gone far up the chain of command.

Finally, rate-of-return rationing is likely to produce more earnings for stockholders, since it directs the flow of funds to their most profitable use by measuring the productivity of capital correctly and comparing it with a relevant standard of acceptable profitability.

MAKING THE ESTIMATES

We have seen that for most companies rate of return is the best yardstick of economic worth. Two problems arise in the practical application of this yardstick. The first concerns the concept for making the empirical projections that are needed to get the three basic determinants of project worth: (a) earnings, (b) economic life, and (c) amount of capital tied up. The second problem (discussed later) is how to combine these determinants in an index of profitability.

Ten Fallacies · The part of this measurement problem which is most often muffed is the job of getting a clear idea of just what needs to be estimated. Why should there be any problem in clarifying the concepts for rate-of-return measurement? The nature of the difficulties and their importance for good measurement can be seen by looking at ten common fallacies.

1. *"No Alternatives."* Perhaps the most common mistake in analyzing a capital proposal is the failure to consider any alternatives. There are always alternatives to an investment proposal, and a systematic analysis of the alternatives is the bench mark for estimating both the investment and the earnings of a capital

project. What will happen if the requested investment is not made measures what the company will get out of it if the investment is made. If, as usual, there are several alternatives differing in the amount of investment required, earnings estimates should logically be built upon the smallest investment alternative which is acceptably profitable. Alternatives which require greater investment are preferable to this one only if the *added* investment over this amount produces enough *added* earnings to yield a satisfactory rate of return.

2. "*'Must' Investment.*" Closely related is the "must" investment fallacy. The common conviction that certain equipment replacements are indispensable for continuing operations implies that top management has no alternatives. True, the alternative is sometimes so catastrophic that it is academic. But even in such a case the reason for making the investment should not be that it is urgent or indispensable, but that its profitability is terrific measured against the catastrophic alternative. Thus the rate of return from replacing a burnt-out pump in an oil pipeline may be astronomical; the investment is small and its earnings are the profits from the whole line, since the only alternative is a complete shutdown.

High-profit investments of this special nature are rarer than realized. Skeptical study of supposed "must" investments will reveal alternatives to many of them and will show that some of them are neither necessary nor even acceptably profitable.

3. "*High Strategy.*" Another fallacy is the notion that some projects are so pivotal for the long-run welfare of the enterprise that they possess high strategic value which overrides mere economic considerations and lifts their evaluation into a mystic realm beyond the ken of economic and financial analysis. For example, the dogma that an integrated oil company should own 75 percent of its crude oil sometimes precludes economic analysis of integration investments.

It is true that some capital expenditures do have benefits which are hard to measure because they are diffused over a wide area of company activity or because they stretch over a protracted time period. And there are some investments which must be made on almost pure faith (e.g., a new research center). Nevertheless, the idea that there is such a thing as strategic value not ultimately rooted in economic worth is demonstrably wrong. If a contemplated investment produces results that do not have any economic value, then directors and stockholders should question its wisdom.

4. *"Routine Replacement."* This fallacy maintains that scheduled periodic replacement of capital facilities is a practical and inexpensive substitute for an investment analysis of the economic desirability of individual replacements. For example, many fleet owners replace motor trucks on a routine basis (i.e., after a certain number of years or a certain number of miles), without determining whether the added net earnings from replacing this or that old truck with a new one will produce an adequate return on the specific added investment. Routine replacement has the virtues of simplicity, orderliness, and predictability. But vintage retirement will not produce as profitable a pattern of investment as will a capital-earnings plan.

5. *"Prediction is Impossible."* Scoffers maintain that since the future cannot be predicted with accuracy, it is futile to try to guess the useful life of a proposed facility or to project its earnings beyond the first year. The consequence of this fallacy is an unwillingness to define concepts in a way that will force explicit projection. People try to duck out by proclaiming that "with a four-year payback, it doesn't matter" or by embracing "unfair" Bureau of Internal Revenue depreciation rates.

The basic mistake is refusing to recognize that forecasting, though difficult and subject to error, is nevertheless necessary in appraising the worth of capital projects. Prediction, whether or not it is done consciously, lies at the heart of any executive judgment about a proposed investment. Usually it is better to *know* what is being done.

6. *"Fair Share of Overhead."* A common error in project analysis is to use allocations of current overhead instead of estimating the added costs that will be caused by the project. This cost-proration fallacy confuses problems of equity with problems of economic consequences. This is illustrated by a question frequently raised: Should a new product line, acquisition of which is being contemplated, carry its full share of the overhead now borne by mature products, or should it get a free ride? Neither of these suggested solutions is correct, at least for estimating project earnings. Old

overheads do not matter—only new overheads. What is needed is not a reallocation of past overheads but a forecast of how future overheads will increase by acceptance as opposed to rejection of the project. This cost increment is wholly unaffected by the conventions of apportionment of common costs.

7. *"Free Ride."* A related fallacy that frequently misguides analysis of capital proposals errs in the opposite direction. It holds that new products or added volume are "plus business" in the sense of incurring negligible additional costs. This "free ride" fallacy leads to the conclusion that earnings from expansion investments are almost equivalent to their revenue. There is something to this notion; long-run incremental costs are often smaller than fully allocated average costs. But they are larger than short-run marginal costs and never negligible.

While short-run marginal costs are relevant for operating decisions, long-run added costs must be used for investment decisions. Herein lies the peril of the "free ride" fallacy. What, for instance, are the earnings from an added gasoline service station when pipeline and bulk plant capacities will just take that added volume? If only the marginal cost of using this bulk-movement capacity is included, rate of return is high. But continued normal growth will soon force expansion of the bulk-movement capacity; the new service station brings this time that much closer. If the full cost of this expansion is included in estimating lifetime earnings, the return of course shows up as much lower.

8. *"Carrying Charge."* The practice of charging the earnings of all projects with an interest cost might be called the "carrying charge" fallacy. Usually this charge is computed by applying the company's short-term borrowing rate to the capitalized portion of the original investment. This approach has the virtue of recognizing that money is not costless, even though no entry is made in the accounts. It has, however, two defects: (*a*) it uses the wrong cost of money, since high-cost equity capital is left out, and (*b*) it introduces cost of money into the capital-management program in the wrong way. Instead of subtracting carrying costs from individual projects, it is better to use cost of capital as a cutoff rate to select acceptably profitable projects.

9. *"Book Value."* Determination of the investment amount looks so easy that it is often done wrong. Bookkeeping is the root

of error here. Accounting conventions that are indispensable for financial reporting give the wrong steer for estimating a project's investment base. The test of what should be included in the investment amount is not how it is handled on the books, which bears only on the tax effects of the proposal, an important but quite separate issue. The test is whether or not the outlay is necessary to produce the stream of earnings contemplated in the proposal.

The "book value" concept would exclude outlays that are expensed (rather than capitalized) from the amount of investment serving as the base for the rate-of-return estimate. Take a proposal to convert an unused portion of a building into a sausage factory requiring $100,000 of capitalizable machinery plus $150,-000 of expensed repairs. The pretax investment amount is the whole $250,000; after deflating the expensed portion for 50 percent income tax rates ($150,000 minus $75,000), the after-tax investment amount is seen to be $175,000. But the book value is only $100,000.

Book value also gives bad investment guidance in propping up, transferring, or abandoning existing assets. The book value of an existing asset is based on recorded historical cost less accumulated depreciation. For investment decisions, its value should be determined by what the company can get for the asset or what the company can do with it in its next best internal use, rather than by the figures that happen to be on the books.

10. *"Taxes Don't Matter."* There is a surprisingly widespread conviction that adjustment for corporate income taxes is academic. This "taxes don't matter" fallacy assumes that the underlying worth of a project is obscured (rather than revealed) by allowing for tax effects, and that the ranking of capital products will be the same whether or not they are deflated for taxes. This beguiling notion is wrong in two respects: (*a*) In order to apply tenable acceptance standards such as the company's outside cost of capital, it is necessary to measure rate of return after taxes, rather than before taxes. (*b*) The impact of taxes differs depending on the time shape of the project; and the after-tax ranking of proposals will differ significantly from their before-tax ranking if taxes are correctly taken into account in computing rate of return. For example, the tax effects of accelerated amortization can con-

vert a border-line project into a highly profitable investment opportunity.

Positive Concepts · Having looked at these ten fallacies, we are in a better position to formulate positive concepts of what needs to be estimated in measuring project earnings and project investment.

A correct estimate of earnings must be based on the simple principle that the earnings from a proposal are measured by the total *added* earnings or savings from making the investment as opposed to not making it. The proper bench mark for computing earnings on a project is the *best alternative* way of doing the job; comparison therewith will indicate the source and amount of the added earnings. Project costs should be unaffected by allocations of existing overheads but should cover all the changes in total overhead (and other) costs that are forecasted to result from the investment, but nothing else—nothing that will be the same regardless of whether the proposal is accepted or rejected.

The value of a proposed investment depends on its future earnings. Hence, the earnings estimate should be based on the best available projections of future volume, wage rates, and price levels. Earnings should be estimated over the economic life of the proposed facilities. Because project earnings vary in time shape, and because this will affect the rate of return, the earnings estimates should reflect the variations in the time trend of earnings.

In estimating economic life of an investment, consideration must be given to (*a*) physical deterioration, (*b*) obsolescence, and (*c*) the possibility that the source of earnings will dry up before either of the first two factors becomes operative.

Interest on investment should not be deducted from project earnings. Charging interest increases the complexity of the rate-of-return computation without adding to the information it provides. Earnings should be stated after corporate income taxes, for only in such form are they relevant for capital attraction and for dividend payment.

The appropriate investment base for calculating rate of return is the added outlay which is occasioned by the adoption of the project as opposed to rejecting it and adopting an alternative which requires less investment. The entire amount of the original added outlay should be included in the investment amount, regardless of how it is treated in the books. Any tax benefit which results from expensing certain items rather than capitalizing them should be reflected. Those repairs which would be made whether or not the proposal is adopted should be excluded from the investment amount, because they are not caused by it.

If the proposal involves a transfer of facilities from another part of the company, the opportunity cost of these facilities (the amount foregone by using them this way rather than another) should be added to the amount of investment. If the opportunity foregone is merely to sell the facilities for scrap, then this will indicate the value to set on the transferred assets.

The amount of the investment should also include the amount of any additional necessary investment in working capital or other auxiliary facilities. Research and promotional expenses to get new products rolling or to develop new methods or to expand business are no less investments than plant and equipment.

CALCULATING RATE OF RETURN

Once the basic estimates of project earnings and investment have been made, there are two major ways of combining them into a rate-of-return measurement. One way—which can be called the "accounting method" because it is closely related to many of the concepts used in conventional accounting procedure—computes rate of return as the ratio of (a) the project's earnings averaged over the life of the proposition to (b) the average lifetime investment. The other—which can be called "discounted cash flow"—computes rate of return as the maximum interest rate which could be paid on the capital tied up over the life of the investment without dipping into earnings produced elsewhere in the company.

Accounting Method · A characteristic of the accounting method is that it has many variants, each of which produces a different rate-of-return figure for any one investment proposal. One set of variants comes from diverse concepts of the investment amount (e.g., the original outlay, $100,000, versus the average amount tied up in the facility over its life, $50,000). Another source of variants is the diverse concepts of the project earnings. Earnings can be either gross or net of depreciation, either before or after taxes. They can be the average for several years or for the first year only. This variety of alternatives produces a tremendous range of rate-of-return results. But they all fall into the category of accounting method, provided the final result is a ratio of earnings to investment.

This shortcoming can be minimized only by arbitrarily standardizing on one variant of the method and making all computations according to this standard.

A more serious drawback to the use of the accounting method is that it is insensitive to variations in the time pattern of investment outlays and earnings. By taking an annual average of earnings over the life of a project this method ignores the earning trends, which may be quite important.

The economic worth of an investment will be affected by the time shape of its lifetime earnings, because near money has greater economic value than distant money. For example, an oil well has a strikingly different time shape than a service station. A well which comes in as a gusher trails off to a pumper. In contrast, a service station in a new area has a rising curve of earnings and is likely to show post-operative losses in the first year or so. Failure to reflect these time-shape disparities in the index of investment worth leads to unprofitable capital-expenditure decisions.

The effect of time shape on economic worth is especially great when the company's cost of capital is high or when the foregone earnings on projects that are passed up are high. Only a company whose investment projects are roughly similar in time shape and in economic life can ignore this feature. For such a firm the added accuracy of the discounted-cash-flow method probably does not justify the transitional pain and effort required to install the system. But any company which has projects that vary significantly in either time shape or longevity has an important stake in using the most sensitive rate-of-return method available.

Discounted Cash Flow · The mechanics of the cash-flow method consist essentially of finding the interest rate that discounts future earnings of a project down to a present value equal to the project cost. This interest rate is the rate of return on that investment. Exhibit 1 illustrates the way in which rate of return can be determined under the cash-flow method for a cost-reducing machine which costs $2,200 and has an anticipated life of five years with no salvage value at the end of that time. In this case, an interest rate of 20 percent is found to make the present value of the future earnings stream equal to the present cost of the machine, so this is the rate of return.

EXHIBIT 1

CASH-FLOW METHOD OF COMPUTING RATE OF RETURN ILLUSTRATED
(Machine costing $2,200 with anticipated life of five years
and no salvage value at the end of that time)

		Present		
	Gross earnings	*value of earnings discounted at*		
Year	*before depreciation*	*18%*	*20%*	*22%*
1	$ 200	$ 184	$ 182	$ 180
2	600	458	446	432
3	800	510	486	462
4	1,200	640	596	556
5	1,200	534	488	448
Total	$4,000	$2,326	$2,198	$2,078

Conceptually, this method is based on the principle that in making an investment outlay we are actually buying a series of future annual incomes—ranging in the example in the exhibit from $200 the first year to $1,200 by the fourth and fifth years. We have an investment in each of those incomes, an investment which compounds in value through time until its own year arrives and it materializes in cash earnings. Thus, for example, the $596 present value of the fourth year's earnings at 20 percent is the amount that would have to be invested at 20 percent now to yield $1,200 gross earnings during the fourth year ($596 compounded at 20 percent for three and one-half years—since the $1,200 would begin to come in at the beginning of the fourth year).

The basic simplicity of this method is brought out by this illustration. Earnings are stated as gross cash receipts (not figuring depreciation). Therefore, it is not necessary to allocate the cost of the machine over its life before computing return. Depreciation is allowed for automatically because the interest rate that discounts the sum of present values to zero is the rate of return on the investment after annual provisions for repaying the principal amount. We are not, as in the accounting method, watching the write-off of original cost; we are watching instead the growth of our investment outlay as we compound it through time.

The method is *simplified* by the fact that there is no need to make a decision as to which earnings base to use (e.g., original outlay, average investment, and so on), nor is there any need to enter interest as a direct cost of the project. Once the data are gathered and set up, there is only one rate-of-return answer possible, and it can be arrived at by straightforward working of charts and interest tables.[1]

Net Superiority of Discounted Cash Flow · The accounting method does have the advantage of familiarity and transparency. Although education would be necessary to get everyone to standardize on one method of averaging earnings and investment, the idea of computing a simple ratio by dividing one number by another is familiar to anyone who went beyond the second grade.

The discounted-cash-flow method admittedly is less familiar. While a method essentially similar to this has been widely used throughout the financial community for computing bond yields, insurance premiums, and rates on leased facilities where accuracy is important and even small errors may cause serious loss, it is new in its application to the measurement of productivity of individual capital-expenditure projects in industry. Hence the job of explaining it to the bookkeeper and the clerk will require time and effort. But its appearance of complexity is deceptive. Once the basic method is understood, it is actually simpler and quicker to use than the accounting method.

Another deterrent to its use is the fact that it does not correspond to accounting concepts about the recording of costs and revenues, so that special analysis is necessary to compute a postmortem on an investment made in the past. But this seems minor in comparison with its imposing superiorities:

1. The discounted-cash-flow method is economically realistic in confining the analysis to cash flows and forgetting about cus-

---

1. [Cases do arise where the rate of return is not unique. See the references in fn. 2 below. *Editor*]

tomary book allocations. The books, although very valuable for other purposes, are irrelevant for the task of measuring investment worth.

2. The use of this method forces guided thinking about the whole life of the project and concentration on the lifetime earnings.

3. It weights the time pattern of the investment outlay and the cash earnings from that outlay in such a way as to reflect real and important differences in the value of near and distant cash flows.

4. It reflects accurately and without ambiguity the timing of tax savings, either from expensing part of the investment outlay or from writing off capitalized costs over the life of the investment—something quite difficult to do by the accounting method.

5. It permits simple allowances for risks and uncertainties and can be adapted readily to increasing the risk allowance over time.

6. It is strictly comparable to cost-of-capital ratios so that decisions can be made quickly and safely on the basis of the relationship between indicated rate of return and the value of money to the company.

CONCLUSION

Examination of the capital-expenditure policies and procedures of some fifty well-managed companies shows that top management is forced to a distressing degree to rely on intuition and authority. Management lacks the skilled analysis and the scientific control needed for sound judgment on these intricate, vital capital decisions. The pivotal problem of capital-expenditure management is the measurement of the investment worth of individual proposals.

Systematic exploration to assure that investment opportunities are ferreted out and objectively analyzed is a prerequisite for the measurement of investment worth. Long-range capital plans and projections enable management to appraise projects in better perspective and to fit them into broader patterns. The comprehensive short-range capital budget which forecasts the timing of probable cash outlays for investment and the timing of cash inflows is essential for determining cut-off points by cash-generation criteria.

For orderly operation of rate-of-return rationing, management needs not only good management of capital productivity but also objective and defensible standards of minimum acceptability. These should generally be based on the company's cost of capital. Candid and economically realistic post-completion audits are indispensable incentives for measuring project profitability accurately; they also provide the systematized experience for improving project measurement in the future.

Special forms and procedures to implement these capital-expenditure management principles also need to be tailored to the particular conditions of the individual company. Above all, good capital-expenditure management must operate in an enlightened intellectual environment throughout the company; all the personnel concerned should understand the economics of capital expenditures and of the measurements and controls which a sound program entails.

For most companies, productivity of capital should be measured by rate of return, rather than by payback or degree of necessity. Estimates of a project's rate of return should be based on concepts of capital investment and projects earnings, which are indicated by what would happen if the company were to go ahead on the project instead of selecting some alternative which requires a smaller investment.

Prediction is essential; project worth depends solely on future earnings—the added earnings that will result from the added investment. These future earnings need to be forecasted over the whole economic life of the facility. Project costs should be unaffected by allocations of existing overhead, but should include all increases in overhead (and in other costs) that will be caused by the project. Earnings should be deflated for taxes. The investment base should be the entire added outlay regardless of bookkeeping —adjusted for corporate income taxes.

The discounted-cash-flow method of computing rate of return is demonstrably superior to existing alternatives in accuracy, realism, relevance, and sensitivity. Acceptance of rate-of-return capital budgeting should not hinge on willingness or reluctance to go this far in breaking with traditional methods.[2]

2. [For further discussion of criteria for choosing investments, see J. Lorie and L. Savage, "Three Problems in Rationing Capital" (1955), E. Solomon, "The Arithmetic of Capital Budgeting Decisions" (1956), and E. Renshaw, "A Note on the Arithmetic of Capital Budgeting Decisions" (1957), all in the *Journal of Business. Editor*]

Risk Analysis in Capital Investment

DAVID B. HERTZ

David B. Hertz is a Principal with McKinsey and Company. This well-known paper appeared in the Harvard Business Review *in 1964.*

Of all the decisions that business executives must make, none is more challenging—and none has received more attention—than choosing among alternative capital investment opportunities. What makes this kind of decision so demanding, of course, is not the problem of projecting return on investment under any given set of assumptions. The difficulty is in the assumptions and in their impact. Each assumption involves its own degree—often a high degree—of uncertainty; and, taken together, these combined uncertainties can multipy into a total uncertainty of critical proportions. This is where the element of risk enters, and it is in the evaluation of risk that the executive has been able to get little help from currently available tools and techniques.

There is a way to help the executive sharpen his key capital investment decisions by providing him with a realistic measurement of the risks involved. Armed with this measurement, which evaluates for him the risk at each possible level of return, he is then in a position to measure more knowledgeably alternative courses of action against corporate objectives.

NEED FOR NEW CONCEPT

The evaluation of a capital investment project starts with the principle that the productivity of capital is measured by the rate of return we expect to receive over some future period. A dollar received next year is worth less to us than a dollar in hand today. Expenditures three years hence are less costly than expenditures of equal magnitude two years from now. For this reason we cannot calculate the rate of return realistically unless we take into account (a) when the sums involved in an investment are spent and (b) when the returns are received.

Comparing alternative investments is thus complicated by the fact that they usually differ not only in size but also in the length of time over which expenditures will have to be made and benefits returned.

It is these facts of investment life that long ago made apparent the shortcomings of approaches that simply averaged expenditures and benefits, or lumped them, as in the number-of-years-to-pay-out method. These shortcomings stimulated students of decision-making to explore more precise methods for determining whether one investment would leave a company better off in the long run than would another course of action.

It is not surprising, then, that much effort has been applied to the development of ways to improve our ability to discriminate among investment alternatives. The focus of all of these investigations has been to sharpen the definition of the value of capital investments to the company. The controversy and furor that once came out in the business press over the most appropriate way of calculating these values has largely been resolved in favor of the discounted cash flow method as a reasonable means of measuring the rate of return that can be expected in the future from an investment made today.

Thus we have methods which, in general, are more or less elaborate mathematical formulas for comparing the outcomes of various investments and the combinations of the variables that will affect the investments.[1] As these techniques have progressed,

1. See, for example, Joel Dean, *Capital Budgeting* (New York, Columbia University Press, 1951); "Return on Capital as a Guide to Managerial Decisions," *National Association of Accounts Research Report No. 35,* Decem-

the mathematics involved has become more and more precise, so that we can now calculate discounted returns to a fraction of a percent.

But the sophisticated businessman knows that behind these precise calculations are data which are not that precise. At best, the rate-of-return information he is provided with is based on an average of different opinions with varying reliabilities and different ranges of probability. When the expected returns on two investments are close, he is likely to be influenced by "intangibles"—a precarious pursuit at best. Even when the figures for two investments are quite far apart, and the choice seems clear, there lurks in the back of the businessman's mind memories of the Edsel and other ill-fated ventures.

In short, the decision-maker realizes that there is something more he ought to know, something in addition to the expected rate of return. He suspects that what is missing has to do with the nature of the data on which the expected rate of return is calculated, and with the way those data are processed. It has something to do with uncertainty, with possibilities and probabilities extending across a wide range of rewards and risks.

The Achilles Heel · The fatal weakness of past approaches thus has nothing to do with the mathematics of rate-of-return calculation. We have pushed along this path so far that the precision of our calculation is, if anything, somewhat illusory. The fact is that, no matter what mathematics is used, each of the variables entering into the calculation of rate of return is subject to a high level of uncertainty. For example:

The useful life of a new piece of capital equipment is rarely known in advance with any degree of certainty. It may be affected by variations in obsolescence or deterioration, and relatively small changes in use life can lead to large changes in return. Yet an expected value for the life of the equipment—based on a great deal of data from which a single best possible forecast has been developed—is entered into the rate-of-return calculation. The same is done for the other factors that have a significant bearing on the decision at hand.

ber 1, 1959; and Bruce F. Young, "Overcoming Obstacles to Use of Discounted Cash Flow for Investment Shares," *NAA Bulletin,* March 1963, p. 15.

Let us look at how this works out in a simple case—one in which the odds appear to be all in favor of a particular decision:

The executives of a food company must decide whether to launch a new packaged cereal. They have come to the conclusion that five factors are the determining variables: *advertising and promotion expense, total cereal market, share of market for this product, operating costs, and new capital investment.* On the basis of the "most likely" estimate for each of these variables the picture looks very bright—a healthy 30 percent return. This future, however, depends on each of the "most likely" estimates coming true in the actual case. If each of these "educated guesses" has, for example, a 60 percent chance of being correct, there is only an 8 percent chance that *all five* will be correct (.60 × .60 × .60 × .60 × .60). So the "expected" return is actually dependent on a rather unlikely coincidence. The decision-maker needs to know a great deal more about the *other* values used to make each of the five estimates and about what he stands to gain or lose from various combinations of these values.

This simple example illustrates that the rate of return actually depends on a specific combination of values of a great many different variables. But only the expected levels of ranges (e.g., worst, average, best; or pessimistic, most likely, optimistic) of these variables are used in formal mathematical ways to provide the figures given to management. Thus, predicting a single most likely rate of return gives precise numbers that do not tell the whole story.

The "expected" rate of return represents only a few points on a continuous curve of possible combinations of future happenings. It is a bit like trying to predict the outcome in a dice game by saying that the most likely outcome is a "7." The description is incomplete because it does not tell us about all the other things that could happen. In Exhibit 1, for instance, we see the odds on throws of only two dice having six sides. Now suppose that each die has 100 sides and there are eight of them! This is a situation more comparable to business investment, where the company's market share might become any one of 100 different sizes and where there are eight different factors (pricing, promotion, and so on) that can affect the outcome.

Nor is this the only trouble. Our willingness to bet on a roll of the dice depends not only on the odds but also on the stakes.

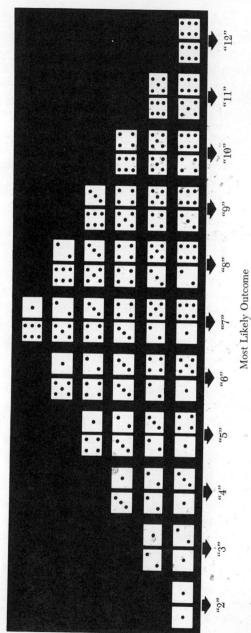

168

David B. Hertz

EXHIBIT 1

DESCRIBING UNCERTAINTY—A THROW OF THE DICE

Most Likely Outcome

"2" "3" "4" "5" "6" "7" "8" "9" "10" "11" "12"

Since the probability of rolling a "7" is 1 in 6, we might be quite willing to risk a few dollars on that outcome at suitable odds. But would we be equally willing to wager $10,000 or $100,000 at those same odds, or even at better odds? In short, risk is influenced both by the odds on various events occurring and by the magnitude of the rewards or penalties which are involved when they do occur. To illustrate again:

Suppose that a company is considering an investment of $1 million. The "best estimate" of the probable return is $200,000 a year. It could well be that this estimate is the average of three possible returns —a 1-in-3 chance of getting no return at all, a 1-in-3 chance of getting $200,000 per year, a 1-in-3 chance of getting $400,000 per year. Suppose that getting no return at all would put the company out of business. Then, by accepting this proposal, management is taking a 1-in-3 chance of going bankrupt.

If only the "best estimate" analysis is used, management might go ahead, however, unaware that it is taking a big chance. If all of the available information were examined, management might prefer an alternative proposal with a smaller, but more certain (i.e., less variable), expectation.

Such considerations have led almost all advocates of the use of modern capital-investment-index calculations to plead for a recognition of the elements of uncertainty. Perhaps Ross G. Walker sums up current thinking when he speaks of "the almost impenetrable mists of any forecast." [2]

How can the executive penetrate the mists of uncertainty that surround the choices among alternatives?

Limited Improvements · A number of efforts to cope with uncertainty have been successful up to a point, but all seem to fall short of the mark in one way or another:

1. *More Accurate Forecasts.* Reducing the error in estimates is a worthy objective. But no matter how many estimates of the future go into a capital investment decision, when all is said and done, the future is still the future. Therefore, however well we forecast, we are still left with the certain knowledge that we cannot eliminate all uncertainty.

2. "The Judgment Factor in Investment Decisions," *Harvard Business Review*, March–April 1961, p. 99.

2. *Empirical Adjustments.* Adjusting the factors influencing the outcome of a decision is subject to serious difficulties. We would like to adjust them so as to cut down the likelihood that we will make a "bad" investment, but how can we do that without at the same time spoiling our chances to make a "good" one? And in any case, what is the basis for adjustment? We adjust, not for uncertainty, but for bias.

For example, construction estimates are often exceeded. If a company's history of construction costs is that 90 percent of its estimates have been exceeded by 15 percent, then in a capital estimate there is every justification for increasing the value of this factor by 15 percent. This is a matter of improving the accuracy of the estimate.

But suppose that new-product sales estimates have been exceeded by more than 75 percent in one-fourth of all historical cases, and have not reached 50 percent of the estimate in one-sixth of all such cases? Penalties for overestimating are very tangible, and so management is apt to reduce the sales estimate to "cover" the one case in six—thereby reducing the calculated rate of return. In doing so, it is possibly missing some of its best opportunities.

3. *Revising Cutoff Rates.* Selecting higher cutoff rates for protecting against uncertainty is attempting much the same thing. Management would like to have a possibility of return in proportion to the risk it takes. Where there is much uncertainty involved in the various estimates of sales, costs, prices, and so on, a high calculated return from the investment provides some incentive for taking the risk. This is, in fact, a perfectly sound position. The trouble is that the decision-maker still needs to know explicitly what risks he is taking—and what the odds are on achieving the expected return.

4. *Three-level Estimates.* A start at spelling out risks is sometimes made by taking the high, medium, and low values of the estimated factors and calculating rates of return based on various combinations of the pessimistic, average, and optimistic estimates. These calculations give a picture of the range of possible results, but do not tell the executive whether the pessimistic re-

sult is more likely than the optimistic one—or, in fact, whether the average result is much more likely to occur than either of the extremes. So, although this is a step in the right direction, it still does not give a clear enough picture for comparing alternatives.

5. *Selected Probabilities.* Various methods have been used to include the probabilities of specific factors in the return calculation. L. C. Grant discusses a program for forecasting discounted cash flow rates of return where the service life is subject to obsolescence and deterioration. He calculates the odds that the investment will terminate at any time after it is made depending on the probability distribution of the service-life factor. After calculating these factors for each year through maximum service life, he then determines an overall expected rate of return.[3]

Edward G. Bennion suggests the use of game theory to take into account alternative market growth rates as they would determine rate of return for various alternatives. He uses the estimated probabilities that specific growth rates will occur to develop optimum strategies. Bennion points out:

Forecasting can result in a negative contribution to capital budget decisions unless it goes further than merely providing a single most probable prediction. . . . [With] an estimated probability coefficient for the forecast, plus knowledge of the payoffs for the company's alternative investments and calculation of indifference probabilities . . . the margin of error may be substantially reduced, and the businessman can tell just how far off his forecast may be before it leads him to a wrong decision.[4]

Note that both of these methods yield an expected return, each based on only one uncertain input factor—service life in the first case, market growth in the second. Both are helpful, and both tend to improve the clarity with which the executive can view investment alternatives. But neither sharpens up the range of

3. "Monitoring Capital Investments," *Financial Executive,* April 1963, p. 19.
4. "Capital Budgeting and Game Theory," *Harvard Business Review,* November–December 1956, p. 123.

"risk taken" or "return hoped for" sufficiently to help very much in the complex decisions of capital planning.

SHARPENING THE PICTURE

Since every one of the many factors that enter into the evaluation of a specific decision is subject to some uncertainty, the executive needs a helpful portrayal of the effects that the uncertainty surrounding each of the significant factors has on the returns he is likely to achieve. Therefore, the method we have developed at McKinsey & Company, Inc., combines the variabilities inherent in all the relevant factors. Our objective is to give a clear picture of the relative risk and the probable odds of coming out ahead or behind in the light of uncertain foreknowledge.

A simulation of the way these factors may combine as the future unfolds is the key to extracting the maximum information from the available forecasts. In fact, the approach is very simple, using a computer to do the necessary arithmetic. (Recently, a computer program to do this was suggested by S. W. Hess and T. A. Quigley for chemical process investments.[5])

To carry out the analysis, a company must follow three steps:

1. Estimate the range of values for each of the factors (e.g., range of selling price, sales growth rate, and so on) and within that range the likelihood of occurrence of each value.

2. Select at random from the distribution of values for each factor one particular value. Then combine the values for all of the factors and compute the rate of return (or present value) from that combination. For instance, the lowest in the range of prices might be combined with the highest in the range of growth rate and other factors. (The fact that the factors are dependent should be taken into account, as we shall see later.)

3. Do this over and over again to define and evaluate the odds of the occurrence of each possible rate of return. Since there

5. "Analysis of Risk in Investments Using Monte Carlo Techniques," *Chemical Engineering Symposium Series 42: Statistics and Numerical Methods in Chemical Engineering* (New York, American Institute of Chemical Engineering, 1963), p. 55.

are literally millions of possible combinations of values, we need to test the likelihood that various specific returns on the investment will occur. This is like finding out by recording the results of a great many throws what percent of "7"s or other combinations we may expect in tossing dice. The result will be a listing of the rates of return we might achieve, ranging from a loss (if the factors go against us) to whatever maximum gain is possible with the estimates that have been made.

For each of these rates the chances that it may occur are determined. (Note that a specific return can usually be achieved through more than one combination of events. The more combinations for a given rate, the higher the chances of achieving it—as with "7"s in tossing dice.) The average expectation is the average of the values of all outcomes weighted by the chances of each occurring.

The variability of outcome values from the average is also determined. This is important since, all other factors being equal, management would presumably prefer lower variability for the same return if given the choice. This concept has already been applied to investment portfolios.[6]

When the expected return and variability of each of a series of investments have been determined, the same technique may be used to examine the effectiveness of various combinations of them in meeting management objectives.

PRACTICAL TEST

To see how this new approach works in practice, let us take the experience of a management that has already analyzed a specific investment proposal by conventional techniques. Taking the same investment schedule and the same expected values actually used, we can find what results the new method would produce and compare them with the results obtained when conventional methods were applied. As we shall see, the new picture of risks and returns is different from the old one. Yet the differences are

6. See Harry Markowitz, *Portfolio Selection, Efficient Diversification of Investments* (New York, John Wiley and Sons, 1959); Donald E. Farrar, *The Investment Decision Under Uncertainty* (Englewood Cliffs, New Jersey, Prentice-Hall, Inc., 1962); William F. Sharpe, "A Simplified Model for Portfolio Analysis," *Management Science,* January 1963, p. 277.

attributable in no way to changes in the basic data—*only to the increased sensitivity of the method to management's uncertainties about the key factors.*

Investment Proposal · In this case a medium-size industrial chemical producer is considering a $10-million extension to its processing plant. The estimated service life of the facility is ten years; the engineers expect to be able to utilize 250,000 tons of processed material worth $510 per ton at an average processing cost of $435 per ton. Is this investment a good bet? In fact, what is the return that the company may expect? What are the risks? We need to make the best and fullest use we can of all the market research and financial analyses that have been developed, so as to give management a clear picture of this project in an uncertain world.

The key input factors management has decided to use are:

1. Market size.
2. Selling prices.
3. Market growth rate.
4. Share of market (which results in physical sales volume).
5. Investment required.
6. Residual value of investment.
7. Operating costs.
8. Fixed costs.
9. Useful life of facilities.

These factors are typical of those in many company projects that must be analyzed and combined to obtain a measure of the attractiveness of a proposed capital facilities investment.

Obtaining Estimates · How do we make the recommended type of analysis of this proposal?

Our aim is to develop for each of the nine factors listed a frequency distribution or probability curve. The information we need includes the possible range of values for each factor, the average, and some ideas as to the likelihood that the various possible values will be reached. It has been our experience that for major capital proposals managements usually make a significant investment in time and funds to pinpoint information about each of the relevant factors. An objective analysis of the values to be assigned to each can, with little additional effort, yield a subjective probability distribution.

Specifically, it is necessary to probe and question each of the experts involved—to find out, for example, whether the estimated cost of production really can be said to be exactly a certain value or whether, as in more likely, it should be estimated to lie within a certain range of values. It is that range which is ignored in the analysis management usually makes. The range is relatively easy to determine; if a guess has to be made—as it often does—it is easier to guess with some accuracy a range rather than a specific single value. We have found from past experience at McKinsey & Company, Inc., that a series of meetings with management personnel to discuss such distributions is most helpful in getting at realistic answers to the a priori questions. (The term "realistic answers" implies all the information management does not have as well as all that it does have.)

The ranges are directly related to the degree of confidence that the estimator has in his estimate. Thus, certain estimates may be known to be quite accurate. They would be represented by probability distributions stating, for instance, that there is only 1 chance in 10 that the actual value will be different from the best estimate by more than 10%. Others may have as much as 100% ranges above and below the best estimate.

Thus, we treat the factor of selling price for the finished product by asking executives who are responsible for the original estimates these questions:

1. Given that $510 is the expected sales price, what is the probability that the price will exceed $550?
2. Is there any chance that the price will exceed $650?
3. How likely is it that the price will drop below $475?

Managements must ask similar questions for each of the other factors, until they can construct a curve for each. Experience shows that this is not as difficult as it might sound. Often information on the degree of variation in factors is readily available. For instance, historical information on variations in the price of a commodity is readily available. Similarly, management can estimate the variability of sales from industry sales records. Even for factors that have no history, such as operating costs for a new product, the person who makes the "average" estimate must have some idea of the degree of confidence he has in his prediction, and therefore he is usually only too glad to express his feelings. Likewise, the less confidence he has in his estimate, the greater will be the range of possible values that the variable will assume.

This last point is likely to trouble businessmen. Does it really make sense to seek estimates of variations? It cannot be emphasized too strongly that the less certainty there is in an "average" estimate, *the more important it is to consider the possible variation in that estimate.*

Further, an estimate of the variation possible in a factor, no matter how judgmental it may be, is always better than a simple "average" estimate, since it includes more information about what is known and what is not known. It is, in fact, this very *lack* of knowledge which may distinguish one investment possibility from another, so that for rational decision-making it *must* be taken into account.

This lack of knowledge is in itself important information about the proposed investment. To throw any information away simply because it is highly uncertain is a serious error in analysis which the new approach is designed to correct.

Computer Runs · The next step in the proposed approach is to determine the returns that will result from random combinations of the factors involved. This requires realistic restrictions, such as not allowing the total market to vary more than some reasonable amount from year to year. Of course, any method of rating the return which is suitable to the company may be used at this point; in the actual case management preferred discounted cash flow for the reasons cited earlier, so that method is followed here.

A computer can be used to carry out the trials for the simulation method in very little time and at very little expense. Thus, for one trial actually made in this case, 3,600 discounted cash flow calculations, each based on a selection of the nine input factors, were run in two minutes at a cost of $15 for computer time. The resulting rate-of-return probabilities were read out immediately and graphed. The process is shown schematically in Exhibit 2.

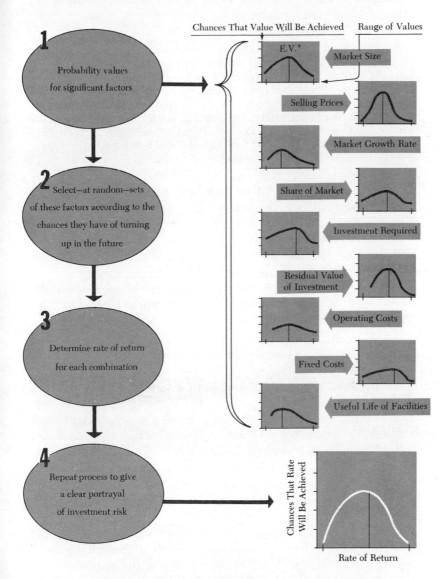

EXHIBIT 2

SIMULATION FOR INVESTMENT PLANNING

* Expected value = highest point of curve.

Data Comparisons · The nine input factors described earlier fall into three categories:

1. *Market analyses.* Included are market size, market growth rate, the firm's share of the market, and selling prices. For a given combination of these factors sales revenue may be determined.
2. *Investment cost analyses.* Being tied to the kinds of service-life and operating-cost characteristics expected, these are subject to various kinds of error and uncertainty; for instance, automation progress makes service life uncertain.
3. *Operating and fixed costs.* These also are subject to uncertainty, but are perhaps the easiest to estimate.

These categories are not independent, and for realistic results our approach allows the various factors to be tied together. Thus, if price determines the total market, we first select from a probability distribution the price for the specific computer run and then use for the total market a probability distribution that is logically related to the price selected.

We are now ready to compare the values obtained under the new approach with the values obtained under the old. This comparison is shown in Exhibit 3.

Valuable Results · How do the results under the new and old approaches compare?

In this case, management had been informed, on the basis of the "one best estimate" approach, that the expected return was 25.2 percent before taxes. When we ran the new set of data through the computer program, however, we got an expected return of only 14.6 percent before taxes. This surprising difference not only is due to the fact that under the new approach we use a range of values; it also reflects the fact that we have weighted each value in the range by the chances of its occurrence.

Our new analysis thus may help management to avoid an unwise investment. In fact, the general result of carefully weighing the information and lack of information in the manner I have suggested is to indicate the true nature of otherwise seemingly satisfactory investment proposals. If this practice were followed by managements, much regretted overcapacity might be avoided.

EXHIBIT 3

COMPARISON OF EXPECTED VALUES UNDER OLD AND NEW APPROACHES

	Conventional "best estimate" approach	New approach
Market analyses		
1. *Market size*		
Expected value (in tons)	250,000	250,000
Range	—	100,000–340,000
2. *Selling prices*		
Expected value (in dollars/ton)	$510	$510
Range	—	$385–$575
3. *Market growth rate*		
Expected value	3%	3%
Range	—	0–6%
4. *Eventual share of market*		
Expected value	12%	12%
Range	—	3%–17%
Investment costs analyses		
5. *Total investment required*		
Expected value (in millions)	$9.5	$9.5
Range	—	$7.0–$10.5
6. *Useful life of facilities*		
Expected value (in years)	10	10
Range	—	5–15
7. *Residual value (at 10 years)*		
Expected value (in millions)	$4.5	$4.5
Range	—	$3.5–$5.0
Other costs		
8. *Operating costs*		
Expected value (in dollars/ton)	$435	$435
Range	—	$370–$545
9. *Fixed costs*		
Expected value (in thousands)	$300	$300
Range	—	250–$375

Note: Range figures in right-hand column represent approximately 1% to 99% probabilities. That is, there is only 1 in a 100 chance that the value actually achieved will be respectively greater or less than the range.

The computer program developed to carry out the simulation allows for easy insertion of new variables. In fact, some programs have previously been suggested that take variability into account.[7] But most programs do not allow for dependence relationships between the various input factors. Further, the program used here permits the choice of a value for price from one distribution, which value determines a particular probability distribution (from among several) that will be used to determine the value for sales volume. To show how this important technique works:

Suppose we have a wheel, as in roulette, with the numbers from 0 to 15 representing one price for the product or material, the numbers 16 to 30 representing a second price, the numbers 31 to 45 a third price, and so on. For each of these segments we would have a different range of expected market volumes; e.g., $150,000–$200,000 for the first, $100,000–$150,000 for the second, $75,000–$100,000 for the third, and so forth. Now suppose that we spin the wheel and the ball falls in 37. This would mean that we pick a sales volume in the $75,000–$100,000 range. If the ball goes in 11, we have a different price and we turn to the $150,000–$200,000 range for a price.

Most significant, perhaps, is the fact that the program allows management to ascertain the sensitivity of the results to each or all of the input factors. Simply by running the program with changes in the distribution of an input factor, it is possible to determine the effect of added or changed information (or of the lack of information). It may turn out that fairly large changes in some factors do not significantly affect the outcomes. In this case, as a matter of fact, management was particularly concerned about the difficulty in estimating market growth. Running the program with variations in this factor quickly demonstrated to us that for average annual growth from 3 percent and 5 percent there was no significant difference in the expected outcome.

In addition, let us see what the implications are of the detailed knowledge the simulation method gives us. Under the method using single expected values, management arrives only at a

7. See Frederick S. Hillier, "The Derivation of Probabilistic Information for the Evaluation of Risky Investments," *Management Science*, April 1963, p. 443.

hoped-for expectation of 25.2 percent after taxes (which, as we have seen, is wrong unless there is no variability in the various input factors—a highly unlikely event). On the other hand, with the method we propose, the uncertainties are clearly portrayed:

Percent return	Probability of achieving at least the return shown
0%	96.5%
5	80.6
10	75.2
15	53.8
20	43.0
25	12.6
30	0

This profile is shown in Exhibit 4. Note the contrast with the profile obtained under the conventional approach. This concept has been used also for evaluation of new product introductions, acquisitions of new businesses, and plant modernization.

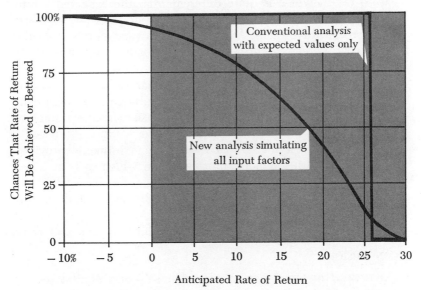

EXHIBIT 4

ANTICIPATED RATES OF RETURN UNDER
OLD AND NEW APPROACHES

COMPARING OPPORTUNITIES

From a decision-making point of view one of the most significant advantages of the new method of determining rate of return is that it allows management to discriminate between measures of (1) expected return based on weighted probabilities of all possible returns, (2) variability of return, and (3) risks.

To visualize this advantage, let us take an example which is based on another actual case but simplified for purposes of explanation. The example involves two investments under consideration, A and B.

When the investments are analyzed, the data tabulated and plotted in Exhibit 5 are obtained. We see that:

• Investment B has a higher expectant return than Investment A.

• Investment B also has substantially more variability than Investment A. There is a good chance that Investment B will earn a return which is quite different from the expected return of 6.8 percent, possibly as high as 15 percent or as low as a loss of 5 percent. Investment A is not likely to vary greatly from the expected 5 percent return. There is virtually no chance of incurring a loss on Investment A.

• Investment B involves far more risk than does Investment A. However, there is 1 chance in 10 of losing money on investment B. If such a loss occurs, its expected size is approximately $200,000.

Clearly, the new method of evaluating investments provides management with far more information on which to base a decision. Investment decisions made only on the basis of maximum expected return are not unequivocally the best decisions.

CONCLUSION

The question management faces in selecting capital investments is first and foremost: What information is needed to clarify the key differences among various alternatives? There is agreement as to the basic factors that should be considered—markets, prices, costs, and so on. And the way the future return on the investment should be calculated, if not agreed on, is at

EXHIBIT 5

COMPARISON OF TWO INVESTMENT OPPORTUNITIES

Selected Statistics

	Investment A	Investment B
Amount of investment	$10,000,000	$10,000,000
Life of investment (in years)	10	10
Expected annual net cash inflow	$ 1,300,000	$ 1,400,000
Variability of cash inflow		
1 chance in 50 of being *greater* than	$ 1,700,000	$ 3,400,000
1 chance in 50 of being *less* * than	900,000	($600,000)
Expected return on investment	5.0%	6.8%
Variability of return on investment		
1 chance in 50 of being *greater* than	7.0%	15.5%
1 chance in 50 of being *less* * than	3.0%	(4.0%)
Risk of investment		
Chance of a loss	Negligible	1 in 10
Expected size of loss		$ 200,000

* In the case of negative figures (indicated by parentheses), "less than" means "worse than."

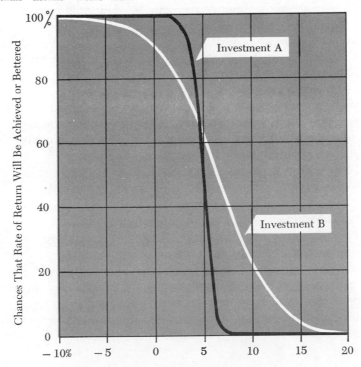

least limited to a few methods, any of which can be consistently used in a given company. If the input variables turn out as estimated, any of the methods customarily used to rate investments should provide satisfactory (if not necessarily maximum) returns.

In actual practice, however, the conventional methods do *not* work out satisfactorily. Why? The reason, as we have seen earlier in this article, and as every executive and economist knows, is that the estimates used in making the advance calculations are just that—estimates. More accurate estimates would be helpful, but at best the residual uncertainty can easily make a mockery of corporate hopes. Nevertheless, there is a solution. To collect realistic estimates for the key factors means to find out a great deal about them. Hence the kind of uncertainty that is involved in each estimate can be evaluated ahead of time. Using this knowledge of uncertainty, executives can maximize the value of the information for decision-making.

The value of computer programs in developing clear portrayals of the uncertainty and risk surrounding alternative investments has been proved. Such programs can produce valuable information about the sensitivity of the possible outcomes to the variability of input factors and to the likelihood of achieving various possible rates of return. This information can be extremely important as a backup to management judgment. To have calculations of the odds on all possible outcomes lends some assurance to the decision-makers that the available information has been used with maximum efficiency.

This simulation approach has the inherent advantage of simplicity. It requires only an extension of the input estimates (to the best of our ability) in terms of probabilities. No projection should be pinpointed unless we are *certain* of it.

The discipline of thinking through the uncertainties of the problem will in itself help to ensure improvement in making investment choices. For to understand uncertainty and risk is to understand the key business problem—and the key business opportunity. Since the new approach can be applied on a continuing basis to each capital alternative as it comes up for consideration and progresses toward fruition, gradual progress may be expected in improving the estimation of the probabilities of variation.

Lastly, the courage to act boldly in the face of apparent uncertainty can be greatly bolstered by the clarity of portrayal of the risks and possible rewards. To achieve these lasting results requires only a slight effort beyond what most companies already exert in studying capital investments.

Investing in the Stock Market

BURTON MALKIEL

Burton Malkiel is Professor of Economics at
Princeton University. This piece is taken
from his book, A Random Walk Down Wall
Street, published by W. W. Norton in 1973.

How to predict future stock prices? That is the investment
question for both amateurs and professionals in the market. It
concerns the brokers who execute your buy and sell orders and
give you advice on stock selection, and also the professional
money managers who invest the billion-dollar pension and retirement funds as well as the popular mutual funds.

Generally the pros take their pick of two approaches to stock
valuation. I call one the "firm-foundation theory" and the other
the "castle-in-the-air theory." Millions have been gained and
lost on these theories. To add to the drama, they appear to be
mutually exclusive. Analysts debate their merits from coast to
coast. Given their hold on the financial community, it is necessary to examine each in some detail. An understanding of these
two approaches is essential to enable you to take your walk down
Wall Street, to interpret much financial news, and to appraise
your broker's advice. It is also a prerequisite for keeping you safe
from serious blunders in the market.

THE FIRM-FOUNDATION THEORY

The firm-foundation theory argues that each common stock has a firm anchor of something called intrinsic value, which can be determined by careful analysis of the company's present position and future prospects. When market prices fall below this firm foundation of intrinsic value a buying opportunity arises, because this fluctuation will eventually be corrected, or so the theory goes. Similarly, should the price of a stock rise considerably above its intrinsic value, the stock is then recommended as a candidate for sale. Investing then becomes a dull but straightforward matter of comparing a stock's actual price with its firm foundation of value.

It is difficult to ascribe to any one individual the credit for originating the firm-foundation theory. S. Eliot Guild is often given this distinction, but the classic development of the technique and particularly the nuances associated with it was worked out by John B. Williams.

In *The Theory of Investment Value*, Williams presented an actual formula for determining the intrinsic value of stock. Williams based his approach on dividend income. In a fiendishly clever attempt to keep things from being simple, he introduced the concept of "discounting" into the process. Discounting basically involves looking at income backwards. Rather than seeing how much money you will have next year (say $1.05 if you put $1 in a savings bank at 5 percent interest), you look at money expected in the future and see how much less it is currently worth (thus, next year's $1 today is work only about 95¢, which could be invested at 5 percent to produce $1 at that time).

Williams was actually serious about this. He went on to argue that the intrinsic value of a stock was equal to the present (or discounted) value of all its future dividends. Investors were advised to "discount" the value of moneys received later. Because so few people understood it, the term caught on and "discounting" now enjoys popular usage among investment people. It received a further boost under the aegis of Professor Irving Fisher of Yale, a distinguished economist and investor.

The logic of the firm-foundation theory is quite respectable.

Wrapped in staid, conservative language, it stresses that stock value ought to consist of the earnings a firm will be able to distribute in the future. But it is here that the tricky little factor of future expectations sneaks in. It stands to reason that a company whose dividends are expected to increase is worth more than one whose dividends are likely to remain static. Thus, security analysts must estimate long-term growth rates. And not only that—they must also try to figure out how long an extraordinary growth rate can be maintained. When the market gets overly enthusiastic about how far in the future growth can continue, it is popularly held on Wall Street that "stocks are discounting not only the future but perhaps even the hereafter."

The point is that the firm-foundation theory relies on some tricky forecasts of the extent and duration of future growth. The mathematical precision with which most intrinsic-value formulas are presented makes it seem easy to specify the worth of a share. Forecasting the future is inherently a very treacherous occupation. Consequently, the anchor of intrinsic value may be a less dependable one than is claimed.

The firm-foundation theory is not confined to economists alone. Thanks to a very influential book, Graham and Dodd's *Security Analysis,* first published in 1934, a whole generation of Wall Street security analysts was converted to the fold. Sound investment management, the practicing analysts learned, simply consisted of buying securities whose prices were temporarily below intrinsic value and selling ones whose prices were temporarily too high. It was that easy. Of course, instructions for determining intrinsic value were furnished and any analyst worth his salt could calculate it with one whisk of the slipstick.

Recently, economists have further enhanced the firm-foundation theory in creating valuation formulas with an additional wrinkle to include an allowance for the risk or quality of the shares. This mathematical legerdemain comes with the spiffy title of capital-asset pricing model. The figures, calculations, and exotic symbols are both impressive and unreadable even for many professional economists. Nevertheless, the *Journal of Finance*—the pinnacle of magazine publishing for the financial economist—continues to sprout pages with terms such as quadratic programming, Riemann surfaces, and bordered Hessian matrices. I do not recommend it for bedtime reading, except to cure insomnia.

THE CASTLE-IN-THE-AIR THEORY

The castle-in-the-air theory of stock prices has nothing to do with intrinsic values. It concentrates on psychic values. Lord Keynes, a famous economist and outstandingly successful investor, enunciated the theory most lucidly in 1936. Keynes felt that intrinsic values—depending as they do on forecasts of the future—are too difficult to determine. It was his opinion that professional investors prefer to devote their energies to an analysis of how the crowd of investors is likely to behave in the future and how during periods of optimism they tend to build their hopes into castles in the air. The successful investor tries to beat the gun by estimating what investment situations are most susceptible to public castle-building and then buying before the crowd.

According to Keynes, the firm-foundation theory involved too much work and was of doubtful value. Keynes practiced what he preached. While London's financial men toiled many weary hours in darkened rooms, he played the market from his bed for half an hour each morning. This leisurely method of investing earned him several million pounds for his own account and a tenfold increase in the market value of the endowment of his college, King's College, Cambridge.

In the depression years in which Keynes gained his fame, most people concentrated on his ideas for stimulating the economy. It was hard for anyone to build castles in the air or to dream that others would do so. Nevertheless, in his book, *General Theory of Employment, Interest and Money,* he devoted an entire chapter to the stock market and to the importance of investor expectations.

Keynes noted the pitfalls of predicting future dividends. No one knows for sure what will influence future earnings prospects and dividend payments. As a result, Keynes says, most persons are "largely concerned, not with making superior long-term forecasts of the probable yield of an investment over its whole life, but with foreseeing changes in the conventional basis of valuation a short time ahead of the general public." Keynes, in

other words, applied psychological principles rather than financial evaluation to the study of the stock market.

[Most persons] are concerned, not with what an investment is really
worth to a man who buys it "for keeps," but with what the market
will value it at, under the influence of mass psycholoy, three months
or a year hence. . . . For it is not sensible to pay 25 for an investment of which you believe the prospective yields to justify a value of
30, if you also believe that the market will value it at 20 three months
hence.

Keynes describes the playing of the stock market in terms
readily understandable to his fellow Englishmen: it is analogous to entering a newspaper beauty-judging contest in which
you have to select the six prettiest faces out of 100 photographs.
The prize goes to the person whose selections most nearly conform to those of the group as a whole.

The smart player recognizes that his personal criteria of beauty
are irrelevant in determining the contest winner. A better
strategy is to select those faces the other players are likely to
fancy. This logic tends to snowball. After all, the other con-
testants are no fools and they are likely to play the game with
at least as keen a perception. Thus the optimal strategy is not to
pick those faces the player thinks are prettiest, or even those he
may believe the other players are likely to fancy, but rather to
predict what the average opinion is likely to think the average
opinion will be or to proceed even further along this sequence.
So much for British beauty contests.

But trying to divine what others will think we think also implies work. Might predicting future dividends be easier after all?
Keynes did not think so: "Investment based on genuine long-
term expectation is so difficult today as to be scarcely practicable." Besides, trying to predict long-run intrinsic values was
terribly boring to Keynes.

Life is not long enough—human nature desires quick results, there is
a peculiar zest in making money quickly, and remoter gains are discounted by the average man at a very high rate. The game of professional investment is intolerably boring and over-exacting to anyone
who is entirely exempt from the gambling instinct; whilst he who has
it must pay this propensity the appropriate toll.

The newspaper-contest analogy represents the ultimate form of a castle-in-the-air theory of price determination. A share of stock is worth one price to a buyer because the expects to sell it to someone else at a higher price. The stock, in other words, holds itself up by its own bootstraps. The new buyer in turn anticipates that future buyers will assign still higher value to the shares.

In this kind of world, there is a sucker born every minute— and he exists to buy your shares at a higher price than you paid for them. Any price will do as long as others may be willing to pay more. There is no reason, only mass psychology. All the smart investor has to do is beat the gun—get in at the very beginning. This theory might less charitably be called the "greater-fool theory." It's perfectly all right to pay three times what a stock is worth as long as later on you can find some innocent to pay five times what it's worth.

The castle-in-the-air theory has many advocates, both in the financial and academic communities. Keynes' newspaper contest is the same game played by "Adam Smith" in *The Money Game*. Mr. Smith also espouses the same view of stock price determination. On the academic side, Oskar Morgenstern has been a leading champion. The views he expresses in *The Theory of Games and Economic Behavior*, of which he is coauthor, have had a significant impact not only on economic theory but also on national security decisions and strategic corporate planning. In 1970 he coauthored another book, *The Determination of Stock Prices*. In this book he and his colleague, Clive Granger, argue that the search for intrinsic value in stocks is a search for the will-o'-the-wisp. In an exchange economy the value of any asset depends on an actual or prospective transaction. Morgenstern believes that every investor should post the following Latin maxim above his desk:

Res tantum valet quantum vendi potest.
(A thing is worth only what someone else will pay for it.)

✿   ✿   ✿

THE SANITY OF INSTITUTIONS

The madness of the crowd can be truly spectacular. Thus, more and more people put their money under the care of a professional—someone who knows what makes the market tick and who can be trusted to act prudently. Thus most of us find that at least a part (and often all) of our investable funds are in the hands of institutional portfolio managers—those who run the large pension and retirement funds, mutual funds, investment counseling organizations and the like. While the crowd may be mad, the institution is above all that. The institution is, to borrow a phrase from Tennyson, "of loyal nature and of noble mind." Very well, let us then take a look at the sanity of institutions.

By 1960, institutions and other professional investors accounted for almost half of the total shares traded on the New York Stock Exchange; in 1969, they had taken a commanding position with a volume of 66 percent. Results of more recent samples of trading activity suggest that institutions accounted for approximately 70 percent of stock exchange volume. Surely, in a market where professional investors dominate trading, the game must have changed. The hard-headed, sharp-penciled reasoning of the pros ought to be a guarantee that the extravagant excesses of the past will be avoided.

And yet in 1969 a company with annual sales of only $16 million was "valued" by the market at $1 billion—the latter value being obtained by multiplying the number of shares outstanding by the price per share. Throughout the past twenty years of institutional domination of the market, prices often gyrated more rapidly and by much greater amounts than could plausibly be explained by apparent changes in their anticipated intrinsic values.

In 1955, for example, General Electric announced that its scientists had created exact duplicates of the diamond. The market became entranced at once, despite the public acknowledgement that these diamonds were not suitable for sale as gems and that they could not be manufactured cheaply enough for industrial use. Within twenty-four hours, the shares of G.E.

.rose 4¼ points. This increased the total market value of all G.E. shares by almost $400 million, approximately twice the then current value of total worldwide diamond sales and six times the value of all industrial diamond sales. Clearly, the price rise was not due to the worth of the discovery to the company, but rather to the castle-building potential this would hold for prospective buyers. Indeed, speculators rushed in so fast to beat the gun that the entire price rise was accomplished in the first minutes of trading during the day following the announcement.

Of course, we should not generalize from isolated instances. Professional investors, however, did participate in three distinct speculative movements during the decade of the 1960's. These were the growth-stock and new-issue craze of the 1959–61 period, the conglomerate boom of the mid-1960's, and the performance cult of the late 1960's, which led to the worship of "concept" stocks. In each case, professional institutions bid actively for stocks not because they felt such stocks were undervalued under the firm-foundation principle, but because they anticipated that some greater fools would take the shares off their hands at even more inflated prices. . . .

THE NEW "NEW ERA": THE GROWTH
STOCK/NEW ISSUE CRAZE

In the 1959–61 period, growth was the magic word. It was the corollary to the "Soaring Sixties," the wonderful decade to come. Growth stocks (those issues for which an extraordinary rate of earnings growth was expected), especially those associated with glamorous new technologies like Texas Instruments and Varian Associates, far outdistanced the standard blue-chip stocks. Wall Street was eager to pay good money for space travel, transistors, klystron tubes, optical scanners, and other esoteric things. Backed by this strong enthusiasm, the price of securities in these businesses rose wildly.

By 1959 the traditional rule that stocks should sell at a multiple of 10 to 15 times their earnings has been supplanted by multiples of 50 to 100 times earnings, or even more for the most glamorous issues. For example, at the peak of the craze in 1961, Control Data, a new computer company, sold for over 200 times its previous year's earnings. Farrington, a handbag manufacturer that had consistently lost money but hoped to manufacture a new electronics device, rose rapidly in the over-the-counter market. The stock later plummeted to 2 and eventually the company went bankrupt. Even large, well-established growth companies with a technological basis rose to unprecedented heights, as the following table illustrates.

| | | 1961 | | 1962 |
| | | | | |
Security	High price	Price-earnings multiple *	Low price	Price-earnings multiple *
IBM	607	80.7	300	34.4
Texas Instruments	206¾	87.6	49	23.0
Microwave Associates	60⅜	85.0	8	12.7
Fairchild Camera	88¼	42.0	31	13.1
Perkin-Elmer	83½	67.3	25	16.7

* Price divided by earnings per share for the year.

Growth took on an almost mystical significance, and questioning the propriety of such valuations became, as in the generation past, almost heretical. These prices could not be justified on firm-foundation principles. But investors firmly believed that later in the wonderful decade of the sixties, buyers would eagerly come forward to pay even higher prices. Lord Keynes must have smiled quietly from wherever it is that economists go when they die.

To be sure, many professionals viewed the market with incredulity. One New York investment manager noted: "I think this market is crazy, just plain crazy. There are still good stocks around, companies selling at 10 to 20 times earnings and with good earnings prospects. But people seem to want to buy stocks selling at 60 or 80 times a company's earnings. I don't know why. This just isn't a thinking man's market."

I had just gone to work on Wall Street during the boom and recall vividly one of the senior partners of my firm shaking his head and admitting that he knew of no one over forty, with any recollection of the 1929–32 crash, who would buy and hold the high-priced growth stocks. But the young Turks held sway. The sky was the limit and the growth stocks were the ones that were going up. *Newsweek* quoted one broker as saying that speculators have the idea that anything they buy "will double overnight. The horrible thing is, it has happened."

But more was to come. Promoters, eager to satisfy the insatiable thirst of investors for the space-age stocks of the soaring sixties, created new offerings by the dozens. A new-issue craze (more were offered in this 1959–62 period than at any other time in history) developed as investors—both individual and institutional—whipped themselves into a speculative frenzy. The new-issue mania of the period rivaled the South Sea Bubble in its intensity and also, regrettably, in the fraudulent practices that were revealed.

It was called the "tronics boom," since the stock offerings often included some garbled version of the word "electronics" in their title even if the companies had nothing to do with the electronics industry. Buyers of these issues didn't really care what the companies made—so long as it sounded electronic, with a suggestion of the esoteric. For example, American Music Guild, whose business consisted entirely of the door-to-door sale of phonograph records and players, changed its name to Space-Tone before "going public." The shares were sold to the public at 2, and within a few weeks rose to 14.

The name was the game. There were a host of "trons" such as Astron, Dutron, Vulcatron, and Transitron, and a number of "onics" such as Circuitronics, Supronics, Videotronics, and several Electrosonics companies. Leaving nothing to chance, one group put together the winning combination, Powertron Ultrasonics. The prices commanded in the market by these companies were unbelievable.

Jack Dreyfus, of Dreyfus and Company, commented on the mania as follows:

Take a nice little company that's been making shoelaces for forty years and sells at a respectable six times earnings ratio. Change the name from Shoelaces, Inc. to Electronics and Silicon Furth-Burners. In today's market, the words "electronics" and "silicon" are worth fifteen times earnings. However, the real play comes from the word "furth-burners," which no one understands. A word that no one understands entitles you to double your entire score. Therefore, we have 6 times earnings for the shoelace business and 15 times earnings for electronic and silicon, or a total of 21 times earnings. Multiply this by two for furth-burners and we now have a score of 42 times earnings for the new company.

In a later investigation of the new-issue phenomenon, the Securities and Exchange Commission uncovered considerable evidence of fraudulence and market manipulation. For example, some investment bankers, especially those who underwrote the smaller new issues, would often hold a substantial volume of securities off the market. This made the market so "thin" at the start that the price would rise quickly in the after market.

*   *   *

The tronics boom came back to earth in 1962. The tailspin started early in the year and exploded in a horrendous selling wave five months later. On Monday, May 28, the worst day of the decline, the Dow-Jones averages of thirty leading industrial stocks fell 34.95 points (this was second only to the drop of 38.33 recorded in 1929). On that single day, the decline in the market value of all stocks listed on the New York Stock Exchange amounted to $20.8 billion. Even on October 28, 1929 only $9.6 billion evaporated, because the total value of listed stocks was smaller on that day. "Something like an earthquake hit the stock market," editorialized the *New York Times*. Growth stocks, even the highest-quality ones, took the brunt of the decline, falling much further than the general market. Yesterday's hot issue became today's cold turkey.

Many professionals refused to accept the fact that they had speculated recklessly. Rather they blamed the decline on President Kennedy's tough stand with the steel industry, which led to a rollback of announced price hikes. Former President Eisenhower blamed the decline on Kennedy's "reckless spending programs," and Walter Lippmann chastised Kennedy for not fulfilling his "promise to bring about something near to the full employment of capital and labor and a rising rate of economic growth."

Others did recognize the speculative mania and said simply that the market, and growth stocks in particular, were "too high" in 1961. As far as steel prices were concerned, with strong foreign competition in steel the price rises would probably have been rescinded anyway. Very few pointed out that it is always easy to look back and say when prices were too high or too low. Fewer still said that no one seems to know the proper price for a stock at any given time.

SYNERGY GENERATES ENERGY: THE CONGLOMERATE BOOM

The market shook off its losses and settled down to ponder its next move. It was not too long in coming.

I've said before that part of the genius of the financial market is that if a product is demanded, it is produced. The product that all investors desired was expected growth in earnings per share. And if growth wasn't to be found in a name, it was only to be expected that someone would find another way to produce it. By the mid-sixties, creative enterpreneurs had discovered that growth was a word and that the word was *synergism*.

Synergism is the quality of having 2 plus 2 equal 5. Thus, it seemed quite plausible that two separate companies with an earning power of $2 million each might produce combined earnings of $5 million if the businesses were consolidated. This magical, mystical, surefire profitable new creation was called a conglomerate.

While antitrust laws kept large companies from purchasing firms in the same industry, it was possible for a while to purchase firms in other industries without interference from the Justice Department. The consolidations were carried out in the name of synergism. Ostensibly, mergers would allow the conglomerate to achieve greater financial strength (and thus greater borrowing capabilities at lower rates); to enhance marketing capabilities through the distribution of complementary product lines; to give greater scope to superior managerial talents; and to consolidate, and thus make more efficient, operating services such as personnel and accounting departments. All this led to synergism—a stimulation of sales and earnings for the combined operation that would have been impossible for the independent entities alone.

In fact, the major impetus for the conglomerate wave of the 1960's was that the acquisition process itself could be made to produce growth in earnings per share. Indeed, the managers of conglomerates tended to possess financial expertise rather than the operating skills required to improve the profitability of the acquired companies. By an easy bit of legerdemain, they could put together a group of companies with no basic potential at all and produce steadily rising per-share earnings. The following example shows how this monkey business was performed.

Suppose we have two companies—the Able Circuit Smasher Company, an electronics firm, and Baker Typewriter Company, which makes typewriters. Each has 200,000 shares outstanding. It's 1965 and both companies have earnings of $1 million a year, or $5 per share. Let's assume neither business is growing and that, with or without merger activity, earnings would just continue along at the same level.

The two firms sell at different prices, however. Since Able Circuit Smasher Company is in the electronics business, the market awards it a price-earnings multiple of 20 which, multiplied by its $5 earnings per share, gives it a market price of $100. Baker Typewriter Company, in a less glamorous business, has its earnings multiplied at only 10 times and, consequently, its $5 per share earnings command a market price of only $50.

The management of Able Circuit would like to become a conglomerate. It offers to absorb Baker by swapping stock at the rate of two for three. The holders of Baker shares would get two shares of Able stock—which have a market value of $200—for every three shares of Baker stock—with a total market value of $150. Clearly this is a tempting proposal, and the stockholders of Baker are likely to accept cheerfully. The merger is approved.

We have a budding conglomerate, newly named Synergon, Inc., which now has 333,333 shares * outstanding and total earnings of $2 million to put against them, or $1 per share. Thus, by 1966 when the merger has been completed, we find that earnings have risen by 20 percent, from $5 to $6, and this growth seems to justify Able's former price-earnings multiple of 20. Consequently, the shares of Synergon (née Able) rise from $100 to $120, everybody's judgment is confirmed, and all go home rich and happy. In addition, the shareholders of Baker

---

* There are 200,000 original shares of Able plus an extra 133,333, which get printed up to exchange for Baker's 200,000 shares according to the terms of the merger.

who were bought out need not pay any taxes on their profits until they sell their shares of the combined company. The top three lines of the following table illustrate the transaction thus far.

	Company	Earnings levels	Number of shares outstanding	Earnings per share	Price-earnings multiple	Price
Before merger (1965)	Able	$1,000,000	200,000	$ 5.00	20	$100
	Baker	1,000,000	200,000	5.00	10	50
After first merger (1966)	Synergon (Able and Baker Combined)	2,000,000	333,333	6.00	20	120
	Charlie	1,000,000	100,000	10.00	10	100
After second merger (1967)	Synergon (Able, Baker, and Charlie Combined)	3,000,000	433,333	6.92	20	138⅜

A year later, Synergon finds Charlie Company, which earns $10 per share or $1 million with 100,000 shares outstanding. Charlie Company is in the relatively risky military-hardware business so its shares command a multiple of only 10 and sell at $100. Synergon offers to absorb Charlie Company on a share-for-share exchange basis. Charlie's shareholders are delighted to exchange their $100 shares for the conglomerate's $120 shares. By the end of 1967, the combined company has earnings of $3 million, shares outstanding of 433,333, and earnings per share of $6.92.

Here we have a case where the conglomerate has literally manufactured growth. Neither Able, Baker, nor Charlie was growing at all; yet simply by virtue of the fact of their merger, the unwary investor who may finger his *Stock Guide* to see the past record of our conglomerate will find the following figures:

Earnings per share

	1965	1966	1967
Synergon, Inc.	$5.00	$6.00	$6.92

Clearly, Synergon is a growth stock and its record of extraordinary performance appears to have earned it a high and possibly even an increasing multiple of earnings.

The trick that makes the game work is the ability of the electronics company to swap its high-multiple stock for the stock of another company with a lower multiple. The typewriter company can only "sell" its earnings at a multiple of 10. But when these earnings are packaged with the electronics company, the total earnings (including those from selling typewriters) could be sold at a multiple of 20. And the more acquisitions Synergon could make, the faster earnings per share would grow and thus the more attractive the stock would look to justify its high multiple.

The whole thing was like a chain letter—no one would get hurt as long as the growth of acquisitions proceeded exponentially. Of course the process could not continue for long, but the possibilities were mind-boggling for those who got in at the start. It seems difficult to believe that Wall Street professionals could be so myopic as to fall for the conglomerate con game, but accept it they did for periods of several years. Or perhaps, as subscribers to the castle-in-the-air theory, they only believed that other people would fall for it.

❉   ❉   ❉

The music slowed drastically for the conglomerates on January 19, 1968. On that day, the granddaddy of the conglomerates, Litton Industries, announced that earnings for the second quarter of that year would be substantially less than had been forecast. It had recorded 20 percent yearly increases for almost an entire decade. The market had so thoroughly come to believe in alchemy that the announcement was treated with disbelief and shock. In the selling wave that followed, conglomerate stocks declined by roughly 40 percent before a feeble recovery set in.

Worse was to come. In July, the Federal Trade Commission announced it would make an in-depth investigation of the conglomerate merger movement. Again the stocks went tumbling down. The Securities and Exchange Commission and the accounting profession finally made their move and began to make attempts to clarify the reporting techniques for mergers and acquisitions.

In January 1969, Litton again announced lower earnings. If that company—believed to be the best managed of the group—was unable to maintain earnings growth, how could the others continue to do so? Perhaps weak parts do not a strong whole make. The sell orders came flooding in. These were closely followed by new announcements from the SEC and the Assistant Attorney General in charge of antitrust, indicating a strong concern about the accelerating pace of the merger movement.

It should be quite a while before the conglomerate castle rises again, although given the propensity of institutions to run in packs after my concept suggesting growth one can't be quite that sure. The aftermath of this speculative phase revealed two disturbing factors. First, conglomerates were mortal and were not always able to control their far-flung empires. Indeed, investors became disenchanted with the conglomerate's new math; 2 plus 2 certainly did not equal 5 and some investors wondered if it even equaled 4. Second, the government and the accounting profesion expressed real concern about the pace of mergers and about possible abuses. These two worries on the part of investors reduced—and in many cases eliminated—the premium multiples that had been paid for the anticipation of earnings from the acquisition process alone. This in itself makes the alchemy game almost impossible, for the acquiring company has to have an earnings multiple larger than the acquired company if the ploy is to work at all.

The combination of lower earnings and flattened price-earnings multiples implied a drastic decline in the prices of conglomerates. . . . Stock prices sank in 1969 as the players in the game all rushed to grab their seats. Even greater declines were suffered in the 1970 bear market.

Interestingly enough, it was the professional investors who were hurt the most in the wild scramble for chairs. Few mutual or pension funds were without large holdings of conglomerate stocks. Castles in the air are not reserved as the sole prerogative of individuals; institutional investors can build them too.

PERFORMANCE COMES TO THE MARKET:
THE BUBBLE IN CONCEPT STOCKS

Despite the prolonged death rattle of the conglomerate, new life stirred elsewhere on Wall Street. It probably came into

being during the mid-sixties when there was heightened competition among mutual funds for the customer's dollar. This
new golden calf was called *performance*. It meant that a fund
performing better than the others (that is, the value of the
stocks in its portfolio went up faster than the stocks in its
competitors' portfolios) was a far easier fund to sell to the
public than one with a less lustrous record.

Some fund managers even suggested that the performance
funds were safer. One mutual fund manager suggested, "The
safest way to preserve capital is by doubling it." The customers
said amen and never bothered to ask why tripling wouldn't be
safer still. And not only that: since performance funds tended
to distribute capital gains rather than dividends, the tax bite was
lower (only half of these gains were subject to tax and the maximum rate was a flat 25 percent). So, with the public buying,
mutual fund salesmen began to clamor for even greater performance.

And perform the funds did—at least over short periods of time.
Fred Carr's highly publicized Enterprise Fund racked up a 117
percent total return (including both dividends and capital gains)
in 1967 and followed this with a 44 percent return in 1968. The
corresponding figures for the Standard & Poor's 500 Stock Index
were 25 percent and 11 percent respectively. This performance
brought large amounts of new money into the fund, and into
other funds that could boast glamorous performances. The public
no longer bet on the horse but rather on the jockey.

How did these jockeys do it? They concentrated the portfolio
in dynamic stocks. Take the Dreyfus Fund and the growth-
oriented Fidelity Funds. Jack Dreyfus, a high-stakes bridge
player, got a running start on the performance record by investing heavily in Polaroid during that company's most rapid growth
stage. Fidelity, run by Edward Johnson and Gerald Tsai, also
held large blocks of stock in a relatively few rapidly growing companies. Johnson and Tsai were not faithful to these companies,
however. At the sign of a better story, they would quickly
switch. Both funds chalked up impressive successes in the mid-
sixties and this led to many imitators. The camp followers were
quickly given the accolade "go-go" funds, and the fund managers
were often called "the youthful gunslingers." "Nothing succeeds

so well as success," Talleyrand once observed, and this was certainly true for the performance funds in their early years—the customers' dollars flowed in.

*   *   *

And so performance investing took hold of Wall Street in the late 1960's. The commandments for fund managers were simple: Concentrate your holdings in a relatively few stocks and don't hesitate to switch the portfolio around if a more desirable investment appears. And because near-term performance was especially important (investment services began to publish monthly records of mutual fund performance) it would be best to buy stocks with an exciting concept and a compelling story. You had to be sure the market would recognize the beauty of your stock now—not far into the future. Hence, the birth of the so-called concept stock.

Xerox was a classic example of a concept stock. The concept was that of a new industry where machines would make dry copies by electrostatic transference. The company, Xerox, with its patent protection and its running head start, could look forward to several years of increased earnings. It was a true story— a believable story, one that would quicken the pulse of any good performance-fund manager.

But even if the story were not totally believable, as long as the investment manager was convinced that the average opinion would think that the average opinion would believe the story, that's all that was needed. The youthful gunslingers became disenchanted with normal security analysts who could tell you how many railroad ties Penn Central had, but couldn't tell you when the company was about to go bankrupt. "I don't want to listen to that kind of security analyst," one of Wall Street's gunslingers told me. "I just want a good story or a good concept."

*   *   *

Minnie Pearl's concept is our last example of the period. Minnie Pearl was a fast-food franchising firm that was as accommodating as all get out. To please the financial community, Minnie Pearl's chickens became "Performance Systems." After all, what better name could be chosen for performance-oriented investors? On Wall Street a rose by any other name does not smell as sweet. The "price-earnings multiple" was infinity. Performance Systems had no earnings at all to divide into the stock's price at the time it reached its high in 1968. Minnie Pearl laid an egg—and a bad one at that. The subsequent performance for this and other such stocks was indeed truly remarkable—although not quite what their buyers had anticipated.

Why did such stocks actually perform so badly? One general answer was that their price-earnings multiples were inflated beyond reason. If a multiple of 100 drops to the more normal multiple of 15 for the market as a whole, you have lost 85 percent of your investment right there. But in addition most of the concept companies of the time ran into severe operating difficulties. The reasons were varied: too rapid expansion, too much debt, loss of management control, etc. These companies were run by men who were primarily promoters, not sharp-penciled operating managers. In addition, fraudulent practices were common. For example, Performance Systems reported profits of $3.2 million in 1969. The SEC claimed that this report was "false and misleading." In 1972 Performance Systems issued a revision of the 1969 report. Apparently a loss of $1.3 million more accurately reflected 1969 operations.

And so when the 1969–71 bear market came, these concept stocks went down just as fast as they went up. In the end it was the pros who were conned most of all. While there is nothing wrong with seeking good performance, the mad rush to outgun the competition week by week had disastrous consequences. The cult of performance and the concept of "concept" stocks were henceforth greeted with disdain when mentioned in Wall Street.

Part Five

Business and Economic Forecasting

PRACTICALLY all problems in managerial economics involve forecasting. The decision of whether or not to build a new plant may depend crucially on forecasts of demand. Whether or not to cut price may depend crucially on forecasts of the price of materials. The opening article from *Business Week* describes the various techniques that are commonly used to forecast economic magnitudes: trend extrapolation, leading series, econometric models, and others. The article by the Conference Board describes the forecasting methods used by five major companies—Kellogg, Eli Lilly, American Radiator, Long Island Lighting, and B. F. Goodrich. Both articles are useful introductions to business forecasting, and include interesting case studies.

The next two papers delve more deeply into the techniques of economic forecasting. The Organization for Economic Cooperation and Development describes how the major Western governments go about forecasting gross national product. Since these government forecasts are used frequently by firms to generate forecasts of their own sales and profits, it is worthwhile looking at the techniques used by the government forecasters. Econometric models are becoming more and more important in business and economic forecasting. In the next paper, F. Gerard Adams and Michael Evans describe the Wharton econometric model.

Finally, turning to the related area of long-term planning, Sidney Alexander argues that this is the area where economists can make their most valuable contribution.

Business and Economic Forecasting

Business Week

The following selection is an abridgement of an article which appeared in the September 24, 1955 issue of Business Week.

Many economists—among them some who have physically left the academic cloisters—still regard economic forecasting as a low and disreputable pursuit for learned men. "We don't know enough about the past to know anything much about the future," they say. So, they suggest, business must wait another hundred years or so before it can expect the savants to say anything meaningful about the future. Meanwhile, they maintain, it is proper that they should qualify all statements about the future to the point of meaninglessness.

But the number of economists who hold to this pure patient view of their calling is shrinking. More and more of them feel that if economics is to have any pretense of being a useful study its claim must rest on its ability to predict developments, and to provide solid foundations for policymakers to build on.

One of the chief reasons for the fact that more of them are overcoming their inhibitions about forecasting, and are concentrating on improving its techniques, is that they are being immersed deeper and deeper in government and business, where eyes are always on the future.

It would take volumes to explain all the forecasting techniques used these days. It is possible, though, to take up the chief techniques that economists use when they are working with any of the three basic strategies of forecasting.

TREND EXTRAPOLATION

Extrapolation is a six-bit word borrowed from the mathematicians. In this case it means predicting the future movements of an economic factor by projecting into the future the trends you know it has taken in the past. On a chart, an extrapolation looks like this:

CHART A

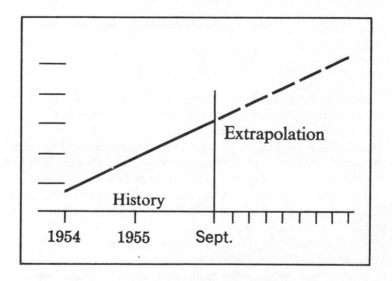

What makes an extrapolation useful to a forecaster is the statistical fact that a trend that is advancing will keep advancing—at least until something else happens. Unfortunately, the technique won't tell you when the "something else" will come. For instance, a wage series that is pushing upward will tend to push prices upward, and that will tend to push wages up again—only not ad infinitum. Eventually, some other series, like a falling sales volume, may halt or reverse the upward wage-price spiral.

But if, in your business, you don't need to care much about cyclical swings around a trend—if, for instance, you are figuring out the number of telephones or kilowatt hours the American people will want to use in the next ten years—trend extrapolation is a useful technique.

Of course, you can put trend extrapolation to work in a more sophisticated way than simply by laying a ruler over the past direction of a business indicator and projecting it on into the future. If you sell books or whiskey you may find your sales correlate nicely with the trend of disposable personal income, or if you sell oil or copper your sales may link up well with the Federal Reserve Index of Production.

"LEADING" SERIES

Andrew Carnegie constructed his own leading series for economic forecasting—by counting the smoking factory chimneys he saw. His was the archetype of the technique.

In the 1920s a hot search was on for a sort of economic philosopher's stone—a single business indicator that would always lead general business development. Some thought it lay in stock market activity; others saw it in interest rates, pig iron production, carloadings, or Dun & Bradstreet's index of business failures. Debate still rages over which of these are "old wives' indicators" and which possess real leading characteristics.

The outstanding hunter for indicators with forecasting value is the National Bureau of Economic Research. It has been scrutinizing masses of business-cycle data for more than three decades. Before World War II, Wesley C. Mitchell, the bureau's guiding genius, and Arthur F. Burns, later chairman of the Council of Economic Advisers under President Eisenhower, examined hundreds of series and picked a set of twenty-one leading, coincident, and lagging indicators, whose movements had regularly traced the course of the business cycle.

After the war, the bureau's Geoffrey H. Moore set to work updating Mitchell's and Burns's work. Moore examined 801 monthly and quarterly indicators and selected twenty-one, some of which were the same as those chosen by Mitchell and Burns. Of the twenty-one, Moore's eight leading series are: residential building contracts, commercial and industrial building contracts, new orders for durable goods, prices of industrial common stocks, wholesale prices of basic commodities, average work week in manufacturing, new incorporations, and business failures.

These indicators do regularly lead the business cycle's turns— though there is argument over just why this happens. But the chief trouble with them is that they are all extremely sensitive. They oscillate a great deal from month to month. So it is hard to know, when making a forecast, whether an up or downturn in one or another of the leading series means the real McCoy, or whether it is only a temporary wiggle.

DIFFUSION INDEXES

To find the meaning of those upturns and downturns, the bureau has invented the diffusion index. The bureau developed the index after it discovered that business cycle movements "have invariably been preceded by a remarkably regular cycle in the proportion of industrial activities undergoing expansion or contraction."

Forecasters make the index by counting the number of indicators in a given group that are rising at a given time. They convert this into a percentage of the number of indicators in the group. The bureau labels this percentage as a diffusion index because it believes it shows how widely diffused economic movements are. The bureau's diffusion indexes generally reach their peaks and troughs six months to twelve months ahead of the peaks and troughs of general business activity.

Not all economists think the diffusion index is much of a step forward. Arthur L. Broida, a Federal Reserve Board economist, maintains that it isolates cyclical turning points from all other changes in the economy's direction some time after the event. He holds that the index shows nothing different from what statisticians have long achieved by noting rates of growth and decline of a series of indicators. Their notes have already shown that a slower rate of increase in an index generally precedes its downturn.

SYSTEMATIC FORECASTING

Test-tube or systematic forecasting is the classic strategy of economic analysis. The technique here is to discover enduring relationships among economic factors and apply them to situations in the past, present, or future.

Analyzing the general business picture and making quantitative estimates of what conditions may be like a year or more ahead requires all the theoretical training, knowledge of institutional and statistical facts, technical skill, and political insight that an economist can command.

In dealing with comprehensive forecasting problems, economists today have two tremendous advantages over those who worked twenty years ago.

The first is economics' own "unified field theory." It is the product of the Keynesian revolution. Before John M. Keynes wrote his *General Theory of Employment, Interest, and Money*, economic theory tended to be fragmented into separate theories of wages, money, foreign trade, and so on. None of these separate principles had much relationship to each other. Economists may argue how much of the Keynesian revolution is attributable to Keynes himself. But there can be little doubt that general comprehension of how all the parts of an economy mesh together has advanced greatly since the mid–1930s.

The second advantage is the system of national income accounts developed since the early 1930s by the Commerce Department and the National Bureau of Economic Research. These give the economist a detailed and comprehensive picture of the national economy.

From unified economic theory and national income accounting stem the two most important techniques for systematic economic forecasting.

The "lost horse" technique is the first. That, anyway, is how it was christened by Sidney Alexander. He took the name from the old gag about how to find a lost horse. You do it by going to where the horse was last seen and asking yourself where you would go from there if you were a horse.

When you take that theory off the farm and put it to work in general business forecasting, each component of the gross national product (consumption, expenditures, gross private domestic investment, net foreign investment, government purchases of goods and services) plays the part of the lost horse. The analyst first finds out where each of these was when last reported by the Commerce Department's National Income Division.

But how he answers the question of where each section of GNP is going depends on his skill, patience, insight, and information

An economist who wants to fake impressively can simply guess figures for each part of the coming year's GNP. (Projecting gross private domestic investment at $49.6 billion is obviously more impressive than projecting it at $50 billion.) If there were state licensing boards for economists, a forecaster caught doing this would be convicted of malpractice and sentenced to run a check-out register in a supermarket for the rest of his days.

But the honest economist will go deeply behind each component of GNP when he prepares his forecast. He will study government plans and policies, analyze budget estimates, weigh the likelihood of the passage of important legislation and attempt to estimate the price tags the various bills will bear.

He will look behind private investment at the factors affecting the capital goods industries, study ratios of inventories to sales and of production to capacity. He will look at the factors that affect building construction, such as credit terms, availability of mortgage money, vacancy rates, rents, and price movements. He will measure his analysis against the findings of capital spending surveys.

He will try to gauge the effect of government fiscal policies on private investment and consumption, estimate the relationship between the growth of investment and consumption. Then he will see how money credit conditions may affect people's spending or saving, their liquid assets, their supplies of durable goods. And he will measure this against the finding of consumer intention surveys.

He must put all these parts together to make a whole—but he must also carry in his mind an image of how the whole will affect the parts. He will also have to sense how non-economic factors—like international relations and national elections—will affect the picture.

Since the task of preparing a forecast of the national economy can be almost endless, the economist must figure out the point at which he has all the information he can handle. But, at best, the time he has for these analyses is always pretty short, since he must base his forecasts on the most current information. If he takes too long, his facts grow cold. The best course for the forecaster is to stay at his task continuously, constantly modifying his forecast on the basis of new information.

The only way to judge whether an economist has done a thoroughly sensitive forecast—or blooped his way through one—is to examine carefully the details of his analysis. Of course, a lost horse analysis depends a lot on the economist's subjective judgments about the data he receives and on his somewhat "artistic" perception of relations. So all of his analysis may not show on paper.

A more rigorous way of tackling the problem of what will happen to the millions of factors and relations that make up the national economy is to build an econometric model of the economy. The method here is related to the lost-horse technique, but it is a lot more elegant, for the practice of econometrics is one of blending economics, mathematics, and statistics.

An economist starts to build a model by first selecting an economic theory, or set of theories, that he believes will take into account all the significant factors likely to affect the general business or particular industry situation that he is forecasting.

He translates the theory into a set of mathematical equations that make up his econometric model. The equations relate the factors he wants to discover (the dependent variables) to the factors he already knows, or can estimate easily (the independent variables). These independent variables can be of two types: first, those that are historic facts, such as last year's profits or inventory spending; and second, future elements, such as government spending, that can be estimated from advance information.

The econometrician bases his forecast on the past relations between the dependent and independent variables. He assumes that relations that were stable in the past will remain stable in the future. Of course, the relation between large economic aggregates, like consumption and income, won't be perfectly stable. So the question the forecaster must first answer is: "Will they be stable enough, within some estimated range of probability, to be used for forecasting?" If it turns out that they aren't stable enough for the job they are supposed to perform, the forecaster can assume that the theory behind his equations is not valid. Even then he has achieved something—and, in this way, econometrics can be a useful technique for junking false economic theories.

Econometric models come in for plenty of criticism from forecasters who stick to other techniques.

One of the chief complaints against them is that they make complex mathematical operations on data that is too rough to permit such manipulation. Stephen M. DuBrul, a General Motors economist, says that to apply intricate econometric techniques to the rough data that is available is "gold-plating crowbars."

But econometricians keep building their models and trying to improve them. They try to fit more factors into their figuring to overcome the complaints that their models are mechanically unsound and insensitive to social movements.

There are plenty of econometric model-builders at work to handle this task of improvement.

At Michigan University's Research Seminar in Quantitative Economics, three econometricians, Lawrence Klein, Daniel Suits, and Arthur S. Goldberger, have built a 25-equation model of the U.S. economy.[1]

They do not look on their model as a once-and-for-all job, but are continuously testing and strengthening it. When a forecast turns out to be off the mark, the Michigan group probes into the machinery of the model to find out just where the fault lies, changes the model to try to correct the mistake next time. And to make the model more realistic, the group is also making intensive studies of particular sectors of the economy, including the construction industry, foreign trade, agriculture, and the money market.

Industry's own economists are beginning to get into the model-building field. For industry's purposes the models have been simplified. Management has found them useful for doing one of the principal jobs for which business is turning to economists:

1. [For a more recent model, see J. Duesenberry, G. Fromm, L. Klein, and E. Kuh, *The Brookings Quarterly Econometric Model of the U.S. Economy* (North Holland, 1965). *Editor*]

helping guide planning for capital spending and expansion programs by producing long-range projections of specific industries' places in the national economy.

Some industry economists say the models provide the best technique yet developed for organizing massive and complex statistical data, for cumulating knowledge and profiting from past errors and successes, and for systematizing the whole forecasting process.

Forecasting in Industry

NATIONAL INDUSTRIAL CONFERENCE BOARD

This article comes from the National Industrial Conference Board's Forecasting in Industry (*Studies in Business Policy*)

1. KELLOGG COMPANY

A typical example of a forecast built up from the grass roots of the sales force is given in the following account of the methods of the Kellogg Company, a large food manufacturer. The company makes two principal types of forecasts. The first, for one year, is used as a basis for planning advertising, promotion and selling expenditures, setting salesmen's quotas, and controlling raw material purchases. The second is a long-range forecast covering three to five years, and is used for planning factory expansion.

Annual Forecast · The annual sales forecast originates in the company's twenty-one sales territories under the direction of the branch sales managers. Each territory is broken up into subdistricts, which are covered by one to five salesmen under the leadership of a subdistrict salesman. In the fall of each year, the branch managers, who head the sales organization of the territories, call in the subdistrict salesmen one by one to discuss the sales outlook. General business conditions in the district, population changes, and other factors which might influence sales are all considered. Sales records for past years, together with A. C. Nielsen Company information on competitive activities, contribute to the development of estimated sales for subdistricts. Assisting the branch manager in this process is a staff of a half dozen or more who handle all of the statistical work. Special forms are printed each year to record data.

Adjustment for Advertising. After the branch manager has completed these meetings, members of the home office sales departments, the advertising department, and representatives of the company's advertising agency meet with each branch office manager to discuss the tentative sales forecast for his territory. In arriving at his estimates, the branch manager does not know the amount of advertising and promotion effort that will be expended in his area. The purpose of these meetings is to determine how much advertising and promotion will be necessary to achieve the forecast. The forecast is revised in the light of probable promotional expenditures.

Production and Purchasing. After these meetings are completed, a recapitulation of the branch sales forecasts is made at the home office and a tentative advertising and promotion budget is set. These are submitted to the production and purchasing departments who determine if it is possible to procure and produce the volume of goods represented by the forecasts. When production and purchase facilities are strained, as in recent years, this review may have an important bearing on the ultimate goal established.

Final Review. The next step is the preparation of a preliminary operating statement for consideration by top management. Members of the sales and advertising departments meet with the top officers of the company and give the sales forecast and the advertising and promotion budget a final review. The president, sales manager, advertising manager, and comptroller are among those who participate in this balancing operation.

Throughout the entire process, previous sales experience, the general business outlook, and changes in the competitive situation are given serious consideration.

The forecast is finally approved by the president and the vice-president in charge of sales. When the year's operating budget comes up for review, the board of directors also adds its approval.

Responsibility. Responsibility for organizing and directing the forecasting procedure rests with the sales supervisor, who is chief assistant to the vice-president in charge of marketing and has charge of the home office sales department and general control over all branch offices.

Revisions · The annual forecast is revised only when some radical change has taken place, such as an important fluctuation in prices, a serious shortage of raw materials, or, as during World War II, when the government sets up restrictions on the use of some items used by the company.

Period Forecasts · Three times a year, however, period forecasts are made. The period forecast is, in a sense, a refinement and revision of the annual forecast. The basic purpose is to estimate sales for each of the ensuing four months. These period forecasts are used for setting production schedules, scheduling shipments of incoming materials, and planning purchases of materials that do not have to be contracted for long in advance.

In making the period forecasts, the subdistrict salesmen are not consulted. Instead, the home office sales staff makes the forecasts on the basis of information obtained during the formulation of the annual forecast plus a study of current sales trends.

Accuracy · To encourage the development of accurate forecasting by the sales force, the branch manager receives each month a comparison of the actual sales with the forecast previously made for each subdistrict of his territory. He can thus observe whether he is meeting his quota. While the normal tendency under such an arrangement would be to make low forecasts so that quotas would be easy to attain, the fact that the advertising and promotion expenditure in his territory is allocated somewhat on the basis of his forecast of sales makes it undesirable for the branch manager to underestimate sales. He knows that if his forecast is low, his allocation for advertising and sales promotion will also be low.

Long-range Forecast · The long-range forecast is largely based upon an averaging of opinions of the sales staff, the market research department, and the comptroller's office. Other things are taken into consideration—the sales trend of the industry for several years past, the economic condition of the country, the sales trend of the company's own brands, new-product development outlook, and competitors' activities.

2. ELI LILLY AND COMPANY

Eli Lilly and Company, manufacturers of drugs and pharmaceuticals, have long made use of correlation analysis between sales and a well-known income series. Study and investigation by company specialists had revealed a very definite relation between the sales of pharmaceuticals and disposable personal income.[1] The company followed this lead and developed a whole system of forecasting based on the relation of sales to movements in disposable personal income.

Industry Forecast · It is usually easier to forecast the sales of an entire industry than those of a particular company. The reason for this is that the foundation of forecasting, the facts and figures, are most generally available on an industry-wide basis. Eli Lilly was most fortunate in having at its disposal reliable data on total industry sales of ethical drugs.

After adjusting both industry sales and the income figures for price changes, the company found through correlation analysis that this relation existed: for every 10-percent growth or decline in disposable personal income, the industry's sales show a corresponding increase or decrease of about 5 percent. Aside from this influence, analysis of the record revealed a steady rate of growth in pharmaceutical sales, which the company attributes to constantly increasing expenditures for research and the resulting new major product developments (see Chart 1). As long as research expenditures continue to increase and new products are evolved the company believes that this trend will continue.

Knowing this trend, and the relationship to personal disposable income, industry sales can be forecast by use of this formula:

Industry Volume = Income (weighted) × Growth Trend

From the visual evidence in Chart 2, it is apparent that the company is in a position to derive a forecast of total industry sales when forecasts of income are made available.

1. Disposable personal income is the income remaining to persons after deduction of personal taxes and other payments to general government.

CHART 1

GROWTH TREND FOR DOMESTIC SALES OF ETHICAL DRUGS, AFTER
ALLOWING FOR CHANGES IN DISPOSABLE PERSONAL INCOME

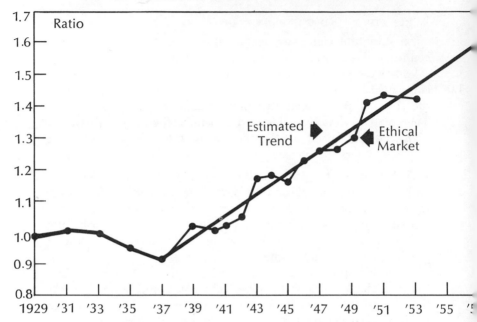

Company Forecast · There still remained the problem of estimating what portion of the forecasted sales of the industry would
be obtained by the company. This estimate is obtained by studying the share of the national market the company obtained in
past years and projecting the trend of company participation into
the future. In order to do a good job, management feels that the
reasons underlying the pattern of past performance must be
understood if future trends are to be evaluated properly. In this
connection, consideration is given to such pertinent details as
relative manufacturing capacity, general customer acceptance
of the company's products, company research expenditures, and
the estimated effect of each of these on past and prospective sales
performance.

District and Product Forecasts · Essentially the same technique
was used to break down the over-all company sales forecast into

CHART 2

U.S. Domestic Sales of Drugs

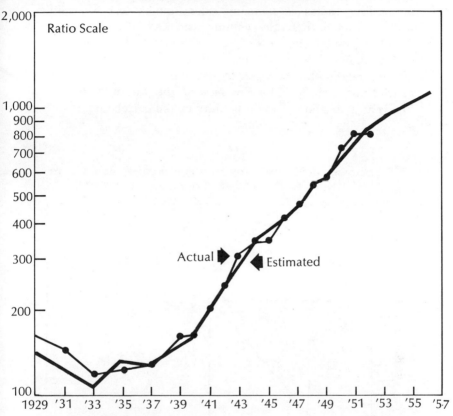

(Source: Eli Lilly and Company)
(Millions of Dollars)

detailed district and product sales forecasts. To obtain district
sales forecasts, past sales were related to the levels of income
for the particular sales district. After allowance was made for
this relationship, the district's rate of sales growth was compared
with the over-all company growth trend. As in the case of the
correlation studies mentioned earlier, the first step was the
preparation of a scatter diagram. In constructing it (Chart 3), the
company plotted district sales volume against company sales

volume, both excluding the estimated effect of income levels. The dot at the lower left-hand corner, for example, indicates that in one year adjusted company sales volume was $15 million and adjusted district sales volume was $300,000.

Judging by the closeness of this relationship, the company was able to draw a line on the scatter diagram which represents the average relationship between total company sales and the sales district under study. The closeness of the various dots to this line is an indication of the reliability of the correlation.

CHART 3

District Sales Volume Adjusted for Income, Related to Company Sales Volume Adjusted for Income

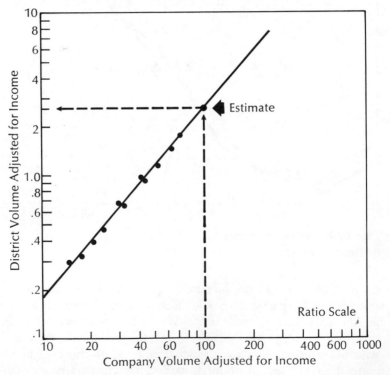

(Source: Company data)

(Millions of Dollars)

On this basis, if company sales are forecast at $100 million on growth factors alone, then this district's figure would be $2.5 million. The sales forecast for the district is then arrived at by adjusting this $2.5 million amount upward or downward, depending upon the forecast of personal disposable income for the district.

Forecasts of sales by product groups are derived by using basically the same methods as for total company sales, but in this case the correlation analysis deals with the single product group and its relation to income instead of the total company operation. Product group sales estimates at the district sales level are likewise obtained by using the basic approach outlined above.

Inasmuch as there are four separate forecasts—total company sales, sales by product groups, sales by districts, and sales by product groups within districts—a reconciliation of the separate forecasts is necessary. This is not too difficult, since the company total is a fixed figure and the other forecasts are proportionately adjusted to this total.

Accuracy · The company reports good success with this method, pointing out that in some recent years forecasts of total company sales, made more than a year in advance, have been within 2 percent of actual sales.

3. AMERICAN RADIATOR COMPANY, PLUMBING AND HEATING DIVISION

The Plumbing and Heating Division of the American Radiator and Standard Sanitary Corporation makes use of a lead-lag correlation, among other methods, in forecasting its sales. Years ago, the company discovered that there was a good correlation between the F. W. Dodge figures on residential building contracts awarded and sales of its plumbing products. Study showed that the demand for the company's products came three to four months after the contracts were awarded. It became possible, therefore, for the company to use the Dodge figures to arrive at reasonable projections of sales probabilities ninety to 120 days in advance, together with some evidence of the sales trend in

the following six to nine months. Chart 4 shows the closeness of
the relationship.

Application · The company uses this correlation in the following
manner. Contract award figures by individual counties are
tabulated into sales territory totals. Dodge contract award figures
covering thirty-seven Eastern states are compared with sales
within the area of the division's twelve sales districts and twenty-
nine sales offices that are covered by such data. A "factor" is
computed for each sales district and sales office within a district
expressing the relationship between contract award figures in
that territory and the past records of company sales. This comparison is aided by the fact that the company's territories are

CHART 4

AMERICAN-STANDARD PLUMBING SALES AND RESIDENTIAL
CONTRACTS AWARDED

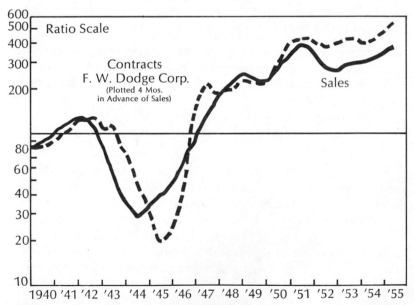

(Source: American Radiator and Standard Sanitary Corporation; F. W.
Dodge Corporation)

(Index numbers: 12-mos. moving averages)

bounded by county lines, and contract award data can be obtained on a county basis.

The factor for each territory is obtained by computing the ratio of sales to contracts, using a twelve-month moving total for comparison. Since contracts lead sales by about four months, sales are recorded with a 120-day lag for the purpose of comparison.

For example, Chart 5 shows the trend of contract awards in a typical territory, plotted four months ahead of sales. The company's latest twelve months sales at the time this chart was drawn averaged 4.63 percent of total contract awards. This factor is first applied to the latest twelve-month figures on contract awards (which precede company's sales by four months), thereby deriving an estimate of sales for the twelve months ending 120 days ahead. From this total, the company then subtracts the actual sales for the preceding eight months, thus deriving an estimate of sales for the following four months, one of which has almost elapsed because of the time required to compile the contract award figures.

Points Considered · The method is not as easy as it seems. The sales contract factor, itself, is not a constant. A territory, for example, may be gradually improving its position. In such a case, the factor would be getting larger. If the rate of growth is fast enough, it must be reckoned with in making the four-month forecast. For that reason the company studies the trends in these ratios. In the case of the territory depicted in Chart 5, the ratio varied from 4.28 percent to 4.63 percent. The general business outlook, industry conditions, and market and building conditions in each territory have to be examined and the basic forecast must be adjusted to reflect an unusual condition.

Even when these things have been taken into consideration, still other factors are at work. Study of past experience indicates that construction prices show a more pronounced reaction to demand changes than do the company's prices of plumbing equipment, and this factor is taken into account in estimating probable ratios of sales to contracts.

This method, like most, is based upon past performance. The factors vary from territory to territory because of differences in the ability of salesmen, the acceptance of the company's products, or the strength of competition. In an effort to bring a low-

CHART 5

AMERICAN-STANDARD PLUMBING SALES IN ONE TERRITORY,
COMPARED WITH RESIDENTIAL BUILDING CONTRACTS AWARDED *

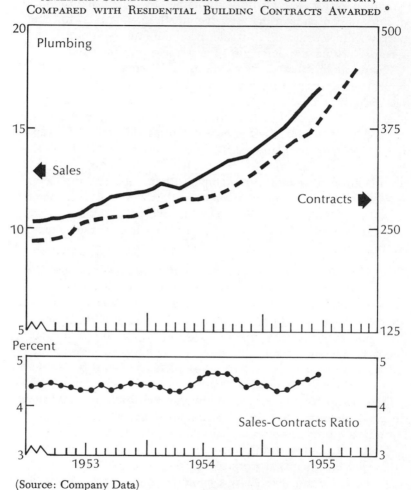

(Source: Company Data)

* Building contracts plotted ahead four months.

producing territory up to par, the company may be prepared to exert greater sales effort or to make a larger promotional expenditure. The forecaster must take these possible influences into consideration before setting the final figure. In short, after applying this method, the forecaster must exercise considerable sound judgment in order to obtain a final figure that reflects current conditions.

Field Information · Because of these considerations, the division's forecasting procedures are designed to give the greatest possible weight to market information available at the sales district level. Each of the twelve districts has a field market analyst who is responsible for preparing a field market report, due the first of each month.

This field market report gives monthly forecasts of district sales, three months in advance, by product categories, in dollars, and in units. These forecasts are based upon order trends evident at the district offices. Since a significant portion of all orders received specify firm future delivery dates, such information can be used as an advance indicator of the level of coming sales. The market field analysts also canvass the sales force on current competitive conditions, sales trends, customer information, and the current level of distributor inventories and distributor inventory policies. This last factor has been found to be very important in making realistic short-term estimates, since month-to-month sales can fluctuate widely, depending upon whether the distributors decide to build up their stocks or reduce them.

In addition, the division's marketing research department provides each field market analyst with the latest comparison of the lead-lag relationship between construction awards and territorial sales on a continuing basis.

Upon approval by the various district sales managers, the monthly field market reports are submitted to the marketing research department. Space is provided on these forms for a comparison of the latest estimates of sales with established sales quotas to help promote consistent forecasting. There is also space for comments regarding information gathered by the market analyst on the following subjects: district construction activity, general business conditions, price levels, corrective action indicated, color trends, product design, sales promotional activity, sales training, and competition.

These comments form the basis for a monthly report distributed by the marketing research department to general management that highlights specific conditions in the various sales territories.

The district sales forecasts are combined and totaled by the marketing research department and are used as a guide in preparing over-all divisional sales forecasts.

Home Office Forecast · The sales forecasting procedure at the home office is as follows. Once a month a forecast preparations committee, which consists of the technical assistant to the general marketing manager and the supervisor of sales analysis, who represents the marketing research department, meet with each of the seven product managers. In this way a unit forecast is arrived at by product, month-by-month, for the succeeding twelve-month period. In progressing to its forecasts, the committee takes into consideration the forecasts from the district sales offices, the latest estimates based on the lead-lag correlation, the record of previous sales estimates, and the current rate of sales, as well as the special knowledge its members bring to bear on the situation. For example, the product managers provide information regarding various sales campaigns and promotions, as well as new product developments in their particular lines and estimate their possible effect on sales.

Once a quarter the forecast review committee meets to consider the recommendations of the forecast preparations committee. Membership consists of the general marketing manager, the general sales manager, the product line managers, the manager of marketing research, and the manager of order handling. Based upon the combined opinion of this committee the forecasts of the forecast preparation committee are accepted or modified as seen fit. This projection is the principal factor in the establishment of the annual sales budget as well as the basis for establishing production schedules and inventory levels.

4. LONG ISLAND LIGHTING COMPANY

The Long Island Lighting Company's forecasts of sales and revenue are the basis of its economic planning. In most businesses, managerial action can guide the course of future events. In the case of public utility companies such control is not so easy.

Must Supply Demand · Houses are built, industries are established, appliances are sold, new equipment is installed, and the local gas and electric company must, by law, supply the new demand. It can promote and encourage use but it cannot refuse or even limit service without serious consequences.

The need for sound sales forecasting is made apparent by the fact that it may take five years to plan and build a new power plant. A transmission line can be constructed more rapidly, but it may take two years to secure the necessary right-of-way, and the design cannot be drawn until the rights-of-way are known. Even small lines and gas mains require considerable time to design and build.

In many utility companies, it is therefore customary to forecast sales at least five years ahead. The Long Island Lighting Company forecasts sales eighteen months ahead by months and five years ahead by years. These forecasts show the probable trend of new customers, of sales, and of revenues, both by classes of business and by location.

Judgment Essential · Although heavy reliance is placed upon statistical methods involving the study and extension of trends, cycles, and seasonal patterns, the company feels that the application of statistical techniques alone will not necessarily produce a reasonable forecast. All company forecasting is therefore centralized in a planning committee which consists of the heads of the following departments: budget, commercial, engineering, operating, rate, research, and sales. Through this committee, independent estimates which encompass all phases of the business are collectively analyzed to produce a mutually acceptable forecast. One of the principal values the company derives from the planning committee is the opportunity to collect independent judgments about the future from the various department heads representing different points of view.

Methods Used · This company's method of forecasting sales evolves about the study of four basic related factors: (1) population; (2) meters or customers; (3) consumption; (4) revenue. Each is studied separately and also in relation to the other three. These interrelationships or "links" serve as cross-checks. They are: (1) the meter ratio (number of people per meter); (2) sales per meter; (3) revenue per meter; and (4) revenue per unit of power sold vs. consumption per meter. With the aid of information from the field, mathematical formulas and sound judgment, the trends of these link factors can be extended into the future.

Population Studies · Changing population is the prime factor affecting company sales, so much time is naturally spent in analyzing and forecasting population trends. Careful and continuous population studies are made of the areas served by the company. These studies take into account the birth and death rates, the migration of people, new construction, and other similar factors. From these studies estimates of current population are made (Chart 6) and a trend of population is established and forecast.

CHART 6

POPULATION OF NASSAU AND SUFFOLK COUNTIES, LONG ISLAND

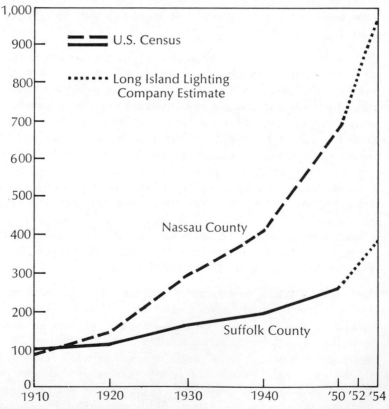

(Source: Company data)

(In thousands)

The company also maintains correlation studies between population and active meters. Regular reports based on field surveys are made by local managers on new construction and new industrial developments in their territories. Each field survey is checked against applications for service on file and against building-permit records in local government offices. The relation between new construction and new meters is generally quite close so that short-range predictions can be made with great accuracy.

These reports are studied also for possible effect on population-meter ratios (Chart 7). By applying the forecast population-meter ratio to estimates of future population, the number of meters in use can be forecast.

CHART 7

NUMBER OF PERSONS PER ELECTRIC METER

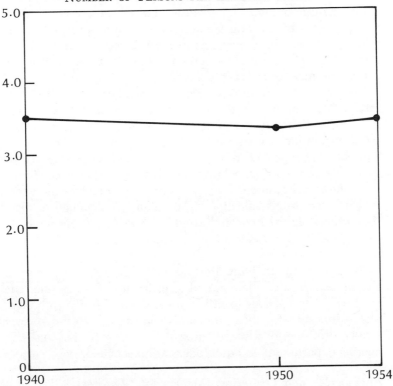

(Source: Company data)

Consumption and Revenue · The next step is to forecast the estimated power consumption per customer. For residential customers, a twelve-month moving average of energy use per customer (or meter) shows a gradual rise, which can be projected into the future by means of a trend line.

The forecast of energy sales is obtained from the combination of the forecast of meters in use and the forecast of estimated use per customer. This forecast is tested in the planning committee against information available to the sales department of electrical appliances in use and of the probable effect of the company's promotional activities.

To obtain a forecast of revenue, the company makes use of the known relation between energy sales per billed meter and revenue per billed meter, both on a billing day basis (Chart 8). From the line of average relation, accurate average revenue rates can be determined for any given level of consumption. Information provided by the rate department regarding prospective rate adjustments can be used to temper the forecast of revenue per kilowatt hour, and then, by applying it to the forecast of energy sales, a revenue forecast is obtained.

The forecast of industrial sales and revenue is handled separately. Most of the short-range information on future demand is obtained from the customers themselves. Any contemplated plant expansions, work-shift changes or installation of new equipment is reported to the company and is taken into account in the forecast of industrial revenue. This technique is confined to large industrial customers who consume about half of the energy sold in this rate classification. The balance is assumed to match proportionately the trend indicated by these large consumers, because much of the small business is subsidiary to the large business in this territory.

The sum of the individual estimates of residential, commercial, and industrial sales when added to estimates of other sales such as street lighting, sales to other utilities and the like, produce a total sales estimate. This estimate is compared with independent estimates of energy demand forecast by the operating and engineering departments and differences are reconciled.

Engineering and Operating Departments' Forecast · The engineering and operating departments' procedure is entirely differ-

CHART 8

RESIDENTIAL CLASS OF BUSINESS—KWH PER BILLED METER PER
BILLING DAY RELATED TO REVENUE PER BILLED METER
PER BILLING DAY, 1953

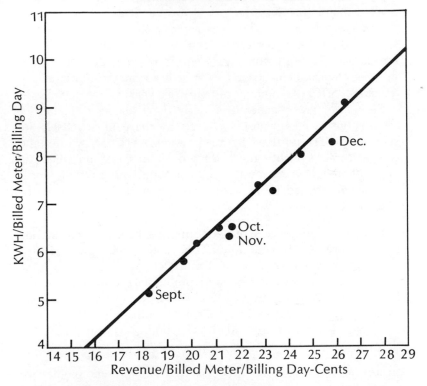

(Source: Company data)

ent, and is based on the relationship between peak demand and
average energy requirements. First, the peak demand in the
previous year is corrected for the estimated effect on demand of
actual versus "normal" weather conditions and is then further
adjusted for any unusual operating conditions in existence at
the time of the actual peak. For instance, a big industrial plant
may have been on strike.

To this corrected peak is added an increment representing demand expected from all new customers. This gives an estimate

of the peak demand for the following years, assuming normal weather and normal operating conditions. The process is then repeated for each of the succeeding four years.

Finally, the trend in the ratio of average kilowatt demand to peak demand (the load factor) is examined and projected for the five-year forecast. This is feasible because this ratio moves slowly and a trend projection is reasonably accurate. Annual forecasts of kilowatt hours generated are then derived as the product of peak demand and average load factor, multiplied by a factor of 8,760 (the number of hours in a year).

From the power generation derived as above, estimates of the amount of energy lost and used by the company itself are subtracted. The resultant figures now represent energy sales and can be compared with the sales projection based on trends in population, customers, and energy consumption. Any differences are then reconciled by applying the consensus judgment of the planning committee.

Revisions · The process of gathering background information for the forecasts is continuous, but new forecasts are issued officially twice a year, on June 1 and October 1. On June 1 the revision for the current year and preliminary estimates for the five succeeding years, by years, are issued. On October 1 final estimates for the next budget year, by months, plus a revision of the five-year forecast are issued. The timing coincides with the dates of budget revision.

Accuracy · The company reports that the present method of forecasting has been in use for about three years. During that time the margin of error has been slightly above 1 percent for forecasts made one year in advance, and between 5 percent and 10 percent for the most distant years. Perhaps as important as accuracy is the ease with which new developments in the use of electricity can be incorporated in the forecast. Also, the establishment of the planning committee has made available more information upon which to base estimates.

Responsibility for Forecasts · Many departments are involved in the company's sales forecasting activities. The budget department, with technical assistance from the commercial research department on statistical techniques, prepares the revenue forecasts from the planning committee's sales forecasts. The sales department supplies information and keeps records on merchandising activity by the company and local dealers. The commercial department keeps records on new customers added. The rate department is responsible for all information dealing with customer bill distributions and rate changes. The system engineering department keeps weather data and makes estimates of its effect on sales. This department also coordinates the work of the engineering, electric operating, and gas operating departments in the forecasts of peak demand.

5. THE B. F. GOODRICH COMPANY

The methods used are well-illustrated by the practices of the B. F. Goodrich Company in forecasting passenger-car tire demand.

Passenger-car tire sales are of two types: Those made to automobile manufacturers, to be used as part of the original equipment, and those sold to car owners to replace worn-out tires.

To estimate sales for original equipment, all a company needs to know is: (1) how many vehicles will be produced; (2) how many and what types and sizes of tires will they be equipped with; and (3) what share of the total sales will the company obtain.

The long-term forecast of passenger-car production involves several steps. In the first step, the number of cars already in use is considered in relation to the nation's level of income. The company's business research department compared the number of passenger cars in operation at the end of each year, for a period of years back to 1930, with the corresponding year's level of disposable personal income, adjusted for changes in purchasing power. It was found that the following relationship existed: for every million dollars of income there were approximately 200 passenger cars in use (see Table 1).

The second step involves the preparation of an estimate of the future trend of disposable personal income based on certain assumptions as to the nation's potential economic growth. The business research department starts by making an economic fore-

TABLE 1

PASSENGER CARS IN OPERATION AND DISPOSABLE
PERSONAL INCOME

Year	Passenger Cars in Operation at End of Year (In Thousands)	Disposable Personal Income (Billions of Constant 1947 Dollars)	Cars per $1 Million Disposable Income
1930........	20,533	105.8	194.0
1940........	25,939	129.6	200.2
1950........	37,619	194.1	193.8
1951........	39,638	199.2	199.0
1952........	40,475	205.1	197.4
1953........	42,945	213.8	200.9

Source: U. S. Department of Commerce and B. F. Goodrich Business Research Department.

cast of gross national product (GNP), which measures the sum total of goods produced by the nation's economy. Analysis has shown that once the effect of changing price levels is removed the rate at which the economy's output grows depends on four factors: population, the proportion of the population employed in the labor force, the length of the average work week, and productivity as measured by gross national product per man-hour of work (see Table 2).

For some components of these factors long-term trends may be calculated and extended into the future. One such factor is output per man-hour of work, which examination of the record has shown to increase over the years at a more or less regular, and predictable rate. For other factors, however, such as the size of the armed forces, flat assumptions must be made, based on the best-informed opinion at the time.

Future levels of gross national product are estimated from the resulting projections of man-hours worked and of gross national product per man-hour (productivity). The forecasts of gross national product are used in turn to estimate the future levels of personal income. This is made possible because of the close connection between GNP and personal income (see Chart 9). Deducting estimated personal tax payments from the estimates of personal income results in a forecast of disposable personal income.

TABLE 2

EMPLOYMENT, MAN-HOURS, AND GROSS NATIONAL PRODUCT

Year	Population Age 15 and Over	Civilian Labor Force	Unemployment	Employed (Including Armed Forces)	Average Hours Per Week	Annual* Man-hours	Gross National Product in 1947 Dollars	Gross National Product per Man-hour (1947$)
	(Millions)	*(Millions)*	*(Millions)*	*(Millions)*		*(Billions)*	*(Billions)*	
1930............	87.1	49.8	4.3	45.8	49.0	116.7	135.2	1.159
1940............	99.0	55.6	8.1	47.9	44.6	111.1	171.6	1.545
1950............	110.0	63.1	3.1	61.5	41.7	133.4	264.7	1.984
1951............	112.1	62.9	1.9	63.9	42.2	140.2	282.9	2.018
1952............	113.1	63.0	1.7	64.7	42.4	142.7	294.2	2.062
1953............	114.2	63.4	1.5	65.8	41.9	143.4	306.6	2.138

* Annual man-hours equals total employed (including armed forces) multiplied by average hours per week, times fifty-two weeks.

Source: U. S. Department of Commerce and B. F. Goodrich Business Research Department.

CHART 9

COMPARISON OF PERSONAL INCOME WITH GROSS
NATIONAL PRODUCT

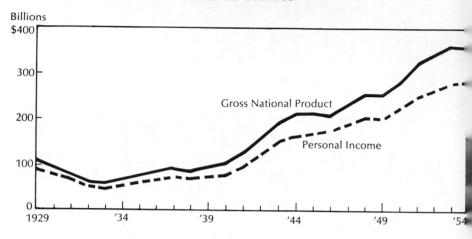

After these estimates have been made, the company is in a position to project the trend of automobile production in future years. Knowing the probable number of cars that will be in use and allowing for anticipated scrappage (which depends upon production in prior years, the average life of cars currently in operation, and economic factors which lead to a rate of scrappage above or below average) the company knows how many cars will probably have been produced in order to replace cars scrapped and to make net additions to the nation's stock of cars.

As this provides only an estimate of new-car production for domestic use, the export demand and the production of military vehicles using passenger-car tires must be estimated and added to get the total.

From these estimates of vehicle production, industry sales forecasts of original equipment tires are derived by applying a factor of about 5.5. The company explains that although new passenger cars are equipped at the factory with five passenger-car tires, original equipment shipments generally exceed this figure somewhat for the reason that these shipments also include passenger car tires used on light trucks and the like (see Table 3).

TABLE 3

ORIGINAL EQUIPMENT PASSENGER-CAR TIRE SHIPMENTS

Year	Passenger Car Total Factory Sales (In Thousands)	Original Equipment Tires Shipped (In Thousands)	Original Equipment Tire Shipments per Passenger Car
1933	1,573	9,031	5.74
1940	3,717	19,560	5.26
1950	6,666	36,678	5.50
1951	5,338	26,422	4.95
1952	4,321	24,034	5.56
1953	6,117	33,082	5.41

Source: B. F. Goodrich Research Department.

Replacement Sales · Replacement sales are dependent upon three factors: (1) the number of cars over two years of age which are in use; [2] (2) the amount of wear tires receive; and (3) the wearing qualities of the tires. Data on past sales of replacement-car tires are collected by the Rubber Manufacturers' Association. The average number of cars over two years of age which are in use is obtained by subtracting from the total number in operation half of the current year's new car sales, all of the first preceding year and half of the second preceding year.

A "replacement tire factor" is obtained by dividing the total number of tire units sold by the total number of passenger cars over two years of age in operation. The company has found that the average automobile user continues to buy tires and keep his automobile in operation despite significant changes in income. A convenient method of allowing for the longer service and higher quality built into tires is to extend into the future the long-run trend of replacement tire shipments per passenger car over two years of age in operation. The annual decline in this ratio from 1933 to 1953 averages out at about 1 percent each year (see Table 4).

The final step in the preparation of the sales forecast is to check carefully all assumptions and extensions of trends and mathematical relationships used in building up the forecast. In

2. Experience has shown that original equipment tires last approximately two years and therefore demand for new tires does not begin until cars reach this age.

TABLE 4

REPLACEMENT PASSENGER-CAR TIRE SHIPMENTS

Year	Average Number of Passenger Cars Over 2 Years of Age in Operation (In Thousands)	Civilian Replacement Tire Shipments (In Thousands)	Replacement Tire Shipments Per Vehicle
1933	16,636	29,138	1.75
1940	19,487	30,903	1.59
1950	25,615	47,103	1.84
1951	27,075	34,121	1.26
1952	29,639	45,315	1.53
1953	32,013	45,787	1.43

Source: Rubber Manufacturers' Association and B. F. Goodrich Business Research Department.

some instances, sound judgment may indicate modifications in the statistical results. The forecast is also checked against other projections of general business and the outlook for the industry. All sales forecasts, whether long-run or short-run, are revised periodically in the light of more recent experience.

How Governments
Forecast GNP

ORGANIZATION FOR ECONOMIC
COOPERATION AND DEVELOPMENT

This piece was taken from Techniques of Economic Forecasting, *a report published by the Organization of Economic Cooperation and Development in 1965.*

A study of the methods used by six countries—Canada, France, the Netherlands, Sweden, the United Kingdom, and the United States—to forecast GNP shows a striking degree of similarity among the methods of forecasting employed in the various countries. There are certainly differences, but these do not seem to be great enough to render an account of a basic common method either impossible or seriously misleading.

All forecasters are attempting to estimate (on the basis of certain assumptions) the future relationship between total demand in the economy and the economy's capacity to meet demands made on it. In all cases some of the items to be forecast are regarded as given, or autonomous; others as functionally derived from known data for the economy or from the autonomous items. An example may make the distinction clearer to the nonprofessional reader. Fixed investment in a succeeding period might in principle be forecast by asking all businessmen what they intended to invest, adding up the answers, and accepting the total, say an increase of *x* percent. This would be regarding investment as entirely autonomous from the forecaster's point of view. Of course, the businessmen would all have had reasons for their decisions: they would be making them on the basis of present and past trends in the economy. But the forecaster would not himself be trying to establish what these reasons were, how investment was in fact being determined. On the other hand, the forecaster might have established to his own satisfaction, from examining the data for previous years, that (to take a deliberately over-simple possibility) investment in any year was always precisely linked to the level of undistributed profits in the previous year. In this case he could forecast investment as a derived variable, needing only to know the previous year's profits.

All countries, then, regard some items as autonomous, some as functionally determined. Moreover, there is a substantial measure of agreement in practice as to which items are regarded in each way. When it comes to constructing a full forecast from the autonomous and the derived variables, there is a difference in approach which has often been emphasized in general comments on forecasting methods: some countries (notably the Netherlands) "solve" their forecast, i.e., find the equilibrium level of expected demand and supply, by solving a set of simultaneous equations; other countries (notably the United Kingdom) solve the forecast by a method of successive approximation. This difference in method, though interesting and important, does not represent a fundamental difference in approach, as will be seen.

We may now proceed to describe the general method of forecasting common to all the participating countries.

We begin with the five main components of demand or expenditure—consumers' expenditure, public expenditure, private fixed investment, investment in stocks, and exports. Of these, public expenditure, private fixed investment, and exports are in practice regarded in most countries as at least largely autonomous from the forecaster's point of view; consumers' expenditure and investment in stocks are regarded as derived or "endogenous" variables.

PUBLIC EXPENDITURE

The forecast of public expenditure (i.e., both current and capital expenditure on goods and services by all public authorities) is based on known plans and programs. In practice a good deal of work is usually necessary: in translating programs from budgetary to national income terms, in estimating the rate of realization of programs, in estimating the relationship between contract placement, cash payments and work done, and sometimes in translating current value figures into constant prices.

EXPORTS

The forecast of exports is usually derived largely from forecasts of activity abroad (which is universally taken as autonomous or "exogenous" to the economy under consideration) together with plausible or established relationships between foreign activity and foreign demand for the country's goods. Export order positions and the views of industrialists, trade associations, commercial attachés abroad, etc., are also taken into account. There are two ways in which export forecasts may be partly determined "endogenously," i.e., derived from the rest of the forecast for the economy. Allowance may be made for expected changes in domestic prices (relative to expected price movements abroad), and for the expected degree of over- or under-utilization of capacity in the economy. All countries are prepared to modify their export forecasts in the light of expected supply limitations or change in competitiveness. In most cases this is done qualitatively; in the case of the Netherlands it is done quantitatively. But in all cases, the exogenous element in the export forecast dominates.

BUSINESS FIXED INVESTMENT

All six countries except the United Kingdom make some use of functional relationships to derive an estimate of business fixed investment. Both financial variables—profits, company taxes, and depreciation allowances, indicators of general liquidity—and nonfinancial variables—capacity utilization, and movements of sales and output—are used. However, in practice most countries do not lay major stress on these relationships and it is only in the Netherlands' first two forecasts that business investment is forecast endogenously from these relationships. For the final Netherlands forecast, information on investment intentions is available and is sometimes used to "disturb" the equations. In some countries estimates of cash flow and liquidities play an important part in "consistency checks" on the plausibility of their forecasts. With the exception of the Netherlands, countries are agreed in relying almost entirely on non-causal or "pre-flow" anticipations data for forecasting business fixed investment. Thus this item is, in practice, regarded as very largely autonomous. Many types of "pre-flow" data are drawn upon. Some countries, especially the United Kingdom and the United States, make use of series of orders for capital goods, building contractors' orders, work on architects' drawing boards, etc. But by far the most important type of pre-flow is investment intentions. All countries carry out surveys of the intentions of a sample of firms several times a year. These must usually be processed and adjusted in many ingenious and sophisticated ways (so that the longer the survey has been in existence the better results it can be made to give), but the final result is normally the most important piece of evidence in coming to a forecast of business fixed investment. The period of the economic forecast, however, frequently exceeds the horizon of the intentions surveys and "causal" relationships are necessary for longer-run forecasts of business fixed investment.

HOUSEBUILDING

Countries vary a good deal in their approach to forecasting housebuilding, but in general it too is regarded as largely autonomous. With knowledge of the average length of time taken to build a house, fairly good forecasts for up to three quarters ahead may often be derived from information on the number of starts and, even better, where they apply, on the number of permits or licenses granted. This evidence is usually supplemented by qualitative expectations of the effects of changes in interest rates and the financial position of building societies, etc. Some work has been done, especially in the United States, on trying to find a way of deriving housebuilding functionally from other data. Thus an aggregate demand-supply model might be built up, the demand for housing being estimated from trends in family formation rates and being compared with the growth in the stock of houses. So far such approaches do not appear to have been very successful, perhaps, as the case of the United States suggests, because the concept of a national housing market is inappropriate: there is, rather, a host of small local markets, developments in which are difficult to assess.

INVESTMENT IN STOCKS [I.E., INVENTORIES]

All countries treat investment in stocks and consumers' expenditure as endogenous, i.e., as functionally determined by known or autonomous items. In attempting to forecast investment in stocks, use is generally made of the concept of some "normal" relationship between stocks and total sales towards which businesses constantly try to move; although some countries (e.g., the United Kingdom) take account of the phasing of stockbuilding in past cycles, in general little is known about what governs the speed at which stocks move towards the normal or equilibrium ratio and this hypothesis has therefore as yet been of only limited help in practice. All countries would try to take account of speculative influences in any particular situation (e.g., rapidly rising prices for a commodity or the expectation of a strike), but apart from the Netherlands none uses any systematic relationship with price changes. There is unanimous agreement that forecasting investment in stocks is the most difficult part of the whole operation. The rate of stockbuilding is everywhere highly volatile; changes in it may be very large in proportion to changes in other items in the short period; and it is common experience to have large errors—even to have the direction of change wrong —in forecasts of stockbuilding. Sweden's latest forecasts, however, include some equations for stockbuilding.

CONSUMERS' EXPENDITURE

Consumers' expenditure is in all countries treated as being primarily a function of personal disposable income. In none of them has the ratio between disposable income and consumption, or between changes in disposable income and changes in consumption, proved stable; but all use modifications of some simple ratio with some success. Most countries find that in the short run consumption is relatively insensitive to changes in income either up or down, adjusting to them only with a lag; but in most countries the fluctuations in the marginal propensity to consume from quarter to quarter are only partly explained on the hypothesis of a lag. In France a rule of thumb which has been used is that in the face of a change in real income households attempt first to maintain the volume of their consumption and the value of their savings, dividing any balance (either plus or minus) in fixed proportions between consumption and savings. Many countries (in particular the United States) find it important to consider expenditure on consumer durables separately from the rest of consumption. Expenditure on non-durables and services tends to exhibit insensitivity to both rises and falls in income while expenditure on durables is highly sensitive to such changes.

A number of countries have tried in different ways to take account of factors other than disposable income which may influence consumption, in particular, consumers' asset/liability and liquidity positions. The Dutch equation for consumption contains, as explanatory variables, time and demand deposits as an index of liquidity as well as price changes and movements of consumption in the recent past. The United Kingdom attempts to take account of movements in outstanding consumer debt and bank loans and changes in controls over consumer credit. The United States also takes changes in liquidity and consumer credit terms into consideration but emphasizes their fundamentally permissive nature which makes it, in United States experience, impossible to derive stable relationships between them and consumption.

If consumption is primarily dependent on personal disposable income, then before it can be added to the other elements of demand to give a forecast of total demand, it is necessary to have an estimate of disposable income. This in turn is regarded as largely dependent on total final demand. There are two ways of proceeding. Either a relationship between total expenditure and disposable income is forecast, and then the resulting equations are solved to give the values of both total demand and the two endogenous components; this is basically what the United States and (in a more complex way) the Netherlands do. Or, on the other hand, one can begin by taking what looks a plausible figure for consumption or personal income (having regard to the forecasts of the non-consumption items and past relationships between non-consumption and consumption) and then derive from the corresponding estimate of total demand a forecast for personal disposable income which will yield in turn a forecast of consumption. If this differs from the estimate first taken, this estimate will have to be altered and the process worked through again, and so on, until a self-consistent forecast is reached. This method of successive approximation is the method followed by Canada, Sweden, and the United Kingdom. It is clear, however, that in either case it is necessary to have a view about the relationship between total final demand and disposable income.

TOTAL OUTPUT ESTIMATED BY THE "SUCCESSIVE APPROXIMATION" METHOD

Consider the successive approximation procedure, as this perhaps shows the reasoning behind the forecasting more easily. A plausible first approximation to the value of consumers' expenditure enables a total of final expenditure to be assumed. This must equal the value of home output produced together with the value of indirect taxes and imports. The value of indirect taxes for any particular total expenditure is fairly easy to determine with reasonable accuracy from a knowledge of the tax rates and some idea of the broad pattern of expenditure. Forecasting imports is more difficult. In general, the method is to assume that imports are determined by movements in total demand after a time lag. Most countries have found that they can improve their estimates by disaggregating total imports and making separate forecasts for particular commodity groups by relating them to expected trends in particular variables: e.g., food imports may be related to personal incomes, raw materials imports to industrial production. Sweden, in particular, appears to have been quite successful with import equations of this kind. In general, countries seem reasonably satisfied with their ability to estimate imports—certainly more satisfied than they are about exports—though at times when there are big movements in stockbuilding or when domestic capacity comes under strain substantial errors can easily be made.

Once indirect taxes and imports have been forecast and subtracted from the forecast of total final expenditure we have an estimate of total output or gross national product (GNP). The next stage is to see what this implies for incomes, prices, employment, and unemployment. For this it is necessary to estimate the growth in the capacity of the economy, i.e., in potential GNP.

This can in principle be thought of as derived from forecasts of the employable labor force and the increase in labor productivity. Most countries can make use of well-established demographic trends for short-term forecasts of the labor force, combined with ad hoc adjustments, for, e.g., a change in the school-leaving age, immigration or emigration, a move out of civil employment into the army (as in 1956 in France) or the reverse (as in 1963 in France).

Given a forecast of the employable labor force, a forecast of actual employment, and hence of unemployment, necessarily implies a forecast of productivity; in each country the latter is in effect regarded as having both a trend and a cyclical component. The trend increase in productivity is largely derived from extrapolation of past trends. Often the aggregate estimate will be built up from a number of estimates for individual industries. Some attempt may be made to allow for the effects of investment in previous periods, but this is usually only where the effects of the investment on productive capacity are relatively easy to see and to measure (e.g., electricity generation). Again, both France and the United Kingdom have found that the change in output attributable to an autonomous change in the labor force (due to conscription or immigration, for example) may have to be estimated on the basis of a different productivity from the average of the economy. But in general such modifications of the trend are likely to be small.

The cyclical element in productivity is another matter. Countries find that when the pressure of demand changes, employment is relatively insensitive—or, as suggested by the case of the United Kingdom, adjusts to the new level of demand only after a time lag—largely perhaps because certain types of labor are "hoarded" by employers, or regarded as overhead. The resultant fluctuations in the ratio of output to employment (i.e., productivity) are often large in relation to the underlying trend and must be carefully forecast on the basis of a judgment about where the economy is in the business cycle and past performance.

In all countries, it is found that as demand rises in relation to supply, not merely does unemployment fall, but the average number of hours worked and the "participation rate" both normally increase. That is, there will be increased overtime working and a number of marginal workers—such as housewives and retired people—will be drawn into employment. These trends must be estimated before any forecast of GNP can be translated into a forecast of unemployment. Several countries—in particular the United Kingdom and the United States—have formulated numerical relationships between changes in GNP and changes in unemployment.

Having forecast employment, the next step is to forecast the increase in average earnings. This is usually regarded as partly autonomous—the forecaster uses any knowledge he may have about pending wage negotiations, etc.—but partly endogenous: the increase in negotiated rates is likely to depend, at least to some extent, on the prevailing pressure of demand, and this may have a further influence on the degree to which actual earnings exceed negotiated rates. Combining employment and average earnings yields the total of wages, the largest component of personal income. The other components are forecast in a relatively routine way: salaries, rent, and self-employed incomes may be estimated partly from extrapolation of past trends, partly by keeping them in some relationship with wages. Government transfers, except for unemployment benefits, are taken as autonomous. Dividend payments may be regarded as a function of profits and hence endogenous to the forecast. An income tax function can then be applied to the total of personal incomes to give disposable income.

When prices are changing rapidly it might be thought that a relationship between consumers' expenditure and disposable income adjusted for price changes would yield better results than a relationship based on nominal values. Only the United Kingdom, however, appears to make the deflation an integral part of their forecast process; the Netherlands and Sweden use a relationship in current prices while the United States and Canada, although making a forecast of consumers' prices, have not stressed this aspect of their forecasting in recent years. If prices are changing significantly, however, it would seem desirable to make explicit allowance for the effects on consumption.

Consumer prices will depend on a number of factors such as import prices, the supply and demand position in the food sector, and movements in unit labor costs. The United Kingdom has developed an interesting theory of price determination in which the important variable is not actual labor costs at any particular time, but *trend* labor costs, derived from the trend in hourly earnings and the trend increase in productivity.

Once consumer prices have been forecast, expected personal disposable income can be deflated to yield a forecast of real personal disposable income. From this may be derived, as has already been discussed, a forecast for consumption. If this derived estimate of consumption differs from the figure assumed at the beginning of the forecasting process, then the whole forecast is obviously inconsistent. A new value for consumption must be assumed and the procedure worked through again to yield a second derived estimate. If assumed and derived estimates still differ, a third estimate must be made, and so on until a value is found which provides a self-consistent forecast.

Though it seems convenient to treat the forecast of potential economic capacity as a separate element in the forecast, it could be argued that this is already implicit in the forecasts of employment, unemployment, and productivity. Thus, an increase in demand greater than the "trend" increase in productivity implies an increase in the pressure of demand, and of "cyclical" productivity, and a decline in unemployment; and vice versa. In practice therefor, the effect of changes in the pressure of demand on the forecasts of demand have to be allowed for. Two other possible interactions between demand and supply should be mentioned. According as the forecast implies a particularly high or low pressure of demand, the "successive approximation" countries may shade their original forecasts of wage increases up or down. The short-term effect of an increase in demand may be considerable and therefore in the case of a forecast over the very short period (e.g., a quarter)any change in wages might call for a revision of the demand forecast. In a longer-term forecast, however, a change in wages is likely to have much less effect on the overall demand forecast since the forecast of prices would also have to be altered. The theories of price determination held by the official forecasters mean that the combined effect of changing wage and price forecasts on expected real personal disposable income and hence on expected real consumption will be small. Again, a particularly high or low pressure of demand is likely to affect the relationship between home supplies and imports and may also affect exports. (Or to put this another way, a forecast "gap" may be reflected in the balance of payments as well as in the level of unemployment.) Thus in some circumstances, forecasters may have to recast their estimate of total demand slightly as a result of taking a higher or lower value for exports. Unless exports are very large in relation to national product, however, such adjustment will tend to be small.

Econometric Forecasting
with the Wharton Model

F. Gerald Adams and
Michael K. Evans

*F. Gerard Adams is Professor of Economics
at the Wharton School of the University of
Pennsylvania, and Michael Evans is President of Chase Econometrics Associates. This
paper appeared in* Business Economics *in
1968.*

As the art of econometric forecasting goes, five years is already a fairly long time. Every three months over the past five
years, the Wharton econometric model has been put through its
paces. National accounts predictions for eight quarters into the
future have been made for a range of possible alternative developments of the exogenous variables of the economy.

This work is part of a program of model building, forecasting,
and research sponsored by some thirty major business firms associated with the Econometric Forecasting Unit. Econometric
forecasting, as it is carried on at Wharton, has become fully
operational. Moreover, the forecasting record shows that it has
also been quite accurate.

WHARTON-EFU MODEL

The development of modern econometric models is an evolutionary process and the Wharton-EFU model is no exception. The

model was originally formulated by merging a short-term forecasting model (two quarter forecasts) developed by L. R. Klein [1] using anticipatory data and a model developed by M. K. Evans [2] which relied entirely on objective variables and was thus capable of predicting over a longer forecasting horizon. The present model not only incorporates many elements from these predecessors but has been frequently altered to incorporate the latest technical expertise and to reflect important economic developments. A recent improvement, for example, has been the development of a non-linear relationship which recognizes the effect of the composition of unemployment as well as its level on the wage rate. A new version of the model is being built which provides a better treatment of profits and which incorporates a more detailed monetary sector.

The Wharton-EFU model is basically a quarterly model of the Keynesian type expanded to explain not only GNP and the major components of aggregate demand but also prices, wages, employment, capacity utilization, and factor shares. There are 47 behavioral and 29 definitional equations. The inter-relationships which make up this system of equations are described elsewhere in detail.[3] In order to get some idea of the most important links in the model, we consider the principal equations very briefly at this point.

The consumption sector is considered first. Consumption of nondurables and services is a function of present and lagged personal disposable income, estimated in a ratio form in order to stress the long-run constancy of the consumption-income ratio. For consumption of durables, stocks of previous purchases are also relevant and additional variables are needed to explain the greater cyclical movements of auto purchases. Here relative prices, supply constraints (such as during strikes), and changes in credit conditions are also quite important, and the rate of

1. L. R. Klein, "A Postwar Quarterly Model," in *Models of Income Determination,* Vol. 28 in Studies in Income and Wealth (Princeton: Princeton University Press for NBER, 1964), pp. 11–30.

2. M. K. Evans, *A Postwar Quarterly Model of the United States Economy,* unpublished Ph.D. dissertation, 1964.

3. For a detailed description of the model see M. K. Evans and L. R. Klein, *The Wharton Econometric Forecasting Model* (Philadelphia: Economics Research Unit, University of Pennsylvania, 1967).

unemployment serves as a general cyclical variable mainly representing consumer attitudes.

The investment sector is more complex and forms the heart of the model. This sector is divided into fixed business investment, residential construction, and inventory investment, with the first being disaggregated further into manufacturing, regulated, and trade-services sectors. The investment equations combine elements of the accelerator-capital stock adjustment and of the financial approaches to investment behavior. A salient feature of these functions is the type of lag structure chosen. Investment planning takes time and it takes additional time to put in place new plant and equipment. While changes in capital requirements or the cost or availability of credit are likely to have only slight effects on investment which is already planned or under way, it is necessary to allow for modifications in the original plans in light of changing real economic conditions. Financial considerations, which affect the rate of investment after a year or so has passed, are introduced through cash flow, the long-term interest rate, and the spread between long- and short-term interest rates, a proxy for availability of credit.

Residential construction is essentially counter-cyclical, increasing when factor resources—labor, materials, and credit—are available and decreasing when these are employed in other forms of investment. Credit conditions as well as personal disposable income and relative costs of construction are the relevant explanatory variables. The inventory investment equations are stock-adjustment formulations with an additional adjustment term incorporating the flexible accelerator, the speed of adjustment in the manufacturing sector being determined by the change in the backlog of unfilled orders.

In the foreign sector equations, imports are disaggregated into food, other raw materials and semimanufactured goods, and other imports (consumer goods and all services). Imports are determined by the appropriate demand variables—personal disposable income, or manufacturing sales and inventory investment—and relative prices. Exports are a function of an index of world trade and of relative prices.

The supply side of the model is considered next. Cobb-Douglas production functions, modified to include utilized labor and capital, are estimated for both the manufacturing and non-manufacturing sectors. Hours worked in the manufacturing sector are cyclically sensitive and depend on both the level and change in output, the index of capacity utilization, and the wage rate. In the non-manufacturing sector, hours worked follow a much smoother path and depend more on long-run influences. The wage rate functions are modified Phillips curves where the spread between the overall unemployment rate and the rate for males age 25–34 is used. When unemployment in this latter group is small, upward pressure on the wage rate is intensified even if other workers still remain unemployed. Additional equations explaining the spread between these two rates and the labor force participation rates are also included. A markup equation relates prices and unit labor costs in the manufacturing sector, with markup margins increasing at higher rates of capacity utilization.

The remaining equations making up the model are sufficiently straightforward to require little comment. Depreciation functions depend on capital stock and changes in the tax laws. The various direct and indirect taxes depend on the income on which they are levied and the tax laws. Income of independent entrepreneurs depends on GNP, rent and interest income on a rent index, and dividends on gross profits including depreciation. The various sector prices depend on the overall price level and various special factors in each sector. Finally, the short-term interest rate is a function of monetary policy variables, and the long-term interest rate depends on the present short-term and past long-term rates.

RAPID COMPUTER SOLUTION

This thumbnail sketch cannot suggest all the reasoning behind the equations or the numerous alternative empirical formulations which have been tried but rejected. However, it may be useful in giving the flavor of the type of model which has been built and which is continually being improved at the Wharton School. In the sectors where relatively poor predictions were obtained or where the present detail is skimpy, further work is currently in progress. This is particularly true for the supply variables and the monetary sector.

Rapid computer solution of the model is the secret to its frequent application for forecasting, simulation, and policy analysis. We are dealing with a large simultaneous equation system which is non-linear because of the presence of current dollar terms (price times quantity), determination of the wage bill (wage rate times man-hours), and the ratio of actual to maximum output. Such a large non-linear system would be most difficult to solve by analytic methods. However, computer programs have been developed at the Wharton School which make possible the solution of the model by iterative procedures; these programs are extremely rapid and convenient.[4] It is only necessary to provide the values of the lagged variables and to estimate the future values of such exogenous variables as government expenditures, tax rates, monetary policy variables, and so on to obtain a solution ahead in time for as many periods as desired. This takes approximately *one second* of computer time for each period forecast. Such versatility makes it possible to provide a complete package of forecasts which incorporates experimentation with numerous reasonable (and even, if desired, unreasonable) alternatives, rather than just a single forecast.

ECONOMETRIC FORECASTING UNIT

A great stimulus to our model building and forecasting work has been the Econometric Forecasting Unit. This is a cooperative effort which brings together economists from business, government, and the Wharton School. Every quarter the assumptions about exogenous developments are carefully evaluated and the forecasts are studied in the context of a forecasting meeting. Economists from major business corporations and banks offer their judgment about such developments as strikes, the outlook in financial markets, and other special situations. Government economists cooperating in this effort provide the latest adjusted statistical information and make the best informed judgments about budgetary developments.

These data are then fed into the model to produce a range of forecasts. These are then further evaluated and additional com-

4. Morris Norman, "Solving a Non-Linear Econometric Model by the Gauss-Seidel Iterative Method." Paper presented at the meetings of the Econometric Society, December, 1967, Washington, D.C.

puter runs are made to produce a final *control solution* and some basic alternatives. Recently, for example, the control solution forecast for 1968 assumed that an 8 percent tax increase would become effective retroactively to January 1st; alternative forecasts assuming no tax surcharge or a surcharge of 10 percent were also provided. Whenever there is a new development, such as the British devaluation, a change in the discount rate, or a strike settlement in the automobile industry, new computer runs are made. The effects of prospective policy alternatives are carefully evaluated in special studies.

In the process of the quarterly meetings and numerous informal contacts a continuous dialogue has developed between the model builders and the users of the forecasts in the business community and in government. This has been helpful not only in sharpening the forecasts, but also in developing the models, improving their structure, directing the research work into areas where it is most needed, and expanding the presentation and analysis of the results. Regular applied prediction is an invaluable discipline for the econometric forecaster. The Econometric Forecasting Unit has also provided the financial support for many aspects of the model building, for computer programming for model estimation and solution, and for many related econometric studies carried out with the assistance of numerous graduate research fellows.

FORECASTING RECORD

The ultimate test of how well the econometric forecasting effort is succeeding is in the record generated by true *ex ante* forecasts. While it is possible to study how the model would perform in the abstract, econometric forecasting is not a mechanical process and the results depend not only on the model but also on how it has been used. This, in turn, depends on judgments about the appropriate values of the exogenous variables—which we obtain largely through the consensus of the econometric forecasting meetings— on the occasional adjustments made to allow for structural or institutional changes in the economy, and on gradual improvement of the model itself. True *ex ante* predictions, *released publicly in advance of the period forecast,* are the best measures of how well we have been able to do.

The tabulation of economic forecasts made annually by the

Federal Reserve Bank of Philadelphia is a useful standard to which the forecasting record can be compared. In the fourth quarter of each year, the Bank collects and then tabulates over fifty forecasts of GNP and other principal economic variables for the coming year. These predictions, which are based on the whole spectrum of forecasting techniques, are made by leading business economists and forecasters. They provide a good idea of the degree of precision which can typically be achieved. In Table 1, we compare the control solutions [5] of the end-of-year forecasts of the Wharton model, the consensus of the Federal Reserve Bank of Philadelphia tabulation, the Council of Economic Advisers forecasts, and the actual *ex post* GNP data.[6] The forecasts made at the end of the year are probably the most important ones because of the preponderance of calendar year planning both by business and by government. They are also probably more accurate than forecasts made at other times of the year because at this time generally more is known than at mid-year about fiscal and monetary policy plans during the next four quarters (though this has not been the case for defense expenditures in recent years).

In comparison to both the Philadelphia Federal Reserve Bank consensus forecasts and the Council predictions, the Wharton-EFU forecasts have a definitely superior record. Admittedly five years is a short period on which to base a judgment, and there has not been a real economic downturn during this time. However, the error of the Wharton-EFU model forecasts for GNP has so far been quite small ($2.8 billion average absolute error), a much better performance than the consensus estimates. While there is no pretense that our record has been perfect, it should discredit any claims that an econometric model cannot be used to generate highly reliable *ex ante* forecasts.

Unfortunately, similar comparisons cannot be made for forecasts of GNP components nor for forecasts of particular quarters.

---

5. As stated earlier, we make several alternative forecasts each quarter. However, in all cases one forecast is clearly designated as the control solution. We have used these forecasts in the following comparisons.

6. Comparison is made with GNP data prior to revisions as appropriate, since later revisions in the data could not have been recognized by forecasters in the *ex ante* forecasts.

TABLE 1

COMPARISONS OF ANNUAL FORECASTS
(End-of-year annual predictions, billions of current dollars)

	Actual Old data *	Actual New data	Wharton-EFU forecasts Forecast	Wharton-EFU forecasts Error	Federal Reserve tabulation Average forecast	Federal Reserve tabulation High	Federal Reserve tabulation Low	Federal Reserve tabulation Error (of avg. forecast)	Council of Economic Advisers Forecast	Council of Economic Advisers Error
1963	584	591	585	+1	573	582	565	−11	578	−6
1964	623	632	625	+2	656	662	647	−10	660	−6
1965	666	684	662	−4	725	735	710	−7	722	−10
1966	732	743	728	−4	785	795	769	+4	787	+6
1967	781	n.a.	784	+3	616	630	607	−7	619	−4
Average absolute error				2.8				7.8		6.4

* Computed as value known in December plus actual change.

In practice, these predictions tend to be somewhat less accurate than the forecast for total GNP over the entire year because there is always some averaging of random error over GNP components and quarters.

Looking first at the GNP components predicted in the end-of-year annual forecasts as above, we compare the average actual annual changes with the average absolute prediction error for the major components of GNP (Table 2). This is a very rigorous

TABLE 2

PREDICTIVE RECORD OF THE WHARTON-EFU MODEL
FOR GNP COMPONENTS
(End-of-year annual predictions in billions of current $)

Component *	Absolute average actual change	Average absolute forecast error
Cns	21.9	0.7
Cd	4.2	2.1
Ip	5.1	1.8
Ih	0.9	1.1
ΔI_1	3.6	2.7
F	1.2	1.9
G	11.9	2.6
GNP	42.5	2.8

* Cns = consumption of non-durables and services
  Cd   = consumption of durables
  Ip   = plant and equipment investment
  Ih   = residential construction investment
  ΔI_1 = inventory investment
  F   = net foreign balance
  G   = government purchases of goods and services
  GNP = gross national product

test, since the magnitude of the forecast error relative to mean annual changes implicit in many forecasting procedures is not often recognized. The performance is, as expected, much better for some categories than for others. Prediction is best (and probably easiest) for consumer non-durables and services. The predictive performance for business investment is quite good and is superior to the results which are obtained from the McGraw-Hill and the OBE-SEC surveys. Considerable problems remain, particularly with inventory investment, which is notably difficult to forecast. Government expenditures are largely exogenous, and for much of this period, the net foreign balance was also largely exogenous to the model.

Quarterly predictions are important because quarterly movements in the economy often define cyclical fluctuation much more clearly than annual averages. Quarterly predictions are, however, more difficult than annual ones. In Table 3 we compare actual

TABLE 3

PREDICTIVE RECORD OF WHARTON-EFU MODEL
FOR QUARTERLY GNP FORECASTS
(Billions of current $)

Forecast	Average absolute actual change	Average absolute forecast error
One quarter ahead	10.8	2.3
Two quarters ahead	21.4	4.3
Three quarters ahead	32.1	5.6
Four quarters ahead	43.9	9.0
Average of Four quarters ahead	26.8	3.6

changes with the predictive error of the Wharton-EFU forecasts over the period of one to four quarters into the future. While the relative error is small in all cases, the error cumulates the further one projects into the future.[7]

It is important to note that much of the error of predictions for particular quarters consists of random variation in the quarterly forecasts, since considerably improved results are obtained when several quarters are averaged. The average for four quarters ahead shows a smaller error than for the second quarter into the future and one can frequently observe that the error for one quarter forward is partly offset by the error for the subsequent quarter. Nevertheless, the quarterly forecasts are valuable for showing cyclical tendencies of the economy or the points when capacity constraints are likely to be felt most strongly. Since there have been no overall turning points in the economy during the period covered, it is not possible to judge how accurately the model

7. Since the equations contain lagged endogenous values, prediction errors in one quarter affect the forecasts for subsequent quarters.

would predict recession and recovery in economic activity on an *ex ante* basis. However, *ex post* forecasts for the sample period reveal that the Wharton-EFU model does show downturns and upturns occurring in the correct quarter for all of the post-war recessions.

PROSPECTS

The Wharton-EFU experience suggests that econometric forecasting has come of age with the development of large flexible macro-models and advanced computer solution techniques. It is possible to make accurate econometric forecasts and to test out numerous alternative assumptions about anticipated exogenous developments and policies. The widespread and rapidly growing interest in our results is evidence of the fact that this work fills an important need in business and government.

The model used for forecasting at the Wharton School is not a static tool but undergoes constant revision and updating. More elaborate models improving the treatment of the monetary sector, price and wage determination, and inventory functions are already on the drawing board. Further likely developments include greater disaggregation of the predictions by major industrial sectors, and ties to econometric models of economic activity in other areas of the world through more elaborate international trade and financial flow equations. These are ambitious objectives and they will naturally take time to accomplish.

In the meantime the Wharton-EFU model continues to be applied regularly for forecasting. It is possible that other models currently available or under development, such as the Brookings model or the FRB-MIT model, will be used similarly. It is important to stress that good econometric forecasting cannot be mechanistic. It is true by definition that once the model has been estimated and the solution has been programmed, anyone can enter exogenous values into the "black box" and obtain a prediction. Yet this is the danger as well as the advantage of econometric forecasting techniques. The model must be used with caution and judgment. The Wharton-EFU experience suggests that in this way superior predictions can be obtained.

Economics and Business Planning

SIDNEY S. ALEXANDER

Sidney Alexander is Professor of Industrial Management at the Massachusetts Institute of Technology. This article is taken from his contribution to Economics and the Policy Maker, *published in 1959.*

While the most obvious task of the economist in the large corporation is short-run forecasting, his most valuable contribution, it seems to me, is in long-run planning. To some extent, this is a consequence of the greater amenability of long-run developments to economic forecasting techniques. While it is often quite hard to estimate whether the fourth quarter of next year will have a gross national product higher or lower than the fourth quarter of this year, it can quite reliably be estimated that the gross national product ten years from now will be some 35 percent higher than it was this year. More precisely, it can be estimated that the long-term trend value that economic historians will come to assign to 1969 will be some 35 percent greater than the long-term trend value they will come to assign to 1959.

The major contribution that an economic mode of thought in particular, or a scientific mode of thought in general, can make to the analysis of business problems, and those of government too, is the reduction of the problems to rational study, the transfer of as much as possible out of the field of the intuitively and implicitly appraised to that of the rationally and explicitly appraised.

The best consultants I know are uniform in their agreement that they contribute to their clients little more than applied common sense. But why can applied common sense be a contribution? Essentially because in attacking the problem the first task is to recognize the problem explicitly, and this is not habitually done by an active type. No discredit is implied here; the contemplative type is probably not very good at making and executing decisions. We should not be surprised that in this activity as in others, productivity can be increased by the division of labor, provided, as always, the extent of the market will support the division of labor. One man can profitably specialize in running a business and meeting its day-to-day problems and another in studying those factors that are likely to affect the business in the long run. Different skills and temperaments are suited to each of these activities.

Many of the critical decisions of long-run planning are once-in-a-decade decisions, some are once in a lifetime. It can hardly be expected that anyone could handle such problems on the basis of his own personal experience. There should be no wonder that this sort of analysis is a field for specialization. Those skills most important for the businessman—skills in negotiation, in execution, and in administration—are not usually associated with the sort of introspective analysis appropriate for the projection into an "as if" world of the future. But the economist is a specialist in the analysis of the "as if." As one Brookings author has stated, "Economic analysis is a substitute for the sixth sense of businessmen." The sixth sense probably does better in sensing the short-run situation, but not as well in sensing the long-run. Even when the businessman himself would be highly skilled at making such a study, the doctrine of comparative advantage suggests that it may be more advantageous to turn the study over to a specialist in analysis while the businessman concentrates on problems of administration and execution.

The characteristic long-run problem of the business enterprise is what business should it be in and on what scale. This is the principal content of business planning, and it centers on capital budgeting.

Long-range planning, or LRP, as it is frequently referred to, is now a big word in business. The devotees of LRP speak of its advantages much as the old line socialists spoke of society under socialism—when everything will be better. "Fuzzy management disappears when LRP is applied." "Crisis management becomes less pronounced." "Short-term dips assume less significance." "New markets are entered as soon as possible." "Money and men come easier." "Long-range planning . . . is a mark of industrial leadership by which good management is made more effective and good companies retain or attain recognition in their industry." These statements, taken out of their context of a discussion of long-range planning in a management journal, possibly give an oversimplified picture of the enthusiasm for long-range planning on the part of its advocates, but they do not exaggerate the intensity of that enthusiasm.

Clearly, planning can confer such benefits only if it is good planning. Most of the literature on planning in business is aimed at the form rather than the substance of planning. Implicit in this is the idea that even a poor plan is better than none at all, since the planning process is unlikely to result in a worse outcome than unplanned behavior. And there is probably some truth in this. Because the very act of planning does require explicit consideration of the relevant factors, it is less likely that an important consideration will be ignored. But most of the literature stops short of the substantive problem of how, in fact, the future is to be projected as the basic assumption for the long-range plans. That is the great opportunity for the economist.

The economist can make a valuable contribution to the solution of long-run business problems because his mode of thought, based on microeconomics and descriptive economics, is particularly attuned to the analysis of the long run, and because his role of outsider affords a broader perspective and leads to explicit examination of practices that would otherwise be taken for granted. Any scientifically trained person would share many of these characteristics, but the economist has the further advantage of familiarity with the class of problems encountered in business and with the data and the techniques of empirical research appropriate to this class of problems.

Part Six

Linear Programming

THE ESSAYS in Part Six provide an introduction to the nature, purpose, and usefulness of linear programming, one of the most important techniques of modern managerial economics. They do not go far into technical details, but concentrate on those aspects of linear programming which a general manager would find useful. Case studies of real-world applications of linear programming are emphasized.

In the opening article, Alexander Henderson and Robert Schlaifer describe how the H. J. Heinz Company used mathematical programming to determine the level of production in various plants as well as the pattern of shipments from plants to warehouses. George Dantzig, in the next article, discusses the basic concepts involved in linear programming and describes the sort of problems that this technique can handle. To be a linear programming model, Dantzig explains, a system must satisfy certain assumptions of proportionality, non-negativity, and additivity. In a classic expository paper, Robert Dorfman uses simple graphical techniques to describe the nature and application of mathematical programming.

The final article, by Garvin and his associates, describes in more detail how linear programming has been used to help solve specific problems in the oil industry. This article is somewhat more difficult than the others in this book, and is for readers with some familiarity with algebra.

Mathematical Programing

ALEXANDER HENDERSON AND
ROBERT SCHLAIFER

*Alexander Henderson was Professor of Eco-
nomics at the Graduate School of Industrial
Administration at Carnegie Institute of Technology. Robert Schlaifer is Professor of Business Administration at Harvard University.
This paper comes from the* Harvard Business
Review of *May 1954.*

In recent years mathematicians have worked out a number of
new procedures which make it possible for management to solve
a wide variety of important company problems much faster, more
easily, and more accurately than ever before. These procedures
have sometimes been called "linear programing." Actually, linear
programing describes only one group of them; "mathematical
programing" is a more suitable title.

Mathematical programing is not just an improved way of getting certain jobs done. It is in every sense a new way. It is new
in the sense that double-entry bookkeeping was new in the Middle
Ages, or that mechanization in the office was new earlier in this
century, or that automation in the plant is new today. Because
mathematical programing is still new, the gap between the scientist and the businessman—between the researcher and the user—
has not yet been bridged. Mathematical programing has made
the news, but few businessmen really understand how it can be of
use in their own companies.

Where to Ship · Let us look at a case where the technique was put to use as a routine operating procedure in an actual company.

The H. J. Heinz Company manufactures ketchup in half a dozen plants scattered across the United States from New Jersey to California and distributes this ketchup from about seventy warehouses located in all parts of the country.

In 1953 the company was in the fortunate position of being able to sell all it could produce, and supplies were allocated to warehouses in a total amount exactly equal to the total capacity of the plants. Management wished to supply these requirements at the lowest possible cost of freight; speed of shipment was not important. However, capacity in the West exceeded requirements in that part of the country, while the reverse was true in the East; for this reason a considerable tonnage had to be shipped from western plants to the East. In other words, the cost of freight could not be minimized by simply supplying each warehouse from the nearest plant.

This problem can immediately be recognized as a problem of programing because its essence is the minimization of cost subject to a fixed set of plant capacities and warehouse requirements. It can be handled by linear programing because the freight bill for shipments between any two points will be proportional to the quantity shipped. (The quantities involved are large enough so that virtually everything will move at carload rates under any shipping program which might be chosen.)

This is, in fact, the simplest possible kind of problem that can be solved by this method. Certain complexities which make solution by trial and error considerably more difficult than usual—in particular, the existence of water-competitive rates, which make it practical to send California ketchup all the way to the East Coast—add no real difficulty to the solution by linear programing. Given the list of plant capacities and warehouse requirements, plus a table of freight rates from every plant to every warehouse, one man with no equipment other than pencil and paper solved this problem for the first time in about twelve hours. After H. J. Heinz had adopted the method for regular use and clerks had been trained to become thoroughly familiar with the routine for this particular problem, the time required to develop a shipping program was considerably reduced.

The actual data of this problem have not been released by the company, but a fair representation of its magnitude is given by the similar but hypothetical examples of Exhibits 1 and 2, which show the data and solution of a problem of supplying twenty warehouses from twelve plants.

Exhibit 1 shows the basic data: the body of the table gives the freight rates, while the daily capacities of the plants and daily requirements of the warehouses are in the margins. For example, factory III, with a capacity of 3,000 cwt. per day, can supply warehouse *G*, with requirements of 940 cwt. per day, at a freight cost of seven cents per cwt.

Any reader who wishes to try his hand will quickly find that without a systematic procedure a great deal of work would be required to find a shipping program which would come reasonably close to satisfying these requirements and capacities at the lowest possible cost. But with the use of linear programing the problem is even easier than the Heinz problem.

Exhibit 2 gives the lowest-cost distribution program. For example, warehouse *K* is to get 700 cwt per day from factory I and 3,000 cwt. per day from factory III. On the other hand, factory III ships nothing to warehouse *A*, although Exhibit 1 shows that factory III could ship at less expense to this warehouse than to any other.

One of the most important advantages gained by the H. J. Heinz Company from the introduction of linear programing was relief of the senior members of the distribution department from the burden of preparing shipping programs. Previously the quarterly preparation of the program took a substantial amount of their time; now they pay only as much attention to this problem as they believe necessary to keep the feel of the situation, while the detailed development of the program has been handed over to clerks. Freed from the burden of working out what is after all only glorified arithmetic, they have this much more time to devote to matters which really require their experience and judgment.

An equally important gain, in the opinion of these officials themselves, is the peace of mind which results from being sure that the program is the lowest-cost program possible.

The direct dollars-and-cents saving in the company's freight bill was large enough by itself to make the use of this technique very

EXHIBIT 1

TABLE OF RATES, REQUIREMENTS, AND CAPACITIES

Factory	I	II	III	IV	V	VI	VII	VIII	IX	X	XI	XII	Daily requirements (cwt.)
					Freight rates (cents per cwt.)								
Warehouse A	16	16	6	13	24	13	6	31	37	34	37	40	1,820
B	20	18	8	10	22	11	8	29	33	25	35	38	1,530
C	30	23	8	9	14	7	9	22	29	20	38	35	2,360
D	10	15	10	8	10	15	13	19	19	15	28	34	100
E	31	23	16	10	10	16	20	14	17	17	25	28	280
F	24	14	19	13	13	14	18	9	14	13	29	25	730
G	27	23	7	11	23	8	16	6	10	11	16	28	940
H	34	25	15	4	27	15	11	9	16	17	13	16	1,130
J	38	29	17	11	16	27	17	19	8	18	19	11	4,150
K	42	43	21	22	16	10	21	18	24	16	17	15	3,700
L	44	49	25	23	18	6	13	19	15	12	10	13	2,560
M	49	40	29	21	10	15	14	21	12	29	14	20	1,710
N	56	58	36	37	6	25	8	19	9	21	15	26	580
P	59	57	44	33	5	21	6	10	8	33	15	18	30
Q	68	54	40	38	8	24	7	19	10	23	23	23	2,840
R	66	71	47	43	16	33	12	26	19	20	25	31	1,510
S	72	58	50	51	20	42	22	16	15	13	20	21	970
T	74	54	57	55	28	53	26	19	14	7	15	6	5,110
U	71	75	57	60	30	44	30	30	41	8	23	37	3,540
Y	73	72	63	56	37	49	40	31	31	10	8	25	4,410
Daily capacity (cwt.)	10,000	9,000	3,000	2,700	500	1,200	700	300	500	1,200	2,000	8,900	40,000

EXHIBIT 2
LOWEST-COST DISTRIBUTION PROGRAM
(DAILY SHIPMENTS FROM FACTORY TO WAREHOUSE IN CWT.)

Warehouse \ Factory	I	II	III	IV	V	VI	VII	VIII	IX	X	XI	XII	Total	Row value
A	1,820												1,820	16
B	1,530												1,530	20
C		2,360											2,360	28
D	100												100	10
E		280											280	28
F		730											730	19
G	940												940	27
H				1,130									1,130	28
J		4,150											4,150	34
K	700		3,000										3,700	42
L	1,360					1,200							2,560	44
M		140		1,570									1,710	45
N	580												580	56
P								30					30	51
Q		1,340			500				500			500	2,840	59
R	810						700						1,510	66
S								90				880	970	57
T												5,110	5,110	42
U	2,160							180		1,200			3,540	71
Y											2,000	2,410	4,410	61
Total	10,000	9,000	3,000	2,700	500	1,200	700	300	500	1,200	2,000	8,900	40,000	
Column value	0	−5	−21	−24	−51	−38	−54	−41	−49	−63	−53	−36		

much worth while. The first shipping program produced by linear programing gave a projected semiannual freight cost several thousand dollars less than did a program prepared by the company's previous methods, and this comparison is far from giving a full measure of the actual freight savings to be anticipated.

Shipping schedules rest on estimates which are continuously subject to revision. The capacity figures in part represent actual stocks on hand at the plants, but in part they are based on estimates of future tomato crops; and the figures for requirements depend almost wholly on estimates of future sales. The fact that schedules are now quickly and accurately prepared by clerks has enabled the company to reschedule monthly rather than quarterly, thus making much better use of new information on crops and sales as it becomes available.

Furthermore, the risk of backhauling is very much reduced under the new system. It had always been company practice early in the season to hold "reserves" in regions of surplus production, in order to avoid the danger of shipping so much out of these regions that it became necessary to ship back into them when production and sales estimates were revised. In fact, these reserves were largely accidental leftovers: when it became really difficult to assign the last part of a factory's production, this remainder was called the reserve. Now the company can look at past history and decide in advance what reserve should be held at each factory and can set up its program to suit this estimate exactly. Since the schedule is revised each month, these reserves can be altered in the light of current information until they are finally reduced to nothing just before the new pack starts at the factory in question.

Many important problems of this same character unquestionably are prevalent in business. One such case, for instance, would be that of a newsprint producer who supplies about 220 customers all over the United States from six factories scattered over the width of Canada.

Similar problems arise where the cost of transportation is measured in time rather than in money. In fact, the first efforts to solve problems of this sort systematically were made during World War II in order to minimize the time spent by ships in ballast. Specified cargo had to be moved from specified origins to specified destinations; there was usually no return cargo, and the problem was to decide to which port the ship should be sent in ballast to pick up its next cargo. An obviously similar problem is the routing of empty freight cars, and a trucker operating on a nationwide scale might face the same problem with empty trucks.

Where to Produce · When ketchup shipments were programed for the H. J. Heinz Company, factory capacities and warehouse requirements were fixed before the shipping program was worked out, and the only cost which could be reduced by programing was the cost of freight. Since management had decided in advance how much to produce at each plant, all production costs were "fixed" so far as the programing problem was concerned.

The same company faces a different problem in connection with another product, which is also produced in a number of plants and shipped to a number of warehouses. In this case, the capacity of the plants exceeds the requirements of the warehouses. The cost of production varies from one plant to another, and the problem is thus one of satisfying the requirements at the least *total* cost. It is as important to reduce the cost of production (by producing in the right place) as it is to reduce the cost of freight (by supplying from the right place). In other words, management must now decide two questions instead of one: (*a*) How much is each factory to produce? (*b*) Which warehouses should be supplied by which factories?

It is tempting to try to solve these two problems one at a time and thus simplify the job, but in general it will not be possible to get the lowest total cost by first deciding where to produce and then deciding where to ship. It is obviously better to produce in a high-cost plant if the additional cost can be more than recovered through savings in freight.

This double problem can be handled by linear programing if we may assume (as businessmen usually do) that the cost of production at any one plant is the sum of a "fixed" cost independent of volume and a "variable" cost proportional to volume in total but fixed per unit, and if these costs are known. The variable cost is handled directly by the linear programing procedure, while the fixed part is handled by a method which will be explained later.

Actually, the problem can be much more complicated and still lend itself to solution by linear programing. For example, we can bring in the possibility of using overtime, or of buying raw materials at one price up to a certain quantity and at another price beyond that quantity.

Exhibit 3 shows the cost information needed to solve a hypothetical example of this sort. It is assumed that there are only four plants and four warehouses, but any number could be brought into the problem.

In our first approximation (which we shall modify later) we shall assume that no plant will be closed down entirely and, therefore, that "fixed costs" are really fixed and can be left out of the picture. Like Exhibit 1, Exhibit 3 shows the freight rates from each plant to each warehouse, the available daily capacity at each plant, and the daily requirements of each warehouse; it also shows the "variable" (fixed-per-unit) cost of normal production at each plant and the additional per-unit cost of overtime production. The total capacity is greater than the total requirements even if the factories work only normal time.

EXHIBIT 3

Cost Information for Double Problem

A. *Warehouse requirements (tons per day)*

Warehouse	A	B	C	D	Total
Requirements	90	140	75	100	405

B. *Factory capacities (tons per day)*

Factory	I	II	III	IV	Total
Normal capacity	70	130	180	110	490
Additional capacity on overtime	25	40	60	30	155

C. *Variable costs (per ton)*

Factory	I	II	III	IV
Normal production cost	$30	$36	$24	$30
Overtime premium	15	18	12	15
Freight rates to:				
Warehouse A	$14	$ 9	$21	$18
B	20	14	27	24
C	18	12	29	20
D	19	15	27	23

On the basis of these data, the lowest-cost solution is given by part *A* of Exhibit 4. It is scarcely surprising that this solution calls for no use of overtime. So long as fixed costs are taken as really fixed, it turns out that it is best to use the entire normal capacity of factories I, II, and III, and to use 25 tons of factory IV's normal capacity of 110 tons per day. The remaining 85 tons of normal capacity at IV are left unused. The total variable cost under this schedule (freight cost plus variable production cost) will be $19,720 per day.

Presented with this result, management would certainly ask whether it is sensible to keep all four factories open when one of

EXHIBIT 4

LOWEST-COST DISTRIBUTION PROGRAM
(DAILY SHIPMENTS IN TONS FROM FACTORY TO WAREHOUSE)

A. With all four factories open

Factory	I	II	III	IV	Total
Warehouse A			90		90
B		80	60		140
C		50		25	75
D	70		30		100
Idle normal capacity				85	85
Total	70	130	180	110	490

B. With factory I closed

Factory		II	III	IV	Total
Warehouse A			90		90
B		130	10		140
C				75	75
D			80	20	100
Idle normal capacity				15	15
Total		130	180	110	420

C. With factory IV closed

Factory	I	II	III		Total
Warehouse A			90		90
B		55	85		140
C		75			75
D	70		30		100
Total	70	130	205		405

them is being left about 80 per cent idle. Even without incurring overtime, factory I, the smallest plant, could be closed and the load redistributed among the other plants. If this is done, the lowest-cost distribution of the requirements among factories II, III, and IV is that given by part *B* of Exhibit 4. Under this program the total variable cost would be $19,950 per day, or $230 per day more than under the program of Exhibit 4A, which depended on the use of all four plants. If more than $230 per day of fixed costs can be saved by closing down factory I completely, it will pay to do so; otherwise it will not.

It might be still better, however, to close down some plant other than factory I even at the cost of a certain amount of overtime. In particular, a very little overtime production (25 tons per day) would make it possible to close factory IV. A person asked to look into this possibility might reason as follows: Under the shipping schedule of Exhibit 4A, the only use of factory IV's capacity is to supply 25 tons per day to warehouse *C*. Looking at Exhibit 3 for a replacement for this supply, he would get the following information on costs per ton:

Factory	Normal cost of production	Overtime premium	Freight to warehouse C	Total
I	$30	$15	$18	$63
II	36	18	12	66
III	24	12	29	65

Apparently the cheapest way of using overtime, if it is to be used at all, would be to produce the needed 25 tons per day at factory I and ship them to warehouse *C* at a total variable cost of $63 per ton. Under the program of Exhibit 4A, with all plants in use, warehouse *C* was supplied from factory IV at a total variable cost of $30 for production plus $20 for freight, or a total of $50 per ton. The change would thus seem to add a total of $325 per day (25 tons times $13 per ton which is the difference between $63 and $50 per ton).

But, in fact, closing factory IV need not add this much to the cost of the program. If we take factory IV out of the picture and then program to find the best possible distribution of the output of the remaining plants, we discover that the program of part *C* of Exhibit 4 satisfies all requirements at a total variable cost of $19,-

995 per day, or only $275 per day more than with all plants in use. The overtime is performed by factory III, which does not supply warehouse C at all.

This last result deserves the reader's attention. *Once a change was made in a single part of the program, the best adjustment was a general readjustment of the entire program.* But such a general readjustment is impractical unless complete programs can be developed quickly and at a reasonable cost. It is rarely clear in advance whether the work will prove profitable, and management does not want to throw a heavy burden of recalculation on senior personnel every time a minor change is made. Mathematical programing avoids these difficulties. Even minor changes in the data can be made freely despite the fact that complete recalculations of the program are required, because the work can be done quickly and accurately by clerks or machines.

We can proceed to compute the lowest possible cost of supplying the requirements with factory II or factory III closed down completely. We can then summarize the results for all alternatives like this:

Total freight plus variable production cost

All four factories in use	$19,720
Factory I closed, no overtime	19,950
Factory II closed, overtime at factory III	20,515
Factory III closed, overtime at factories I, II, and IV	21,445
Factory IV closed, overtime at factory III	19,995

Management now has the information on variable costs which it needs in order to choose rationally among three alternatives: (1) operating all four plants with a large amount of idle normal capacity; (2) shutting down factory I and still having a little idle normal capacity; (3) shutting down factory II, III, or IV and incurring overtime. Its choice will depend in part on the extent to which fixed costs can be eliminated when a particular plant is completely closed; it may depend even more on company policies regarding community relations or some other nonfinancial consideration. Mathematical programing cannot replace judgment, but it can supply some of the factual information which management needs in order to make judgments.

Problems of this general type are met in purchasing as well as in producing and selling. A company which buys a standard raw material at many different geographical locations and ships it to a number of scattered plants for processing will wish to minimize the total cost of purchase plus freight; here the solution can be obtained in exactly the same way as just discussed. The Department of Defense is reported to have made substantial savings by using linear programing to decide where to buy and where to send certain standard articles which it obtains from a large number of suppliers for direct shipment to military installations.

Linear Programming:
Examples and Concepts

GEORGE DANTZIG

George Dantzig is head of the Operations
Research Center at the University of California, Berkeley. This article comes from his
book, Linear Programming and Extensions,
published in 1963.

THE PROGRAMMING PROBLEM

Industrial production, the flow of resources in the economy, the
exertion of military effort in a war theater—all are complexes of
numerous interrelated activities. Differences may exist in the
goals to be achieved, the particular processes involved, and the
magnitude of effort. Nevertheless, it is possible to abstract the
underlying essential similarities in the management of these seemingly disparate systems. To do this entails a look at the structure
and state of the system, and at the objective to be fulfilled, in
order to *construct a statement of the actions to be performed, their
timing, and their quantity (called a "program" or "schedule"),
which will permit the system to move from a given status toward
the defined objective.*

If the system exhibits a structure which can be represented by a
mathematical equivalent, called a mathematical model, and if the
objective can also be so quantified, then some computational
method may be evolved for choosing the best schedule of actions

among alternatives. Such use of mathematical models is termed mathematical programming. The observation that a number of military, economic, and industrial problems can be expressed (or reasonably approximated) by mathematical systems of linear inequalities and equations[1] has helped give rise to the development of linear programming.

The following three examples are typical programming problems which can be formulated linearly; they are analogous to the ones which originated research in this area. It is well to have them in mind before we discuss the general characteristics of linear programming problems.

The objective of the system in each of the three examples to be considered happens to be the minimization of total costs measured in monetary units. In other applications, however, it could be to minimize direct labor costs or to maximize the number of assembled parts or to maximize the number of trained students with a specified percentage distribution of skills, etc.

1. *A cannery example.* Suppose that the three canneries of a distributor are located in Portland (Maine), Seattle, and San Diego. The canneries can fill 250, 500, and 750 cases of tins per day, respectively. The distributor operates five warehouses around the country, in New York, Chicago, Kansas City, Dallas, and San Francisco. Each of the warehouses can sell 300 cases per day. The distributor wishes to determine the number of cases to be shipped from the three canneries to the five warehouses so that each warehouse should obtain as many cases as it can sell daily at the minimum total transportation cost.

The problem is characterized by the fifteen possible *activities* of shipping cases from each of the canneries to each of the warehouses (Fig. 1). There are fifteen *unknown activity levels* (to be determined) which are the *amounts* to be shipped along the fifteen routes. This *shipping schedule* is generally referred to as the *program.* There are a number of constraints that a shipping schedule must satisfy to be feasible: namely, the schedule must

---

1. The reader should especially note we have used the word *inequalities.* Systems of linear inequalities are quite general; linear inequality relations such as $x \geq 0$, $x + y \leq 7$ can be used to express a variety of common restrictions, such as quantities purchased, x, must not be negative or the total amount of purchases, $x + y$, must not exceed 7, etc.

FIGURE 1

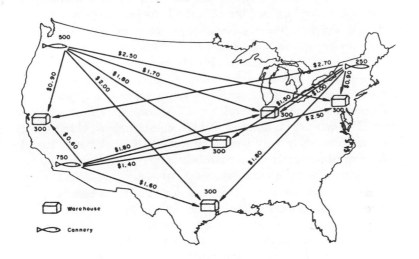

The problem: find a least cost plan of shipping from canneries to warehouses (the costs per case, availabilities and requirements are as indicated).

show that each warehouse will receive the required number of cases and that no cannery will ship more cases than it can produce daily. (Note there is one constraint for each warehouse and one for each cannery.) Several *feasible shipping schedules* may exist which would satisfy these constraints, but some will involve larger shipping costs than others. The problem then is to determine an *optimal shipping schedule*—one that has least costs.

2. *The housewife's problem.* A family of five lives on the modest salary of the head of the household. A constant problem is to determine the weekly menu after due consideration of the needs and tastes of the family and the prices of foods. The husband must have 3,000 calories per day, the wife is on a 1,500-calorie reducing diet, and the children require 3,000, 2,700, and 2,500 calories per day, respectively. According to the prescription of the family doctor, these calories must be obtained for each member by eating not more than a certain amount of fats and carbohydrates and not less than a certain amount of proteins. The diet, in fact, places emphasis on proteins. In addition, each member of

the household must satisfy his or her daily vitamin needs. The problem is to assemble menus, one for each week, that will minimize costs according to Thursday food prices.

This is a typical linear programming problem: the possible activities are the purchasing of foods of different types; the program is the amounts of different foods to be purchased; the constraints on the problem are the calorie and vitamin requirements of the household, and the upper or lower limits set by the physician on the amounts of carbohydrates, proteins, and fats to be consumed by each person. The number of food combinations which satisfy these constraints is very large. However, some of these feasible programs have higher costs than others. The problem is to find a combination that minimizes the total expense.

3. *On-the-job training.* A manufacturing plant is contracting to make some commodity. Its present work force is considerably smaller than the one needed to produce the commodity within a specified schedule of different amounts to be delivered each week for several weeks hence. Additional workers must, therefore, be hired, trained, and put to work. The present force can either work and produce at some rate of output, or it can train some fixed number of new workers, or it can do both at the same time according to some fixed rate of exchange between output and the number of new workers trained. Even were the crew to spend one entire week training new workers, it would be unable to train the required number. The next week, the old crew *and* the newly trained workers may either work or train new workers, or may both work and train, and so on. The commodity is semi-perishable so that amounts produced before they are needed will have to be stored at a specified cost. The problem is to determine the hiring, production, and storage program that will minimize total costs.

This, too, is a linear programming problem, although with the special property, not shared with the previous two examples, of *scheduling activities through time.* The activities in this problem are the assignment of old workers to either of two jobs, production or training, and the hiring of new workers each week. The quantities of these activities are restricted by the number of workers available at the beginning of each week and by the instructor-student ratio. The cumulative output produced by all workers through the number of weeks in the contractual period has to equal or exceed the required output. A possible production-training program is shown in Fig. 2. The problem can now be stated

FIGURE 2

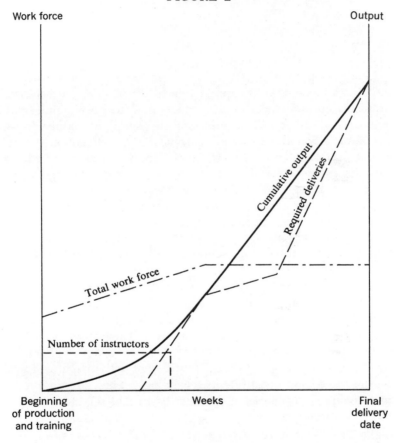

The problem: determine a least-cost hiring, production and storage program to meet required deliveries.

more precisely: determine the proper balance between hiring and training of workers, between teaching and production, and between over- and under-production in order to minimize total costs.

LINEAR PROGRAMMING DEFINED

We shall use the term *model building* to express the process of putting together of symbols representing objects according to certain rules, to form a structure, *the model,* which corresponds to a system under study in the real world. The symbols may be small-scale replicas of bricks and girders or they may be, as in our application, algebraic symbols.

Linear programming has a certain philosophy or approach to building a model that has application to a broad class of decision problems encountered in government, industry, economics, and engineering. It probably possesses the simplest mathematical structure which can be used to solve the practical scheduling problems associated with these areas. Because it is a method for studying the behavior of systems, it exemplifies the distinguishing feature of management science, or operations research, to wit: "Operations are considered as an entity. The subject matter studied is not the equipment used, nor the morale of the participants, nor the physical properties of the output, it is the combination of these in total as an economic process." (Cyril Herrmann and John Magee, 1953).

Linear programming[2] is concerned with describing the interrelations of the components of a system. As we shall see, the first step consists in regarding a system under design as composed of a number of elementary functions that are called "activities."[3] As a consequence, T. C. Koopmans introduced the term *activity analysis* to describe this approach. The different activities in which a system can engage constitute its technology. These are the representative building blocks of different types that might be recombined in varying amounts to rear a structure that is self-supporting, satisfies certain restrictions, and attains as well as possible a stated objective. Representing this structure in mathematical terms often results in a system of linear inequalities and equations; when this is so, it is called a linear programming model. Like

2. The term "linear programming" was suggested to the author by T. C. Koopmans in 1951 as an alternative to the earlier form, "programming in a linear structure."

3. The term "activity" in this connection is military in origin. It has been adopted in preference to the term "process," used by von Neumann in "A Model of General Economic Equilibrium."

architects, people who use linear programming models manipulate "on paper" the symbolic representations of the building blocks (activities) until a satisfactory design is obtained. The theory of linear programming is concerned with scientific procedures for arriving at the best design, given the technology, the required specifications, and the stated objective.

To be a linear programming model, the system must satisfy certain assumptions of proportionality, nonnegativity, and additivity. How this comes about will be discussed below. It is important to realize in trying to construct models of real-life situations, that life seldom, if ever, presents a clearly defined linear programming problem, and that simplification and neglect of certain characteristics of reality are as necessary in the application of linear programming as they are in the use of any scientific tool in problem solving.

The rule is to *neglect the negligible.* In the cannery example, for instance, the number of cases shipped and the number received may well differ because of accidental shipping losses. This difference is not known in advance and may be unimportant. In the optimum diet example the true nutritional value of each type of food differs from unit to unit, from season to season, from one source of food to another. Likewise, production rates and teaching quality will vary from one worker to another and from one hour to another. In some applications it may be necessary to give considerable thought to the differences between reality and its representation as a mathematical model to be sure that the differences are reasonably small and to assure ourselves that the computational results will be operationally useful.

What constitutes the proper simplification, however, is subject to individual judgment and experience. People often disagree on the adequacy of a certain model to describe the situation.

BASIC CONCEPTS

Suppose that the system under study (which may be one actually in existence, or one which we wish to design) is a complex of machines, people, facilities, and supplies. It has certain over-all reasons for its existence. For the military it may be to provide a striking force, or for industry it may be to produce certain types of products.

The linear programming approach is to consider a system as decomposable into a number of elementary functions, the *activities*. An activity is thought of as a kind of "black box"[4] into which flow tangible inputs, such as men, material, and equipment, and out of which may flow the products of manufacture, or the trained crews of the military. What happens to the inputs inside the "box" is the concern of the engineer or of the educator; to the programmer, only the rates of flow into and out of the activity are of interest. The various kinds of flow are called *items*.

The quantity of each activity is called the *activity level*. To change the activity level it is necessary to change the flows into and out of the activity.

Assumption 1: Proportionality · In the linear programming model the quantities of flow of various items into and out of the activity are always proportional to the activity level. If we wish to double the activity level, we simply double all the corresponding flows for the unit activity level. For instance, in Example 3, if we wish to double the number of workers trained in a period, we would have to double the number of instructors for that period and the number of workers hired. This characteristic of the linear programming model is known as the proportionality assumption.

Assumption 2: Nonnegativity · While any positive multiple of an activity is possible, negative quantities of activities are not possible. For instance, in Example 1, a negative number of cases cannot be shipped. Another example occurs in a well-known classic: the Mad Hatter, you may recall, in *Alice's Adventures in Wonderland*, was urging Alice to have some more tea, and Alice was objecting that she couldn't see how she could take more when she hadn't had any. "You mean, you don't see how you can take *less* tea," said the Hatter, "it is very easy to take more than nothing." Lewis Carroll's point was probably lost on his pre-linear-programming audience, for why should one emphasize the obvious fact that the activity of "taking tea" cannot be done in negative quantity? Perhaps it was Carroll's way of saying that mathemati-

4. Black box: Any system whose detailed internal nature one willfully ignores.

cians had been so busy for centuries extending the number system from integers, to fractions, to negative, to imaginary numbers, that they had given little thought on how to keep the variables of their problems in their original nonnegative range. This characteristic of the variables of the linear programming model is known as the nonnegativity assumption.

Assumption 3: Additivity · The next step in building a model is to specify that the system of activities be complete in the sense that a complete accounting by activity can be made of each item. To be precise, for each item it is required that the total amount specified by the system as a whole equals the sum of the amounts flowing into the various activities minus the sum of the amounts flowing out. Thus, each item, in our abstract system, is characterized by a *material balance equation*, the various terms of which represent the flows into or out of the various activities. In the cannery example, the number of cases sent into a warehouse must be completely accounted for by the amounts flowing out of the shipping activities from various canneries including possible storage or disposal of any excess. This characteristic of the linear programming model is known as the additivity assumption.

Assumption 4: Linear Objective Function · One of the items in our system is regarded as "precious" in the sense that the total quantity of it produced by the system measures the payoff. The precious item could be skilled labor, completed assemblies, an input resource that is in scarce supply like a limited monetary budget. The contribution of each activity to the total payoff is the amount of the precious item that flows into or out of each activity. Thus, if the objective is to maximize profits, activities that require money contribute negatively and those that produce money contribute positively to total profits. The housewife's expenditures for each type of food, in Example 2, is a negative contribution to total "profits" of the household; there are no activities in this example that contribute positively. This characteristic of the linear programming model is known as the linear objective assumption.

The Standard Linear Programming Problem · The determination of values for the *levels* of activities, which are positive or zero, such that flows of each item (for these activity levels) satisfy the material balance equations and such that the value of the payoff is a maximum is called the standard linear programming problem. The representation of a real system, as in any one of the three examples above, as a mathematical system which exhibits the above characteristics, is called a linear programming model. The problem of programming the activities of the real system is thus transformed into the problem of finding the solution of the linear programming model.

Mathematical, or "Linear," Programming: A Non-mathematical Exposition

Robert Dorfman

Robert Dorfman is Professor of Economics at Harvard University. This well-known expository article appeared in the American Economic Review in 1953.

This paper is intended to set forth the leading ideas of mathematical programming [1] purged of the algebraic apparatus which has impeded their general acceptance and appreciation. This will be done by concentrating on the graphical representation of the method. While it is not possible, in general, to portray mathematical programming problems in two dimensional graphs, the conclusions which we shall draw from the graphs will be of general validity and, of course, the graphic representation of

1. The terminology of the techniques which we are discussing is in an unsatisfactory state. Most frequently they are called "linear programming" although the relationships involved are not always linear. Sometimes they are called "activities analysis," but this is not a very suggestive name. The distinguishing feature of the techniques is that they are concerned with programming rather than with analysis, and, at any rate, "activities analysis" has not caught on. We now try out "mathematical programming"; perhaps it will suit.

multidimensional problems has a time-honored place in economics.

The central formal problem of economics is the problem of allocating scarce resources so as to maximize the attainment of some predetermined objective. The standard formulation of this problem—the so-called marginal analysis—has led to conclusions of great importance for the understanding of many questions of social and economic policy. But it is a fact of common knowledge that this mode of analysis has not recommended itself to men of affairs for the practical solution of their economic and business problems. Mathematical programming is based on a restatement of this same formal problem in a form which is designed to be useful in making practical decisions in business and economic affairs. That mathematical programming is nothing but a reformulation of the standard economic problem and its solution is the main thesis of this exposition.

The motivating idea of mathematical programming is the idea of a "process" or "activity." A process is a specific method for performing an economic task. For example, the manufacture of soap by a specified formula is a process. So also is the weaving of a specific quality of cotton gray goods on a specific type of loom. The conventional production function can be thought of as the formula relating the inputs and outputs of all the processes by which a given task can be accomplished.

For some tasks, e.g., soap production, there are an infinite number of processes available. For others, e.g., weaving, only a finite number of processes exist. In some cases, a plant or industry may have only a single process available.

In terms of processes, choice in the productive sphere are simply decisions as to which processes are to be used and the extent to which each is to be employed. Economists are accustomed to thinking in terms of decisions as to the quantities of various productive factors to be employed. But an industry or firm cannot substitute factor A for factor B unless it does some of its work in a different way, that is, unless its substitutes a process which uses A in relatively high proportions for one which uses B. Inputs, therefore, cannot be changed without a change in the way of doing things, and often a fundamental change. Mathematical programming focuses on this aspect of economic choice.

The objective of mathematical programming is to determine the optimal levels of productive processes in given circumstances. This requires a restatement of productive relationships in terms of processes and a reconsideration of the effect of factor scarcities on production choices. As a prelude to this theoretical discussion, however, it will be helpful to consider a simplified production problem from a commonsense point of view.

I. AN EXAMPLE OF MATHEMATICAL PROGRAMMING

Let us consider a hypothetical automobile company equipped for the production of both automobiles and trucks. This company, then, can perform two economic tasks, and we assume that it has a single process for accomplishing each. These two tasks, the manufacture of automobiles and that of trucks, compete for the use of the firm's facilities. Let us assume that the company's plant is organized into four departments: (1) sheet metal stamping, (2) engine assembly, (3) automobile final assembly, and (4) truck final assembly—raw materials, labor, and all other components being available in virtually unlimited amounts at constant prices in the open market.

The capacity of each department of the plant is, of course, limited. We assume that the metal stamping department can turn out sufficient stampings for 25,000 automobiles or 35,000 trucks per month. We can then calculate the combinations of automobile and truck stampings which this department can produce. Since the department can accommodate 25,000 automobiles per month, each automobile requires 1/25,000 or 0.004 percent of monthly capacity. Similarly each truck requires 0.00286 percent of monthly capacity. If, for example, 15,000 automobiles were manufactured, they would require 60 percent of metal stamping capacity and the remaining 40 percent would be sufficient to produce stampings for 14,000 trucks. Then 15,000 automobiles and 14,000 trucks could be produced by this department at full operation. This is, of course, not the only combination of automobiles and trucks which could be produced by the stamping department at full operation. In Figure 1, the line labeled "Metal Stamping" represents all such combinations.

Similarly we assume that the engine assembly department has monthly capacity for 33,333 automobile engines or 16,667 truck engines or, again, some combination of fewer automobile and truck engines. The combinations which would absorb the full capacity of the engine assembly department are shown by the "Engine Assembly" line in Figure 1. We assume also that the automobile assembly department can accommodate 22,500 automobiles per month and the truck assembly department 15,000 trucks. These limitations are also represented in Figure 1.

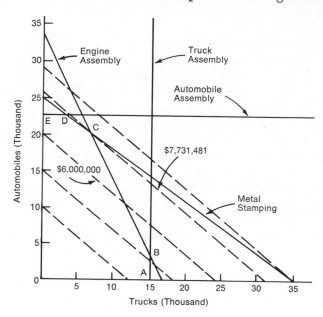

FIGURE 1

CHOICES OPEN TO AN AUTOMOBILE FIRM

We regard this set of assumptions as defining two processes: the production of automobiles and the production of trucks. The process of producing an automobile yields, as an output, one automobile and absorbs, as inputs, 0.004 percent of metal stamping capacity, 0.003 percent of engine assembly capacity, and 0.00444 percent of automobile assembly capacity. Similarly the process of producing a truck yields, as an output, one truck and absorbs, as inputs, 0.00286 percent of metal stamping capacity, 0.006 percent of engine assembly capacity, and 0.00667 percent of truck assembly capacity.

The economic choice facing this firm is the selection of the numbers of automobiles and trucks to be produced each month, subject to the restriction that no more than 100 percent of the capacity of any department can be used. Or, in more technical phraseology, the choice consists in deciding at what level to employ each of the two available processes. Clearly, if automobiles alone are produced, at most 22,500 units per month can be made, automobile assembly being the effective limitation. If only trucks are produced, a maximum of 15,000 units per month can be made because of the limitation on truck assembly. Which of these alternatives should be adopted, or whether some combination of trucks and automobiles should be produced, depends on the relative profitability of manufacturing trucks and automobiles. Let us assume, to be concrete, that the sales value of an automobile is $300 greater than the total cost of purchased materials, labor, and other direct costs attributable to its manufacture. And, similarly, that the sale value of a truck is $250 more than the direct cost of manufacturing it. Then the net revenue of the plant for any month is 300 times the number of automobiles produced plus 250 times the number of trucks. For example, 15,000 automobiles and 6,000 trucks would yield a net revenue of $5,000,000. There are many combinations of automobiles and trucks which would yield this same net revenue; 10,000 automobiles and 12,000 trucks is another one. In terms of Figure 1, all combinations with a net revenue of $6,000,000 lie on a straight line, to be specific, the line labeled $6,000,000 in the figure.

A line analogous to the one which we have just described corresponds to each possible net revenue. All these lines are parallel, since their slope depends only on the relative profitability of the two activities. The greater the net revenue, of course, the higher the line. A few of the net revenue lines are shown in the figure by the dashed parallel lines.

Each conceivable number of automobiles and trucks produced corresponds to a point on the diagram, and through each point there passes one member of the family of net revenue lines. Net revenue is maximized when the point corresponding to the number of automobiles and trucks produced lies on the highest possible net revenue line. Now the effect of the capacity restrictions is to limit the range of choice to outputs which correspond to points lying inside the area bounded by the axes and by the broken line *ABCDE*. Since net revenue increases as points move out from the origin, only points which lie on the broken line need be considered. Beginning with point *A* and moving along the broken line we see that the boundary of the accessible region intersects higher and higher net revenue lines until point *C* is reached. From there on, the boundary slides down the scale of net revenue lines. Point *C* therefore corresponds to the highest attainable net revenue. At point *C* the output is 20,370 automobiles and 6,481 trucks, yielding a net revenue of $7,731,481 per month.

The reader has very likely noticed that this diagram is by no means novel. The broken line *ABCDE* tells that maximum number of automobiles which can be produced in conjunction with any given number of trucks. It is therefore, apart from its angularity, a production opportunity curve or transformation curve of the sort made familiar by Irving Fisher, and the slope of the curve at any point where it has a slope is the ratio of substitution in production between automobiles and trucks. The novel feature is that the production opportunity curve shown here has no defined slope at five points and that one of these five is the critical point. The dashed lines in the diagram are equivalent to conventional price lines.

The standard theory of production teaches that profits are maximixed at a point where a price line is tangent to the production opportunity curve. But, as we have just noted, there are five points where our production opportunity curve has no tangent. The tangency criterion therefore fails. Instead we find that profits are maximized at a corner where the slope of the price line is neither less than the slope of the opportunity curve to the left of the corner nor greater than the slope of the opportunity curve to the right.

Diagrammatically, then, mathematical programming uses angles where standard economics uses curves. In economic terms, where does the novelty lie? In standard economic analysis we visualize production relationships in which, if there are two products, one may be substituted for the other with gradually increasing difficulty. In mathematical programming we visualize a regime of production in which, for any output, certain factors will be effectively limiting but other factors will be in ample supply. Thus, in Figure 1, the factors which effectively limit production at each point can be identified by noticing on which limitation lines the point lies. The rate of substitution between products is determined by the limiting factors alone and changes only when the designation of the limiting factors changes. In the diagram a change in the designation of the limiting factors is represented by turning a corner on the production opportunity curve.

We shall come back to this example later, for we have not exhausted its significance. But now we are in a position to develop with more generality some of the concepts used in mathematical programming.

II. THE MODEL OF PRODUCTION IN
MATHEMATICAL PROGRAMMING

A classical problem in economics is the optimal utilization of two factors of production, conveniently called capital and labor. In the usual analysis, the problem is formulated by conceiving of the two factors as cooperating with each other in accordance with a production function which states the maximum quantity of a product which can be obtained by the use of stated quantities of the two factors. One convenient means of representing such a production function is an "isoquant diagram," as in Figure 2. In this familiar figure, quantities of labor are plotted along the horizontal axis and quantities of capital along the vertical. Each of the arcs in the body of the diagram corresponds to a definite quantity of output, higher arcs corresponding to greater quantities.

If the prices per unit of capital and labor are known, the combinations of labor and capital which can be purchased for a fixed total expenditure can be shown by a sloping straight line like CC' in the figure, the slope depending only on the relative prices. Two interpretations follow immediately. First, the minimum unit cost of producing the output represented by any isoquant can be achieved by using the combination of labor and capital which corresponds to the point where that isoquant is tangent to a price line. Second, the greatest output attainable

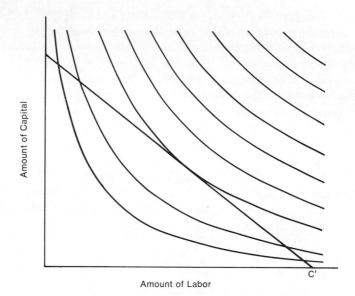

FIGURE 2

An Isoquant Diagram

with any given expenditure is represented by the isoquant which is tangent to the price line corresponding to that expenditure.

This diagram and its analysis rest upon the assumption that the two factors are continuously substitutable for each other in such wise that if the amount of labor employed be reduced by a small amount it will be possible to maintain the quantity of output by a *small* increase in the amount of capital employed. Moreover, this analysis assumes that each successive unit decrement in the amount of labor will require a slightly larger increment in the amount of capital if output is to remain constant. Otherwise the isoquants will not have the necessary shape.

All this is familiar. We call it to mind only because we are about to develop an analogous diagram which is fundamental to mathematical programming. First, however, let us see why a new diagram and a new approach are felt to be necessary.

The model of production which we have just briefly sketched very likely is valid for some kinds of production. But for most manufacturing industries, and indeed all production where elaborate machinery is used, it is open to serious objection. It is characteristic of most modern machinery that each kind of machine operates efficiently only over a narrow range of speeds and that the quantities of labor, power, materials, and other factors which cooperate with the machine are dictated rather inflexibly by the machine's built-in characteristics. Furthermore, at any time there is available only a small number of different kinds of machinery for accomplishing a given task. A few examples may make these considerations more concrete. Earth may be moved by hand shovels, by steam or diesel shovels, or by bulldozers. Power shovels and bulldozers are built in only a small variety of models, each with inherent characteristics as to fuel consumption per hour, number of operators and assistants required, cubic feet of earth moved per hour, etc. Printing type may be set by using hand-fonts, linotype machines, or monotype machines. Again, each machine is available in only a few models and each has its own pace of operation, power and space requirements, and other essentially unalterable characteristics. A moment's reflection will bring to mind dozens of other illustrations: printing presses, power looms, railroad and highway haulage, statistical and accounting calculation, metallic ore reduction, metal fabrication, etc. For many economic tasks the number of processes available is finite, and each process can be regarded as inflexible with regard to the ratios among factor inputs and process outputs. Factors cannot be substituted for each other except by changing the levels at which entire technical processes are used, because each process uses factors in fixed characteristic ratios. In mathematical programming, accordingly, process substitution plays a role analogous to that of factor substitution in conventional analysis.

We now develop an apparatus for the analysis of process substitution. For convenience we shall limit our discussion to processes which consume two factors, to be called capital and labor, and produce a single output. Figure 3 represents such a process. As in Figure 2, the horizontal axis is scaled in units of labor and the vertical axis in units of capital. The process is represented by the ray, *OA*, which is scaled in units of output. To each output there corresponds a labor requirement found by locating the appropriate mark on the process ray and reading

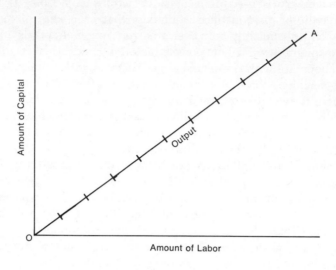

FIGURE 3

A Process

straight down. The capital requirement is found in the same manner by reading straight across from the mark on the process line. Similarly, to each amount of labor there corresponds a quantity of output, found by reading straight up, and a quantity of capital, found by reading straight across from the output mark.

It should be noted that the quantity of capital in this diagram is the quantity used in a process rather than the quantity owned by an economic unit; it is capital-service rather than capital itself. Thus, though more or less labor may be combined with a given machine—by using it more or fewer hours—the ratio of capital to labor inputs, that is, the ratio of machine hours to labor hours—is regarded as technologically fixed.

Figure 3 incorporates two important assumptions. The fact that the line *OA* is straight implies that the ratio between the capital input and the labor input is the same for all levels of output and is given, indeed, by the slope of the line. The fact that the marks on the output line are evenly spaced indicates that there are neither economies or diseconomies of scale in the use of the process, i.e., that there will be strict proportionality between the quantity of output and the quantity of either input. These assumptions are justified rather simply on the basis of the notion of a process. If a process can be used once, it can be used twice or as many times as the supplies of factors permit. Two linotype machines with equally skilled operators can turn out just twice as much type per hour as one. Two identical mills can turn out just twice as many yards of cotton per month as one. So long as factors are available, a process can be duplicated. Whether it will be economical to do so is, of course, another matter.

If there is only one process available for a given task there is not much scope for economic choice. Frequently, however, there will be several processes. Figure 4 represents a situation in

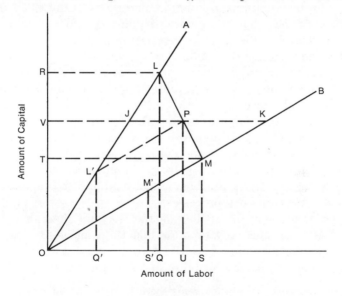

FIGURE 4

Two Processes

which two procedures are available, Process A indicated by the line *OA* and Process B indicated by *OB*. We have already seen how to interpret points on the lines *OA* and *OB*. The scales by which output is measured on the two rays are not necessarily the same. The scale on each ray reflects the productivity of the factors when used in the process represented by that ray and has no connection with the output scale on any other process ray. Now suppose that points L and M represent production of the same output by the two processes. Then LM, the straight line between them, will represent an isoquant and each point on this line will correspond to a combination of processes A and B which produces the same output as OL units of Process A or OM units of Process B.

To see this, consider any point P on the line LM and draw a line through P parallel to OB. Let L' be the point where this line intersects OA. Finally mark the point M' on OB such that $OM' = L'P$. Now consider the production plan which consists of using Process A at level OL' and Process B at level OM'.[2] It is easy to show that this production plan uses OU units of labor, where U is the labor coordinate of point P, and OV units of capital, where V is the capital coordinate of point P.[3]

Since the coordinates of point P correspond to the quantities of factors consumed by OL' units of Process A and OM' units of Process B, we interpret P as representing the combined production plan made up of the specified levels of the two processes. This interpretation implies an important economic assumption, namely, that if the two processes are used simultaneously they will neither interfere with nor enhance each other, so that the inputs and outputs resulting from simultaneous use of two processes at any levels can be found by adding the inputs and outputs of the individual processes.

In order to show that P lies on the isoquant through points L and M it remains only to show that the sum of the outputs corresponding to points L' and M' is the same as the output corresponding to point L or point M. This follows at once from

2. An alternative construction would be to draw a line through point P parallel to OA. It would intersect OB at M'. Then we could lay off OL' equal to $M'P$ on OA. This would lead to exactly the same results as the construction used in the text. The situation is analogous to the "parallelogram of forces" in physics.

3. Proof: Process A at level OL' uses OQ' units of labor, Process B at level OM' uses OS' units of labor; together they use $OQ' + OS'$ units of labor. But, by construction, $L'P$ is equal and parallel to OM'. So $Q'U = OS'$. Therefore, $OQ' + OS' = OQ' + Q'U = OU$ units of labor. The argument with respect to capital is similar.

the facts that the output corresponding to any point on a process ray is directly proportional to the length of the ray up to that point and that the triangles *LL'P* and *LOM* in Figure 4 are similar.[4] Thus if we have two process lines like *OA* and *OB* and find points *L* and *M* on them which represent producing the same output by means of the two processes, then the line segment connecting the two equal-output points will be an isoquant.

We can now draw the mathematical programming analog of the familiar isoquant diagram. Figure 5 is such a diagram with four process lines shown. Point *M* represents a particular output by use of Process A and points *L, K, J* represent that same output by means of Processes B, C, D, respectively. The succession of line segments connecting these four points is the isoquant for that same output. It is easy to see that any other succession of line segments respectively parallel to those of *MLKJ* is also an isoquant. Three such are shown in the figure. It is instructive to compare Figure 5 with Figure 2 and note the strong resemblance in appearance as well as in interpretation.

We may draw price lines on Figure 5, just as on the conventional kind of isoquant diagram. The dashed lines *XX'* and *YY'* represent two possible price lines. Consider *XX'* first. As that line is drawn, the maximum output for a given expenditure can be obtained by use of Process C alone, and, conversely, the minimum cost for a given output is also obtained by using Process C alone. Thus, for the relative price regime represented by *XX'*, Process C is optimal. The price line *YY'* is drawn parallel to the isoquant segment *JK*. In this case Process C is still optimal, but Process D is also optimal and so is any combination of the two.

It is evident from considering these two price lines, and as many others as the reader wishes to visualize, that an optimal production program can always be achieved by means of a single process, which process depending, of course, on the slope of the

4. Proof: Let Output (X) denote the output corresponding to any point, X, on the diagram. Then Output (M')/Output (M) = OM'/OM and Output (L')/Output (L) = OL'/OL. By assumption: Output (L) = Output (M). So Output (M')/Output (L) = OM'/OM. Adding, we have:

$$\frac{\text{Output (M')} + \text{Output (L')}}{\text{Output (L)}} = \frac{OM'}{OM} + \frac{OL'}{OL} = \frac{L'P}{OM} + \frac{OL'}{OL} = \frac{L'L}{OL} + \frac{OL'}{OL} = 1.$$

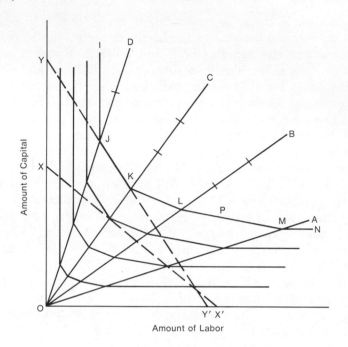

FIGURE 5

Four Processes

price line. It should be noted, however, that the conventional tangency criterion is no longer applicable.

We found in Figure 5 that an optimal economic plan need never use more than a single process for each of its outputs.[5] That conclusion is valid for the situation depicted, which assumed that the services of the two factors could be procured in any amounts desired at constant relative prices. This assumption is not applicable to many economic problems, nor is it used much in mathematic programming. We must now, therefore, take factor supply conditions into account.

III. FACTOR SUPPLIES AND COSTS

In mathematical programming it is usual to divide all factors of production into two classes: unlimited factors, which are

5. Recall, however, that we have not taken joint production into account nor have we considered the effects of consideration from the demand side.

available in any amount desired at constant unit cost, and limited or scarce factors, which are obtainable at constant unit cost up to a fixed maximum quantity and thereafter not at all. The automobile example illustrates this classification. There the four types of capacity were treated as fixed factors available at zero variable cost; all other factors were grouped under direct costs which were considered as constant per unit of output.

The automobile example showed that this classification of factors is adequate for expressing the maximization problem of a firm dealing in competitive markets. In the last section we saw that when all factors are unlimited, this formulation can be used to find a minimum average cost point.

Both of these applications invoked restrictive assumptions, and, furthermore, assumptions which conflict with those conventionally made in studying resource allocation. In conventional analysis we conceive that as the level of production of a firm, industry, or economy rises, average unit costs rise also after some point. The increase in average costs is attributable in part to the working of the law of variable proportions,[6] which operates when the inputs of some but not all factors of production are increased. As far as the consequences of increasing some but not all inputs are concerned, the contrast between mathematical programming and the marginal analysis is more verbal than substantive. A reference to Figure 4 will show how such changes are handled in mathematical programming. Point *J* in Figure 4 represents the production of a certain output by the use of process A alone. If it is desired to increase output without increasing the use of capital, this can be done by moving to the right along the dotted line *JK*, since this line cuts successively higher isoquants. Such a movement would correspond to using increasingly more of Process B and increasingly less of Process A and thus, indirectly, to substituting labor for capital. If, further, we assume that unit cost of production is lower for Process A than for Process B this movement would also correspond to increasing average cost of production. Thus both marginal analysis and mathematical programming lead to the same conclusion when factor proportions are changed: if the change starts from a mini-

6. Cf. J. M. Cassels, "On the Law of Variable Proportions," in W. Fellner and B. F. Haley, eds., *Readings in the Theory of Income Distribution* (Philadelphia, 1946), pp. 103–18.

mum cost point the substitution will lead to gradually increasing unit costs.

But changing input proportions is only one part of the story according to the conventional type of analysis. If output is to be increased, any of three things may happen. First, it may be possible to increase the consumption of all inputs without incurring a change in their unit prices. In this case both mathematical programming and marginal analysis agree that output will be expanded without changing the ratios among the input quantities, and average cost of production will not increase.[7] Second, it may not be possible to increase the use of some of the inputs. This is the case we have just analyzed. According to both modes of analysis the input ratios will change in this case and average unit costs will increase. The only difference between the two approaches is that if average cost is to be plotted against output, the marginal analyst will show a picture with a smoothly rising curve while the mathematical programmer will show a broken line made up of increasingly steep line segments. Third, it may be possible to increase the quantities of all inputs but only at the penalty of increasing unit prices or some kind of diseconomies of scale. This third case occurs in the marginal analysis, indeed it is the case which gives long-run cost curves their familiar shape, but mathematical programming has no counterpart for it.

The essential substantive difference we have arrived at is that the marginal analysis conceives of pecuniary and technical diseconomies associated with changes in scale while mathematical programming does not.[8] There are many important economic problems in which factor prices and productivities do not change in response to changes in scale or in which such variations can be disregarded. Most investigations of industrial capacity, for example, are of this nature. In such studies we seek the maximum output of an industry, regarding its inventory of physical

7. Cf. F. H. Knight, *Risk, Uncertainty and Profit* (Boston, 1921), p. 98.

8. Even within the framework of the marginal analysis the concept of diseconomies of scale has been challenged on both theoretical and empirical grounds. For examples of empirical criticism see Committee on Price Determination, Conference on Price Research, *Cost Behavior and Price Policy* (New York, 1943). The most searching theoretical criticism is in Piero Sraffa, "The Laws of Returns under Competitive Conditions," *Econ. Jour.*, Dec. 1926, pp. 535–50.

equipment as given and assuming that the auxiliary factors needed to cooperate with the equipment can be obtained in the quantities dictated by the characteristics of the equipment. Manpower requirement studies are of the same nature. In such studies we take both output and equipment as given and calculate the manpower needed to operate the equipment at the level which will yield the desired output. Studies of full employment output fall into the same format. In such studies we determine in advance the quantity of each factor which is to be regarded as full employment of that factor. Then we calculate the optimum output obtainable by the use of the factors in those quantities.

These illustrations should suffice to show that the assumption made in mathematical programming can comprehend a wide variety of important economic problems. The most useful applications of mathematical programming are probably to problems of the types just described, that is, to problems concerned with finding optimum production plans using specified quantities of some or all of the resources involved.

IV. ANALYSIS OF PRODUCTION WITH LIMITED FACTORS

The diagrams which we have developed are readily adaptable to the analysis of the consequences of limits on the factor supplies. Such limits are, of course, the heart of Figure 1, where the four principal lines represent limitations on the process levels which result from limits on the four factor quantities considered. But Figure 1 cannot be used when more than two processes have to be considered. For such problems diagrams like Figures 3, 4, and 5 have to be used.

Figure 6 reproduces the situation portrayed in Figure 5 with some additional data, to be explained below. Let *OF* represent the maximum amount of capital which can be used and thus show a factor limitation. The horizontal line through *F* divides the diagram into two sections: all points above the line correspond to programs which require more capital than is available; points on and below the line represent programs which do not have excessive capital requirements. This horizontal line will be called the capital limitation line. Points on or below it are called "feasible," points above it are called "infeasible."

The economic unit portrayed in Figure 6 has the choice of

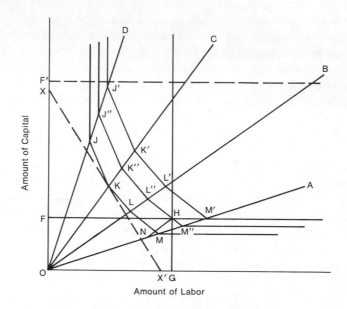

FIGURE 6

FOUR PROCESSES, WITH LIMITATIONS

operating at any feasible point. If maximum output is its objective, it will choose a point which lies on the highest possible isoquant, i.e., the highest isoquant which touches the capital limitation line. This is the one labeled $J'K'L'M'$, and the highest possible output is attained by using Process A.

Of course, maximum output may not be the objective. The objective may be, for example, to maximize the excess of the value of output over labor costs. We shall refer to such an excess as a "net value." The same kind of diagram can be used to solve for a net value provided that the value of each unit of output is independent of the number of units produced [9] and that the cost of each unit of labor is similarly constant. If these provisos are met, each point on a process ray will correspond to a certain physical output but also to a certain value of output, cost of la-

9. This is a particularly uncomfortable assumption. We use it here to explain the method in its least complicated form.

bor, and net value of output. Further, along any process ray the net value of output will equal the physical output times the net value per unit and will therefore be proportional to the physical output. We may thus use a diagram similar to Figure 6 except that we think of net value instead of physical output as measured along the process rays and we show isovalue lines instead of isoquants. This has been done on Figure 7, in which the maximum net value attainable is the one which corresponds to the isovalue contour through point *P*, and is attained by using Process C.

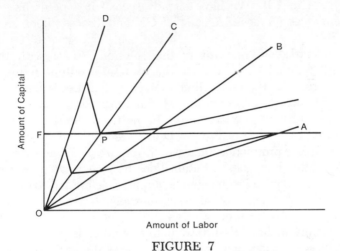

FIGURE 7

FOUR PROCESSES WITH ISOVALUE LINES

It should be noted in both Figures 6 and 7 that the optimal program consisted of a single process, that shifts in the quantity of capital available would not affect the designation of the optimal process though they would change its level, and that the price lines, which are crucial in Figure 5, played no role.

The next complication, and the last one we shall be able to consider, is to assume that both factors are in limited supply. This situation is portrayed in Figure 6 by adding the vertical line through point *G* to represent a labor limitation. The available quantity of labor is shown, of course, by the length *OG*. Then the points inside the rectangle *OFHG* represent programs which can be implemented in the sense that they do not require more than the available supplies of either factor. This is the rectangle of feasible programs. The greatest achievable output is the one which corresponds to the highest isoquant which touches the rectangle of feasible programs. This is the isoquant $J''K''L''M''$, and furthermore, since the maximum isoquant touches the rectangle at H, H represents the program by which the maximum output can be produced.

This solution differs from the previous ones in that the solution point does not lie on any process ray but between the rays for Processes A and B. We have already seen that a point like H represents using Process A at level ON and Process B at level NH.

Two remarks are relevant to this solution. First: with the factor limitation lines as drawn, the maximum output requires two processes. If the factor limitation lines had been drawn so that they intersected exactly on one of the process rays, only one process would have been required. If the factor limitation lines had crossed to the left of Process D or to the right of Process A, the maximizing production plan would require only one process. But, no matter how the limitation lines be drawn, at most two processes are required to maximize output. We are led to an important generalization: maximum output may always be obtained by using a number of processes which does not exceed the number of factors in limited supply, if this number is greater than zero. The conclusions we drew from Figures 6 and 7 both conform to this rule, and it is one of the basic theorems of mathematical programming.

Second: although at most two processes are required to obtain the maximum output, which two depends on the location of the factor limits. As shown, the processes used for maximum output were Processes A and B. If somewhat more capital, represented by the amount OF', were available, the maximizing processes would have been Processes C and D. If two factors are limited, it is the ratio between their supplies rather than the absolute supplies of either which determines the processes in the optimum program. This contrasts with the case in which only one factor is limited. Just as the considerations which determine the optimum set of processes are more complicated when two factors are limited than when only one is, so with three or more limited factors the optimum conditions become more complicated still

and soon pass the reach of intuition. This, indeed, is the *raison
d'être* of the formidable apparatus of mathematical programming.

We can make these considerations more concrete by applying
them to the automobile example. Referring to Figure 1, we note
that the optimum production point, *C*, lay on the limitation lines
for engine assembly and metal stamping, but well below the
limits for automobile and truck assembly. The limitations on
automobile and truck assembly capacity are, therefore, ineffective and can be disregarded. The situation in terms of the two
effectively limiting types of capacity is shown in Figure 8.

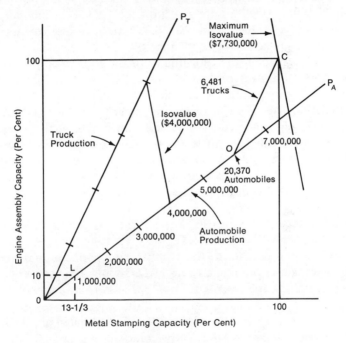

FIGURE 8

AUTOMOBILE EXAMPLE, OPTIMAL PLAN

In Figure 8 the ray P_A represents the process of producing
automobiles and P_T the process for producing trucks. These
two processes can be operated at any combination of levels
which does not require the use of more than 100 percent of either
metal stamping or engine assembly capacity. Thus the rectangle

in the diagram is the region of feasible production programs. The optimal production program is the one in the feasible region which corresponds to the highest possible net revenue.[10] Thus it will be helpful to construct isorevenue lines, as we did in Figure 7. To do this, consider automobile production first. Each point on P_A corresponds to the production of a certain number of automobiles per month. Suppose, for example, that the scale is such that point L represents the production of 3,333 automobiles per month. It will be recalled that each automobile yields a net revenue of $300. Therefore, 3,333 automobiles yield a revenue of $1,000,000. Point L, then, corresponds to a net revenue of $1,000,000 as well as to an output of 3,333 automobiles per month. Since (see Figure 1) 3,333 automobiles require 13⅓ percent of metal stamping capacity and 10 percent of engine assembly capacity, the coordinates of the $1,000,000 net revenue point on P_A are established at once. By a similar argument, the point whose coordinates are 26⅔ percent of metal stamping capacity and 20 percent of engine capacity is the $2,000,000 net revenue point on P_A. In the same manner, the whole ray can be drawn and scaled off in terms of net revenue, and so can P_T, the process ray for truck production. The diagram is completed by connecting the $4,000,000 points on the two process lines in order to show the direction of the isorevenue lines.

The optimum program is at point C, where the two capacity limits intersect, because C lies on the highest isorevenue line which touches the feasible region. Through point C we have drawn a line parallel to the truck production line and meeting the automobile production line at D. By our previous argument, the length OD represents the net revenue from automobile production in the optimal program and the length DC represents the net revenue from trucks. If these lengths be scaled off, the result, of course, will be the same as the solution found previously.

V. IMPUTATION OF FACTOR VALUES

We have just noted that the major field of application of mathematical programming is to problems where the supply of

10. Since the objective of the firm is, by assumption, to maximize revenue rather than physical output, we may consider automobile and truck production as two alternative processes for producing revenue instead of as two processes with disparate outputs.

one or more factors of production is absolutely limited. Such scarcities are the genesis of value in ordinary analysis, and they generate values in mathematical programming too. In fact, in ordinary analysis the determination of outputs and the determination of prices are but two aspects of the same problem, the optimal allocation of scarce resources. The same is true in mathematical programming.

Heretofore we have encountered prices only as data for determining the direct costs of processes and the net value of output. But of course the limiting factors of production also have value although we have not assigned prices to them up to now. In this section we shall see that the solution of a mathematical programming problem implicitly assigns values to the limiting factors of production. Furthermore, the implicit pricing problem can be solved directly and, when so solved, constitutes a solution to the optimal allocation problem.

Consider the automobile example and ask: how much is a unit (1 percent) of each of the types of capacity worth to the firm? The approach to this question is similar in spirit to the familiar marginal analysis. With respect to each type of capacity we calculate how much the maximum revenue would increase if one more unit were added, or how much revenue would decrease if one unit were taken away. Since there is a surplus of automobile assembly capacity, neither the addition nor the subtraction of one unit of this type would affect the optimum program or the maximum net revenue. Hence the value of this type of capacity is nil. The analysis and result for truck assembly are the same.

We find, then, that these two types of capacity are free goods. This does not imply that an automobile assembly line is not worth having, any more than, to take a classic example, the fact that air is a free good means that it can be dispensed with. It means that it would not be worthwhile to increase this type of capacity at any positive price and that some units of these types could be disposed of without loss.

The valuation of the other types of capacity is not so trivial. In Figure 9 possible values per percent of engine assembly capacity are scaled along the horizontal axis and values per percent of metal stamping capacity are scaled along the vertical axis. Now consider any possible pair of values, say engine assembly capacity worth $20,000 per unit and metal stamping

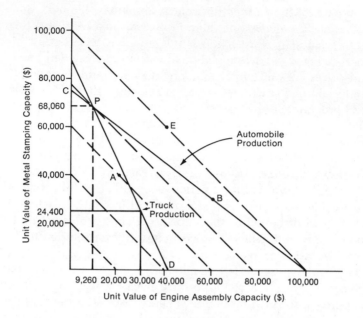

FIGURE 9

AUTOMOBILE EXAMPLE, IMPLICIT VALUES

worth $40,000. This is represented by point *A* on the figure. Applying these values to the data on pages 293–294, the values of capacity required for producing an automobile is found to be $(0.004 \times \$40,000) + (0.003 \times \$20,000) = \$220$ which is well under the value of producing an automobile, or $300.[11] In the same way, if engine assembly capacity is worth $60,000 per percent of capacity and metal stamping capacity is valued at $30,000 per unit (point *B*), the cost of scarce resources required to produce an automobile will be exactly equal to the value of the product. This is clearly not the only combination of resource values which will precisely absorb the value of output when the resources are used to produce automobiles. The automobile production line on the figure, which passes through point *B*, is the locus of all such value combinations. A similar

11. These unit values are also marginal values since costs of production are constant.

line has been drawn for truck production to represent those combinations of resource values for which the total value of resources used in producing trucks is equal to the value of output. The intersection of these two lines is obviously the only pair of resource values for which the marginal resource cost of producing an additional automobile is equal to the net value of an automobile and the same is true with respect to trucks. The pair can be found by plotting or, with more precision, by algebra. It is found that 1 percent of engine assembly capacity is worth \$9,259 and 1 percent of metal stamping capacity is worth \$68,056.

To each pair of values for the two types of capacity, there corresponds a value for the entire plant. Thus to the pair of values represented by point *A* there corresponds the plant value of (100 $\times$ \$20,000) + (100 $\times$ \$40,000) — \$6,000,000. This is not the only pair of resource values which give an aggregate plant value of \$6,000,000. Indeed, any pair of resource values on the dotted line through *A* corresponds to the same aggregate plant value. (By this stage, Figure 9 should become strongly reminiscent of Figure 1.) We have drawn a number of lines parallel to the one just described, each corresponding to a specific aggregate plant value. The dashed line which passes through the intersection of the two production lines is of particular interest. By measurement or otherwise this line can be found to correspond to a plant value of \$7,731,500 which, we recall, was found to be the maximum attainable net revenue.

Let us consider the implications of assigning values to the two limiting factors from a slightly different angle. We have seen that as soon as unit values have been assigned to the factors an aggregate value is assigned to the plant. We can make the aggregate plant value as low as we please, simply by assigning sufficiently low values to the various factors. But if the values assigned are too low, we have the unsatisfactory consequence that some of the processes will give rise to unimputed surpluses. We may, therefore, seek the lowest aggregate plant value which can be assigned and still have no process yield an unimputed surplus. In the automobile case, that value is \$7,731,500. In the course of finding the lowest acceptable plant value we find specific unit values to be assigned to each of the resources.

In this example there are two processes and four limited resources. It turns out that only two of the resources were effectively limiting, the others being in relatively ample supply. In general, the characteristics of the solution to a programming problem depend on the relationship between the number of limited resources and the number of processes taken into consideration. If, as in the present instance, the number of limited resources exceeds the number of processes, it will usually turn out that some of the resources will have imputed values of zero and that the number of resources with positive imputed values will be equal to the number of processes.[12] If the number of limited resources equals the number of processes all resources will have positive imputed values. If, finally, the number of processes exceeds the number of limited resources, some of the processes will not be used in the optimal program. This situation, which is the usual one, was illustrated in Figure 6. In this case the total imputed value of resources absorbed will equal net revenue for some processes and will exceed it for others. The number of processes for which the imputed value of resources absorbed equals the net revenue will be just equal to the number of limited resources, and the processes for which the equality holds are the ones which will appear at positive levels in the optimal program. In brief, the determination of the minimum acceptable plant value amounts to the same thing as the determination of the optimal production program. The programming problem and the valuation problem are not only closely related they are basically the same.

This can be seen graphically by comparing Figures 1 and 9. Each figure contains two axes and two diagonal boundary lines. But the boundary lines in Figure 9 refer to the same processes as the axes in Figure 1, and the axes in Figure 9 refer to the same resources as the diagonal boundary lines in Figure 1. Furthermore, in using Figure 1 we sought the net revenue corresponding to the highest dashed line touched by the boundary; in using Figure 9 we sought the aggregate value corresponding to the lowest dashed line which has any points on or outside the boundary; and the two results turned out to be the same. Formally

12. We say "usually" in this sentence because in some special circumstances the number of resources with positive imputed values may exceed the number of processes.

stated, these two figures and the problems they represent are *duals* of each other.

The dualism feature is a very useful property in the solution of mathematical programming problems. The simplest way to see this is to note that when confronting a mathematical programming problem we have the choice of solving the problem or its dual, whichever is easier. Either way we can get the same results. We can use this feature now to generalize our discussion somewhat. Up to now when dealing with more than two processes we have had to use relatively complicated diagrams like Figure 6 because straightforward diagrams like Figure 1 did not contain enough axes to represent the levels of the processes. Now we can use diagrams modeled on Figure 9 to depict problems with any number of processes so long as they do not involve more than two scarce factors. Figure 10 illustrates a diagram for four pro-

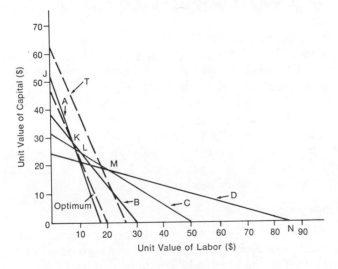

FIGURE 10

THE VALUATION PROBLEM, FOUR PROCESSES

cesses and is, indeed, derived from Figure 6. In Figure 10, line *A* represents all pairs of factor values such that Process A would yield neither a profit nor a loss. Lines *B, C,* and *D* are similarly interpreted. The dashed line *T* is a locus along which the aggregate value of the labor and capital available to the firm (or industry) is constant. Its position is not relevant to the analysis; its slope, which is simply the ratio of the quantity of available labor to that of capital, is all that is significant. The broken line *JKLMN* divides the graph into two regions. All points on or above it represent pairs of resource values such that no process gives rise to an unimputed surplus. Let us call this the acceptable region. For each point below that broken line there is at least one process which does have an unimputed surplus. This is the unacceptable region. We then seek for that point in the acceptable region which corresponds to the lowest aggregate plant value. This point will, of course, give the set of resource values which makes the accounting profit of the firm as great as possible without giving rise to any unimputed income. The point which meets these requirements is *K*, and a dotted line parallel to *T* has been drawn through it to indicate the minimum acceptable aggregate plant value.

At point *K*, processes A and B yield zero profits, and processes C and D yield losses. Hence processes A and B are the ones which should be used, exactly as we found in Figure 6. To be sure, this diagram does not tell the levels at which A and B should be used, any more than Figure 6 tells the valuations to be placed on the two resources. But finding the levels after the processes have been selected is a comparatively trivial matter. All that is necesssary is to find the levels which will fully utilize the resources which are not free goods. This may be done algebraically or by means of a diagram like Figure 8.

VI. APPLICATIONS

In the first section we asserted that the principal motivation of mathematical programming was the need for a method of analysis which lent itself to the practical solution of the day-to-day problems of business and the economy in general. Immediately after making that claim we introduced a highly artificial problem followed by a rather extended discussion of abstract and formal relationships. The time has now come to indicate the basis for saying that mathematical programming is a practical method of analysis.

The essential simplification achieved in mathematical programming is the replacement of the notion of the production function by the notion of the process. The process is a highly observable unit of activity and the empirical constants which characterize it can be estimated without elaborate analysis. Furthermore in many industries the structure of production corresponds to operating a succession of processes, as we have conceived them. Many industrial decisions, like shutting down a bank of machines or operating an extra shift, correspond naturally to our concept of choosing the level of operation of a process. In brief, mathematical programming is modeled after the actual structure of production in the hope that thereby it will involve only observable constants and directly controllable variables.

Has this hope been justified? The literature already contains a report of a successful application to petroleum refining.[13] I have made a similar application which, perhaps, will bear description. The application was to a moderate-sized refinery which produces premium and regular grades of automotive gasoline. The essential operation studied was blending. In blending, ten chemically distinct kinds of semirefined oil, called blending stocks, are mixed together. The result is a salable gasoline whose characteristics are approximately the weighted average of the characteristics of the blending stocks. For example, if 500 gallons of a stock with octane rating of 80 are blended with 1,000 gallons of a stock with octane rating of 86 the result will be $500 + 1,000 = 1,500$ gallons of product with octane rating of $(\frac{1}{3} \times 80) + (\frac{2}{3} \times 86) = 84$.

The significant aspect of gasoline blending for our present purposes is that the major characteristics of the blend—its knock rating, its vapor pressure, its sulphur content, etc.—can be expressed as linear functions of the quantities of the various blending stocks used. So also can the cost of the blend if each of the blending stocks has a definite price per gallon. Thus the problem of finding the minimum cost blend which will meet given quality specifications is a problem in mathematical programming.

Furthermore, in this refinery the quantities of some of the blending stocks are definitely limited by contracts and by refining capacity. The problem then arises: what are the most profitable quantities of output of regular and premium gasoline, and how

13. A. Charnes, W. W. Cooper, and B. Mellon, "Blending Aviation Gasolines," *Econometrica*, Apr. 1952, pp. 135–59.

much of each blending stock should be used for each final product? This problem is analogous to the artificial automobile example, with the added complication of the quality specifications. The problem is too complicated for graphic analysis but was solved easily by arithmetical procedures. As far as is known, mathematical programming provides the only way for solving such problems. Charnes and Cooper have recently published the solution to a similar problem which arose in the operations of a metal-working firm.[14]

An entirely different kind of problem, also amenable to mathematical programming, arises in newsprint production. Freight is a major element in the cost of newsprint. One large newsprint company has six mills, widely scattered in Canada, and some two hundred customers, widely scattered in the United States. Its problem is to decide how much newsprint to ship from each mill to each customer so as, first, to meet the contract requirements of each customer, second, to stay within the capacity limits of each mill, and third, to keep the aggregate freight bill as small as possible. This problem involves 1,200 variables (6 mills × 200 customers), in contrast to the two- or four-variable problems we have been discussing. In the final solution most of these variables will turn out to be zero—the question is which ones. This problem is solved by mathematical programming and, though formidable, is not really as formidable as the count of variables might indicate.

These few illustrations should suffice to indicate that mathematical programming is a practical tool for business planning. They show, also, that it is a flexible tool because both examples deviated from the format of the example used in our expansion. The petroleum application had the added feature of quality specification. In the newsprint application there were limits on the quantity of output as well as on the quantities of the inputs. Nevertheless mathematical programming handled them both easily.

On the other hand, it should be noted that both of these were

14. A. Charnes, W. W. Cooper, and Donald Farr and Staff, "Linear Programming and Profit Preference Scheduling for a Manufacturing Firm," *Journal of the Operations Research Society of America,* May 1953, pp. 114–29.

small-scale applications, dealing with a single phase of the operation of a single firm. I believe that this has been true of all successful applications to date. Mathematical programmers are still a long way from solving the broad planning problems of entire industries or an entire economy. But many such broad problems are only enlarged versions of problems which have been met and solved in the context of the single firm. It is no longer premature to say that mathematical programming has proved its worth as a practical tool for finding optimal economic programs.

VII. CONCLUSION

Our objective has been only to introduce the basic notions of mathematical programming and to invest them with plausibility and meaning. The reader who would learn to solve a programming problem—even the simplest—will have to look elsewhere,[15] though this paper may serve as a useful background.

Although methods of solution have been omitted from this exposition, we must emphasize that these methods are fundamental to the whole concept of mathematical programming. Some eighty years ago Walras conceived of production in very much the same manner as mathematical programmers, and more recently A. Wald and J. von Neumann used this view of production and methods closely allied to those of mathematical programming to analyze the conditions of general economic equilibrium.[16] These developments, however, must be regarded merely as precursors of mathematical programming. Programming had no independent existence as a mode of economic analysis until 1947 when G. B.

15. The standard reference is T. C. Koopmans, ed., *Activity Analysis of Production and Allocation* (New York, 1951). Less advanced treatments may be found in A. Charnes, W. W. Cooper, and A. Henderson, *An Introduction to Linear Programming* (New York, 1953); and my own *Application of Linear Programming to the Theory of the Firm* (Berkeley, 1951).

16. Walras' formulation is in *Eléments d'économie politique pure ou théorie de la richesse sociale*, 2d ed. (Lausanne, 1889), 20ᵉ Leçon. The contributions of A. Wald and J. von Neumann appeared originally in *Ergebnisse eines mathematischen Kolloquiums*, Nos. 6, 7, 8. Wald's least technical paper appeared in *Zeitschrift für Nationalökonomie*, VII (1936) and has been translated as "On some Systems of Equations of Mathematical Economics," *Econometrica*, Oct. 1951, pp. 368–403. Von Neumann's basic paper appeared in translation as "A Model of General Economic Equilibrium," *Rev. Econ. Stud.*, 1945–46, pp. 1–9.

Dantzig announced the "simplex method" of solution which made practical application feasible.[17] The existence of a method whereby economic optima could be explicitly calculated stimulated research into the economic interpretation of mathematical programming and led also to the development of alternative methods of solution. The fact that economic and business problems when formulated in terms of mathematical programming can be solved numerically is the basis of the importance of the method. The omission of methods of solution from this discussion should not, therefore, be taken to indicate that they are of secondary interest.

We have considered only a few of the concepts used in mathematical programming and have dealt with only a single type of programming problem. The few notions we have considered, however, are the basic ones; all the rest of mathematical programming is elaboration and extension of them. It seems advisable to mention two directions of elaboration, for they remove or weaken two of the most restrictive assumptions which have here been imposed.

The first of these extensions is the introduction of time into the analysis. The present treatment has dealt with a single production period in isolation. But in many cases, successive production periods are interrelated. This is so, for example, in the case of a vertically integrated firm where the operation of some processes in one period is limited by the levels of operation in the preceding period of the processes which supply their raw materials. Efficient methods for analyzing such "dynamic" problems are being investigated, particularly by George Dantzig.[18] Although the present discussion has been static, the method of analysis can be applied to problems with a time dimension.

The second of these extensions is the allowance for changes in the prices of factors and final products. In our discussion we regarded all prices as unalterable and independent of the actions of the economic unit under consideration. Constant prices are, undeniably, a great convenience to the analyst, but the method

17. G. B. Dantzig, "Maximization of a Linear Function of Variables Subject to Linear Inequalities," T. C. Koopmans, ed., op. cit., pp. 339–47.

18. "A Note on a Dynamic Leontief Model with Substitution" (abstract), *Econometrica*, Jan. 1953, p. 179.

can transcend this assumption when necessary. The general mathematical theory of dealing with variable prices has been investigated [19] and practical methods of solution have been developed for problems where the demand and supply curves are linear.[20] The assumption of constant prices, perhaps the most restrictive assumption we have made, is adopted for convenience rather than from necessity.

Mathematical programming has been developed as a tool for economic and business planning and not primarily for the descriptive, and therefore predictive, purposes which gave rise to the marginal analysis. Nevertheless it does have predictive implications. In so far as firms operate under the conditions assumed in mathematical programming it would be unreasonable to assume that they acted as if they operated under the conditions assumed by the marginal analysis. Consider, for example, the automobile firm portrayed in Figure 1. How would it respond if the price of automobiles were to fall, say by $50 a unit? In that case the net revenue per automobile would be $250, the same as the net revenue per truck. Diagrammatically, the result would be to rotate the lines of equal revenue until their slope was 45 degrees. After this rotation, point C would still be optimum and this change in prices would cause no change in optimum output. Mathematical programming gives rise, thus, to a kinked supply curve.

On the other hand, suppose that the price of automobiles were to rise by $50. Diagrammatically this price change would decrease the steepness of the equal revenue lines until they were just parallel to the metal stamping line. The firm would then be in a position like that illustrated by the YY' line in Figure 5. The production plans corresponding to points on the line segment DC in Figure 1 would all yield the same net revenue, and all would be optimal. If the price of automobiles were to rise by more than $50 or if a $50 increase in the price of automobiles were accom-

19. See H. W. Kuhn and A. W. Tucker, "Non-Linear Programming," in J. Neyman, ed., *Proceedings of the Second Berkeley Symposium on Mathematical Statistics and Probability* (Berkeley, 1951), pp. 481–92.

20. I reported one solution of this problem to a seminar at the Massachusetts Institute of Technology in September 1952. Other solutions may be known.

panied by any decrease in the price of trucks, the point of optimal production would jump abruptly from point C to point D.

Thus mathematical programming indicates that firms whose choices are limited to distinct processes will respond discontinuously to price variations: they will be insensitive to price changes over a certain range and will change their levels of output sharply as soon as that range is passed. This theoretical deduction surely has real counterparts.

The relationship between mathematical programming and welfare economics is especially close. Welfare economics studies the optimal organization of economic effort; so does mathematical programming. This relationship has been investigated especially by Koopmans and Samuelson.[21] The finding, generally stated, is that the equilibrium position of a perfectly competitive economy is the same as the optimal solution of the mathematical programming problem embodying the same data.

Mathematical programming is closely allied mathematically to the methods of input-output analysis or interindustry analysis developed largely by W. W. Leontief.[22] The two methods were developed independently, however, and it is important to distinguish them conceptually. Input-output analysis finds its application almost exclusively in the study of general economic equilibrium. It conceives of an economy as divided into a number of industrial sectors each of which is analogous to a process as the term is used in mathematical programming. It then takes either of two forms. In "open models" an input-output analysis starts with some specified final demand for the products of each of the sectors and calculates the level at which each of the sector-processes must operate in order to meet this schedule of final demands. In "closed models" final demand does not appear but attention is concentrated on the fact that the inputs required by each sector-process must be supplied as outputs by some other sector-processes. Input-output analysis then calculates a mutually

21. T. C. Koopmans, "Analysis of Production as an Efficient Combination of Activities," in T. C. Koopmans, ed., op. cit., pp. 33–97; P. A. Samuelson, "Market Mechanisms and Maximization" (a paper prepared for the Rand Corp., 1949).

22. W. W. Leontief, *The Structure of American Economy 1919–1939*, 2nd. ed. (New York, 1951).

compatible set of output levels for the various sectors. By contrast with mathematical programming the conditions imposed in input-output analysis are sufficient to determine the levels of the processes and there is no scope for finding an optimal solution or a set of "best" levels. To be sure, input-output analysis can be regarded as a special case of mathematical programming in which the number of products is equal to the number of processes. On the other hand, the limitations on the supplies of resources which play so important a role in mathematical programming are not dealt with explicitly in input-output analysis. On the whole it seems best to regard these two techniques as allied but distinct methods of analysis addressed to different problems.

Mathematical programming, then, is of significance for economic thinking and theory as well as for business and economic planning. We have been able only to allude to this significance. Indeed, apart from the exploration of welfare implications, very little thought has been given to the consequences for economics of mathematical programming because most effort has been devoted to solving the numerous practical problems to which it gives rise. The outlook is for fruitful researches into both the implications and applications of mathematical programming.

Applications of Linear Programming in the Oil Industry

W. W. Garvin, H. W. Crandall, J. B. John, and R. A. Spellman

The authors of this article, which appeared in Management Science *in 1957, are officials of Standard Oil of California and California Research Corporation.*

As technology advances and improves, problems become more interwoven and complex. The problems of the oil industry are no exception. They can logically be grouped into categories according to the different phases of our business as shown in Figure 1. An integrated oil company must first of all carry out exploration activities to determine the spots where oil is most likely to be found. The land must then be acquired or leased and an exploratory well or "wildcat" as it is called is drilled. If luck is with us, we hit oil. Additional wells are drilled to develop the field and production gets under way. The oil is transported by various means to the refinery, where a variety of products are manufactured from it. The products in turn leave the refinery, enter the distribution system, and are marketed.

Needless to say, each of the areas shown in Figure 1 is full of unanswered questions and problems. Different methods exist for exploring the oil potentialities of a region. How should they be combined for maximum effectiveness? An oil field can be produced in many different ways. Which is best? The complexity of a modern refinery is staggering. What is the best operating plan? And what precisely do we mean by "best"? Of course, not all the problems in these areas lend themselves to linear programming but some of them do. What we would like to do is to pick out a few representative *LP* type problems from each area, show how they were formulated, and, in some cases, discuss the results that were obtained.

FIGURE 1

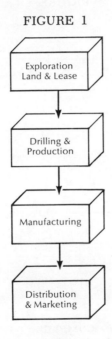

We had hoped to find applications [of linear programming] in all four of the areas shown in Figure 1. Unfortunately, we were successful only in three. We did not find any nonconfidential applications in the field of exploration. Exploration is one of the most confidential phases of our business and it is for that reason that oil companies are not very explicit about their studies in this field. We can state, however, from personal experience, that a number of applications to exploration are under investigation.

Let us therefore turn our attention to the remaining three areas of Drilling and Production, Manufacturing, and Distribution and Marketing. Out of the Drilling and Production area the problem of devising a model for a producing complex was selected. In the case of Manufacturing, the selection was difficult because historically this was the first area of application and much work has been done in this field. The problem of incremental product costs illustrates the technique of parametric programming and also shows what can happen if too many simplifications are introduced.

FIGURE 2

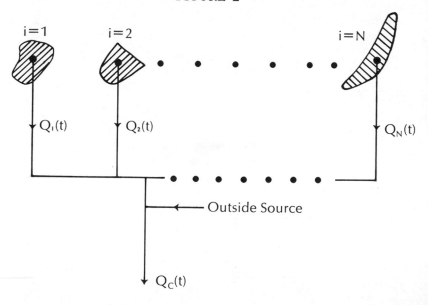

MODEL OF A PRODUCING COMPLEX

Let us now turn our attention to the model of a producing complex. We are indebted to the Field Research Laboratory of Magnolia Petroleum Company and to Arabian American Oil Company for contributing this application. Consider N oil fields or reservoirs ($i=1, 2 \cdots N$), as shown in Figure 2, which are producing at rates $Q_i(t)$ where t is the time. The total production of the N reservoirs is to be adjusted to meet a commitment $Q_c(t)$ (such as keeping a pipe line full or a refinery supplied). An outside source of crude oil is also available. Let the profit realizable per barrel be $c_i(t)$ and consider that the operation is to be run on this basis for a period of T years. Production limitations exist which require that the $Q_i(t)$ do not exceed certain values and that the pressures in the reservoirs do not fall below certain values. These limits may be functions of time. We shall consider the case where these fields are relatively young so that development drilling activity will occur during the time period under consideration. The problem is to determine a schedule of $Q_i(t)$ such that the profit over T years is a maximum.

By splitting up the period T into time intervals ($k=1, 2 \cdots K$) and bringing in the physics of the problem, it can be shown that the condition that the field pressures are not to fall below certain minimum values assumes the form:

$$\sum_{j=1}^{k} (f_{i,k-j+1} - f_{i,k-j})Q_{ij} \leqq P_{i0} - P_{i \min} \tag{1}$$

for all i and k. The f's describe the characteristics of the fields and are known. The right-hand side is the difference between the initial and the minimum permissible pressure of the ith field. The variable is Q_{ij} which is the production rate of the ith field during the jth period. Additional constraints on the Q_{ij}'s are that the total production for any time period plus the crude oil possibly purchased from the outside source, Q_j, be equal to the commitment for that time period:

$$\sum_{i=1}^{N} Q_{ij} + Q_j = Q_{cj}, j = 1, 2 \cdots K \tag{2}$$

Furthermore, production limitations exist such that:

$$Q_{ij} \leqq Q_{ij \max} \tag{3}$$

which are simple under bound constraints. The objective function expressing profit over the time period considered is:

$$\sum_{j=1}^{K} \sum_{i=1}^{N} c_{ij}Q_{ij} + \sum_{j=1}^{K} c_jQ_j = \max \tag{4}$$

which completes the formulation of the linear programming problem. The coefficients c_{ij} and c_j are the profit per barrel of the ith reservoir at time j and correspondingly for purchased crude oil.

Thus far, everything has been rather straightforward. But now, the time has come to clutter up the theory with facts. Let us take a closer look at the coefficients c_{ij}. If we plot revenue versus a particular production rate Q_{ij}, we get a straight line passing through the origin as shown in Figure 3. Cost versus Q_{ij} is also more or less a straight line which, however, does not pass through the origin. The cost function is discontinuous at the origin, corresponding to a set-up charge such as building a road, a pipeline, or harbor facilities, or installing a gas-oil separator.

FIGURE 3

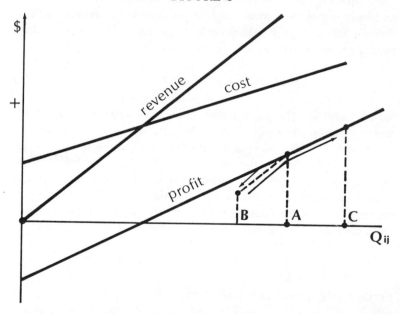

It drops to zero when $Q_{ij}=0$ because this corresponds to not yet developing the field. Also shown in Figure 3 is profit versus Q_{ij} which is the difference between revenue and cost. The profit function thus is the straight line shown plus the origin. Hence, we can say that profit from Q_{ij} production is $c_{ij}Q_{ij}-s_{ij}$ where s_{ij} is zero if Q_{ij} is zero and s_{ij} is a constant if $Q_{ij}>0$. This is a particularly difficult constraint. No general methods are available for handling this except a cut-and-try approach. This type of fixed set-up charge constraint occurs in many practical problems and we shall meet it again later on.

One other complicating feature should be mentioned. Consider that during a certain time period, Q_{ij} was at level "A" as shown in Figure 3 and that in the succeeding time period $Q_{i, j+1}$ has dropped to level "B." The profit at level "B" is not obtained by following the profit line to operating level "B" but rather by following a line as shown which is parallel to the revenue line. The reduction in level from "A" to "B" involves merely turning a few valves and essentially does not entail any reduction in operating costs. If, on the other hand, we go from "A" to "C" in succeeding time periods, then we do follow the profit line because an increase in production necessitates drilling additional wells assuming that all the wells at "A" are producing at maximum economic capacity. If we should go from "A" to "B" to "C" in succeeding time periods and if "A" was the maximum field development up to that time, then in going from "B" to "C" we would follow the broken path as shown in Figure 3.

This state of affairs can be handled by building the concept of "production capacity" into the model and requiring that production capacity never decreases with time. But this can be done only at the expense of enlarging the system appreciably.

There exist other factors and additional constraints which must be taken into account. As is so often the case, we are dealing here with a system which on the surface looks rather simple but which becomes considerably more complex as we get deeper into it to make it more realistic. Nevertheless, the simple system or modest extensions of it enables an entire producing complex to be studied, thus providing a good basis upon which to build more realistic models.

INCREMENTAL PRODUCT COSTS

Let us now leave the problems of petroleum production behind us and venture into the petroleum refinery. As was indicated before, a great deal of work has been done in this area. The few problems we shall discuss will be illustrative of what is going on in this field.

We shall consider at first a simple but nevertheless instructive example. A refinery produces gasoline, furnace oil and other products as shown in Figure 4. The refinery can be supplied with a fairly large number of crude oils. The available crude oils have different properties and yield different volumes of finished products. Some of these crudes must be refined because of long-term minimum volume commitments or because of requirements for specialty products. These crudes are considered fixed and yield

FIGURE 4

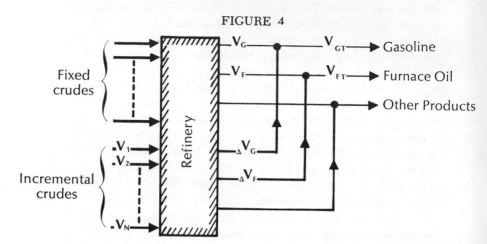

gasoline and furnace oil volumes V_G and V_F respectively. From the remaining crudes and from those crudes which are available in volumes greater than their minimum volume commitment must be selected those which can supply the required products most economically. These are the incremental crudes. Denote the gasoline and furnace oil volumes which result from the incremental crudes by ΔV_G and ΔV_F and the total volumes (fixed plus incremental) by V_{GT} and V_{FT}. The problem is to determine the minimum incremental cost of furnace oil as a function of incremental furnace oil production keeping gasoline production and general refinery operations fixed.

The formulation of this problem is straightforward:

$$\sum_1^N a_{Gi} V_i = V_{GT} - V_G = \Delta V_G \qquad (5)$$

$$\sum_1^N a_{Fi} V_i = V_{FT} - V_F = \Delta V_F \qquad (6)$$

$$V_i \leqq V_{i\,max} \qquad (7)$$

$$\sum_1^N c_i V_i = min \qquad (8)$$

where a_{Gi} and a_{Fi} are the gasoline and furnace oil yields of the *i*th crude, V_i and $V_{i\,max}$ are the volume and availability of the *i*th incremental crude and c_i is the cost of producing incremental gasoline plus incremental furnace oil per barrel of the *i*th crude. This cost is made up of the cost of crude at the refinery, the incremental processing costs and a credit for the by-products produced at the same time.

The procedure now consists of assuming a value for ΔV_F and obtaining an optimal solution. The shadow price of equation (6) will then be equal to the incremental cost of furnace oil because it represents the change in the functional corresponding to a change of one barrel in ΔV_F. The incremental cost thus obtained, however, is valid only over ranges of variation of ΔV_F which are sufficiently small so that the optimum solution remains feasible. Beyond that permissible range of ΔV_F the basis must be changed with a resulting change in the shadow price. For problems of this type, the so-called "parametric programming" procedure can be used. This procedure has been incorporated into the IBM 704 LP code. It starts with an optimal solution and then varies in an arbitrary but preassigned manner the constants on the right-hand side until one of the basic variables becomes zero. The computer then prints out the optimal solution which exists at that time, changes the basis to an adjacent extreme point which is also optimum, and repeats this process until a termination is reached.

An actual problem was run with the model shown in Figure 4. Thirteen incremental crudes were available and incremental gasoline production was fixed at 14,600 barrels daily. The results are shown in Figure 5 which shows the minimum total incremental cost as a function of incremental furnace oil production. Ignore the dashed line for the moment. The circles represent points at which the optimum basis had to be changed. The functional is a straight line between these points. It turned out that incremental furnace-oil production was possible only in the range from about 7,100 bpd to about 11,200 bpd. Between the two extremes, the functional exhibits a minimum at about 8,000 bpd. The reason for the minimum is to be found in the fact that near the two extremes of furnace oil production, little choice exists in the composition of the crude slate. Volume is the limitation and economics plays a secondary part. Away from the two

FIGURE 5

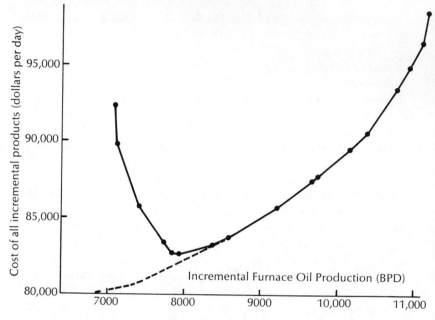

extremes, however, we have greater flexibility in crudes run and thus have the freedom to pick the cheapest crude combination. Figure 6 shows the incremental cost of furnace oil as a function of furnace oil production. It is a staircase type function because the shadow price remains unchanged as long as the optimum basis remains feasible and jumps discontinuously whenever the basis is changed. At low levels of incremental furnace oil production, the incremental cost becomes negative because in that region it is *more* expensive to make *less* furnace oil.

If we now were to show our model and our results to the refiner, he would immediately detect a fly in the ointment. The negative incremental cost at low furnace oil production runs counter to his intuitive feeling for the problem. He would point out, and rightly so, that the formulation of our model is not complete. Common sense would dictate the making of the larger volumes of furnace oil at lower cost and disposing of the excess furnace oil in some manner. For example, this excess can be mixed into heavy fuel production. If all the heavy fuel that is made can be sold, the net cost of the furnace oil overproduction

FIGURE 6

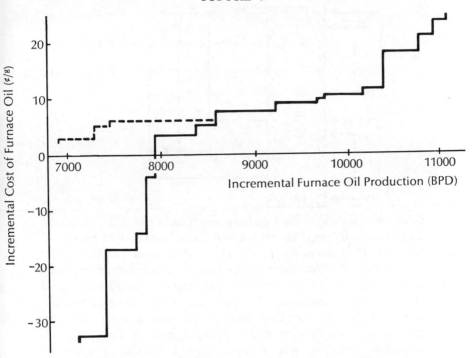

would be the negative of the value of heavy fuel indicating a credit we receive for increasing heavy fuel production.

We are tempted, therefore, to try the formulation shown in Figure 7 where we permit the diversion of some furnace oil to heavy fuel. The equation for gasoline production remains unchanged but the furnace oil equation now reads:

$$\sum_{1}^{N} a_{iF} V_i - s_1 = \Delta V_F \tag{9}$$

and the objective form is:

$$\sum_{1}^{N} c_i V_i - v_{HF} s_1 = \min \tag{10}$$

where s_1 is a slack variable indicating the volume of furnace oil diverted to heavy fuel and v_{HF} is the value per barrel of heavy fuel. It is not possible, however, to divert unlimited amounts of furnace oil into heavy fuel without violating heavy fuel's speci-

FIGURE 7

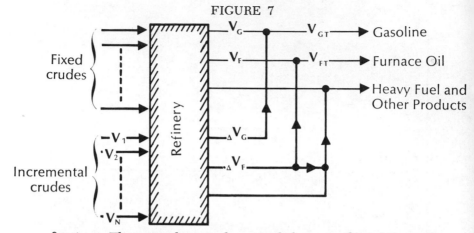

fications. The upper limit on how much furnace oil can be mixed
into heavy fuel depends on the volume of heavy fuel produced
which in turn is related to the crude slate, and would depend
also on the specifications of heavy fuel. Furthermore, if we bring
heavy fuel into the picture explicitly, the cost coefficients used
before must be modified. The problem is beginning to become
more complex. To take these effects into account would form the
basis of an entirely new study. For purposes of the present illustration, however, the situation can be handled roughly as
follows. It turns out from experience and by considering the
volumes involved that the excess furnace oil production should
be less than or at most equal to about 15 percent of the incremental furnace oil production if all the excess is to go to heavy
fuel and specifications on heavy fuel are to be met. Therefore,
the additional constraint

$$\sum_1^N a_{iF} V_i + s_2 = 1.15 \Delta V_F \tag{11}$$

was added to the system where s_2 is a slack variable. This constraint insures that no undue advantage is taken of the freedom
introduced by excess furnace oil production.

The results for this second formulation of the problem are
shown by the dashed lines in Figures 5 and 6. The abscissa now
refers to that part of incremental furnace oil production which
leaves the refinery as furnace oil. Excess furnace oil is produced
below incremental furnace oil production of about 8,600 bpd.

FIGURE 8

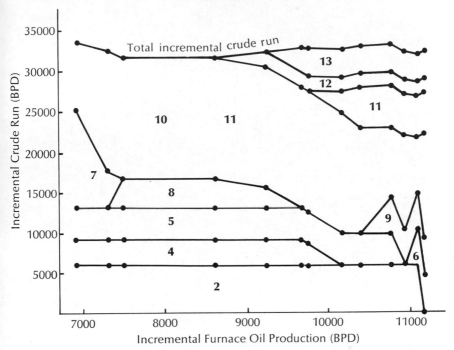

Above that level, it is not economic to produce more furnace oil than required and, consequently, there is no difference between the two formulations of the problem. Constraint (11) is limiting for incremental furnace oil production below about 7,500 bpd. Figure 8 shows the composition of the optimum crude slate for the second formulation as a function of incremental furnace oil production. This is useful information to have on hand. Note that no changes occur in the range of incremental furnace oil production from 7,500 to 8,600 bpd. In this range, actual incremental furnace oil production remains fixed at 8,600 bpd with any excess going into heavy fuel.

The modern refinery is a complicated system with strong interdependence among the activities within it. The example just described illustrates this point and shows the importance of the refiner's experience in correctly isolating portions of the refinery which can be separately considered.

Part Seven

Decision Theory and Scheduling Techniques

IN RECENT YEARS, firms have come to use various types of decision-theoretic and scheduling techniques to help them arrive at better decisions. Part Seven is devoted to a discussion of these techniques. The opening article, from *Fortune,* describes statistical decision theory and various scheduling techniques in a relatively simple way. Going a step further, John Pratt, Howard Raiffa, and Robert Schlaifer present elements of modern statistical decision theory, including a description of decision trees. In a brief note, Martin Shubik discusses some alternative theories of decision-making under uncertainty. A. A. Walters then presents a detailed application of decision theory to a specific example, the problem being to determine whether or not a tax should be imposed on a particular commodity and whether a survey should be carried out to obtain relevant information.

In the final article, Jerome D. Wiest discusses the nature and significance of heuristic programming. A heuristic is "a rule of thumb used to solve a particular problem . . . [and] a heuristic program is a collection or combination of heuristics. . . ." Wiest describes how heuristic programming can be used to help solve scheduling problems, as well as a variety of other types of problems.

Decision Theory and Program Scheduling

Fortune MAGAZINE

The author, George A. W. Boehm, is an associate editor of Fortune; this article appeared in the April 1962 issue.

Throughout history men have employed elaborate rituals for making up their minds. They have poured libations and sacrificed oxen in hopes of persuading a capricious and possibly hostile Nature to reward their decisions. They have consulted sibyls and watched the flight of birds to discover what the future holds in store. They have put their faith in proverbs and rules of thumb devised to take some of the guesswork out of living. They have sought divine guidance, as did George Romney, former president of American Motors, when he fasted and meditated before deciding to seek the Republican nomination for governor of Michigan.

In managing the affairs of modern business and government more scientific decision methods are needed. Unaided, the human mind cannot possibly weigh the manifold complexities involved in the development of a missile, the erection of a forty-story office building, the operation of an enterprise producing hundreds of products for millions of customers. Thousands of decisions go into scheduling jobs, ordering supplies, managing inventories, negotiating with contractors, hiring labor, pricing goods, and planning production facilities. The executive is further harassed by such uncertainties as the unpredictable tastes of consumers and the speculative nature of economic forecasts and research and development programs. Thus all too often he must act largely on hunch and intuition—and go home with the gnawing suspicion that he might have decided more wisely.

In recent years scientists have been showing the executive how to avoid some of the perplexity that attends decision making. They have been putting together a voluminous bundle of mathematical techniques for evaluating possible courses of action. In attempting to rationalize the process of deciding, they have developed "decision theory." This is not really a single theory of how to make decisions, but rather a collection of techniques for weighing many factors in logical fashion. Some of the techniques are best suited to situations in which, though all the factors are known or predictable, the complexity is so confusing that the human mind cannot arrive at a wholly rational decision. Other techniques cope with "risks"—chances that can be accurately measured or calculated, such as the probability that a given number of insurance policyholders will die within a year. Still others deal with "uncertainties" (which scientists carefully distinguish from "risks")—chances that can be estimated only roughly at best, because, for example, they depend on future developments or the behavior of a competitor. All decision theory, however, has a common purpose: to show decision makers surer ways to attain their goals.

Decision theorists use some tools that were developed several decades ago, notably statistical sampling, and some that are less familiar, such as linear programing, a short-cut method of finding the best way to allocate scarce resources. In addition, some brand-new techniques are being perfected. Two of the most successful, PERT and CPM (which will be explained later), are now used to schedule most United States space programs and many large construction jobs. To date, the various kinds of mathematical decision aids have been effectively applied to controlling inventory levels, arranging bus schedules, planning preventive maintenance, determining the best operating conditions for oil refineries, and scheduling many other industrial and military logistic operations that depend on the making of many routine but intricately related decisions.

Decision theory caught on first in the petroleum industry, which has a tradition of exploiting scientific techniques to control its production and marketing procedures. Other research-minded enterprises, including most of the big chemical and electrical firms, are now also making wide use of decision theory, and a few other industries are beginning to adopt it.

The techniques are too complicated to be applied by amateurs; the executive must call upon a specialist. Many big companies have staffs of decision experts, who are usually designated by some other name—e.g., planning, applied mathematics, or operations research. The executive without such a staff can turn to any of more than a score of consultants, many of whom specialize in industrial production, economic planning, or some other field of decision making. The Air Force has its own group of decision-theory consultants—the Rand Corporation. Serving private industry are a number of consulting firms that are capable of inventing new decision techniques for special applications.

Any group of decision experts is likely to include men with varied backgrounds, for the theoretical ideas stem from a wide range of scientific disciplines: mathematics, physics, systems engineering, econometrics, statistics, and servomechanism theory, which originally applied to automatic controls. But whatever his approach, the decision theorist must understand how to use computers. The techniques usually demand a prodigious amount of calculation. To apply them on large-scale problems without a computer would be as unthinkable as to work out a complex engineering design with Roman numerals.

The new scientific approach might suggest the possibility that even the most far-reaching business decisions could be turned over entirely to computers. But executives have no reason to fear that they will be replaced by machines producing decisions "untouched by human brains." Hunch and intuition are still invaluable. Indeed, most decision theorists today are looking for ways to incorporate expert judgment with their mathematics. They want to take full advantage of the comprehensiveness of the human mind to augment the precision of computers. For his part, the executive of the future will depend on the tools of decision theory much as an airplane pilot relies on his instruments. If he can learn to understand the theory well enough to appraise its applications, he can free himself from many routine responsibilities and broaden the scope of his thinking.

This inclusion of judgment is making decision theory more realistic, but at the same time it may cost the theory some of its mathematical incisiveness. Some leaders in the field used to cherish the somewhat arrogant hope that pure mathematics might produce perfectly precise and automatic decisions. Now they are aware that decision theory will be used less to dictate optimal courses of action, more to present the human decision maker with a choice of feasible actions and help him choose a good one.

The marriage of judgment to mathematics requires considerable ingenuity. Not infrequently the decision theorist must be a virtuoso psychologist in order to translate intuition and opinions into the numbers and mathematical functions that a computer can process. People tend to think about their jobs in one way, describe them in another, and actually perform them in a third way. For example, the warehouse manager who claims he has never been late on a promised delivery date may be talking quite frankly; but perhaps he has achieved his remarkable record by setting back the date whenever he has foreseen a jam. He may also find it difficult to assess the value of some quite ordinary factors—e.g., how much an inventory shortage might cost his company in lost sales and irate customers. He might be able, however, to estimate the cost indirectly in different terms, such as the amount he would be willing to spend for air freight in an emergency.

Far knottier problems arise because people are often erratic and inarticulate when they try to explain what they want to accomplish. Theoretical economists conceive of a marvelously rational being whom they call "economic man": he has a clear idea of what ends he wants to attain, and, given alternatives, he has the wisdom to calculate which one will be most rewarding in terms of his personal scale of values. But the very fact that personal values are part of the equation casts doubt on whether there can ever be an authentic "economic man." One of the most valuable services a decision theorist can perform is to list alternative courses of action and spell out the risks and payoffs associated with each. But if he is actually going to recommend an acceptable decision, he may first have to determine his client's attitude toward taking chances, which is an element in the client's personal scale of values. Several gambling strategies have been formulated mathematically so that they can be incorporated in some decision methods. For the pessimist who regards himself as an underdog faced by hostile Nature, there is the "minimax" strategy. This guides him to choose the course of action that entails the minimum risk of disaster, although it may also reduce his chance of winning. Against a wise and powerful adversary, "minimax" is clearly the prudent policy. For the unbridled optimist who likes to plunge on long shots, this is "maximax." This enables him to shoot for big gains although he runs a big risk of large loss. And for the patient man who regards life as an unending series of gambles and expects his luck to average out, there is the "maximum expected value" strategy. Given about an even number of good and bad breaks, this will maximize his chances of profiting in the long run.

Interest in decision theory is now booming, thanks largely to the striking success of two new scheduling procedures: Critical Path Method (CPM) and Program Evaluation and Review Technique (PERT), which differ from each other only in a few details. They enable managers to keep tight control of the timing and budgets of even the most complex and widely scattered projects. Scheduling of such programs actually consists of a multitude of interrelated decisions—e.g., when to promise delivery, how many electricians to hire for a given week, when to order materials and how to ship them, which contractor to employ. The new procedures are relatively simple to apply and interpret. Yet they produce many decisions almost automatically, while giving the manager wide scope to use his judgment and without burdening him with mathematical details.

In both CPM and PERT, the first step is to analyze all the work that must be done, break it down into individual tasks, and then estimate how long each will probably take and how much it will cost. This information is then diagramed as a network showing what activities must await the completion of other jobs and what work can be carried on in parallel with other phases of the project.

The scheduling network is based on the obvious logic that people commonly apply to any number of everyday activities. For example, a methodical hostess planning a party might make a list including all that will have to be done: order meat and vegetables, bake a cake, polish the silver, hire a maid, buy liquor, buy a new dress, get a permanent, set up a bar, set the table, etc. And she will have a good idea of the timing of every item on the list. Similarly, most able industrial managers presumably have kept in the backs of their minds at least a vague idea of a job network. But until the advent of electronic computers, it would have been futile actually to draw detailed networks. Projects large enough to require elaborate planning are usually represented by networks that are far too complicated for the unaided human mind to analyze and adjust—over 1,000 steps for the construction of a modest industrial plant, up to perhaps 30,000 for the development of a large missile.

A modern computer, however, can derive all sorts of useful information from the network. All the time and cost estimates and the relation of every job to all the others are reduced to a numerically coded program. Then, in a matter of minutes, the computer can calculate how long the project will take and how much it will cost. The over-all time estimate depends on a key concept: the "critical path." This is a sequence of jobs in which any slowdown will delay the completion of the entire project. Conversely, if these jobs are rushed, the whole project will be completed earlier. Generally, most jobs do not lie along the critical path; if they take a little longer than expected, the project will still finish on time. In principle, a human being could apply this concept just as a computer does, and take steps to shorten the time along the critical path. But it might take him days, even weeks, to find just which path is critical. The computer also does what no human mind could possibly accomplish: it shows continually how plans should be changed to keep the project on schedule and within the budget. Users of network scheduling avoid costly over-all crash programs; they have found that even in emergencies they seldom have to expedite more than ten per cent of the work. Besides, they don't have to waste time in tedious coordinating conferences.

The inventors of CPM and PERT started with somewhat different objectives but wound up with the same basic concepts. Early in 1957 a group of operations-research specialists from E. I. du Pont de Nemours got together with computer-applications experts at the Remington Rand division of Sperry Rand to design a procedure for scheduling chemical-plant construction. CPM was the result, and much of the credit for it belongs to James E. Kelley Jr., then with Remington Rand. Kelley not only exploited the critical-path concept but also introduced ways of "crashing" a project in an economical fashion. CPM caught on almost immediately in the construction industry.

CHART 1

How a Computer Decides the Cheapest Schedule for a Project

Job	Normal days	cost	Crash days	cost	Cost of crashing dollars per day
A	3	$140	2	$210	$70
B	6	215	5	275	60
C	2	160	1	240	80
D	4	130	3	180	50
E	2	170	1	250	80
F	7	165	4	285	40
G	4	210	3	290	80
H	3	110	2	160	50
Total		$1300		$1890	

Major industrial projects, such as the building of a ship or a factory or the development of a missile, involve so many activities that no human mind can keep close track of all that is going on, much less schedule every detail in the most efficient way. New mathematical techniques, however, are giving project managers a clearer view of their work and a better opportunity to use their judgment effectively. The essential steps in one of these new techniques, Critical Path Method, are demonstrated by the analysis of a tiny hypothetical project. The manager begins the scheduling by listing all the jobs that must be done (see chart above) together with estimates of normal time and cost for each. Next he estimates how much it would cost to rush each job to completion by a crash program. All this information is fed into a computer. As the totals show, the manager could get each job done as fast as possible by spending an extra $590. But he may be able to shorten the time of completing the whole project without "crashing" every job. This is what the computer will investigate.

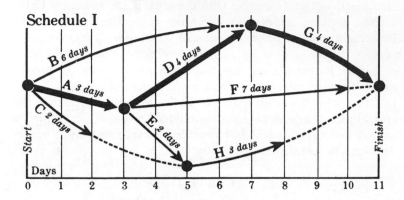

Schedule I

The manager diagrams the order in which the jobs must be done. This shows, for example, that C can be done in parallel with A but that D cannot be started until A is finished. The computer calculates the "critical path" (heavy black line) from this information. The jobs on this path determine the time (eleven days) needed to complete the whole project; the rest can be delayed somewhat (broken lines) without affecting the over-all schedule.

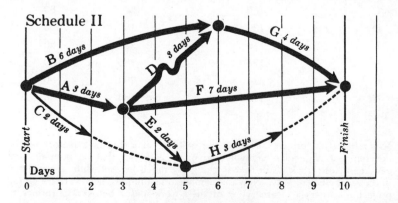

Schedule II

Next the computer calculates ways to shorten the over-all schedule by crashing some of the jobs. There may be several ways, but the computer selects the cheapest. The diagram above shows that if D is accelerated to three days instead of four, the over-all schedule can be reduced to ten days. Two more jobs, B and F, become part of a critical path, but there is still some leeway in C, E, and H. The cost of crashing D is an extra $50.

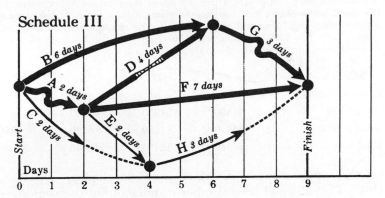

Again rescheduling the project so that it can be finished in nine days, the computer finds that it is best to crash both A and G by one day. Surprisingly, the extra effort put on these jobs makes it possible to relax a bit on D and allot the normal four days for its completion. Crashing A and G will cost a total of $150, but the relaxation of D saves $50, so the acceleration of the whole project from ten to nine days costs only $100 more.

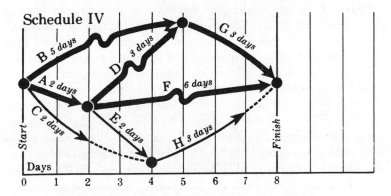

If the manager wants to lop another day from the schedule, he can do so most economically by crashing three jobs: B, D, and F. Although the chart shows that F could be shortened by as much as three days, the extra hurry would have no effect on the over-all schedule, so F is shortened by only one day. The manager has now spent $300 on the crash program, compared with the $590 he might have spent to crash all the jobs.

To decide which schedule is actually best from all viewpoints, the manager can instruct the computer to take other factors into account. There may be a penalty for failing to complete the project on schedule. Sometimes in actual practice contractors have found that they can make more profit by proceeding slowly and paying a penalty rather than paying heavy overtime. The chart below shows how the computer might include on its calculations indirect costs—e.g., overhead or penalties. In this example the indirect costs amount to a flat $110 per day, and the chart tells the manager that the cheapest schedule is the one that takes nine days.

Schedule	I	II	III	IV
Duration (days)	11	10	9	8
Direct cost	$1300	$1350	$1450	$1600
Indirect cost	$1210	$1100	$990	$880
Total cost	$2510	$2450	$2440	$2480

Other applications of CPM are now developing. Du Pont, Union Carbide, and several other manufacturing companies are using it to schedule maintenance on large plants. Most production lines have to be shut down and overhauled from time to time. By scheduling hundreds of maintenance steps in an optimal way CPM can often shorten the shutdown period and save thousands of dollars of production that would otherwise be lost.

PERT (Program Evaluation Review Technique) was born of sheer desperation. In 1956, during the early stages of the Navy's Polaris submarine-missile development program, a Special Projects Office was set up to manage this immense project. The men in charge found that all the conventional managerial methods were hopelessly inadequate to keep track of the schedule. Superimposed on the job of coordinating the efforts of 11,000 contractors was a degree of uncertainty as to when crucial research and development stages might be completed. So, Willard Fazar of the SPO, with the help of Lockheed's Missile and Space Division and consultants from Booz, Allen & Hamilton, devised PERT as a network flow chart with built-in uncertainty. Instead of assigning a single time estimate to each task, as Kelley had done with CPM, Fazar called for three estimates: optimistic, normal, and pessimistic. Such multiple estimating made the computations somewhat more difficult but they were still well within the capability of a high-speed computer.

PERT worked well from the time it was put into operation in 1958. Polaris chief Vice Admiral W. F. Raborn, Jr. has given the technique much credit for the fact that the development of the first Polaris missile required two years' less time than originally estimated. PERT is also beginning to find uses outside government projects. The most noteworthy to date was a schedule for the production of a Broadway play. PERT kept track of some 200 steps the producers had to take before the play opened—e.g., rent the theatre, sign the stars, hire a scenery designer, buy props, dispense publicity, and set a date for the dress rehearsal.

Both CPM and PERT are still in the evolutionary stage. Kelley has worked out a way to schedule a number of simultaneous projects that must share available resources, such as labor, machines, space, or money.

Most executive decisions hinge on the question of how to make the most of whatever is available—time, money, raw materials, manpower, production facilities, storage space, shipping. A manager may have to decide how many of each of three items he should produce. For example, the first item must be painstakingly assembled by hand; the second needs a great deal of machining; the third is bulky. If he were to concentrate on any one item, he would run short of labor, machines, or warehouse space. The decision technique called linear programing, a method older than and somewhat different from CPM or PERT, can tell him precisely the most profitable combination of the three items.

Some linear programs, such as those that portray the entire distribution system of a large company, involve several hundred interrelated variables. The programer starts by putting down in mathematical terms all the relations among the variables. Some are in the form of equations, others in the form of "inequalities"— e.g., mathematical statements that say a machine can produce *no more than* so many items per hour. By a mathematical stratagem the inequalities are then converted to equations. The variables outnumber the equations, so there is no unique algebraic solution. But such a system of equations can be made to yield optimum solutions—i.e., solutions that maximize profits, minimize costs, or make some other element in the business as small or large as possible. This is the purpose of linear programing.

The mathematical procedure generally used to find optimal solutions is the "simplex" method, invented in 1947 by George Dantzig. The method belies its name; it is extremely complicated. It is essentially a trial-and-error approach. But the groping for a solution is entirely methodical. It guarantees finding a better solution at each step and an optimal solution in a finite number of steps. Most practical linear-programming problems would take months, even years, to solve by hand, but a fast computer usually handles them in a few minutes.

Linear programing has been so thoroughly studied and so widely applied that experts usually classify problems into a number of standard types. They schedule truck and airline fleets with the transportation type. Another linear program, sometimes called the nutrition problem, decides how to mix animal feed so as to meet nutritional specifications at minimum cost; it is also used for blending gasoline to meet octane-number specifications. Paper and sheet-steel mills rely on the trim-loss reduction program to minimize waste when small orders are cut from large rolls.

Linear programing is especially valuable to the petroleum industry. There it is used more or less routinely for scheduling the distribution of products, balancing availability of raw crude with refinery operations so as to produce the most profitable assortment of products, blending gasoline, and even deciding where new refineries are needed.

In recent years linear programing has gained an important new dimension. In 1949, Albert W. Tucker, Harold W. Kuhn, and David Gale, following up a conjecture by the late John von Neumann, proved that every linear program has a shadow, called its "dual program." When a mathematician sets up a linear program to achieve one objective, he can in an easy step solve the dual program and thereby achieve a different objective. For example, the original program might find a production scheme that minimized costs for a fixed labor force and consumption of raw materials; the dual program would determine a system of internal pricing that would maximize the value of net output while balancing the direct costs of labor and raw materials. Looking at the solutions of both the original program and its dual gives the manager another degree of flexibility in making decisions. In addition to learning how to make the most profit with the machines at hand, he may be able to tell how to increase profits by installing more or different machines. Related mathematical techniques indicate what would happen if some of the variables were to change slightly. The same procedures also reveal how critical an error in the data might be; thus the manager knows when he can get away with an offhand estimate and when he has to make a careful study. The significance of all this additional information is that it enables the non-mathematical executive to ask questions he would naturally want to ask, even those that may not have occurred to him when the programing was begun. The decision theorist is able to use this kind of analysis also to increase the realism of his technique by blending hunches and judgments with the mathematics.

New mathematical inventions are beginning to break through some of the limitations of linear programing. Many programs are unwieldy; even the fastest computer takes several hours to perform the 200 million calculations needed to solve a program with 400 equations. Recently, however, Dantzig and Philip Wolfe worked out a computational shortcut, which they call the "decomposition" principle. It seems particularly applicable to situations that are not very tightly knit—e.g., the production scheduling of a company with many plants, each specializing in a few products that it feeds into a centralized marketing system. Decomposition is a mathematical way of chopping a huge program into many smaller ones and then solving each and coordinating the results in succession. As yet there have been no industrial applications, but several computer-service groups are coding the decomposition principle so that it can be fed into computers.

Another limitation of linear programing stems from the fact that it fails to distinguish between fractions and whole numbers. In some real problems only whole numbers are feasible. A program for scheduling a fleet of planes might, for example, tell an airline that 8.26 planes should be assigned to one particular route and 3.74 to another. The obvious step would be to round off the numbers to eight and four. But actually this is not safe; oddly enough, it might well prove more economical to assign six planes to each route. For such linear-programing problems Ralph E. Gomory, a young I.B.M. mathematician, has invented a brand-new technique called "integer programing." It usually requires a good deal more computation than the conventional simplex method, but it produces the best solution that can be expressed in whole numbers. Its greatest potential application appears to be in such problems as determining the overall costs of a new production plant where there is a major initial cost of building the plant as well as the continuing variable costs of its operation.

Elements of uncertainty complicate the decision process, often to such an extent that linear programing cannot produce a realistic solution in a reasonable time. In extreme cases a decision maker starts with almost total ignorance as to what decisions are possible, what the consequences might be, how long the situation will last, or even what goals he should seek. He gropes along, committing himself when he has to and changing his mind as his view becomes clearer. A new decision technique called "dynamic programing" formulates this groping in a logical way so that the decision maker behaves optimally at every stage—optimally, at least, within the limits of his knowledge at each stage.

The basic logic and the mathematics of dynamic programing are directly related to the theory of servomechanisms, the feedback controls that, for example, enable an autopilot to sense variations in an airplane's flight and bring it back on course. Richard Bellman, a Rand mathematician who is the leading exponent of dynamic programing, aims at a more sophisticated kind of control. Whereas an autopilot is designed for a specific goal—to keep the plane steady in flight—Bellman would like to design controls that would learn from experience what their goals should be and how best to attain them.

Bellman's theory is comprehensive enough to embrace decision making in business, economics, biology, and statistics, as well as engineering. The computational difficulties are formidable in many applications, but in the long run, dynamic programing promises to solve many hitherto intractable decision problems. It may, for example, help solve the dilemma of a physician who is testing a drug to determine whether it will cure a lethal disease. He is confronted with partly conflicting goals. As a scientist, he wants to prove conclusively whether the drug is effective, and he resolves to give it to only half his patients. But by following this plan he will almost surely doom the rest of the patients and so, as a practitioner, he is tempted to give the drug to all. Ordinarily, he must decide either to carry out a scientifically impeccable experiment or to do everything possible to cure patients. In principle, dynamic programing offers the physician a partial escape from this burdensome decision. He may be able to alter the testing procedure as he accumulates experimental results. If in the early stages of testing the drug seems to be effective, dynamic programing should tell him better than previous techniques how to administer it to a larger proportion of patients without casting doubts on the scientific validity of the test.

Dynamic programing is actually an extension of some concepts that have brought statistics into the realm of decision theory. During World War II a Columbia University statistician, Abraham Wald, devised a new way to decide how much statistical evidence was needed to support a conclusion.

Wald's "sequential" decision theory was based on earlier ideas that had been developed in the early thirties by Egon S. Pearson and Jerzy Neyman in England. Pearson and Neyman had included in their statistical methods the risks and consequences of drawing wrong conclusions. To these Wald had added another variable: the cost of sampling and testing. His methods had obvious practical appeal. Testing—indeed, acquiring knowledge of any sort—costs something, and the faster a statistician can make up his mind, the more money he saves.

As a consequence of Wald's theory, human judgment had to be embodied in statistical analysis. The statistician had to invent some formal procedure for deciding when to stop testing, and this procedure inevitably depended on expert opinion as to the consequences of drawing a wrong conclusion.

Some further attempts to extend the use of human judgment in statistics have aroused a major controversy. One group of statisticians advocates using expert opinion as if it were experimental evidence; this group is called the "neo-Bayesian" school after the Reverend Thomas Bayes, an eighteenth-century British contributor to the mathematics of probability theory. The neo-Bayesians use judgment to determine a priori probabilities—i.e., assumptions of likelihood—which can then be used mathematically to help calculate the probability that a given hypothesis is true. Neyman and most other conventional statisticians go along with this idea, but only up to a point. They employ a priori probabilities only when they are derived from repetitive observations of relevant data. In such cases there is a clear relationship between probability and frequency. They balk at the notion of applying a priori probabilities and judgment to analysis of once-in-a-lifetime situations.

These, significantly, are the situations that are involved in most major executive decisions—e.g., whether to merge with a company in another field, whether to bid on a missile contract, whether to open a plant in Europe. The neo-Bayesians would ask the executive for an opinion of his chances of success and they would use this "expert" opinion as if it were the result of an actual experiment.

The use of judgmental probability makes it possible to reinforce the subjective beliefs of a business executive—or a military commander—with a good deal of objectivity in the form of decision theory. Nevertheless, over-reliance on opinion can lead to bad decisions. Samuel S. Wilks cautions: "The danger is that you may be accepting a bad guess when you really should be buying more experimental knowledge."

Sir Solly Zuckerman, a British scientist who is one of the fathers of operations research, is greatly concerned because military analysts are applying probability laws that pertain to repetitive situations to once-in-a-lifetime situations. Writing in *Foreign Affairs*, Zuckerman warns: "If one decides wrongly about the use of nuclear weapons, we shall be in a situation which may never repeat itself. . . ."

Introduction to Statistical
Decision Theory

JOHN PRATT, HOWARD RAIFFA,
AND ROBERT SCHLAIFER

John Pratt, Howard Raiffa, and Robert Schlaifer are professors in the Graduate School of Business Administration at Harvard University. This article is taken from their book, Introduction to Statistical Decision Theory, *published in 1965.*

THE PROBLEM OF DECISION UNDER UNCERTAINTY

When all of the facts bearing on a business decision are accurately known—when the decision is made "under certainty"—careless thinking or excessive computational difficulty are the only reasons why the decision should turn out, after the fact, to have been wrong. But when the relevant facts are not all known—when the decision is made "under uncertainty"—it is impossible to make sure that every decision will turn out to have been right in this same sense. Under uncertainty, the businessman is forced, in effect, to gamble. His previous actions have put him in a position where he must place bets, hoping that he will win but knowing that he may lose. Under such circumstances, a right decision consists in the choice of the best possible bet, whether it is won or lost after the fact. A businessman who buys fire insurance does not censure himself if his plant has not burned down by the time the insurance expires, and the following example is typical of other decisions which must be made and judged in this way.

An oil wildcatter who holds an option on a plot of land in an oil-producing region must decide whether to drill on the site before the option expires or to abandon his rights. The profitability of drilling will depend on a large number of unknowns— the cost of drilling, the amount of oil or gas discovered, the price at which the oil or gas can be sold, and so forth—none of which can be predicted with certainty. His problem is further complicated by the fact that it is possible to perform various tests or experiments that will yield a certain amount of information on the geophysical structure below the land on which he has an option. Since some structures are more favorable to the existence of oil than others, this information would be of considerable help in deciding whether or not to drill; but the various tests cost a substantial amount of money, and hence it is not at all obvious that any of the available tests should be performed. The wildcatter must nevertheless decide which if any of the tests are to be performed, and ultimately, if not now, he must decide whether or not to drill.

Decision Trees · The essential characteristics of this example are two in number:
1. A *choice* or in some cases a sequence of choices must be made among various possible courses of action.
2. This choice or sequence of choices will ultimately lead to some *consequence*, but the decision maker cannot be sure in advance what this consequence will be because it depends not only on his choice or choices but on an unpredictable *event* or sequence of events.

The essence of any such problem can be brought out very clearly by a type of diagram known as a *decision tree*.

As an example that will illustrate all the essential points involved in the construction of a decision tree without useless complexities, we shall take a somewhat simplified version of the oil-drilling problem described just above. For our present purpose we shall assume that:
1. If the well is drilled at all, it will be drilled on a fixed-price contract for $100,000;

2. If oil is struck, the wildcatter will immediately sell out to a major producer for $450,000;

3. Only one type of test or experiment, namely a seismic sounding, can be performed before deciding whether or not to drill. This experiment costs $10,000; if it is performed, it will reveal with certainty whether the structure is of Type *A* (very favorable to the existence of oil), Type *B* (less favorable), or Type *C* (very unfavorable).

On these assumptions the wildcatter's decision problem can be represented by the tree shown as Figure 1. We imagine the decision-maker as standing at the base of the tree (the left side of the diagram) and as being obliged to choose first between having the seismic sounding made and not having it made. If the wildcatter's choice is to have the sounding made, one of three events will occur: the subsurface structure will be revealed to be of Type *A*, *B*, or *C*. If the wildcatter's choice is not to have the sounding made, then only one event can occur: no information.

Whatever the wildcatter's first-stage choice may be and whatever the first-stage event, the wildcatter must now enter a second stage by making a choice between drilling and abandoning the option. If he drills, then one or the other of two events will occur: oil or dry hole; if he chooses to abandon the option, the only possible "event" is "option rights lost."

Finally, at the end (right) of the tree we write down a description of the consequence of each possible sequence of choices and events. If the wildcatter chooses not to have the sounding made and to abandon his option, the consequence is simply $0—we neglect whatever he may originally have paid for the option because this is a sunk cost that cannot be affected by any present decision and therefore is irrelevant to the decision problem. Suppose, on the contrary, he decides to drill even though he has learned nothing about the subsurface structure; if he strikes a dry hole, he loses the $100,000 drilling cost, whereas if he strikes oil, his profit is the $450,000 for which he sells the rights less the $100,000 cost of drilling. If in the first stage he decides to have the sounding made, then the consequences of abandoning the option, drilling a dry hole, or striking oil are all reduced by the $10,000 cost of the sounding.

FIGURE 1

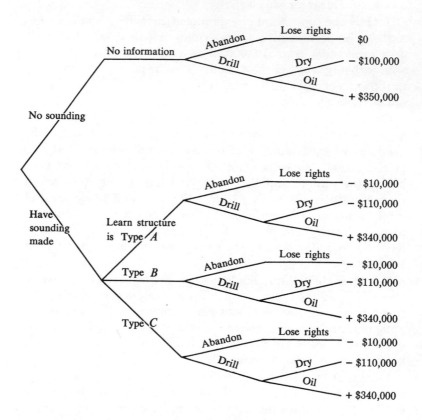

THE PROBLEM OF ANALYSIS

Analysis of the Simplest Problems · Before we even try to say
what we mean by a "reasoned solution" of a complex decision
problem of the kind we have just described, let us try to get a
start by seeing what a sensible businessman might do when
he solves a much simpler problem.

We consider an example. A manufacturer, Mr. L. K. Jones,
has recently experienced a serious decline in demand for his
product and as a result will be forced to lay off a substantial
portion of his work force, spend money for protective treatment

of idle machinery, and so forth, unless he can obtain a large order which the XYZ Company is about to place with some supplier. To have a chance at obtaining this order, Jones will have to incur considerable expense both for the making of samples and for sending a team of sales engineers to visit the XYZ Company; he must now decide whether or not to incur this expense. Formally, his problem can be described by the tree shown in Figure 2, where the three possible consequences of the two possible acts are represented by symbols:

C_1 = layoff of substantial part of work force, cost of protecting machinery;

C_2 = same as C_1, and in addition the cost of unsuccessful attempt to obtain order;

C_3 = substantial monetary profit on order, less cost of obtaining it.

FIGURE 2

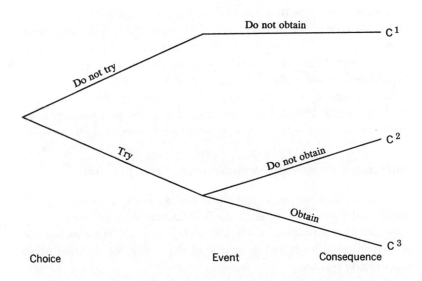

The structure of *this* problem is simple enough to make quite clear to anyone the issues that are involved in its solution. Jones (or any other sensible businessman faced with a problem of this sort) will feel that his decision will depend on two separate considerations: (1) his judgment concerning his chances of getting the order if he tries, and (2) a comparison of the cost of trying with the advantages which will accrue to him if he succeeds. If the cost is quite small relative to the advantages which would accompany success, he will make the attempt even if he thinks the chances of success are quite small; if, on the other hand, the cost of trying to get the order is so large that it would eat up most of the profits, he will not make the attempt unless he feels virtually sure that the attempt will succeed.

Sometimes a businessman who is thinking about a problem of this kind will go even further and *quantify* some if not all of his reasoning. He may say, for example, that there is so much to be gained by obtaining the order that he would try to obtain it even if there were only 1 chance in 3 of success; he may then conclude either (*a*) that he *will* make the attempt because in his opinion the chances are at least as good as 1 in 3, or else (*b*) that he *will not* make the effort because in his opinion the chances of success are less than 1 in 3. Alternatively, the businessman may start from the other side of the problem, say that in his opinion he has about 1 chance in 3 of getting the order if he tries, and then conclude either (*a*) that he *will* make the attempt because the gains which would accrue from success are so great that a 1/3 chance of obtaining them is well worth the cost of trying, or else (*b*) that he *will not* make the attempt because the gains are too small to warrant the cost when there is only 1 chance in 3 of success.

THE BASES OF DECISION: PREFERENCE AND JUDGMENT

The problem we have just discussed suffices to make it quite clear that there is in general no "objectively correct" solution to *any* decision problem. Since Jones is personally responsible for the decision to try or not to try to get the order, his decision must *necessarily* rest on:

1. How good *he feels* the chances of obtaining the order would have to be to make it worth his while to try;

2. How good *in his opinion* the chances of obtaining the order actually are.

What the businessman actually does when he answers questions of type 1 is quantify his *personal preference* for C_1 relative to C_2 and C_3; what he does when he answers questions of type 2 is quantify his *personal judgment* concerning the relative strengths of the factors that favor and oppose certain events. If he behaves reasonably, he then chooses the solution of the problem which is *consistent* with this personal preference and this personal judgment.

ANALYSIS OF COMPLEX PROBLEMS;
THE ROLE OF FORMAL ANALYSIS

Since reasonable decisions in even the simplest problems must rest necessarily on the responsible decision maker's personal judgments and personal preferences, it is intuitively quite clear that these same elements must be involved in the solution of complex problems represented by decision trees with many levels and many branches at each level. It would be folly, in other words, to look for a method of analysis that will lead to an "objectively correct" solution of the oil-drilling problem we have used. A reasonable decision-maker wants his decision to agree with his preferences and his best judgments, and he will have (and should have) no use for any proposal that purports to solve his problem by some "formula" that does *not* incorporate his preferences and judgments. This assertion does not of course imply that the decision-maker should ignore objective evidence that is relevant and available.

Stated in another way, the reason why a decision-maker might want help in analyzing a decision problem like our oil-drilling example, when Jones needed no help in deciding whether or not to try for the order from the XYZ Company, is that Jones could easily see the *implications* of his preferences and judgments whereas the wildcatter cannot. The wildcatter may feel quite sure that, for example, he would decide to drill if he knew that the structure was of Type A or B and would decide not to drill if he knew that the structure was of Type C; however, his immediate problem is to decide whether or not to spend \$10,000 in order to learn what the structure is, and while it is obvious that this information has value, it is not at all clear whether the value is greater or less than the \$10,000 the information will cost.

Any decision problem, no matter how complex, can in principle be reduced to a number of problems each of which individually has the same simple structure as the problem described by the tree of Figure 2.

If, in each of these simple problems, the decision-maker will

1. Quantify his *preference* by telling us how good the chances of obtaining C_3 *would have to be* to make him willing to gamble on C_2 or C_3 rather than to take C_1 for certain, and

2. Quantify his *judgment* by telling us how good in his opinion the chances of obtaining C_3 *actually are,*

and if, in addition, he accepts certain simple principles of "reasonable," "consistent," or "coherent" behavior, then it is possible by purely logical deduction to find that solution of the complex problem which is *logically consistent with the decision-maker's own preferences and judgments.*

Naturally we are concerned with decision problems where this kind of analysis by decomposition and evaluation produces fruitful results. There are, of course, many problems—some would say "most problems"—where although in principle such an analysis could be made it would not be profitable to do so. In many situations, the incremental advantage to be gained from formal analysis cannot be expected to repay the effort, time, and cost of the analysis; in others, the decision maker may not be able, especially without training, to quantify his preference and judgments in the way required for a formal analysis; in still others, the decision problem may be faithfully abstracted into the proper form only to prove to be too complicated for the analytical tools we have available. Even after granting all these exceptions, however, there remain many problems in which formal analysis can be of considerable help to a businessman who wishes to take advantage of it.

A Note on Decision-making under Uncertainty

MARTIN SHUBIK

Martin Shubik is Professor of Industrial Administration at Yale University. This is an excerpt from his article, "Approaches to the Study of Decision-making Relevant to the Firm," which appeared in The Journal of Business *in 1961.*

By introducing considerations of probability, an attempt can be made to extend the economic theory of choice to conditions involving uncertainty. The heroic assumption must be made that the situations to be modeled are such that it is valid and useful to utilize the theory of probability. This has given rise to discussions concerning subjective probability and a large literature on probabilistic preferences and the theory of utility. Problems concerning gambling and risk preference have been examined, and several alternatives for optimal behavior have been suggested. For example, Savage has offered a man who wishes to minimize regret. In other words, after the event, when he looks back, he wishes to have acted in such a manner that he will be least sorry concerning the outcome.

Bayesian and "maximin" principles[1] have also been suggested as manners in which the individual should cope with lack of

1. [The "maximin" principle is often called the "minimax" principle. *Editor*]

knowledge. The simple examples given here illustrate the behaviors manifested in following these different principles. In Figure 1 a simple 2×2 payoff matrix is presented. The decision-maker must choose between one of two actions, knowing that "Nature," or the environment, may also make a choice which affects him. For example, if both select their second alternative, the payoff is 7 to the decision-maker. The principle he follows will depend upon his view of the forces and motivations present in his environment.

"Nature"

The Decision-maker

	1	2
1	1	9
2	2	7

FIGURE 1

The Bayesian assumption says that all the actions of "Nature" are equiprobable, and thus the optimal behavior under this assumption will be to select the first alternative, with an expected payoff of:

$$\tfrac{1}{2}\,(1) + \tfrac{1}{2}\,(9) = 5.$$

The maximin assumption has the decision-maker believe that the environment is "out to get him." In this case he will select his second alternative, assuming that, since the worst will happen, he can at least guarantee 2 for himself.

"Nature"

The Decision-maker

	1	2
1	1	0
2	0	2

FIGURE 2

The "regret payoff" is illustrated in Figure 2 for the same situation. If he selected his second alternative and the environment did likewise, he would obtain 7 (Fig. 1) but could have obtained 9 (by selecting his first alternative); hence his regret is 2.

Shackle has constructed a "potential surprise function" which he feels dominates many major decisions which must be made in face of uncertainty which cannot be adequately portrayed by considerations of probability. All the methods noted above depend upon assumptions as to how to deal with uncertainty. Which is the "best" assumption depends upon the application and knowledge of human behavior.

In spite of the limitations of models of probability, operations research and industrial statistics have, however, flourished by applying normative models of economic man acting under probabilistically portrayed uncertainty. Theoretical models of inventory, sequential sampling, and various queueing problems have been actively applied. These have already influenced the inventory levels of the whole economy and have had an effect on the understanding of reliability and risk in areas as diverse as individual credit risks, quality control in production, and stockpiling for emergency.

One area in which the applications have been fewer but the implications deeper is that of dynamic programming. This methodology deals with situations where at each period the decision-maker chooses an action which influences a sequence of events stretching off into the possibly indefinite future. In subsequent periods he has the opportunity to modify the effects of previous decisions by current action. Although this theory still deals with statistical uncertainty and mathematical expectations, the rules of decision generated as dynamic program solutions have more of the flavor of over-all long-range strategic decisions. Dividend and investment policies can be studied as dynamic programs. However, the mathematics of functional equations used in dynamic programming is, unfortunately, difficult and still relatively underdeveloped.

Decision Theory: An Example

A. A. WALTERS

A. A. Walters is Professor of Econometrics and Social Statistics at the University of Birmingham. This piece comes from his book Introduction to Econometrics, published by Norton in 1970.

It is often claimed that the ultimate purpose of any investigation is to enable us to make better decisions. From a judgment of the state of the world we evaluate the consequences of each potential course of action. We then decide to pursue one of these courses of action according to our view of the attractiveness of the consequences. For example, suppose we are concerned with finding the optimum tax to impose on confectionery and that we know that the elasticity of supply is infinite; then the question turns on the elasticity of demand. With the traditional approach we would either estimate the elasticity of demand or examine certain hypotheses about the elasticity. Let us suppose, for simplicity, that the elasticity of demand is *either* unity *or* 0.5. We might then set up our experiment to discover which hypothesis has the highest likelihood—using either Bayesian methods or the traditional methods of hypothesis testing. At this stage the statistician's job *per se* is completed and the decision-maker takes over.

With decision theory, however, the statistical problem is extended to consider the costs of making various decisions if certain hypotheses hold. Again let us simplify and assume that there are only two possible courses of action—to tax at 10 percent or not to tax at all. Then we can characterize the four outcomes by the following costs:

| | Elasticity | |
	1	0.5
Tax	$10 million	0
No tax	0	$5 million

Now if the main purpose of the tax is to raise revenue, it is clear that taxing confectionery when the elasticity is unity involves expense and no tax revenue—so we have supposed that the cost is $10 million which has been entered in the appropriate box of the table of outcomes. If, on the other hand, we impose a tax and the elasticity is only 0.5, we have taxed 'correctly' and we reckon the cost at zero. Similarly, if we do not tax when we should not, the cost can be taken as zero. If we miss an opportunity for taxing, i.e. no tax when the elasticity is 0.5, we incur a cost of $5 million.

Now let us suppose that we have *already carried out the survey* and found that the chance of unit elasticity is 0.2 and the likelihood of 0.5 elasticity is 0.8. Then we can find the expected costs of adopting the tax as

$$[(\$10 \text{ million}) \times 0.2] + [(\$0 \text{ million}) \times 0.8] = \$2 \text{ million}.$$

This is simply the sum of the outcome multiplied by the likelihood of that outcome. Similarly, the expected costs of not adopting the tax is

$$[(\$0 \text{ million}) \times 0.2] + [(\$5 \text{ million}) \times 0.8] = \$4 \text{ million}.$$

So we have

Strategy	Expected costs
Tax	$2 million
No tax	$4 million

and it is clearly the best strategy to tax confectionery.

This result is, however, critically dependent on the criteria we have adopted—that is, the minimizing of expected costs. There is nothing sacrosanct about this aim; and it is natural to consider alternative approaches. One such is to find the strategy which results in as low a value as possible for the *maximum* loss. In short the strategy is concerned with minimizing the maximum loss—or even shorter "minimax."

In our table we see that, if we tax, the maximum possible loss is $10 million. If we do not tax, the maximum possible loss is $5 million. Clearly the maximum loss is minimized if we then choose not to tax confectionery—and we are ensured that the maximum loss is $5 million. This is a different solution from that developed for the "expected loss" criterion. The minimax strategy represents a "safety-first" attitude to decision-making. In this strategy the numerical value of the likelihoods, provided they exceed zero, do not play a part—whereas in the "expected loss" case they play a critical role.

There are, of course, many other criteria for decision-making. But there is no obvious rule for choosing between the criteria available. Each must be chosen according to the "utility function" of the decision-maker. An ultra-cautious individual may choose "minimax," a less cautious man the "expected loss" criterion. If it is possible to describe each situation by means of a utility function we can generalise the choice criterion to one of maximizing expected utility (or minimizing expected disutility). This will then enable us to take account of the fact that a large loss, for example, has enormous disutility, while a small loss has proportionately less disutility. For example, we may assume that the disutility function is simply the *square* of the loss so that we have the disutility table in "utils":

	Elasticity	
	1	0
Tax	100	0
No tax	0	25

Units: utils.

And now calculating expected disutility

for tax $(100 \times 0.2) + (0 \times 0.8) = 20$ utils;

for no tax $(0 \times 0.2) + (25 \times 0.8) = 20$ utils.

There is a tie! It does not matter whether we choose to tax confectionery or not—they have equal disutility. If the disutility function had been the *cube* of the loss, then we should have been better off *not* introducing a tax. For the rest of this discussion we shall adopt only one of the various criteria discussed above—we shall use the simple "expected loss" formulation.

Up to now we have supposed that the experiment (the survey) had already taken place and that we were concerned with making a decision on the basis of its results about the likelihoods. But frequently we find ourselves in the situation where *whether to do a survey or not is actually part of the decision-making procedure*. In other words we start our decision-making process *before* the sample; we ask whether it is worthwhile sampling or not. This is a question in addition to those about choosing an action strategy, i.e. whether to tax or not.

Obviously the question of whether to sample or not will depend on two things: first the cost of the sample itself and secondly our ideas about how the sample result is likely to affect our views about the likelihoods of the elasticities. To develop the latter point suppose that *if the elasticity is actually unity* there is a very high chance (say 0.9) that the experiment will produce the correct result (elasticity = 1.0), and only a low chance (0.1) that the experiment will produce the wrong result, i.e. falsely allege that the elasticity is 0.5.

Now let us suppose that, as before, we can, before we decide whether or not to sample, ascribe probabilities to the hypotheses elasticity = 1, and 0.5, and let us suppose that these are respectively 0.3 and 0.7. These figures measure our degree of belief in the validity of the hypothesis before the sample is carried out. (They correspond to the values of 0.8 and 0.2 which we assumed in the previous example, when we assumed that we had already sampled and incorporated the results in these two likelihoods.) We can now calculate the chances of *both* the elasticity being unity *and* the experiment producing evidence showing that it is unity (and we use the mnemonic "prob" for probability):

$$\text{prob}\left[\begin{array}{cc} \text{elasticity}=1, & \text{sample} \\ & \text{indicates unity} \end{array}\right]$$

$$=\text{prob}\left[\begin{array}{c|c} \text{sample} & \text{elasticity} \\ \text{indicates unity} & =1 \end{array}\right] \cdot \text{prob}[\text{elasticity}=1]$$

by the ordinary laws of conditional probability.[1]

---

1. Prob [event x | event y] is the probability that event x occurs *given that event y occurs*: it is a conditional probability. On the other hand, prob [event x, event y] is the probability that *both* event x and event y occur. Clearly, prob [event x, event y] = prob [event x | event y] · prob [event y] · [*Editor.*]

Numerically

$$\text{prob}\left[\text{elasticity}=1, \begin{array}{l}\text{sample}\\ \text{indicates unity}\end{array}\right]=0.9\times0.3$$

$$=0.27.$$

Similarly

$$\text{prob}\left[\text{elasticity}=1, \begin{array}{l}\text{sample}\\ \text{indicates } 0.5\end{array}\right]=0.1\times0.3$$

$$=0.03$$

—this shows the likelihood that *both* the elasticity is unity *and* the sample evidence indicated that it is (wrongly) 0.5.

We have dealt with the case when the elasticity is unity; now we examine the case when the elasticity is 0.5. Suppose now that in fact the elasticity were 0.5. Then let us assume that the likelihood of the sample survey pointing to the correct result (i.e. elasticity$=0.5$) is 0.6, and the likelihood of it indicating the wrong result (unity) is 0.4. One can then construct the chances of the outcomes:

$$\text{prob}\left[\text{elasticity}=0.5, \begin{array}{l}\text{sample indicates}\\ \text{elasticity}=0.5\end{array}\right]$$

$$=\text{prob}\left[\begin{array}{l}\text{sample indicates}\\ \text{elasticity}=0.5\end{array}\middle| \text{elasticity}=0.5\right]\cdot\text{prob}\left[\text{elasticity}=0.5\right]$$

$$=0.6\times0.7=0.42.$$

Similarly

$$\text{prob}\left[\text{elasticity}=0.5, \begin{array}{l}\text{sample indicates}\\ \text{elasticity}=1\end{array}\right]$$

$$=\text{prob}\left[\begin{array}{l}\text{sample indicates}\\ \text{elasticity}=1\end{array}\middle| \text{elasticity}=0.5\right]\cdot\text{prob}\left[\text{elasticity}=0.5\right]$$

$$=0.4\times0.7=0.28.$$

These chances give us a measure of how the sample is likely to influence our views of the elasticity. We can portray them in a table which gives us the chances of outcomes when it is *assumed that we have decided to sample*. Notice that the sum of the joint chances over the sample outcomes gives us the prior probabilities

TABLE 1

Joint Chance of Sample Outcome and Actual Elasticity

| | | Actual elasticity: | | *Sum* Prior probability of sample outcomes |
		0.5	1.0	
Sample indicates elasticity to be	0.5	0.42	0.03	0.45
	1.0	0.28	0.27	0.55
Sum	Prior probability of actual elasticity	0.70	0.30	1.00

of the elasticities, 0.7 and 0.3. The sum horizontally gives the prior probabilities of the sample outcomes.

Now we can specify the decisions open to us and the costs associated with each eventuality. Let us assume that the survey costs $2 million. The costs of the various outcomes can be tabulated as follows:

Costs in $ million

| Strategy | Elasticity | |
	0.5	1.0
Sample and tax	2	12
Sample and no tax	7	2
No sample and tax	0	10
No sample and no tax	5	0

We have simply incorporated the cost of the sample in this Table. Thus when we sample and tax and the elasticity is actually unity we incur the total cost of $12 million, of which $2 million was spent on the sample.

We might set out the process of decision-making in the form of a "tree." We begin on the left with the problem whether or not to sample—and there are two branches, the upper one representing no sample and the bottom one representing the decision to sample. The bottom branch is then split into two according to the results of the sample—the upper one indicating the sample outcome favorable to the elasticity being 0.5, and the lower one favorable to the elasticity being 1.0. To each of these outcomes of the sample we can attach the prior probabilities (given that the sample has been carried out) indicated in the last column of Table 1—0.45 for the elasticity = 0.5, and 0.55 for the elasticity = 1.0. We then continue our tree with the *action* branch—to tax or not to tax. The two sample branches, as well as the upper "do not-sample" branch, are each split into two, so that we have six possible positions at the end of the action stage. Note that there are no probabilities attached to the action stage—we choose one course or another, just as we choose whether or not to sample. The last stage is the actual *realization* of the elasticity, i.e. whether it is 0.5 or 1.0. The costs of each of the outcomes, as described in the table above, is now attached to each of the final branch-ends. (Note that we have assumed that the outcome of the sample makes no difference to the branch-end costs.)

The problem is now tackled in reverse. We start at the branch-ends and work backwards to the root of the tree. Consider, for example, the topmost action branch—(do not sample)→(tax). Now we know that two possibilities arise—the elasticity may be 0.5 with prior probability 0.7 and the elasticity may be 1.0 with prior probability 0.3. So we can find the expected costs as

$$(\$0 \text{ million}) \times 0.7 + (\$10 \text{ million}) \times 0.3 = \$3 \text{ million}.$$

Now consider the "no tax" strategy, the second action branch, and we calculate expected costs as

$$(\$5 \text{ million}) \times 0.7 + (\$0 \text{ million}) \times 0.3 = \$3.5 \text{ million}.$$

We insert these values on the diagram at the appropriate junctions and encircle them. Clearly this calculation makes the no-tax strategy (when we have already decided *not* to sample) redundant—the expected costs of taxing are $0.5 *less*. Thus, effectively, the expected costs of not sampling—and then following the best policy of taxing—are $3 million, so enter that value, duly encircled at the junction at the beginning of the action branch.

More difficulties are involved with the sampling branches. Again let us start at the top branch-end—the process of: (sample) —(outcome favorable to elasticity = 0.5—(tax)—(elasticity = 0.5). Working backwards from the branch-ends we see that the final process is the probabilistic realization that the elasticity is either

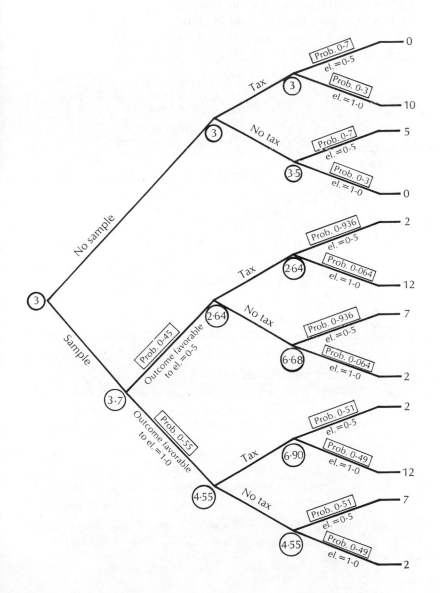

ACTION	PROBABILITY	ACTION	PROBABILITY	COSTS
To sample or not to sample	Outcome of sample	To tax or not to tax	Realized elasticity	

0.5 (1st branch) or 1.0 (2nd branch), each of which has associated costs \$2 million and \$12 million. These probabilities are conditional upon the fact that we (i) chose to sample; (ii) observed an outcome of the sample favorable to elasticity $=0.5$; (iii) chose to tax. On (ii) looking back to Table 1 we can see that the prior probability of the sample indicating an elasticity of 0.5 is given as 0.45. (And if we get a sample which indicates this elasticity we would choose to tax.) So we can write

$$\text{prob}\left[\text{elasticity}=0.5 \,\middle|\, \begin{matrix} \text{(i) sample} \\ \text{(ii) outcome of sample} \\ \text{favorable to 0.5} \end{matrix} \right]$$

$$=\text{prob}\left[\text{elasticity}=0.5 \,\middle|\, \begin{matrix} \text{outcome of} \\ \text{sample favorable} \\ \text{to 0.5} \end{matrix} \right],$$

since (i) sampling is already implied in (ii) the particular sample outcome favorable to 0.5. So we can construct:

$$\text{prob}\left[\text{elasticity}=0.5 \,\middle|\, \begin{matrix} \text{outcome of} \\ \text{sample favorable} \\ \text{to 0.5} \end{matrix} \right]$$

$$=\frac{\text{prob}\left[\text{elasticity}=0.5, \begin{matrix} \text{outcome of} \\ \text{sample favorable} \\ \text{to elasticity}=0.5 \end{matrix} \right]}{\text{prob}\left[\begin{matrix} \text{outcome of} \\ \text{sample favorable} \\ \text{to elasticity}=0.5 \end{matrix} \right]},$$

by the ordinary rules of conditional probability. Returning to Table 1 we see that this is

$$\text{prob}\left[\text{elasticity}=0.5 \,\middle|\, \begin{matrix} \text{outcome of sample} \\ \text{favorable to elasticity}=0.5 \end{matrix} \right]=\frac{0.42}{0.45}$$
$$= 0.936,$$

and

$$\text{prob}\left[\text{elasticity}=1.0 \,\middle|\, \begin{matrix} \text{outcome of sample} \\ \text{favorable to elasticity}=0.5 \end{matrix} \right]=\frac{0.03}{0.45}$$
$$= 0.064.$$

One can now calculate the expected costs of the strategy of sampling and taxing if the outcome is favorable to 0.5. We have, as expected, costs

($2 million) $\times 0.936 + ($12 million$) \times 0.064 = 2.64 million,

which we enter, duly encircled, at the appropriate junction. Secondly let us examine the no-tax branch of the "outcome-favorable-to-0.5" case. This, of course, should be the same as the case considered immediately above. Only the decision tax or no tax differs.

Now consider the other main branch of the sample result where the evidence favors an elasticity of 1.0. Taking the "tax" branch first, we calculate the probability of an elasticity of 0.5 emerging, given that the sample outcome favored 1.0.

$$\text{prob}\left[\text{elasticity}=0.5 \left| \begin{array}{l} \text{outcome of sample} \\ \text{is favorable to } 1.0 \end{array} \right. \right]$$

$$= \frac{\text{prob}\left[\begin{array}{l} \text{elasticity}=0.5, \quad \begin{array}{l} \text{outcome of sample is} \\ \text{favorable to } 1.0 \end{array} \end{array}\right]}{\text{prob}\left[\begin{array}{l} \text{outcome of sample is} \\ \text{favorable to } 1.0 \end{array}\right]},$$

which from Table 1 is

$$\frac{0.28}{0.55}=0.51.$$

The probability of the other branch where elasticity is unity is then $1-0.51=0.49$. These two probabilities are repeated for the last "no tax" branches. To find the expected costs at this last stage we repeat the operation—for cxample, for the last two branches

$\{(7 \text{ million}) \text{ with prob}=0.51\} + \{($2 \text{ million}) \text{ with prob}=$

$$0.49\} = 3.57 + 0.98 = $4.55 \text{ million}$$

which we enter in a circle at the junction.

In the action of choosing to tax or not we clearly wish to consider only those which have the lowest cost. Thus if we find ourselves at the point of having sampled and found that the evidence favored the elasticity of 0.5 we should clearly tax, since the expected cost $2.64 million would be lower than not taxing. We enter then $2.64 million at the junction of sample outcome and tax. Similarly if the sample outcome were favorable to elasticity$=1.0$, then the choice is clearly "no tax" with an expected cost of $4.55 million.

Lastly we see whether it is worth while sampling. From the sample branch there are two outcomes:

(i) an expected cost of $2.64 million with an associated probability of 0.45;

(ii) an expected cost of $4.55 million with an associated probability of 0.55.

We then form the expected costs of sampling as

($2.64 million) × 0.45 + ($4.55 million) × 0.55 = $3.7 million.

Now it is clearly not efficient to sample the population since the expected costs of sampling are $3.7 million whereas, in the no-sample branch the expected costs are only $3 million. The optimum policy, therefore, is *not* to sample, and to introduce the tax. This completes the analysis of the decision-making process.

One of the results of this example is that it is not worth while to sample. We can get a more direct measure of why this is the case. The sample, we assumed, costs us $2 million, and if we sampled the minimum costs, including the sample costs, are $3.7 million, i.e.

Sample costs	$2 million
Other expected costs	$1.7 million
Total	$3.7 million

To be worth while the sample would have to cost less than $1.3 million; this would give a total cost less than $3 million—so it would be then preferable to sample before making the decision. As it stands, however, the sample information is worth less than it costs to acquire it.

We must now touch on some of the problems of the decision-theory approach. One which will certainly have occurred to the reader is that of attributing costs to each possible outcome. Often one just cannot formulate what the costs are likely to be. It is, however, a compelling argument that one always in fact behaves *as if* there were costs attributable to every outcome. Surely it is a good discipline to have to formulate them explicitly. In practice one often uses useful shortcuts; one commonly used rule is to use the square of the deviation of the estimate of the unknown parameter from its true value as the "loss function." Thus in our example the relative 'loss' would be measured by the square of the estimated elasticity from its true value, e.g.

Loss when elasticity $=1.0$ and we judge it to be $0.5 = (0.5 - 1.0)^2$

$$= 0.25.$$

When the elasticity is estimated at its correct value, the loss is zero. This loss function is, of course, quite arbitrary, but statisticians have found in practice that this is a useful loss function to use in the absence of any detailed cost specification.

Another major difficulty lies in attaching values to the probabilities which need to be quantified in using decision functions. This involves specifying the prior probabilities of the elasticities assuming certain values, and the more complex task of stating the probabilities of the sample indicating the correct and incorrect elasticities. This is merely a way of evaluating what the sample is going to tell us—but it is not at all easy to put quantities on the probability of the sample results revealing the true facts.

Our example is extremely simple. We have not considered the enormous number of opportunities which occur in practical cases. For example, we might consider many samples of various size, complexity and cost. Formally it is easy to extend the theory to deal with multiple opportunities, but the problems of specifying the probabilities of the outcomes are not simplified! Even so, it is often useful to draw a decision tree, or at least certain of the main branches, to clear one's mind about the decision problem.

Heuristic Programs for Decision-making

JEROME D. WIEST

Jerome D. Wiest is Professor of Management at the University of Utah. This article appeared in the Harvard Business Review *in 1966.*

In an age of rapidly expanding technology and methodology, the language of science has inevitably crept into the vocabulary of the business world, with the result that the businessman has ceased to be surprised (though he is still slightly perplexed, perhaps) by strange words like cybernetics and cryogenics. Sometimes (as with cybernetics) the words are new; sometimes they are old with new or expanded meanings. An example of the latter kind—one that is appearing with increasing frequency in literature of interest to the thoughtful businessman—is *heuristic.* Often it appears in such terms as *heuristic programming* or *heuristic problem-solving.*

The word has an old and venerable meaning; as used recently, however, it refers to a particular approach to decision-making that is rapidly growing in application and importance. In recent years, for example, heuristic programs have been applied with varying degrees of success to such problems as:

- Assembly line balancing.
- Facilities layout.
- Portfolio selection.
- Job shop scheduling.
- Electric motor design.
- Warehouse location.
- Inventory control.
- Resource allocation to large projects.

Although notable in their own right, these programs are just forerunners of what promises to be a significant new development in programmed decision-making—a development with which the informed businessman will want to keep abreast.

In order to better understand the significance of heuristic problem-solving, let us first examine the traditional meaning of the word *heuristic*, and then note the developments which have expanded this meaning and led to the current interest in heuristic problem-solving. Actually, the basic notion of heuristic problem-solving is not new, and a mere definition of the term is likely to leave most managers with the impression that the notion is trivial. But some rather sophisticated extensions of a basically simple concept, when combined with the computational power of a computer, enable the problem-solver to deal successfully with many problems that have not yielded previously to established problem-solving techniques. As we shall see, it is this combination of ideas and developments that gives significance to the concept.

MEANING AND SIGNIFICANCE

Anciently, *heuristic* (as a noun) was the name of a branch of study belonging to logic or philosophy, the aim of which was to investigate the methods of discovery and invention.[1] In present usage the meaning has expanded somewhat. A *heuristic* is itself an aid to discovery—especially the discovery of a solution to a problem. Going one step further, we may describe a heuristic

---

1. See György Polya, *How To Solve It* (Garden City, New York: Doubleday & Co., Inc., 1957).

as any device or procedure used to reduce problem-solving effort —in short, a rule of thumb used to solve a particular problem.

Familiar Examples · We all use heuristics in our daily living, drawing them from our knowledge and experience. To help us face the countless problem-solving situations that confront us each day, we devise simple rules of thumb that free us from the task of solving the same or similar problems over and over again. For example, consider the rule, "When the sky is cloudy, take an umbrella to work." The problem at hand is how to defend one-self against the potential discomforts of the weather. This simple heuristic avoids more complicated problem-solving procedures such as reading the weather report, calling the weather bureau, analyzing barometer readings, and so forth. For many problems of this kind, we lack the time or inclination to employ more thorough problem-solving procedures. A simple (if not infallible) rule serves us best.

Businessmen frequently develop and follow various heuristics in their own operations, perhaps without realizing that they are employing a type of heuristic problem-solving. The following examples should be familiar:

- *Stock market investing*—"Buy when prices move rapidly in one direction with heavy volume." Or, "Sell when the good news is out."
- *Inventory control*—"When the stock gets down to four, that's the time to buy some more." (Such heuristics are called "trigger-level" rules.)
- *Accounting*—"Value at cost or market, whichever is lower." Or, "First in, first out."
- *Job scheduling*—"First come, first served. Or, "Schedule the red-flag jobs first."
- *Management*—"Handle only the exceptional problems; let sub-ordinates decide routine matters."

I could cite other and more complex examples of heuristics, but these should suffice to indicate their general nature. While heuristics may not lead to the best solution in a particular case, experience over time has proved their general usefulness in finding good solutions to recurring problems with a minimum of effort.

All of the above heuristics could be improved by further

elaboration to take into account exceptional circumstances or additional information. Thus the inventory control rule might also take into consideration recent trends in usage rates and expectations of future demand for a stocked item. Instead of a simple rule of thumb, a combination of rules might be better. This leads us to the heuristic program.

HEURISTIC PROGRAMMING

In simplest terms a heuristic program is a collection or combination of heuristics used for solving a particular problem. If the program is sufficiently complex, it may require a computer for its solution. As a matter of fact, most of the interesting developments in heuristic programming that have appeared in the literature recently have relied on computers. Such heuristic programs take the form of a set of instructions for directing the computer to solve a problem—the way a manager might do it if he had enough time. To cover all contingencies likely to occur in a difficult problem setting, a group of heuristics may become quite complicated—too difficult to follow through at man's pace of problem-solving. Hence the need for a computer.

Why resort to heuristic programming in the first place? Why not use other techniques that mathematicians and operations researchers have devised in recent years? There seems to be no end to their bag of tools—many of them highly acclaimed and of proved usefulness, such as linear programming, waiting-line models, statistical decision theory, linear decision rules, and so on. There are essentially two answers to these questions.

Large Problems · Some problems—although they can be reduced to numbers and equations—are too large to solve by analytical techniques, even with the aid of a computer. Linear programming, for instance, has been widely used to solve many problems of resource allocation (transportation routing, machine scheduling, product mix, oil refinery operations, and so forth); but some problems are just too large for it—job shop scheduling, for instance. Conceptually, linear programming could lead to an optimum assignment of start times for the thousands of jobs to be scheduled in a large shop, given some criterion like "minimize idle machine time"; but the number of steps necessary to reach the optimum solution—though finite—is so large as to render the method useless. In this application, linear programming is computationally inefficient.

Heuristic programming, on the other hand, attempts to short-cut computations. It is not so concerned with finding the one best answer after a lengthy search as with rapidly reaching a satisfactory one. In other words, it is willing to trade a guaranteed optimum solution for a "good" one if it can do so with considerably less computational effort.

Ill-Structured · The other reason for employing heuristic programming is that some problems are "ill structured"—they cannot be expressed in mathematical terms. Judgment, intuition, creativity, and learning are important elements of the problem and its solution, and these variables are qualitative rather than numerical. Quantitative techniques are not available or are not suitable for solving such problems.

Heuristic means of dealing with ill-structured problems have been explored by a number of researchers in the field of "artificial intelligence." Their object has been to develop computer programs that imitate certain human problem-solving processes. Among their efforts have been programs which prove mathematical theorems, play chess, write music, and solve problems like the "cannibal and missionary" problem.

A business manager may ask: What relevance do chess-playing and theorem-proving programs have to solutions of ill-structured business problems? None of the programs of the foregoing type have a business orientation; but if the programs were successful, they would indeed have implicit relevance, for they deal with problem-solving situations in which judgment, intuition, and even creativity play an important part. If a computer could be "taught" to exercise these qualities in a game context, it might be programmed to display them when dealing with the ill-structured problems so ubiquitous in the manager's world.

Results to date, however, are mixed. While there are some programs that have demonstrated these human-like qualities to some degree, the problems with which they have dealt differ in complexity by several orders of magnitude from typical ill-structured managerial problems. It is not clear that a straightforward extension of these programming concepts plus an increase in computer size and speed is all that is needed to bridge the gap. We need to learn much more about the brain and cognitive processes before we can claim success in dealing with such problems mechanically. Accomplishments in artificial intelligence, while substantial, seem not to have kept pace with early successes and hopes, as the complexity of problems facing researchers has become more apparent. For example:

- Language translation programs, after early apparent gains, have experienced considerable difficulties and are far from being generally useful.
- Pattern-recognition programs, despite much excellent work, do not even approach the flexibility of human pattern-recognition processes. Automatic reading devices are able to handle only typed or handprinted material of great uniformity in type and layout. A person's tolerance for ambiguity and his ability to decipher various styles of type and handwriting seem even further beyond mechanical duplication than they did a few years ago when early successes led to high optimism.
- Even chess-playing programs are still poor novices at the game, despite some predictions in the late 1950's that a computer would be the world's champion chess player in 1967.

Nevertheless, these efforts are increasing our ability to understand and to deal with qualitative phenomena. It is reasonable to suppose that the boundary between what we consider structured and ill-structured problems—between problems which have yielded to programmed solutions and those which have not—will continue to change. Such developments are still in the future, however, and must await the researcher's exploration of human thinking and complex problem-solving processes. Whether these can be efficiently imitated or simulated by digital computers remains to be proved.

Thus we come back to the application of heuristic programming to problems which are too large (or not suitable) for solution by analytical means. It is this area that is of current interest to businessmen. An idea of the kinds of problems which have yielded—or conceivably might yield—to solution by heuristic techniques should indicate the range of their usefulness as well as their limitations.

WIDE-RANGING USES

Most business-oriented heuristic programs apply to what may be characterized as combinatorial problems because of the extremely large number of ways in which a series of decisions can be made. A problem may be likened to a maze consisting of a sequence of decision points; at each point a number of paths are available, but only one can be chosen. Thus, as illustrated schematically in the "tree diagram" shown in Exhibit 1, there are numerous combinations of paths which lead from the initial point to some terminal point.

Each node represents a decision point; lines represent various possible decisions that could be made, and lead either to another decision point or to a terminal node. The heavy line indicates a path, or series of decisions, leading to a particular solution to the problem. Thus each terminal node represents a possible solution —a plan of action.

One method of finding the optimum solution is to enumerate each possible path, evaluate the end result according to some criteria, and select the best path. Obviously, if the problem contains many decision points and various paths at each of these points, the number of possible combinations becomes enormous. For example, a series of ten distinct decisions, each of which could be made in five different ways, leads to almost ten million different solutions or combinations of decisions. (Since the decisions at each step are considered to differ from decisions at previous or subsequent steps, the number of branches at each decision point is raised to the power of the number of decision points. In this example, $5^{10} = 9,765,625$.)

Most of the combinatorial-type decisions to which heuristic programming has been applied are actually much larger than this. Even with the aid of a high-speed computer, enumeration is not a feasible solution method for large problems. Accordingly, the heuristic technique is to prune the tree—eliminate some branches from the start so a much smaller maze remains to be searched. This is illustrated in the "pruned" tree diagram in Part B of Exhibit 1.

The danger in pruning the tree, of course, is that a good branch may be cut off by mistake. A path that appears to be

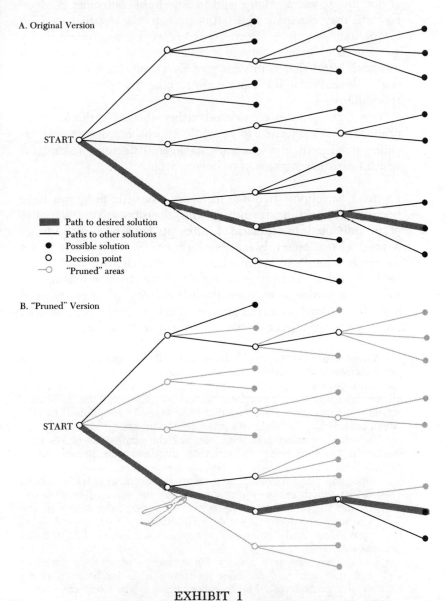

A. Original Version

START

Path to desired solution
Paths to other solutions
● Possible solution
○ Decision point
–○ "Pruned" areas

B. "Pruned" Version

START

EXHIBIT 1

REPRESENTATION OF A PROBLEM

of doubtful value may later lead to a desirable outcome. A given heuristic may eliminate that path—perhaps the one that leads to the optimum solution. However, as noted before, sacrifice of a guaranteed optimum solution is the price paid for the reduction in search effort that heuristics provide. (But, then, a guarantee is of little real value if the price of reaching the optimum solution is prohibitive.)

Now that we have considered rather abstractly the kinds of problems that may yield to heuristic approaches, let us next examine some particular cases of managerial decision-making for which heuristic programs have been written.

Portfolio Selection · In some instances, heuristic programs have been written to simulate the existing decision-making activities of an individual; in other cases, attempts have been made to go beyond what is presently feasible for humans. An example of the former is a heuristic approach to the investment of trust funds held by banks.[2] The program simulates the decision-making (in this case a particular trust investment officer) in his selection of a portfolio, based on information available to him at the time he makes a decision. In brief, the program operates as follows:

• A preference list of stocks is established and stored in the computer memory. It includes some eighty issues, categorized by industry and representing the working list of stocks from which the investment officer will make all his portfolio selections. The preference list, designed to cover various economic conditions and updated by the officer periodically, is taken as a given by the program.
• Various data associated with each of the companies represented in the list (such as price, growth rate, dividend rate, price-earnings ratio, expected earnings, and so forth) are also stored.
• From this list a portfolio is generated, based on rules of thumb (heuristics) which relate information about the client, the securities market, and the economy to the selection of particular stocks in the list. The heuristics were compiled from a study of past decisions of the trust officer and "protocols" or verbalizations of his decision processes.
• The program keeps a history (in memory) of its past decisions and their outcomes and modifies its future behavior by eliminating unsuccessful procedures. For instance, if a certain stock were more volatile than originally believed, the selling rate might be increased

2. See Geoffrey P. Clarkson and Allan H. Meltzer, "Portfolio Selection: A Heuristic Approach," *Journal of Finance*, December 1960, p. 465.

in a falling market. Thus the program "learns" from its previous experience—paralleling to some degree human learning processes.

Two things should be noted about this kind of program:

(1) It simulates the decisions of a *particular* investment officer. No attempt is made to determine if some other person in this position has superior heuristics. Thus the program is not prescriptive in nature; it is descriptive, and only in a narrow sense (i.e., it describes only one person rather than trust officers in general).

(2) The human activity described is sufficiently simple to be formalized. The portfolio selection rules followed by the trust officer are explicable to a large degree and can be set down in terms of unambiguous rules (and hence can be programmed for a computer). The determination and translation of these rules are not perfect, as the computer-produced portfolios have differed slightly from the trust officer's, but they are remarkably close.

Many business decision processes are of this type; that is, the decision rules may be clearly identified and formalized. In all such cases the process may be simulated by means of heuristic programming. We should note that, in some of these instances, a computer is not a necessary adjunct to the process. A human can follow the programming instructions and perform each step as required. If the heuristics are numerous and complicated, however, humans are much less efficient at the task than computers are.

Assembly Line Balancing · A production management problem that occurs frequently in industries where products are assembled on a conveyor line is balancing the line—assigning elemental assembly tasks to work stations situated along the line. In general, each work station is manned by a single operator. Ideally, the sum of task times at each station is the same as that at all other stations; the line is then said to be perfectly balanced. An out-of-balance line requires more operators than the ideal line, since operators are idle during part of each work cycle at some of the stations and the lost time has to be compensated for by additional work stations.

The assignment of elementary tasks to work stations is an example of the combinatorial type of problem which I described earlier. There are many ways of combining tasks—too many to enumerate for large, real-life problems. Several heuristic approaches have been suggested, however, which attempt to narrow in on some smaller set of "good" combinations.[3] Some of the heuristics employed are quite sophisticated and are not necessarily attempts to duplicate the procedures a human line balancer would go through. One technique, for example, capitalizes on the speed of a computer in order to rapidly generate many solutions on a trial-and-error basis—a process for which a human, at his plodding pace, would be grossly inefficient. The solutions are not completely random samples from the set of all possible combinations, however, but are biased (this is where the heuristics come into play) in favor of more promising combinations. In one application the program was able to find an optimum balance of 1,000 elemental tasks distributed to 200 work stations—all in three minutes of computer time.[4]

Job Shop Scheduling · The problem of job shop scheduling appears in many guises outside of the typical machine shop, but it is most familiar in that setting. It may be characterized as a continuous inflow of jobs, each of which requires one or more operations (perhaps in a given sequence) to be performed on one or more machines. The problem is to schedule the operations on the machines in such a way as to minimize idle machine time or total time of jobs in the system, or to meet some other criterion. A similar problem exists in many office operations, where letters or other paperwork (jobs) are assigned to secretaries or clerks or other "processors." Engineering departments, drafting rooms, mail-order operations, printing shops, computer centers, and

---

3. See Fred M. Tonge, *A Heuristic Program for Assembly Line Balancing* (Englewood Cliffs, New Jersey: Prentice-Hall, Inc., 1961); Maurice Kilbridge and Leon Wester, "A Heuristic Method of Assembly Line Balancing," *Journal of Industrial Engineering*, July–August 1961, p. 292; W. B. Helgeson and D. P. Birnie, "Assembly Line Balancing Using the Ranked Positional Weight Technique," *Journal of Industrial Engineering*, November–December 1961, p. 394; and Albert Arcus, *An Analysis of a Computer Method of Sequencing Assembly Line Operations* (unpublished doctoral dissertation, University of California, Berkeley, September 1963).

4. See Albert Arcus, op. cit.

surgery wards—to name just a few examples—all have scheduling problems characteristic of job shop operations.

When the number of operations to be completed is large, the number of possible solutions (different schedules, in this case) is enormous. Before the advent of the computer, job-shop scheduling for large operations had to be decentralized. Due dates for jobs were established by the production control office (with plenty of slack time allowed), but it was the foreman—or workers—who decided on the start time of each job operation. High in-process inventories, delays in schedules, and broken promises to customers were all common management problems.

Heuristic techniques, aided by the use of a computer, permit greater centralization of job-shop scheduling, and thus enable the manager of the operation to exercise more effective control. At the heart of heuristic scheduling programs are rules for deciding which jobs will be scheduled on particular machines and when. Each machine may be viewed as a service facility with a waiting line of jobs to be serviced. The simplest heuristic for determining the order in which the waiting jobs will be taken is "first come, first served," but many others are possible—for instance, "schedule first the job which can be finished first," and "schedule the longest jobs first." Scheduling programs use these rules, or some combination of them, modified as necessary to take into account sequencing constraints, machine capabilities, special priority jobs, and so forth—all integrated in a program which specifies unambiguously the order in which jobs are to be processed and on what facilities.[5]

At least one large-scale installation of a heuristic-based job shop scheduling program has been reported:

The shop, a gear producer with 1,000 machine tools handling up to 2,000 orders at any one time, found that the computerized scheduling program increased production 5 percent to 10 percent, decreased lead time up to three months, and boosted on-time deliveries by 30 percent. Top managers feel that they are finally "in control" of the operations of the plant; the project schedule enables them to predict order delivery dates more confidently, as well as plan purchases of new equipment. Foremen like the program because it frees them from the

5. William S. Gere, Jr., "A Heuristic Approach to Job Shop Scheduling" (unpublished doctoral dissertation, Carnegie Institute of Technology, 1962).

responsibility of scheduling jobs (and the frequent negotiation of schedule changes with other foremen) and allows them to devote more time to quality control and supervision of employees.[6]

Facilities Location · In the same context as the job shop scheduling problem is the facilities location problem. When the nature of products and demand patterns suggests a process-controlled (or functional) layout, then the relative location of various machine groups or types of equipment is an important problem for management to solve. That arrangement which leads to the lowest costs for moving all orders through the shop is generally regarded as the best solution (assuming, of course, that other constraints, such as necessary adjacent locations of related facilities, can be observed).

Again, the problem is a large combinatorial one. Just twelve departments can be arranged in over a million non-redundant patterns of relative location. The problem may be conceptualized analytically, but there is no way to promise the best possible solution. However, a heuristic program has been written for successively exchanging pairs of departments in a given location pattern until no further reductions in transportation costs can be obtained.[7] An optimum pattern is not assured, but the solutions reached have been better than those obtained by other techniques.

Inventory Control · Numerous mathematical techniques for minimizing costs in an inventory system are available for use by the inventory manager. The techniques start with the simple economic lot-size formulas and proceed through highly sophisticated models. Many companies—especially those whose inventory stock includes thousands of different items—find it difficult to fit the models to their own requirements and conditions. Assumptions of the model are not met in practice, demand patterns are unpredictable, cost data are unavailable, or the sheer size of the problem frustrates attempts at analytical solutions.

6. See "Computer Planning Unsnarls the Job Shop," *Business Week*, April 2, 1966, p. 60.

7. See, for example, Elwood S. Buffa, Gordon C. Armour, and Thomas E. Vollmann, "Allocating Facilities With CRAFT," *Harvard Business Review*, March–April 1964, p. 136.

As a result, heuristic inventory rules are widely used by business managers, whether in the form of trigger-level rules or more complex procedures. Computerized systems containing both analytical and heuristic elements are used by a number of companies for purposes of inventory control.[8] The problem, especially when considered in the larger context of an operational system, is exceedingly complex, somewhat ill structured, and a likely candidate for solution by heuristic programming techniques. Since inventory decisions have implications for marketing and finance functions as well as for production, top managers in these areas should be aware of, and have some part in establishing, the heuristics which underlie the inventory control system.

Warehouse Sites · Business or government operations which require large-scale distribution networks face the problem of determining the number and location of regional warehouses. The geographical pattern of locations which just matches the expense of establishing and operating warehouses with the resulting savings in transportation costs and incremental profits from more rapid delivery is most profitable. The number of possible patterns and the complexity of the problem (as exemplified by transportation rate structures) rule out the feasibility of mathematical solutions. As a result, most distribution systems have grown, not toward some optimal pattern, but one warehouse at a time, each located at what appears to be the best site at the particular moment. This is clearly not the way to maximize profits in the long run.

Various heuristic approaches to the problem have been suggested.[9] One of these selects from all possible sites the relatively few that appear promising, calculates the net savings that would result from locating a warehouse at each of these sites, adds warehouses one at a time to the best of these until no

8. For several examples, see Joseph Buchan and Ernest Koenigsberg, *Scientific Inventory Management* (Englewood Cliffs, New Jersey: Prentice-Hall, Inc., 1963).

9. See Alfred A. Kuehn and Michael J. Hamburger, "A Heuristic Program for Locating Warehouses," *Management Science*, July 1963, p. 643; and Leon Cooper, "Location-Allocation Problems," *Operations Research*, May–June 1963, p. 331.

further savings result, and then "bumps and shifts" warehouses in the selected sites until no further improvement is apparent. Kuehn and Hamburger report that the program can handle several hundred sites and several thousand shipment destinations. Results from trials on small-scale problems have been equal to or better than those from alternative methods available.

Engineering Design · Heuristic programs have also been reported which can solve certain engineering design problems that lend themselves to formal structuring. The design of electric motors is a case in point. Because of the great range of customer specifications for voltage, power, size, metallurgical properties, environmental conditions, and so forth, large electrical equipment manufacturers will build hundreds of motors and transformers whose designs differ from basic types in varying degrees. Heuristic programs, with the help of a computer, relieve engineers of the rather tedious task of designing a motor for each new customer order that differs from a standard design.

Large-Project Scheduling · Large projects, such as the construction of buildings and plants, missile development programs, large-scale maintenance projects, and so forth, present scheduling problems similar to those for job shop scheduling except that the activities (jobs) which comprise a large project have more complex sequencing relationships and the project has an end point. The project manager must be able to schedule, with some degree of precision, the start and completion dates for all of the major activities. Also, he must have a workable means of measuring ongoing progress for purposes of control and for redirecting resources to activities which are behind schedule.

Such planning and scheduling techniques as PERT and CPM have been widely used by large-project managers in recent years, but in their conventional form they fail to consider the constraints imposed on activity scheduling when resources are limited. The usual problem facing project managers is allocating scarce resources among the various activities to be scheduled in such a way as to keep the project on schedule and to minimize costs of resources used. The number of possible schedules for activity start and completion times and for resource use, given sequencing relationships, estimated durations, and limited resources, is enormously large for all but the smallest projects. No manager even with the aid of a computer, could enumerate them all and find the best one.

Because of the great interest in large-project management during recent years much research effort has been devoted to the problem of resource scheduling; and most of the suggested scheduling techniques are based on heuristic programming. The programs in general are quite flexible. They enable the manager to ask questions such as:

• What if we double the number of engineers assigned to propulsion system design in the next six months?
• What if we lease five additional earth-movers during the summer season?
• What if the funding of the new by-pass highway system is decreased 10 percent beginning January?
• How would these changes in resource availabilities affect the progress and anticipated finish date of the project?

Heuristic programs can be used to generate project schedules under varying conditions, simulating for the manager the anticipated effects of proposed resource changes or other scheduling constraints.

As a further illustration of heuristic programming and how heuristics are combined to make decisions, an example of a project scheduling program is developed in the Appendix. Some of the basic scheduling heuristics and their interrelationships are displayed in a simplified flow diagram.

CURRENT USEFULNESS

The foregoing illustrations of heuristic programs, while not exhaustive, indicate the range of current applications and suggest in part the kinds of problems that might be solved by this technique. There remains the practical question: Has heuristic problem-solving developed to the point where it is really useful for the businessman today?

The question cannot be given an unqualified answer because the evidence is mixed and subject to at least some controversy. Several heuristic programs have proved to be feasible and efficient, and they are in use today. For instance, the program for designing electric motors was first reported to be in use eight years ago and presumably is still functional. And at least one machine shop is scheduling job operations by an extensive heuristic program, apparently with considerable success. Several other companies are in the process of installing similar systems. Large-project scheduling programs also have been used by many firms. One proprietary program has been available for over three years; other programs have been or are in the process of being developed by several companies to match their own particular requirements. Line-balancing programs have been tested by a number of companies, notably those in the automobile industry, with results as yet unpublished. Likewise, no report has been made of a large-scale application of a warehouse location program. The process-layout program has been utilized in a variety of firms—from factories to movie studios to engineering departments—with reported success.

The problem of evaluating heuristic programs is twofold. First, much of the work in the field has been done by researchers who are primarily concerned with conceptualizing a problem and its heuristic solution. Testing a model in the "real world" and subjecting it to the mundane problems (often unanticipated by the researcher) that inevitably complicate matters require time and often different talents. Thus real-world applications and evaluation quite naturally lag behind research developments.

Secondly, there is the problem of standards. How does a manager determine what is a "good" heuristic program? In most instances, results cannot be compared to an optimal solution because the latter is generally not available. The minimum-length schedule for a large project with limited resources, for example, is frequently incalculable. The relevant and, in most cases, the only comparison that can be made is with results from traditional techniques. A manager should examine the output of a heuristic program with the following four questions in mind:

• Does it produce better results than our present methods do?
• Are there incremental savings in resources?
• Are computational effort and expense reduced without sacrificing the quality of work?
• Is the information produced more timely, and are decisions reached earlier, than by present methods?

In summary, a few existing programs have been tried and have passed the above test; some have not been tried at all; and the evidence on others has not come in yet. We should note that in all cases heuristic programs which have been applied to problems of business decision-making are *special-purpose* programs; they have been designed specifically to solve a particular problem. None of them are general problem solvers in the sense that the procedures used adapt to the particular tasks given to them.

EFFECT ON MANAGEMENT

Last rites have been pronounced more than once for the middle manager since the advent of the computer, while his health and resilience in an age of change have been praised by others. Most of the disagreement is based on differences of opinion about the proportion of his job that is well structured (i.e., has clear-cut objectives and straightforward decision procedures) and that which is ill structured (i.e., concerns vaguely defined problems) and thus not as susceptible to programming.

It is not my purpose here to enter into that debate, except to note that heuristic methods of decision-making have made some inroads into the ill-structured problems or at least have changed our minds about what should be considered ill structured. In any event it is apparent that the role of the middle manager is changing as methods are found of programming more and more problem-solving activities. In view of the total scope of his activities, however, the inroads appear relatively minor.

What seems relevant is not how much of his job will be taken away, but how the remaining activities will change. Heuristic as well as analytic techniques of decision-making yield computer outputs which in most cases have to be combined and tempered with managerial judgment and acumen. The computer is a partner of, rather than replacement for, the manager. Instead of

trying to replace the human decision maker *in toto,* we should
concentrate on discovering which elements of a manager's task
are best handled by him and which by the computer. As Hu-
bert L. Dreyfus suggests:

We must couple [the computer's] capacity for fast and accurate
calculation with the [human's] short-cut processing made possible by
the fringes of consciousness and ambiguity tolerance. . . . In problem
solving once the problem is structured and planned, a machine could
take over to work out the details (as in the case of machine shop
allocation or investment banking). A mechanical dictionary would be
useful in translation. In pattern recognition, machines are able to
recognize certain complex patterns that the natural prominences in
our experience force us to exclude.[10]

In short, the combination of man and computer can lead to
accomplishments that neither is capable of alone.

Beyond the technological capabilities of computers and heuristic programs is the question of economics. Sunlight is free,
and we know how to convert it into electricity; but it has not
replaced coal as a source of energy for generating power. Likewise, computer technology has outpaced its economic feasibility
in some applications. Humans are still less expensive decision-
makers than computers are for many problems that both are
capable of solving. We should add, however, that computers are
decreasing in cost (per computation) while humans are increasing in cost. The break-even point is changing continually.

CONCLUSION

Surveying the field of heuristic programming, we may summarize progress to date by noting that several programs have
proved the usefulness of a heuristic approach to decision-making
when applied to certain problems that we have characterized as
large combinatorial types. Some programs are in actual operation; others are being developed. Additionally, researchers are
extending the boundaries of programmable decision-making into
the area of ill-structured problems. They are showing that some
decision processes can be formalized and described in terms of
heuristic decision rules. All heuristic programs that have been
applied to business problems, I again emphasize, have been

10. "Alchemy and Artificial Intelligence," The RAND Corporation, Vol.
P–3244, December 1965, p. 82.

special-purpose programs, tailored to a specific and narrowly defined problem.

Some early successes in heuristic programs—computer programs that played chess, recognized patterns, and proved mathematical theorems—led many competent researchers to conclude that human decision-making involving judgment, intuition, and creativity could be simulated by a computer and that decision-making by mechanical means was no longer confined to well-structured problems. The view has been well stated by Herbert A. Simon and Allen Newell:

"With recent developments in our understanding of heuristic processes and their simulation by digital computers, the way is open to deal scientifically with ill-structured problems—to make the computer co-extensive with the human mind." [11]

Though widely supported, this view has been subjected to some recent debate. Skeptics have noted that recent progress in artificial intelligence has failed to match the rate of early successes, as the complexities of problems facing researchers have become apparent. Dreyfus recently observed:

There is . . . evidence that human and mechanical information processing proceed in entirely different ways. At best, research in artificial intelligence can write programs which allow the digital computer to *approximate,* by means of discrete [stepwise] operations, the results which human beings achieve [by much more efficient techniques]. . . .[12]

Because of this, Dreyfus sees a limit to how far we can go in cognitive simulation using the present heuristic approach, even with newer and faster machines, better programming languages, and more clever heuristics.

A new appreciation for the human being as a problem-solver has resulted. It now appears that radical advances in programmed solution procedures for most ill-structured management problems are not just around the corner, as supposed, or even yet on the horizon, and that advancements will be made more slowly than earlier supposed. Meanwhile, however, there

11. "Heuristic Problem Solving: The Next Advance in Operations Research," *Operations Research,* January–February 1958, p. 9.

12. Dreyfus, op. cit., p. 63.

are many opportunities for applying heuristic problem-solving techniques. They can be used on well-structured but difficult-to-solve problems and also on problems which, though apparently not well structured, may yield to formalization with careful analysis and some degree of ingenuity. Business managers can profitably search for opportunities of these kinds.

APPENDIX. SCHEDULING PROJECTS

A simplified version of a heuristic program for scheduling a large project is shown in the flow diagram in Figure A. The program is based essentially on three heuristics:

(1) Allocate resources serially in time. That is, start on the first day and schedule all jobs possible, then do the same for the second day, and so on.

(2) When several jobs compete for the same resources, give preference to the jobs with the least slack.

(3) Reschedule non-critical jobs, if possible, in order to free resources for scheduling critical (non-slack) jobs.

To illustrate how these heuristics operate in the program, let us apply them to one part of the main project. This smaller project consists of ten jobs, each of which requires a certain amount of time and a given number of men (crew). For simplicity, let us assume that all the men are interchangeable. In practical situations, however, the various jobs may require men of different skills as well as other resources such as machines, materials, money, and so forth.

For technological reasons, some jobs must be completed before others can begin. Thus in the project list in Figure B, Job 9 cannot begin until Jobs 2 and 6 have been completed. To simplify this exposition, I have chosen a crew size for each job which is identical to its job number. Thus Job 1 requires one man, Job 5 requires five men, and so forth.

The small project is best visualized as a network diagram in which each job appears as an arrow, and the connections of arrows indicate the predecessor relationships. The arrow for Job 9, for example, is directly preceded by the arrows for Jobs 2 and 6. (See Figure C.) If we draw the diagram on a horizontal time scale in such a way that a job arrow's placement and

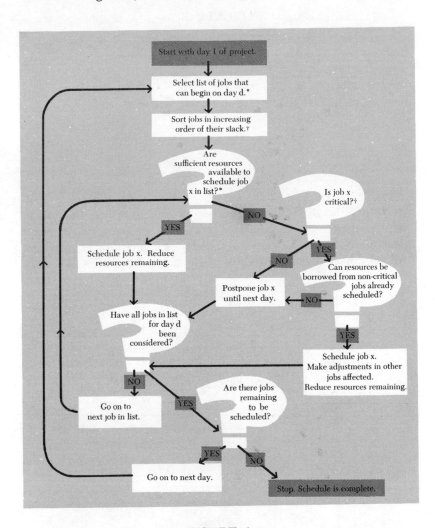

FIGURE A

* Day d is day under consideration; Job x is job under consideration.
† *Slack* is a measure of the number of days a job may be delayed without delaying the project as a whole. A job is *critical* if it has no slack.

FIGURE B

Job number	Predecessor jobs	Length (days)	Crew size
1	7	3	1
2	4	2	2
3	7	2	3
4	7	3	4
5	7	2	5
6	3	3	6
7	(none)	1	7
8	1	2	8
9	2,6	1	9
10	9,5	3	10

horizontal length indicate the period during which the job is active, then we can illustrate both the project and its time schedule. Figure C shows a schedule for our project in which all jobs have been started as early as their predecessors will

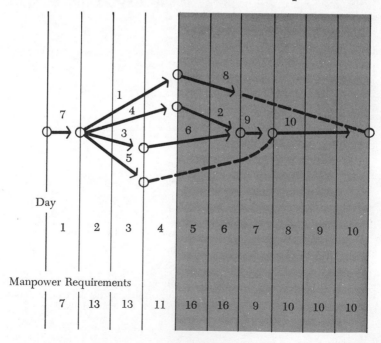

FIGURE C

allow. (Dashed lines indicate ordering relationships and are necessary when a job's successors do not begin immediately following its completion.) The number above each arrow identifies the job and its crew size. Job 4, for example, requires four men on each of Days 2, 3, and 4. Thus we can calculate daily manpower requirements for the schedule by summarizing vertically the crew sizes of all jobs active on a given day. In the schedule graph in Figure C, manpower requirements start at seven on Day 1, climb to thirteen on Days 2 and 3, and so on.

Suppose, however, that only ten men are available to assign to the project on any one day. How should the project be scheduled in order not to exceed this constraint but still to complete it as soon as possible? One way to find the shortest feasible schedule would be to enumerate all possible schedules. For example, on the first day there is just one possible choice of jobs (Job 7). On the second day, with four jobs available, there are thirteen feasible combinations: four consisting of a single job, six consisting of pairs of jobs, and three consisting of triples of jobs. (The remaining combinations exceed the manpower limit of ten.) Each of these thirteen choices represents a branch on a tree diagram, and multiple choices fan out from each of these on succeeding days. The tree of all possible schedules is very large, even for this small project.

DAY-TO DAY DECISIONS

The heuristic program diagrammed in Figure C trims the tree drastically; it selects just one branch at each decision point (one combination of jobs each day), only occasionally retracing its steps to see if a better branch could be found. Scheduling day by day (as required by the first heuristic mentioned earlier), the program would make the following decisions.

Day 1 · Only one job (7) is available to start in this period, and there are sufficient men to schedule it.

Schedule Job 7 (slack = 0, as it is calculated relative to jobs on the critical path, which are defined to have no slack); three men remain.

Day 2 · Four jobs (1, 3, 4, and 5) can be started on Day 2, but there are not enough men to schedule them all. The second heuristic calls for scheduling the jobs with the least slack first.

> Schedule Job 3 (slack = 0); seven men remain.
> Schedule Job 4 (slack = 0); three men remain.

Jobs 1 and 5 both have four days slack; but since there are just 3 men unassigned, Job 5 must be delayed.

> Schedule Job 1 (slack = 4); two men remain.
> Postpone Job 5 (slack = 4).

Day 3 · We assume that jobs cannot be interrupted once started; partially completed jobs have first call on the available resources.

> Continue Job 3 (slack = 0); seven men remain.
> Continue Job 4 (slack = 0); three men remain.
> Continue Job 1 (slack = 1); two men remain;

Since there are still not enough men for Job 5, it must be delayed again.

> Postpone Job 5 (slack = 3).

At this point the schedule graph appears as shown in Figure D. Heavy lines indicate jobs already scheduled; light lines are projected schedules—which still must be checked for feasibility.

Note that Job 5, which has been postponed two days, now has only two days slack (possible slippage) remaining.

Day 4 ·

> Continue Job 4 (slack = 0); six men remain.
> Continue Job 1 (slack = 4); five men remain.

Job 6 has no slack and hence is critical, but only five men are still unassigned. The third heuristic is now brought into play: Are there non-critical jobs still active which could be postponed without delaying the project? Job 1 satisfies this requirement and hence is reassigned to begin later.

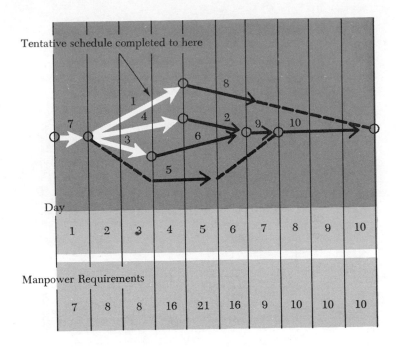

FIGURE D

Reschedule Job 1; six men remain.
Schedule Job 6 (slack = 0); zero men remain.
Postpone Job 5 (slack = 2).

The schedule graph at the end of Day 4 is shown in Figure E.

Day 5 ·

Continue Job 6 (slack = 0); four men remain.
Schedule Job 2 (slack = 0); two men remain.
Schedule Job 1 (slack = 1); one man remains.
Postpone Job 5 (slack = 1).

Day 6 ·

Continue Job 6 (slack = 0); four men remain.
Schedule Job 2 (slack = 0); two men remain.

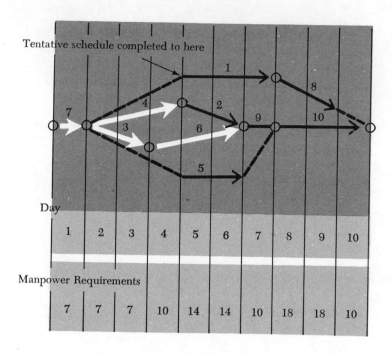

FIGURE E

Schedule Job 1 (slack $= 1$); one man remains.
Postpone Job 5 (slack $= 0$).

Job 5 has now become critical, as shown in Figure F. Note that the projected finish date has been delayed a day.

Day 7 ·

Continue Job 1 (slack $= 2$); nine men remain.
Schedule Job 5 (slack $= 0$); four men remain.
Postpone Job 9 (slack $= 1$).

Day 8 ·

Continue Job 5 (slack $= 0$); five men remain.
Postpone Job 9 (slack $= 0$); no non-critical jobs can be rescheduled).
Postpone Job 8 (slack $= 2$).

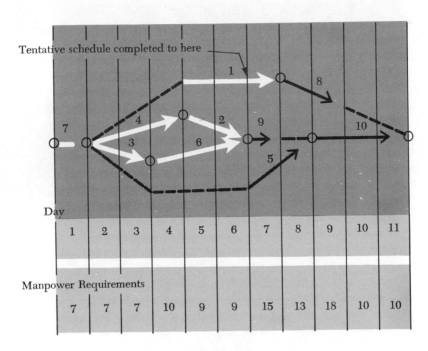

FIGURE F

At the end of Day 8, the schedule graph appears as shown in Figure G.

Remaining Period · The program decisions for the remaining six days are as follows:

Day 9—Schedule Job 9 (slack = 0); one man remains. Postpone Job 8 (slack = 2).

Day 10—Schedule Job 10 (slack = 0); no men remain. Postpone Job 8 (slack = 1).

Day 11—Continue Job 10 (slack = 0); no men remain. Postpone Job 8 (slack = 0).

Day 12—Continue Job 10 (slack = 1); no men remain. Postpone Job 8 (slack = 0).

Day 13—Schedule Job 8 (slack = 0); two men remain.

Day 14—Continue Job 8 (slack = 0); two men remain.

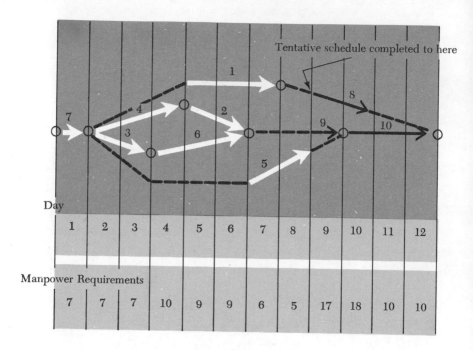

FIGURE G

All jobs are now scheduled. The final schedule graph appears in Figure H.

Thus the manpower limit of ten men per day has resulted in a four-day increase in the project length, compared with the un-limited resource schedule. In this application the heuristic program has found an optimal schedule. There are other feasible schedules, but none shorter than fourteen days.

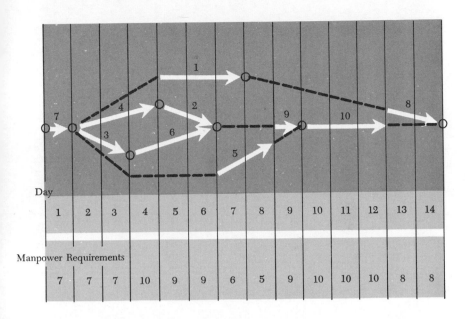

FIGURE H

Part Eight

Game Theory, Inventory Policy, and Queuing Analysis

GAME THEORY, inventory models, and queuing analysis are all important tools of managerial economics. The first two papers of Part Eight are concerned with the theory of games. John McDonald discusses one-person, two-person, and three-person games, using the liquor industry to illustrate games with more than two persons. J. D. Williams shows how conflict situations must be described in order to be amenable to game-theory analyses; the basic elements are the number of persons, the payoff, the strategy, and the game matrix.

The next three papers in this part are an introduction to inventory theory. The short piece by Thomson M. Whitin introduces the reader to the lot-size formula used to calculate economical purchase quantities. As Whitin points out, this formula is by no means new. The following paper by John Magee provides a very readable and useful account of the basic inventory techniques in use; the discussion is sprinkled liberally with references to particular cases. Finally, William Baumol describes the salient characteristics of queuing problems, which have received a great deal of attention from managerial economists and operations researchers, and shows how Monte Carlo techniques can be used to solve them.

The "Game" of Business

JOHN McDONALD

John McDonald is an editor of Fortune Magazine. This article is taken from his book, Strategy in Poker, Business, and War, *first published in 1050.*

The core of business is the market. The core of the market is the relationship of buyer and seller, whether either is an individual or a corporation. The theory of games investigates the interior of this relationship with game models.

From the standpoint of the individual there are three possible economic situations on earth: one man alone, two men, or three or more men. One man is Robinson Crusoe alone on an island. He plays there the game of solitaire, maximizing his gain uncomplicated by anything but the forces of nature, which are predictable, at least in such terms as probable rainfall and the probability of a tornado.

If there are two men on earth, the individual enters into the relation of exchange (buyer-seller), in which the problem of the other fellow appears; he can no longer maximize his gain but must seek a limitation of the possibilities in an optimum. But if there are three men, the novelty occurs that two of them may gain more by combining against the third (e.g., two sellers against a buyer, or vice versa). These three situations are the same as those found in games.

Any industry serves as an example of strategical game play. Take the liquor industry, which like steel, oil or automobiles has only a few sellers. The following story was told at length in *Fortune* magazine. Samuel Bronfman of Seagram had come down from Canada at the time of repeal and built his organization on blended whiskey in the tradition of Canadian and Scotch whiskeys. U.S. distillers, slow to adopt blends, preferred to sell the traditional American rye and bourbon. But blended whiskey could be nationally advertised to better advantage (rye and bourbon being largely regional); and Bronfman made the most of it. His marketing strategy consisted of blends, brand names and mild taste. Eventually there was a contest for leadership in the industry between Seagram and Schenley. Lewis Rosenstiel of Schenley, an old-school U.S. distiller, divided his attention between blends and straights. Now whiskey is made at one time to be sold four or more years later, and there is a corresponding risk in the inventory. Keep too little and you may run short. Keep too much and you may get stuck (whiskey consumption roughly follows the income curve; and as in any industry total inventories can get out of hand, resulting, in the absence of mandatory fair trade laws, in occasional price wars). "Holidays" during World War II had eliminated several crops of whiskey and inventories generally were low. Rosenstiel is known as an inventory strategist. He came out of the war period with brand sales off but with perhaps half of the remaining aged whiskey inventory in the U.S. Bronfman of Seagram had used up a large part of his whiskey inventory in gaining record brand sales. In this situation, they had a contest for the leadership, a kind of two-man game within the industry.

Facing a forthcoming shortage, Bronfman could either buy scarce bulk whiskey at a losing price and maintain Seagram's brand sales with a decline in profits, or maintain his rate of profit out of his remaining inventory with a decline in brand sales—or follow a mixed policy. In any event he could not maximize both brand sales and profits. Rosenstiel could sell the inventory to Bronfman at high bulk prices and no sales cost and thus maximize profits in the immediate circumstance; or he could put the inventory into Schenley brands with an expensive and risky sales campaign to raise brand sales at less profit. Like Bronfman, but for different reasons, he could not maximize both brand sales and profits.

Nor could the policies of the antagonists fail to conflict; for Rosenstiel, who, having the better inventory, had the dominant choice, could reconcile their difference only by taking profit and giving Bronfman the market (brand sales), i.e., take short-term gains at the cost of long-term losses. Within limits, Bronfman would have been glad to buy the market (take short-term losses with long-term gains)—if Rosenstiel would let him. But Rosenstiel wouldn't. Each sought an optimum move on a strategical basis. The game broadened out with larger numbers as Bronfman got some whiskey from another source. Rosenstiel opened a "back-label" campaign to make his aged stocks pay off. The consequences of the struggle have not been told, but whatever they are, they are the consequences of conscious strategy. Theoretically, Seagram and Schenley had another alternative, namely, to combine. There are good reasons why they would not, yet each of these corporate individuals like so many others in industry had grown large through combination.

The three-man coalition game can be played as an auction with one seller and two buyers. The seller has a reserve price of, say, $10 on the object to be sold. The first buyer is willing to go to not more than $15; the second buyer to not more than $20. Clearly the second buyer being the stronger will get the object. Ordinarily he is expected to get it for something over $15. But suppose the second buyer approaches the first and makes a deal to eliminate competitive bidding. He can then get the object for something over $10. The deal, however, requires a division of the spoils. The second, stronger buyer must pay the first, weaker buyer something for making the coalition. That payment must be enough to yield the second buyer the "best" profit, and yet enough to ensure that his partner will remain in the coalition: two maximums which must be resolved. For another, rival deal is possible —in game theory but not in classical economics—namely this: The seller may cross the market and break up the coalition by paying something to the second buyer to restore the bidding and thereby push the selling price back above $15. Thus each two-man game in this three-man game is under the influence of the other possible two-man games, in arriving at the distribution payment.

In the theory of games a number of solutions, i.e., distribution schemes, are possible, some of which are enforceable and therefore dominate others. In classical theory the weaker buyer gets nothing; in game theory he gets a bribe, and the bribe will be expressed in the price. Here the difference between classical economics and game theory can be shown with simple numbers. In classical theory the price is between $15 and $20 (all going to the seller). In game theory it is between $10 and $20, depending on the bargaining ability of the players.

The basic strategy of organizers of industry from the beginning has been to substitute combination for large-number competition. The value which J. P. Morgan put on combination was indicated in the capitalization of the United States Steel Corporation in 1901. The Corporation, which brought together about 65 percent of the steel capacity of the United States, was capitalized at about twice the tangible value given to its separate properties before combination. The specific combinative value (about three-quarters of a billion dollars minus an unknown value put on "good will") was expressed in the new common stock—attacked as "watered stock"—which eventually paid off as the technical and strategical market advantages of combination were realized. The Corporation later met rivalry from other combinations which were organized in opposition to it.

Rockefeller's genius similarly expressed itself in combinations. But some of these early combinations, as they were organized, were unwieldy. Standard Oil stockholders probably benefited from the trust's court-ordered dissolution in 1911. It became impolitic thereafter, under the Sherman Act, for one organization to hold an overwhelming share of the market. For that reason or because its ability to compete against counter-combinations was injured by organizational and management defects, the Steel Corporation retreated to its present holdings of about one-third of the industry's ingot capacity. Its present leadership of the industry is maintained by modern market techniques described in oligopoly and game theory.

Introduction to Game Theory

J. D. WILLIAMS

J. D. Williams is head of the mathematics department at the RAND Corporation. This article comes from his book, The Compleat Strategyst, *published in 1954.*

The number of persons involved is one of the important criteria for classifying and studying games, 'person' meaning a distinct set of interests. Another criterion has to do with the payoff: What happens at the end of the game? Say at the end of the hand in poker? Well, in poker there is usually just an exchange of assets. If there are two persons, say you (Blue) and we (Red), then if you should win $10, we would lose $10. In other words,

$$\text{Blue winnings} = \text{Red losses}$$

or, stated otherwise,

$$\text{Blue winnings} - \text{Red losses} = 0$$

We may also write it as

$$\text{Blue payoff} + \text{Red payoff} = \$10 - \$10 = 0$$

by adopting the convention that winnings are positive numbers and that losses are negative numbers.

It needn't have turned out just that way; i.e., that the sum of the payoffs is zero. For instance, if the person who wins the pot has to contribute 10 percent toward the drinks and other incidentals, as to the cop on the corner, then the sum of the pay-offs is not zero; in fact

$$\text{Blue payoff} + \text{Red payoff} = \$9 - \$10 = -\$1$$

The above two cases illustrate a fundamental distinction among games: It is important to know whether or not the sum of the payoffs, counting winnings as positive and losses as negative, to all players is zero. If it is, the game is known as a *zero-sum game*. If it is not, the game is known (mathematicians are not very imaginative at times) as a *non-zero-sum game*. The importance of the distinction is easy to see: In the zero-sum case, we are dealing with a good, clean, closed system; the two players and the valuables are locked in the room. It will require a certain effort to specify and to analyze such a game. On the other hand, the non-zero-sum game contains all the difficulties of the zero-sum game, plus additional troubles due to the need to incorporate new factors. This can be appreciated by noting that we can restore the situation by adding a fictitious player—Nature, say, or the cop. Then we have

$$\text{Blue payoff} = \$9$$
$$\text{Red payoff} = -\$10$$
$$\text{Cop payoff} = \$1$$

so now

$$\text{Blue payoff} + \text{Red payoff} + \text{Cop payoff} = \$9 - \$10 + \$1 = 0$$

which is a *three-person zero-sum* game, of sorts, where the third player has some of the characteristics of a millstone around the neck. But recall that we don't like three-person games so well as we do two-person games, because they contain the vagaries of coalitions. So non-zero-sum games offer real difficulties not present in zero-sum games, particularly if the latter are two-person games.

Parlor games, such as poker, bridge, and chess, are usually zero-sum games, and many other conflict situations may be treated as if they were. Most of the development of game theory to date has been on this type of game. Some work on non-zero-sum games has been done, and more is in progress, but the subject is beyond our scope. A troublesome case of particular interest is the two-person game in which the nominally equal payoffs differ in utility to the players; this situation occurs often even in parlor games.

STRATEGIES

Just as the word "person" has a meaning in game theory somewhat different from everyday usage, the word 'strategy' does too. This word, as used in its everyday sense, carries the connotation of a particularly skillful or adroit plan, whereas in game theory it designates any *complete* plan. *A strategy is a plan so complete that it cannot be upset by enemy action or Nature;* for everything that the enemy or Nature may choose to do, together with a set of possible actions for yourself, is just part of the description of the strategy.

So the strategy of game theory differs in two important respects from the conventional meaning: It must be utterly complete, and it may be utterly bad; for nothing is required of it except completeness. Thus, in poker, all strategies must make provision for your being dealt a royal flush in spades, and some of them will require that you fold instantly. The latter are not very glamorous strategies, but they are still strategies—after all, a bridge player once bid 7 no-trump while holding 13 spades. In a game which is completely amenable to analysis, we are able—conceptually, if not actually—to foresee all eventualities and hence are able to catalogue all possible strategies.

We are now able to mention still another criterion according to which games may be classified for study, namely, the number of strategies available to each player. Thus, if Blue and Red are the players, Blue may have three strategies and Red may have five; this would be called a 3×5 game (read 'three-by-five game').

When the number of players was discussed, you will recall that certain numbers—namely, one, two, and more-than-two—were especially significant. Similarly, there are critical values in the number of strategies; and it turns out to be important to distinguish two major categories. In the first are games in which the player having the *greatest* number of strategies still has a finite number; this means that he can count them, and finish the task within some time limit. The second major category is that in which at least one player has infinitely many strategies,

or, if the word 'infinitely' disturbs you, in which at least one
player has a number of strategies which is larger than any
definite number you can name. (This, incidentally, is just precisely what 'infinitely large' means to a mathematician.)

While infinite games (as the latter are called) cover many interesting and useful applications, the theory of such games is
difficult. 'Difficult' here means that there are at least some problems the mathematician doesn't know how to solve, and further
that we don't know how to present any of it within friendly
pedagogical limits; such games require mathematics at the level
of the calculus and beyond—mostly beyond. Therefore we here
resolve to confine our attention to finite games.

THE GAME MATRIX

We are now in a position to complete the description of games,
i.e., conflict situations, in the form required for game theory
analysis. We will freely invoke all the restrictions developed so
far. Hence our remarks will primarily apply to finite, zero-sum,
two-person games.

The players are Blue and Red. Each has several potential
strategies which we assume are known; let them be numbered
just for identification. Blue's strategies will then bear names,
such as Blue 1, Blue 2, and so on; perhaps, in a specific case, up
to Blue 9; and Red's might range from Red 1 through Red 5.
We would call this a nine-by-five game and write it as '9×5
game.' Just to demonstrate that it is possible to have a 9×5
game, we shall state one (or enough of it to make the point). Consider a game played on the following page.

The rules require that Blue travel from *B* to *R*, following the
system of roads, without returning to *B* or using the same segment twice during the trip. The rules are different for Red, who
must travel from *R* to *B*, always moving toward the west. Perhaps Blue doesn't want to meet Red, and has fewer inhibitions
about behavior. You may verify that there are nine routes for
Blue and five for Red.[1]

1. To avoid even the possiblity of frustrating you this early in the game,

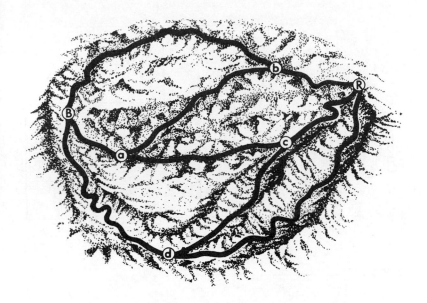

The rules must also contain information from which we can determine what happens at the end of any play of the game: What is the payoff when, say, Blue uses the strategy Blue 7 (the northern route, perhaps) and Red uses Red 3 (the southern route, perhaps)? There will be $9 \times 5 = 45$ of these pairs and hence that number of possible values for the payoff; and these must be known. Whatever the values are, it is surely possible to arrange the information on the kind of bookkeeping form shown on Chart 1, page 188.

Such an array of boxes, each containing a payoff number, is called a *game matrix*. We shall adopt the convention that a positive number in the matrix represents a gain for Blue and hence a loss for Red, and vice versa. Thus if two of the values in the game matrix are 3 and -8, as shown in Chart 2 (page 188), the

---

we itemize the routes. Blue may visit any of the following sets of road junctions (beginning with *B* and ending with *R* in each case):

      b, bac, bacd, ab, ac, acd, dcab, dc, d

Red may visit

      b, ba, ca, cd, d

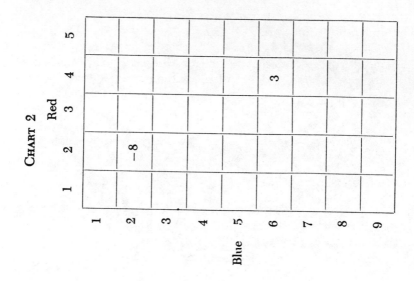

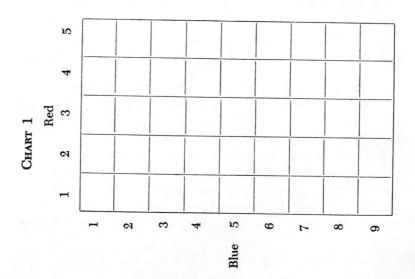

meaning is: When Blue uses Blue 6 and Red uses Red 4, Blue wins 3 units, whereas when Blue 2 is used vs. Red 2, Red wins 8 units.

When the original problem has been brought to this form, a game theory analysis may begin, for all the relevant information is represented in the descriptions of the strategies whose signatures border the matrix and in the payoff boxes. This is the game theory model of the conflict, and the applicability of the subsequent analysis will depend completely on the adequacy of this form of representation—a set of strategies and a payoff matrix.

THE CRITERION

A perennial difficulty in modelmaking of the analytical (as opposed to wooden) variety is the illness which might well be known as criterion-trouble. What is the criterion in terms of which the outcome of the game is judged? Or should be judged?

To illustrate the wealth of possible criteria in a homely example, consider a housewife who has $5 to spend on meat. What should she buy? If her criterion is simply quantity, she should buy the cheapest kind and measure the payoff in pounds. If it is variety, she should buy minimum, useful quantities of several kinds, beginning with the cheapest kinds; she measures the payoff by the number of kinds she buys. Or she may be interested in protein, fat, or calories. She may have to satisfy various side conditions, or work within certain constraints, such as allergies, tastes, or taboos. She may be interested in least total effort, in which case she may say, "I want five dollars worth of cooked meat—the nearest, of course—and deliver it sometime when you happen to be down our way."

Generally speaking, criterion-trouble is the problem of what to measure and how to base behavior on the measurements. Game Theory has nothing to say on the first topic, but it advocates a very explicit and definite behavior-pattern based on the measurements.

It takes the position that there is a definite way that rational people should behave, if they believe in the game matrix. The notion that there is some way people ought to behave does not refer to an obligation based on law or ethics. Rather it refers to a kind of mathematical morality, or at least frugality, which claims that the *sensible object of the player is to gain as much from the game as he can, safely, in the face of a skillful opponent who is pursuing an antithetical goal.* This is our model of rational behavior. As with all models, the shoe has to be tried on each time an application comes along to see whether the fit is tolerable; but it is well known in the Military Establishment, for instance, that a lot of ground can be covered in shoes that do not fit perfectly.

Let us follow up the consequences of this model in a zero-sum game, which, you will recall, is a closed system in which assets are merely passed back and forth between the players. It won't affect anything adversely (except Red), and it will simplify the discussion, if we assume for a moment that all payoffs in the game matrix are *positive;* this means that the strategy options available to the players only affect how many valuables Red must give to Blue at the end of a play of the game; this isn't a fair game for Red, but we will let him suffer for the common weal.

Now the viewpoint in game theory is that *Blue wishes to act in such a manner that the least number he can win is as great as possible, irrespective of what Red does;* this takes care of the safety requirement. *Red's comparable desire is to make the greatest number of valuables that he must relinquish as small as possible, irrespective of Blue's action.* This philosophy, if held by the players, is sufficient to specify their choices of strategy. If Blue departs from it, he does so at the risk of getting less than he might have received; and if Red departs from it, he may have to pay more than he could have settled for.

The above argument is the central one in game theory. There is a way to play every two-person game that will satisfy this criterion. However, as in the case of the housewife buying meat, it is not the only possible criterion; for example, by attributing to the enemy various degrees of ignorance or stupidity, one could devise many others. Since game theory does not attribute these attractive qualities to the enemy, it is a conservative theory.

You will note an apparent disparity in the aims of Blue and Red as stated above; Blue's aims are expressed in terms of winning and Red's in terms of losing. This difference is not a real one, as both have precisely the same philosophy. Rather, it is a consequence of our convention regarding the meaning of positive and negative numbers in the game matrix. The adoption of a uniform convention, to the effect that Blue is always the maximizing player and Red the minimizing player, will reduce technical confusion (once it becomes fixed in your mind); but let's not pay for this mnemonic by coming to believe that there is an essential lack of symmetry in the game treatment of Blue and Red.

Introduction to the Lot-size Formula

THOMSON M. WHITIN

Thomson M. Whitin is Professor of Economics at Wesleyan University. This is an excerpt from his article, "Inventory Control in Theory and Practice," which appeared in the Quarterly Journal of Economics *in 1952.*

The best known "scientific" inventory control system involves the calculation of economical purchase quantities and reorder point quantities. Several authors independently arrived at the same basic formula for determining economical purchase quantities in the 1920s. A number of different factors contributed to the development of such formulas.

First of all, the increasing size of business establishments has played an important role. It was possible for most firms in the past to make use of highly inefficient inventory control methods and yet still maintain profit margins. Modern large-scale enterprises often operate with small profit margins which might well be eliminated by poor inventory control methods. Furthermore, size in itself makes obvious the existence of possibilities of substantial savings through improvement in inventory control.

Secondly, during the past century, there has been an enormous increase in the amount of business training. High schools now offer some business preparatory courses, and the growth of business administration colleges has been extremely rapid. This additional training has made recent generations of businessmen more aware of improvement possibilities. Also, trade publications on market research, purchasing, retailing, standardization, and many other topics have contributed much to businessmen's understanding of the various problems which confront them.

A third factor that has aided the transition to modern inventory control methods is the increased emphasis that has been placed on the importance of engineers in business. The entrance of many trained engineers into business has brought with it the "scientific" approach, including scientific methods of production control, factory layout, standardization, etc. Also, cost accounting has helped entrepreneurs to evaluate the performance of various departments of their establishments, thus indicating specific areas where better control may be needed.

A final factor that gave impetus to research on inventory control was the "inventory depression" of 1921, which taught businessmen to be extremely wary of inventory accumulation. As a result of these factors, formulas for determining economic purchase quantities have been derived. These formulas involve a simple application of elementary differential calculus to inventory control.

The economic purchase quantity may be determined in the following manner. Two different sets of cost factors must be considered, namely, those which increase as purchase quantities increase and those which decrease as purchase quantities increase. Among those costs which increase are interest, obsolescence, risk, depreciation, storage, etc., while the forces making for decreasing costs include such items as quantity discounts, freight differentials, and procurement costs. In the following example, assume that the expense of procurement is constant and that interest, risk, depreciation, obsolescence, etc., may be lumped into one percentage figure (I). Let Y designate expected yearly sales (in \$), Q be the economic purchase quantity (in \$) and S be the procurement expense (in \$). Then total annual variable costs involved in ordering and carrying purchase quantities may be expressed as follows: $TVC = \dfrac{Q}{2}I + \dfrac{Y}{Q}S$. Differentiating with respect to the purchase quantity, Q, and setting the derivative equal to zero, the solution

$$Q = \sqrt{\frac{2YS}{I}}$$

results, where Q is the purchase quantity that minimizes combined ordering costs and carrying charges. This economical purchase quantity is thus seen to vary with the square root of sales and inversely with the square root of the carrying charges. This formula has been used in business and its use has been accompanied by good results.

Guides to Inventory Policy:
Functions and Lot Sizes

John F. Magee

*John F. Magee is Vice President of Arthur
D. Little, Inc. This article appeared in the
Harvard Business Review in 1956.*

"Why are we always out of stock?" So goes the complaint of great numbers of businessmen faced with the dilemmas and frustrations of attempting simultaneously to maintain stable production operations, provide customers with adequate service, and keep investment in stocks and equipment at reasonable levels.

But this is only one of the characteristic problems business managers face in dealing with production planning, scheduling, keeping inventories in hand, and expediting. Other questions— just as perplexing and baffling when managers approach them on the basis of intuition and pencil work alone—are: How often should we reorder, or how should we adjust production, when sales are uncertain? What capacity levels should we set for job-shop operations? How do we plan production and procurement for seasonal sales? And so on, and so on.

In this series of articles, I will describe some of the technical developments which aim at giving the business manager better control over inventory and scheduling policy. While these techniques sometimes employ concepts and language foreign to the line executive, they are far from being either academic exercises or mere clerical devices. They are designed to help the business manager make better policy decisions and get his people to follow policy more closely.

As such, these techniques are worth some time and thought, commensurate with the central importance of production planning and inventory policy in business operations. Indeed, many companies have found that analysis of the functions of inventories, measurement of the proper level of stocks, and development of inventory and production control systems based on the sorts of techniques described in this and following sections can be very profitable. For example:

• Johnson & Johnson has used these techniques for studying inventory requirements for products with seasonally changing demand, and also to set economical inventory goals balancing investment requirements against additional training and overtime costs.
• The American Thread Company, as a supplier to the fashion goods industry, plagued with large in-process inventories, day-to-day imbalances among production departments, labor turnover, and customer service difficulties, found these methods the key to improved scheduling and control procedures. Now these improved procedures help keep an inventory of tens of thousands of items in balance and smooth out production operations even in the face of demand showing extremely erratic fluctuations due to fashion changes.
• The Lamp Division of the General Electric Company has reported using these methods to survey its finished inventory functions and stock requirements in view of operating conditions and costs. This survey indicated how an improved warehouse reorder system would yield inventory cuts at both factories and warehouses, and pointed to the reorder system characteristics that were needed; it led to the installation of a new reorder and stock control system offering substantial opportunities for stock reduction. The analytic approach can also be used to show clearly what the cost in inventory investment and schedule changes is to achieve a given level of customer service.
• An industrial equipment manufacturer used these methods to investigate inventory and scheduling practices and to clear up policy ambiguities in this area, as a prelude to installing an electronic computer system to handle inventory control, scheduling, and purchase requisitions. In general, the analytic approach has proved a valuable help in bringing disagreements over inventory policy into the open, helping each side to recognize its own and the others' hidden assumptions, and to reach a common agreement more quickly.
• The Procter & Gamble Company recently described how analysis

of its factory inventory functions and requirements, using these methods, has pointed out means for improved scheduling and more efficient use of finished stock. The analysis indicated how the company could take advantage of certain particular characteristics of its factories to cut stocks needed to meet sales fluctuations while still maintaining its long-standing policy of guaranteed annual employment.

These are only a few instances of applications. Numerous others could be drawn from the experience of companies ranging from moderate to large size, selling consumer goods or industrial products, with thousands of items or only a few, and distribution in highly stable, predictable markets or in erratically changing and unpredictable circumstances.

In the present article major attention will be devoted to (a) the conceptual framework of the analytic approach, including the definition of inventory function and the measurement of operational costs; and (b) the problem of optimum lot size, with a detailed case illustration showing how the techniques are applied.

This case reveals that the appropriate order quantity and the average inventory maintained do not vary directly with sales, and that a good answer to the lot-size question can be obtained with fairly crude cost data, provided that a sound analytical approach is used. The case also shows that the businessman does not need calculus to solve many inventory problems (although use has to be made of it when certain complications arise).

INVENTORY PROBLEMS

The question before management is: How big should inventories be? The answer to this is obvious—they should be just big enough. But what is big enough?

This question is made more difficult by the fact that generally each individual within a management group tends to answer the question from his own point of view. He fails to recognize costs outside his usual framework. He tends to think of inventories in isolation from other operations. The sales manager commonly says that the company must never make a customer wait; the production manager says there must be long manufacturing runs for lower costs and steady employment; the treasurer says

that large inventories are draining off cash which could be used
to make a profit.

Such a situation occurs all the time. The task of all production
planning, scheduling, or control functions, in fact, is typically
to balance conflicting objectives such as those of minimum purchase or production cost, minimum inventory investment, minimum storage and distribution cost, and maximum service to
customers.

Production vs. Time · Often businessmen blame their inventory
and scheduling difficulties on small orders and product diversity:
"You can't keep track of 100,000 items. Forecasts mean nothing.
We're just a job shop." Many businessmen seem to feel that
their problems in this respect are unusual, whereas actually the
problems faced by a moderate-size manufacturer with a widely
diversified product line are almost typical of business today.

The fact is, simply, that under present methods of organization
the costs of paper work, setup, and control, in view of the
diversity of products sold, represent an extremely heavy drain
on many a company's profit and a severe cost to its customers.
The superficial variety of output has often blinded management
to the opportunities for more systematic production flow and for
the elimination of many of the curses of job-shop operation by
better organization and planning.

The problem of planning and scheduling production or inventories pervades all operations concerned with the matter of
production versus time—i.e., the interaction between production,
distribution, and the location and size of physical stocks. It occurs at almost every step in the production process: purchasing,
production of in-process materials, finished production, distribution of finished product, and service to customers. In multiplant
operations, the problem becomes compounded because decisions
must be made with reference to the amount of each item to be
produced in each factory; management must also specify how
the warehouses should be served by the plants.

Action vs. Analysis · The questions businessmen raise in connection with management and control of inventories are basically
aimed at action, not at arriving at answers. The questions are

stated, unsurprisingly, in the characteristic terms of decisions to be made: "Where shall we maintain how much stock?" "Who will be responsible for it?" "What shall we do to control balances or set proper schedules?" A manager necessarily thinks of problems in production planning in terms of centers of responsibility.

However, action questions are not enough by themselves. In order to get at the answers to these questions as a basis for taking action, it is necessary to back off and ask some rather different kinds of questions: "Why do we have inventories?" "What affects the inventory balances we maintain?" "How do these effects take place?" From these questions, a picture of the inventory problem can be built up which shows the influence on inventories and costs of the various alternative decisions which the management may ultimately want to consider.

This type of analytic or functional question has been answered intuitively by businessmen with considerable success in the past. Consequently, most of the effort toward improved inventory management has been spent in other directions; it has been aimed at better means for recording, filing, or displaying information and at better ways of doing the necessary clerical work. This is all to the good, for efficient data-handling helps. However, it does not lessen the need for a more systematic approach to inventory problems that can take the place of, or at least supplement, intuition.

As business has grown, it has become more complex, and as business executives have become more and more specialized in their jobs or farther removed from direct operations, the task of achieving an economical balance intuitively has become increasingly difficult. That is why more businessmen are finding the concepts and mathematics of the growing field of inventory theory to be of direct practical help.

One of the principal difficulties in the intuitive approach is that the types and definitions of cost which influence appropriate inventory policy are not those characteristically found on the books of a company. Many costs, such as setup or purchasing costs, are hidden in the accounting records. Others, such as inventory capital costs, may never appear at all. Each cost may be clear to the operating head primarily responsible for its control;

since it is a "hidden" cost, however, its importance may not be clear at all to other operating executives concerned. The resulting confusion may make it difficult to arrive at anything like a consistent policy.

In the last five years in particular, operations research teams have succeeded in using techniques of research scientists to develop a practical analytic approach to inventory questions, despite growing business size, complexity, and division of management responsibility.

INVENTORY FUNCTIONS

To understand the principles of the analytic approach, we must have some idea of the basic functions of inventories.

Fundamentally, inventories serve to uncouple successive operations in the process of making a product and getting it to consumers. For example, inventories make it possible to process a product at a distance from customers or from raw material supplies or to do two operations at a distance from one another (perhaps only across the plant). Inventories make it unnecessary to gear production directly to consumption or, alternatively, to force consumption to adapt to the necessities of production. In these and similar ways, inventories free one stage in the production-distribution process from the next, permitting each to operate more economically.

The essential question is: At what point does the uncoupling function of inventory stop earning enough advantage to justify the investment required? To arrive at a satisfactory answer we must first distinguish between (a) inventories necessary because it takes time to complete an operation and to move the product from one stage to another; and (b) inventories employed for organizational reasons, i.e., to let one unit schedule its operations more or less independently of another.

Movement Inventories · Inventory balances needed because of the time required to move stocks from one place to another are often not recognized, or are confused with inventories resulting from other needs—e.g., economical shipping quantities (to be discussed in a later section).

The average amount of movement inventory can be determined from the mathematical expression $I = S \times T$ in which S

represents the average sales rate, T the transit time from one stage to the next, and I the movement inventory needed. For example, if it takes two weeks to move materials from the plant to a warehouse, and the warehouse sells 100 units per week, the average inventory in movement is 100 units per week times 2 weeks, or 200 units. From a different point of view, when a unit is manufactured and ready for use at the plant, it must sit idle for two weeks while being moved to the next station (the warehouse); so, on the average, stocks equal to two weeks' sales will be in movement.

Movement inventories are usually thought of in connection with movement between distant points—plant to warehouse. However, any plant may contain substantial stocks in movement from one operation to another—for example, the product moving along an assembly line. Movement stock is one component of the "float" or in-process inventory in a manufacturing operation.

The amount of movement stock changes only when sales or the time in transit is changed. Time in transit is largely a result of method of transportation, although improvements in loading or dispatching practices may cut transit time by eliminating unnecessary delays. Other somewhat more subtle influences of time in transit on total inventories will be described in connection with safety stocks.

Organization Inventories · Management's most difficult problems are with the inventories that "buy" organization in the sense that the more of them management carries between stages in the manufacturing-distribution process, the less coordination is required to keep the process running smoothly. Contrariwise, if inventories are already being used efficiently, they can be cut only at the expense of greater organization effort—e.g., greater scheduling effort to keep successive stages in balance, and greater expediting effort to work out of the difficulties which unforeseen disruptions at one point or another may cause in the whole process.

Despite superficial differences among businesses in the nature and characteristics of the organization inventory they maintain, the following three functions are basic:

(1) *Lot-size inventories* are probably the most common in

436   *John F. Magee*

business. They are maintained wherever the user makes or
purchases material in larger lots than are needed for his immediate purposes. For example, it is common practice to buy
raw materials in relatively large quantities to order to obtain
quantity price discounts, keep shipping costs in balance, and
hold down clerical costs connected with making out requisitions,
checking receipts, and handling accounts payable. Similar reasons lead to long production runs on equipment calling for expensive setup, or to sizable replenishment orders placed on factories by field warehouses.

(2) *Fluctuation stocks,* also very common in business, are held
to cushion the shocks arising basically from unpredictable fluctuations in consumer demand. For example, warehouses and
retail outlets maintain stocks to be able to supply consumers on
demand, even when the rate of consumer demand may show
quite irregular and unpredictable fluctuations. In turn, factories
maintain stocks to be in a position to replenish retail and field
warehouse stocks in line with customer demands.

Short-term fluctuations in the mix of orders on a plant often
make it necessary to carry stocks of parts of subassemblies, in
order to give assembly operations flexibility in meeting orders as
they arise while freeing earlier operations (e.g., machining) from
the need to make momentary adjustments in schedules to meet
assembly requirements. Fluctuation stocks may also be carried in
semifinished form in order to balance out the load among manufacturing departments when orders received during the current
day, week, or month may put a load on individual departments
which is out of balance with long-run requirements.

In most cases, anticipating all fluctuations is uneconomical, if
not impossible. But a business cannot get along without some
fluctuation stocks unless it is willing and able always to make its
customers wait until the material needed can be purchased conveniently or until their orders can be scheduled into production
conveniently. Fluctuation stocks are part of the price we pay
for our general business philosophy of serving the consumers'
wants (and whims) rather than having them take what they can
get. The queues before Russian retail stores illustrate a different
point of view.

(3) *Anticipation stocks* are needed where goods or materials

are consumed on a predictable but changing pattern through the year, and where it is desirable to absorb some of these changes by building and depleting inventories rather than by changing production rates with attendant fluctuations in employment and additional capital capacity requirements. For example, inventories may be built up in anticipation of a special sale or to fill needs during a plant shutdown.

The need for seasonal stocks may also arise where materials (e.g., agricultural products) are *produced* at seasonally fluctuating rates but where consumption is reasonably uniform; here the problems connected with producing and storing tomato catsup are a prime example.[1]

Striking a Balance · The joker is that the gains which these organization inventories achieve in the way of less need for coordination and planning, less clerical effort to handle orders, and greater economies in manufacturing and shipping are not in direct proportion to the size of inventory. Even if the additional stocks are kept well balanced and properly located, the gains become smaller, while at the same time the warehouse, obsolescence, and capital costs associated with maintaining inventories rise in proportion to, or perhaps even at a faster rate than, the inventories themselves. To illustrate:

Suppose a plant needs 2,000 units of a specially machined part in a year. If these are made in runs of 100 units each, then twenty runs with attendant setup costs will be required each year.

If the production quantity were increased from 100 to 200 units, only ten runs would be required—a 50 percent reduction in setup costs, but a 100 percent increase in the size of a run and in the resulting inventory balance carried.

If the runs were further increased in length to 400 units each, only five production runs during the year would be required—only 25 percent more reduction in setup costs, but 200 percent more increase in run length and inventory balances.

The basic problem of inventory policy connected with the three types of inventories which "buy" organization is to strike

1. See Alexander Henderson and Robert Schlaifer, "Mathematical Programing: Better Information for Better Decision-making," *Harvard Business Review*, May–June 1954, p. 73. [This paper also appears in this volume.— Ed.]

a balance between the increasing costs and the declining return earned from additional stocks. It is because striking this balance is easier to say than to do, and because it is a problem that defies solution through an intuitive understanding alone, that the new analytical concepts are necessary.

INVENTORY COSTS

This brings us face to face with the question of the costs that influence inventory policy, and the fact, noted earlier, that they are characteristically not those recorded, at least not in directly available form, in the usual industrial accounting system. Accounting costs are derived under principles developed over many years and strongly influenced by tradition. The specific methods and degree of skill and refinement may be better in particular companies, but in all of them the basic objective of accounting procedures is to provide a fair, consistent, and conservative valuation of assets and a picture of the flow of values in the business.

In contrast to the principles and search for consistency underlying accounting costs, the definition of costs for production and inventory control will vary from time to time—even in the same company—according to the circumstances and the length of the period being planned for. The following criteria apply:

(1) *The costs shall represent "out-of-pocket" expenditures, i.e., cash actually paid out or opportunities for profit foregone.* Overtime premium payments are out-of-pocket; depreciation on equipment on hand is not. To the extent that storage space is available and cannot be used for other productive purposes, no out-of-pocket cost of space is incurred; but to the extent that storage space is rented (out-of-pocket) or could be used for other productive purposes (foregone opportunity), a suitable charge is justified. The charge for investment is based on the out-of-pocket investment in inventories or added facilities, not on the "book" or accounting value of the investment.

The rate of interest charged on out-of-pocket investment may be based either on the rate paid banks (out-of-pocket) or on the rate of profit that might reasonably be earned by alternative uses of investment (foregone opportunity), depending on the financial policies of the business. In some cases, a bank rate may be used on short-term seasonal inventories and an internal rate for long-term, minimum requirements.

Obviously, much depends on the time scale in classifying a given item. In the short run, few costs are controllable out-of-pocket costs; in the long run, all are.

(2) *The costs shall represent only those out-of-pocket expenditures or foregone opportunities for profit whose magnitude is affected by the schedule or plan.* Many overhead costs, such as supervision costs, are out-of-pocket, but neither the timing nor the size is affected by the schedule. Normal material and direct labor costs are unaffected in total and so are not considered directly; however, these as well as some components of overhead cost do represent out-of-pocket investments, and accordingly enter the picture indirectly through any charge for capital.

Direct Influence · Among the costs which directly influence inventory policy are (a) costs depending on the amount ordered, (b) production costs, and (c) costs of storing and handling inventory.

Costs that depend on the amount ordered—These include, for example, quantity discounts offered by vendors; setup costs in internal manufacturing operations and clerical costs of making out a purchase order; and, when capacity is pressed, the profit on production lost during downtime for setup. Shipping costs represent another factor to the extent that they influence the quantity of raw materials purchased and resulting raw stock levels, the size of intraplant or plant-warehouse shipments, or the size and the frequency of shipments to customers.

Production costs—Beyond setup or change-over costs, which are included in the preceding category, there are the abnormal or non-routine costs of production whose size may be affected by the policies or control methods used. (Normal or standard raw material and direct labor costs are not significant in inventory control; these relate to the total quantity sold rather than to the amount stocked.) Overtime, shakedown, hiring, and training represent costs that have a direct bearing on inventory policy.

To illustrate, shakedown or learning costs show up wherever

output during the early part of a new run is below standard in quantity or quality.[2] A cost of undercapacity operation may also be encountered—for example, where a basic labor force must be maintained regardless of volume (although sometimes this can be looked on as part of the fixed facility cost, despite the fact that it is accounted for as a directly variable labor cost).

Costs of handling and storing inventory—In this group of costs affected by control methods and inventory policies are expenses of handling products in and out of stock, storage costs such as rent and heat, insurance and taxes, obsolescence and spoilage costs, and capital costs (which will receive detailed examination in the next section).

Inventory obsolescence and spoilage costs may take several forms, including (1) outright spoilage after a more or less fixed period; (2) risk that a particular unit in stock or a particular product number will (a) become technologically unsalable, except perhaps at a discount or as spare parts, (b) go out of style, or (c) spoil.

Certain food and drug products, for example, have specified maximum shelf lives and must either be used within a fixed period of time or be dumped. Some kinds of style goods, such as many lines of toys, Christmas novelties, or women's clothes, may effectively "spoil" at the end of a season, with only reclaim or dump value. Some kinds of technical equipment undergo almost constant engineering change during their production life; thus component stocks may suddenly and unexpectedly be made obsolete.

Capital Investment · Evaluating the effect of inventory and scheduling policy upon capital investment and the worth of capital tied up in inventories is one of the most difficult problems in resolving inventory policy questions.

Think for a moment of the amount of capital invested in inventory. This is the out-of-pocket, or avoidable, cash cost for material, labor, and overhead of goods in inventory (as distinguished from the "book" or accounting value of inventory).

2. See Frank J. Andress, "The Learning Curve as a Production Tool," *Harvard Business Review*, January–February 1954, p. 87.

For example, raw materials are normally purchased in accordance with production schedules; and if the production of an item can be postponed, buying and paying for raw materials can likewise be put off.

Usually, then, the raw material cost component represents a part of the out-of-pocket inventory investment in finished goods. However, if raw materials must be purchased when available (e.g., agricultural crops) regardless of the production schedule, the raw material component of finished product cost does not represent avoidable investment and therefore should be struck from the computation of inventory value for planning purposes.

As for maintenance and similar factory overhead items, they are usually paid for the year round, regardless of the timing of production scheduled; therefore these elements of burden should not be counted as part of the product investment for planning purposes. (One exception: if, as sometimes happens, the maintenance costs actually vary directly with the production rate as, for example, in the case of supplies, they should of course be included.)

Again, supervision, at least general supervision, is usually a fixed monthly cost which the schedule will not influence, and hence should not be included. Depreciation is another type of burden item representing a charge for equipment and facilities already bought and paid for; the timing of the production schedule cannot influence these past investments and, while they represent a legitimate cost for accounting purposes, they should not be counted as part of the inventory investment for inventory and production planning purposes.

In sum, the rule is this: for production planning and inventory management purposes, the investment value of goods in inventory should be taken as the cash outlay made at the time of production that could have been delayed if the goods were not made then but at a later time, closer to the time of sale.

Cost of Capital Invested. This item is the product of three factors: (a) the capital value of a unit of inventory, (b) the time a unit of product is in inventory, and (c) the charge or imputed interest rate placed against a dollar of invested cash. The first factor was mentioned above. As for the second, it is fixed by management's inventory policy decisions. But these decisions can be made economically only in view of the third factor. This factor depends directly on the financial policy of the business.

Sometimes businessmen make the mistake of thinking that cash tied up in inventories costs nothing, especially if the cash to finance inventory is generated internally through profits and depreciation. However, this implies that the cash in inventories would otherwise sit idle. In fact, the cash could, at least, be invested in government bonds if not in inventories. And if it were really idle, the cash very likely should be released to stockholders for profitable investment elsewhere.

Moreover, it is dangerous to assume that, as a "short-term" investment, inventory is relatively liquid and riskless. Businessmen say, "After all, we turn our inventory investment over six times a year." But, in reality, inventory investment may or may not be short-term and riskless, depending on circumstances. No broad generalization is possible, and each case must be decided on its own merits. For example:

• A great deal of inventory carried in business is as much a part of the permanent investment as the machinery and buildings. The inventory must be maintained to make operations possible as long as the business is a going concern. The cash investment released by the sale of one item from stock must be promptly reinvested in new stock, and the inventory can be liquidated only when the company is closed. How much more riskless is this than other fixed manufacturing assets?

• To take an extreme case, inventory in fashion lines or other types of products having high obsolescence carries a definite risk. Its value depends wholly on the company's ability to sell it. If sales are insufficient to liquidate the inventory built up, considerable losses may result.

• At the other extreme, inventory in stable product lines built up to absorb short-term seasonal fluctuations might be thought of as bearing the least risk, since this type of investment is characteristically short-term. But even in these cases there can be losses. Suppose, for instance, that peak seasonal sales do not reach anticipated levels and substantially increased costs of storage and obsolescence have to be incurred before the excess inventory can be liquidated.

Finally, it might be pointed out that the cost of the dollars invested in inventory may be underestimated if bank interest rate is used as the basis, ignoring the risk-bearing or entrepreneur's compensation. How many businessmen are actually satisfied with uses of their companies' capital funds which do not earn more than a lender's rate of return? In choosing a truly appropriate rate—a matter of financial policy—the executive must answer some questions:

1. Where is the cash coming from—inside earnings or outside financing?
2. What else could we do with the funds, and what could we earn?
3. When can we get the investment back out, if ever?
4. How much risk of sales disappointment and obsolescence is really connected with this inventory?
5. How much of a return do we want, in view of what we could earn elsewhere or in view of the cost of money to us and the risk the inventory investment entails?

Investment in Facilities. Valuation of investment in facilities is generally important only in long-run planning problems—as, for example, when increases in productive or warehouse capacity are being considered. (Where facilities already exist and are not usable for other purposes, and where planning or scheduling do not contemplate changing these existing facilities, investment is not affected.)

Facilities investment may also be important where productive capacity is taxed, and where the form of the plan or schedule will determine the amount of added capacity which must be installed either to meet the plan itself or for alternative uses. In such cases, considerable care is necessary in defining the facilities investment in order to be consistent with the principles noted above: i.e., that facilities investment should represent out-of-pocket investment, or, alternatively, foregone opportunities to make out-of-pocket investment elsewhere.

Customer Service · An important objective in most production planning and inventory control systems is maintenance of reasonable customer service. An evaluation of the worth of customer service, or the loss suffered through poor service, is an important part of the problem of arriving at a reasonable inventory policy. This cost is typically very difficult to arrive at, including as it does the paper-work costs of rehandling back orders and, usually much more important, the effect that dissatisfaction of customers may have on future profits.

In some cases it may be possible to limit consideration to the cost of producing the needed material on overtime or of purchasing it from the outside and losing the contribution to profit which it would have made. On the other hand, sometimes the possible loss of customers and their sales over a substantial time may outweigh the cost of direct loss in immediate business, and it may be necessary to arrive at a statement of a "reasonable" level of customer service—i.e., the degree of risk of running out of stock, or perhaps the number of times a year the management is willing to run out of an item. In other cases, it may be possible to arrive at a reasonable maximum level of sales which the company is prepared to meet with 100 percent reliability, being reconciled to have service suffer if sales exceed this level.

One of the uses of the analytic techniques described below is to help management arrive at a realistic view of the cost of poor service, or of the value of building high service, by laying out clearly what the cost in inventory investment and schedule changes is to achieve this degree of customer service. Sometimes when these costs are clearly brought home, even a 100 percent service-minded management is willing to settle for a more realistic, "excellent" service at moderate cost, instead of striving for "perfect" service entailing extreme cost.

OPTIMUM LOT SIZE

Now, with this background, let us examine in some detail one of the inventory problems which plague businessmen the most —that of the optimum size of lot to purchase or produce for stock. This happens also to be one of the oldest problems discussed in the industrial engineering texts—but this does not lessen the fact that it is one of the most profitable for a great many companies to attack today with new analytic techniques.

Common Practices · This problem arises, as mentioned earlier, because of the need to purchase or produce in quantities greater than will be used or sold. Thus, specifically, businessmen buy raw materials in sizable quantities—carloads, or even trainloads —in order to reduce the costs connected with purchasing and control, to obtain a favorable price, and to minimize handling and transportation costs. They replenish factory in-process stocks of parts in sizable quantities to avoid, where possible, the costs of equipment setups and clerical routines. Likewise, finished stocks maintained in warehouses usually come in shipments substantially greater than the typical amount sold at once, the motive again being, in part, to avoid equipment setup and paperwork costs and, in the case of field warehouses, to minimize shipping costs.

Where the same equipment is used for a variety of items, the equipment will be devoted first to one item and then to another in sequence, with the length of the run in any individual item to be chosen, as far as is economically possible, to minimize change-over cost from one item to another and to reduce the production time lost because of clean-out requirements during change-overs. Blocked operations of this sort are seen frequently, for example, in the petroleum industry, on packaging lines, or on assembly lines where change-overs from one model to another may require adjustment in feed speeds and settings and change of components.

In all these cases, the practice of replenishing stocks in sizable quantities compared with the typical usage quantity means that inventory has to be carried; it makes it possible to spread fixed costs (e.g., setup and clerical costs) over many units and thus to reduce the unit cost. However, one can carry this principle only so far, for if the replenishment orders become too large, the resulting inventories get out of line, and the capital and handling costs of carrying these inventories more than offset the possible savings in production, transportation, and clerical costs. Here is the matter, again, of striking a balance between these conflicting considerations.

Even though formulas for selecting the optimum lot size are presented in many industrial engineering texts,[3] few companies make any attempt to arrive at an explicit quantitative balance of inventory and change-over or setup costs. Why?

For one thing, the cost elements which enter into an explicit solution frequently are very difficult to measure, or are only very hazily defined. For example, it may be possible to get a fairly accurate measure of the cost of setting up a particular machine,

3. See, for example, Raymond E. Fairfield, *Quantity and Economy in Manufacture* (New York, D. Van Nostrand Company, Inc., 1931).

but it may be almost impossible to derive a precise measure of the cost of making out a new production order. Again, warehouse costs may be accumulated separately on the accounting records, but these rarely show what the cost of housing an *additional* unit of material may be. In my experience the capital cost, or imputed interest cost, connected with inventory investment never appears on the company's accounting records.

Furthermore, the inventory is traditionally valued in such a way that the true incremental investment is difficult to measure for scheduling purposes. Oftentimes companies therefore attempt to strike only a qualitative balance of these costs to arrive at something like an optimum or minimum-cost reorder quantity.

Despite the difficulty in measuring costs—and indeed because of such difficulty—it is eminently worthwhile to look at the lot-size problem explicitly formulated. The value of an analytic solution does not rest solely on one's ability to plug in precise cost data to get an answer. An analytic solution often helps clarify questions of principle, even with only crude data available for use. Moreover, it appears that many companies today still have not accepted the philosophy of optimum reorder quantities from the over-all company standpoint; instead, decisions are dominated from the standpoint of some particular interest such as production or traffic and transportation. Here too the analytic solution can be of help, even when the cost data are incomplete or imperfect.

Case Example · To illustrate how the lot-size problem can be attacked analytically—and what some of the problems and advantages of such an attack are—let us take a fictitious example. The situation is greatly oversimplified on purpose to get quickly to the heart of the analytic approach.

Elements of the Problem. Brown and Brown, Inc., an automotive parts supplier, produces a simple patented electric switch on long-term contracts. The covering is purchased on the outside at $0.01 each, and 1,000 are used regularly each day, 250 days per year.

The castings are made in a nearby plant, and B. and B. sends its own truck to pick them up. The cost of truck operation, maintenance, and the driver amounts to $10 per trip.

The company can send the truck once a day to bring back 1,000 casings for that day's requirements, but this makes the cost of a casing rather high. The truck can go less frequently, but this means that it has to bring back more than the company needs for its immediate day-to-day purposes.

The characteristic "saw-tooth" inventory pattern which will result in shown in Exhibit 1, where 1,000 Q casings are picked up each trip (Q being whatever number of days' supply is obtained per replenishment trip). These are used up over a period of Q days. When the inventory is depleted again, another trip is made to pick up Q days' supply or 1,000 Q casings once more, and so on.

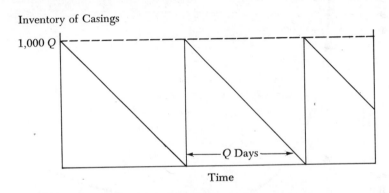

EXHIBIT 1

PATTERN OF INVENTORY BALANCE
(1,000 Q CASINGS OBTAINED PER REPLENISHMENT TRIP;
1,000 CASINGS USED PER DAY)

B. and B. estimates that the cost of storing casings under properly controlled humidity conditions is $1 per 1,000 casings per year. The company wants to obtain a 10 percent return on its inventory investment of $10 (1,000 times $0.01), which means that it should properly charge an additional $1 (10 percent of $10), making a total inventory cost of $2 per 1,000 casings per year.

(Note that, in order to avoid undue complications, the inventory investment charge is made here only against the purchase price of the casings and not against the total delivery cost including transportation. Where transportation is a major component of total cost, it is of course possible and desirable to include it in the base for the inventory charge.)

Graphic Solution. Brown and Brown, Inc., can find what it should do by means of a graph (see Exhibit 2) showing the annual cost of buying, moving, and sorting casings:

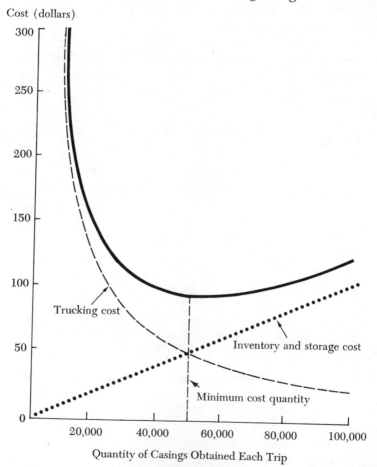

Cost (dollars)

Quantity of Casings Obtained Each Trip

EXHIBIT 2

ANNUAL COST OF BUYING, MOVING, AND STORING CASINGS
COMPARED WITH REORDER QUANTITY

The broken line shows total trucking costs versus the size of the individual purchase quantity:

• If 1,000 casings are purchased at a time, the total cost is $10 times 250 trips, or $2,500 per year.
• If 10,000 casings are purchased at one time, only 25 trips need be made, for a total cost of $250 per year.
• If 100,000 casings are purchased, only 2½ trips, on the average, have to be taken each year, for a total of $25.

The dotted line shows the inventory cost compared with the size of the purchased quantity:

• If 10,000 casings are purchased at one time, the inventory at purchase will contain 10,000, and it will gradually be depleted until none are on hand, when a new purchase will be made. The average inventory on hand will thus be 5,000 casings. The cost per year will be $2 times 5,000 casings, or $10.
• Similarly, if 100,000 casings are purchased at one time, the average inventory will be 50,000 casings, and the total inventory and storage cost will be $100.

The solid line is the total cost, including both trucking and inventory and storage costs. The total cost is at a minimum when 50,000 casings are purchased on each trip and five trips are made each year.

The solution to B. and B.'s problem can be reached algebraically as well as graphically. Exhibit 3 shows how the approach works in this very simple case.

Similar Cases · The problem of Brown and Brown, Inc., though artificial, is not too far from the questions many businesses face in fixing reorder quantities.

Despite the simplifications introduced—for example, the assumption that usage is known in advance—the method of solution has been found widely useful in industries ranging from mail order merchandising (replenishing staple lines), through electrical equipment manufacturing (ordering machined parts to replenish stockrooms), to shoe manufacturing (ordering findings and other purchased supplies). In particular, the approach

---

EXHIBIT 3

EXAMPLE OF ALGEBRAIC SOLUTION OF SAME INVENTORY PROBLEM AS EXHIBIT 2

The total annual cost of supplying casings is equal to the sum of the direct cost of the casings, plus the trucking cost, plus the inventory and storage cost.

Let:

T = total annual cost

b = unit purchase price, \$10 per 1,000 casings

s = annual usage, 250,000 casings

A = trucking cost, \$10 per trip

N = number of trips per year

i = cost of carrying casings in inventory at the annual rate of \$2 per 1,000, or \$0.002 per casing

x = size of an individual purchase ($x/2$ = average inventory)

Then the basic equation will be:

$$T = bs + AN + ix/2$$

The problem is to choose the minimum-cost value of x (or, if desired, N). Since x is the same as s/N, N can be expressed as s/x. Substituting s/x for N in the above equation, we get:

$$T = bs + As/x + ix/2$$

From this point on we shall use differential calculus. The derivative of total cost, T, with respect to x will be expressed as:

$$dT/dx = -As/x^2 + i/2$$

And the minimum-cost value of x is that for which the derivative of total cost with respect to x equals zero. This is true when:

$$x = \sqrt{2As/i}$$

Substituting the known values for A, s, and i:

$$x = \sqrt{2 \cdot 10 \cdot 250{,}000/.002} = 50{,}000 \text{ casings}$$

---

has been found helpful in controlling stocks made up of many low-value items used regularly in large quantities.

A number of realistic complications might have been introduced into the Brown and Brown, Inc., problem. For example:

• In determining the size of a manufacturing run, it sometimes is important to account explicitly for the production and sales rate. In this case, the inventory balance pattern looks like Exhibit 4 instead of the saw-tooth design in Exhibit 1. The maximum inventory point is not equal to the amount produced in an individual run, but to that quantity less the amount sold during the course of the run. The maximum inventory equals $Q (1 - S/P)$, where Q is the amount produced in a single run, and S and P are the daily sales and production rates respectively.

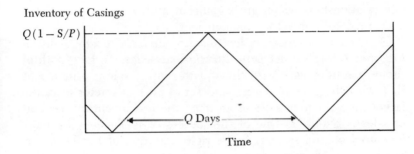

EXHIBIT 4

INFLUENCE OF PRODUCTION AND SALES RATE ON
PRODUCTION CYCLE INVENTORY

This refinement can be important, particularly if the sales rate is fairly large compared with the production rate. Thus, if the sales rate is half the production rate, then the maximum inventory is only half the quantity made in one run, and the average inventory equals only one-fourth the individual run quantity. This means that substantially more inventory can be carried—in fact, about 40 percent more.

• When a number of products are made on a regular cycle, one after another, with the sequence in the cycle established by economy in change-over cost, the total cycle length can be obtained in the same ways as described above. Of course, it sometimes happens that there is a periodic breach in the cycle, either to make an occasional run of a product with very low sales or to allow for planned maintenance of equipment; the very simple run-length formulas can be adjusted to allow for this.

• Other kinds of costs can also be included, such as different sorts of handling costs. Or the inventory cost can be defined in such a way as to include transportation, obsolescence, or even capital and storage cost as part of the unit value of the product against which a charge for capital is made. When a charge for capital is included as part of the base value in computing the cost of capital, this is equivalent to requiring that capital earnings be compounded; this can have an important bearing on decisions connected with very low volume items which might be purchased in relatively large, long-lasting quantities.

Complications such as the foregoing, while important in practice, represent changes in arithmetic rather than in basic concept.

Significant Conclusions · When the analytic approach is applied to Brown and Brown's problem and similar cases, it reveals certain relationships which are significant and useful to executives concerned with inventory management:

(1) *The appropriate order quantity and the average inventory maintained do not vary directly with sales.* In fact, both of these quantities vary with the square root of sales. This means that with the same ordering and setup cost characteristics, the larger the volume of sales of an item, the less inventory per unit of sales is required. One of the sources of inefficiency in many inventory control systems is the rigid adoption of a rule for ordering or carrying inventory equivalent to, say, one month's sales.

(2) *The total cost in the neighborhood of the optimum order quantity is relatively insensitive to moderately small changes in the amount ordered.* Exhibit 2 illustrates this proposition. Thus, all that is needed is just to get in the "right ball park," and a good answer can be obtained even with fairly crude cost data. For example, suppose the company had estimated that its total cost of holding 1,000 casings in inventory for a year was $1 when it actually was $2 (as in our illustration). Working through the same arithmetic, the company would have arrived at an optimum order quantity of 70,000 casings instead of 50,000. Even so, the total cost would have been (using the correct $2 annual carrying cost):

3.6 trips per year @ $10	= $36
35,000 casings average inventory @ $0.002	= 70
Total annual cost	= $106

Thus, an error of a factor of 2 in one cost results in only 6 percent difference in total cost.

In summary, Brown and Brown's problem, despite its oversimplification, provides an introduction to the analytic approach to inventory problems.

In particular, it illustrates the first essential in such an approach—i.e., defining an inventory function. In this case the function is to permit purchase or manufacture in economical order quantities or run lengths; in other cases it may be different. The important point is that this basic function can be identified wherever it may be found—in manufacturing, purchasing, or warehouse operation.

The only way to cut inventories is to organize operations so that they are tied more closely together. For example, a company can cut its raw materials inventory by buying in smaller quantities closer to needs, but it does so at a cost; this cost results from the increased clerical operations needed to tie the purchasing function more closely to manufacturing and to keep it more fully informed of manufacturing's plans and operation. The right inventory level is reached when the cost of maintaining any additional inventory cushion offsets the saving that the additional inventory earns by permitting the plant to operate in a somewhat less fully organized fashion.

B. and B.'s problem also illustrates problems and questions connected with defining and making costs explicit. The inventory capital cost is usually not found on a company's books, but it is implied in some of the disagreements over inventory policy. Here, again, bringing the matter into the open may help each side in a discussion to recognize its own and the others' hidden assumptions, and thus more quickly to reach a common agreement.

Queuing Analysis and
Monte Carlo Methods

William J. Baumol

William Baumol is Professor of Economics at
Princeton University. This article is taken
from his book, Economic Theory and Operations Analysis, published in 1961.

QUEUING ANALYSIS

Queuing theory is one of the subjects which has loomed large
in the literature of operations research. Any operation in which
the objects to be dealt with arrive at irregular intervals, and in
which the operating facilities are of limited capacity, is a queuing
problem. Automobiles waiting to be serviced in a garage, subway riders waiting to get through a turnstile, and telephone
callers waiting for a clear line all constitute queues. Among the
real problems to which queuing theory has been applied are the
landing of aircraft, the parking of automobiles, the timing of
traffic lights, the processing of films, and the servicing of travelers
through customs.

One of the key characteristics of a queue is the random pattern
of arrivals, which can therefore only be described in probabilistic
terms. There will be times, which cannot be predicted precisely,
when the number of arrivals will be unusually large, and as a
result, it will then take longer to be serviced. For example, in a
supermarket, customer delays at the checkout counters may be

caused by the arrival of a large number of customers at the same time, or by the coincidental arrival of several customers each of whom has many groceries in her shopping basket, so that the average checkout time is materially increased.

Suppose the manager of the supermarket wishes to know what sort of delays his customers are likely to encounter. The analyst requires information about two frequency distributions, one describing customer arrivals and the other the length of time it takes a clerk to handle a customer's purchases. Once both of these have been found, mathematical analysis permits us, in many cases, to find out such things as the expected average customer waiting time, the expected length of the waiting lines at different times of the day or week, etc.

The basic idea of the calculation is relatively simple, although the details are ingenious and complicated. The probability that there will be, say, 25 customers waiting now is equal to the sum of probabilities of the several alternative series of events which can produce this result. For example, there would now be 25 customers in line if 24 customers were there one minute ago, none has since been serviced, and one more customer has just arrived. Since we know the probability of a customer's having been serviced during any one minute and of a customer's arriving during any one minute, we can find out the relationship between the probability that there were 24 customers a minute ago and the probability that there are 25 customers in line now. Similarly, we can find the probability that the lines will grow from 25 to 26 customers in this way; and we can trace, customer by customer, the expected growth of the queues in the supermarket from the time it opens in the morning with zero customers.

One of the most interesting results of the theory states, in effect, that service facilities must have excess capacity built into them if service is not to break down altogether. More specifically, suppose the service facilities, if they were always kept fully occupied, were just sufficient to meet the needs of all the store's customers. Then queues would just grow longer and longer, without limit, and ultimately the operations would collapse. The basic reason for this result is, of course, that customer arrivals are *not* spread evenly in time, and so during some periods the facility will temporarily be idle whereas at other times it will be overcrowded. But, by assumption, the facilities would be of sufficient capacity only if there were no such oscillations in customer arrival time. To permit them to cope with bunched arrivals, therefore, the capacity of service facilities must be increased.

The theory also permits us, at least in principle, to investigate how much the expected length of queue lines will be reduced when a number of new checkout counters are added in our supermarket. This immediately raises an optimality question— just how many checkout counters should the supermarket have? More counters cost money to install and operate. Too many counters will therefore be wasteful, but too small a number of counters will slow down service and lose customers. The optimality problem, then, is to determine the intermediate number of counters which best serves management's purposes. Unfortunately, these probabilistic optimality calculations are often likely to grow very complex; therefore, instead of a direct approach to the problem, the operations researcher frequently resorts to the methods described in the following section.

ARTIFICIAL EXPERIMENTATION: MONTE CARLO TECHNIQUES

Before we can hope to find out the consequences of a course of action, it is necessary to have some sort of data. For example, suppose, as before, that it is desired to test some proposed service facilities to see how often customers will be kept waiting, and how long they will have to wait, on the average. These figures, of course, depend on the fluctuations in the number of customer arrivals—how frequently their number will exceed a particular magnitude.

In solving such a problem, experimentation is not a real possibility. It can be costly in customer relations to try very much more meager service facilities just to see what will happen. It may be that some information can be obtained from the experience of other supermarkets. But this may be too limited in range and in quantity to be of much assistance.

The operations researcher has, however, invented another very effective way to gather the relevant data: that is, to make them up himself, or rather to let the mathematical statistician make them up for him! But one may well ask, how can improvised statistics help us to foresee what will happen in the real world?

The answer is that the numbers are invented in a manner which carefully employs the analytical methods of mathematical statistics in order to stretch as far as possible such few actual data as are available to begin with. At some particular moment in the week we may assume that customers will arrive randomly, in a pattern somewhat similar to outcomes in successive throws of a pair of dice. The pattern of customer arrivals may then be described in terms of a frequency distribution, which indicates how many weeks in a year customer arrivals per hour can be expected to fall between 100 and 110 units, how often the number will lie in the 110 to 120 range, etc.

Now, from the available information *and the nature of the problem,* the statistician can often decide which frequency distribution best describes the pattern of expected customer arrivals. From this frequency distribution it is then possible to construct an artificial history of customer arrivals by choosing randomly among all the possibilities, but in a way which is "loaded" to produce the right frequencies. To give a very simple illustration, suppose we consider two possibilities: *A,* fewer than 100 arrivals per hour and *B,* at least 100 arrivals. If, on some basis, the odds are computed to be 2 to 1 in favor of *A,* we can generate an artificial demand history as follows: Toss the (unbiased) die. If it falls, 1, 2, 3, or 4, put down an *A;* if it falls 5 or 6, put down a *B.* This might yield a pattern for weekly demands such as the following:

TABLE 1

		Arrival "history"	
"Week"	*Face of die*	*Under 100*	*100 or more*
First	3	A	
Second	1	A	
Third	3	A	
Fourth	5		B
Fifth	6		B
Sixth	2	A	
Seventh	2	A	

This, incidentally, indicates the reason for the term "Monte Carlo method."

In practice, it is not actually necessary to toss any dice. Instead, we can use tables called "tables of random numbers" which have been worked out in advance. Moreover, the computations can be made by high-speed electronic computers which are able, in a few minutes or hours, to run off thousands of cases and manufacture data whose collection would, otherwise, require many years. But although this method is economical and powerful, it must be used only with the greatest care and caution. As we have seen, everything depends on the choice of frequency distribution (i.e., the odds of the various outcomes), and unless there is some assurance that these have been picked well, the entire calculation can be worthless.

Once this artificial experience has been generated, it can be used to find approximate solutions to optimality problems such as that of determining the number of checkout counters which was described in the last section—problems where straightforward computational methods are too complex. To illustrate the approach, consider the (unrelated) problem of finding an approximate root of the equation

$$X^2 - 6X + 9.1 = 0.$$

Instead of using the standard formula, we can go about it indirectly by trial and error, first, say, substituting $X = 1$ to find that the expression takes the value

$$(1)^2 - 6(1) + 9.1 = 4.1.$$

Clearly, $X = 1$ is not our root. So we try again, this time using, say, $X = 0$, and we see that this value of X makes the expression equal 9.1—i.e., it has only made things worse. We therefore infer that we have been going in the wrong direction, so this time we go up and try $X = 2$, etc. The results of several such trials can be tabulated as follows:

Trial value of X	1	0	2	3	4
Value of $X^2 - 6X + 9.1$	4.1	9.1	1.1	0.1	1.1

Clearly, this suggests that there is a root located very close to $X = 3$, at which the value of the expression is very close to zero, and we can take this as the approximate value of the root we are seeking.

The finding of optimal solutions in queuing problems and many other difficult operations problems can be approached in somewhat the same spirit with the aid of Monte Carlo methods. A number of alternative possibilities (number of possible checkout counters) can be postulated, and their consequences over a long period can then be simulated and reported on by the computer with the aid of Monte Carlo predictions of customer arrivals. If our objective is to minimize some sort of over-all cost function (which includes the costs of operating additional checkout counters as well as the costs of customer delays), we would take the optimal solution to be approximated by that trial (number of checkout counters) for which the machine reported the lowest over-all expected costs.

Unfortunately, this description, although correct in essence, is somewhat misleading in its simplicity. Particularly where decisions involve the assignment of values to a number of interrelated variables and where the ranges of possible values are considerable, there are difficult problems in deciding on what combination of values to try out next. It is by no means easy to design a procedure which converges with reasonable rapidity toward an optimal solution.

It is to be emphasized that the use of Monte Carlo methods is not limited to queuing problems. They can be used in inventory analysis, replacement analysis (when to stop repairing a piece of equipment and replace it with a new one), and a wide variety of other situations in which a prominent role is played by probabilistic elements such as the timing and magnitudes of customer demands or of the need for repairs.

Part Nine

The Role of the Computer in Industrial Management

THE electronic computer has had an enormous impact on management practices, and its full influence has yet to be felt. The computer allows managers to control the firm and assess its environment with new effectiveness because it enables them to get the relevant facts quickly and to understand their changing relationships. The papers in Part Nine are concerned with the role of the computer in industrial management. The article by Gilbert Burck of *Fortune* describes the Westinghouse Electric Corporation's use of computers both to reduce the length of time required to obtain management information and to simulate various aspects of its business.

Harold Leavitt and Thomas Whisler try to predict the impact of the electronic computer on managerial organization. In their judgment, the boundary between planning and performance will move upward, and there will be a tendency toward recentralization and a radical reorganization of middle management. John Dearden, in the following article, argues that the Leavitt-Whisler conclusions are incorrect. Herbert Simon is also concerned with the changes that will take place in the job of the manager during the next generation. He concludes that "the change in occupation profile depends on a well-known economic principle, the doctrine of comparative advantage. . . . [Thus,] if computers are a hundred times faster than executives in making investment decisions, but only ten times faster in handling employee grievances (the quality of the decisions being held constant), then computers will be employed in making investment decisions, while executives will be employed in handling grievances."

"On Line" in "Real Time"

GILBERT BURCK

*This article appeared in the April 1964 issue
of* Fortune. *Its author, Gilbert Burck, is an
editor of that magazine.*

Members of Westinghouse Electric Corporation's executive
committee recently filed into a small room in the company's new
Tele-Computer Center near Pittsburgh and prepared to look
at their business as no group of executives had ever looked at
business before. In front of them was a large video screen, and
to one side of the screen was a "remote inquiry" device that
seemed a cross between a typewriter and a calculator. As the
lights dimmed, the screen lit up with current reports from many
of the company's important divisions—news of gross sales, orders,
profitability, inventory levels, manufacturing costs, and various
measures of performance based on such data. When the officers
asked the remote-inquiry device for additional information or
calculations, distant computers shot back the answers in seconds.

This was only an experimental performance, designed to show
how the corporation's decision makers could someday be provided with practically all the timely and relevant information they
need to run the company. No computer system can do that yet,
and a few academicians doubt that such a system will ever do it.
But top managers in companies like Westinghouse are enthusi-
astically supporting the efforts of their systems men to convert
common business data into useful knowledge with the computer.

The computer is making such rapid, continuous progress in converting knowledge into efficiency and dollar savings that no man can yet be sure of its potential.

Knowledge is power and control, provided it is timely, ample, and relevant. Only a businessman who knows what is happening inside his company as soon as it happens can truly adjust his means to his aims; and only one who understands what is happening in the marketplace as soon as it happens can really make sound decisions about his aims. But even a lot of timely facts is not enough. Most facts are either dead the moment they are born, or are the remnants of autopsies on history. Unless a man understands how they are related, and particularly how their relationships are changing, he knows very little.

Today's advanced electronic computer enables a man to control his business and to assess its environment with incomparable effectiveness because it enables him both to lay hands on relevant facts swiftly and to understand their changing relationships. Besides supplying him with facts in historical time, or after they have happened, it supplies him with facts "on line," i.e., as soon as they are born, and in "real time," i.e., promptly and abundantly enough to control the circumstances they describe while those circumstances are developing. The computer helps the businessman understand the changing relationships of facts chiefly by a technique known as simulation, or the imitation of experience with models. Without the computer, he must build many models and compare them laboriously, or even construct pilot plants, and both methods cost much time and money. With the computer he needs only to translate an appropriate number of models into mathematical formulas and instruct the computer to compare them and pick the likeliest. He can also simulate part or all of his operation in a computer, and test it in dozens of different situations.

The simulation technique grows in effectiveness when a corporation can repeatedly inspect its past performance and gauge its objectives accordingly—that is, after the business has become "computerized," and the records of its "transactions" over the years have been stored in the machine's memory. Given such a "continuum" of information, the businessman can keep on refining his model by taking it apart, nailing down its variables, rejiggering its weights. As time passes, his model gets better and better, and he can make millions of telling comparisons in a few minutes. He knows precisely what has happened and why, what should be happening and why, and he has an excellent notion of what is likely to happen, and what is the best way of capitalizing on it all. He can rely less and less on guesses and hunch and more and more on analysis. As somebody once remarked hyperbolically, an executive is a genius if he is right fifty-two percent of the time. Whatever the correct percentage, computer men argue, the machine can help him expand and elevate his native intuitive powers to new levels.

The vast bulk of United States businesses' fourteen thousand computer installations are still confined to routine data processing —preparing payrolls and paychecks for nearly every kind of business, recording and sorting bank checks, making out bills for telephone and electric utilities, analyzing personnel data, preparing financial results for corporate annual reports, and performing all manner of scientific calculations. But now that the practicality of real-time applications has been demonstrated, more and more corporations are starting the arduous process of putting themselves at least partly on real time lest competitors get the jump on them. By 1970, computer sages predict, nearly all new electronic data-processing systems will be on line in real time.

Westinghouse Electric Corporation is said to use computers in a wider range of applications than any other United States company; whether it does or not, it has a clear notion of what it wants to do with them. The aim of the company's business-systems department, says Lou Hague, its director, is to shrink the lead time in the management information cycle to practically nothing, and eventually to be able to prepare a final report that will include just about everything top management needs to make its decisions. Some are skeptical. John Dearden of the Harvard Business School argues that flooding high-level management with operational information is "sheer nonsense." But Hague points out that no competent computer-system man proposes to inundate managers with useless information, and anyway no good top manager would stand for it. The phrase for what he and other systems men want to present to managers is "exception information," or information that calls for attention and action.

How the computer monitors exception information is illustrated by an example the business-systems department uses for internal education. Costs in a certain plant have been normal for a while, but begin to rise steeply. Without the computer, these costs would get far out of line before being noticed, and would not be brought back for a week or more; but with real-time control they get only a little out of line before being noticed, and are brought back promptly. The cumulative effect on profits can be enormous.

Westinghouse's business-systems department is tackling one problem at a time; Hague says it doesn't yet know enough to do the job all at once, and he doubts that anyone else does. And the company keeps expansion within realistic limits by making computer operations pay off in identifiable savings. Last year Westinghouse spent $16,200,000 for machine rentals and programing and research. But it realized $20,700,000 and thus saved $4,500,000 or nearly 30 percent on its outlays, not including indirect benefits such as better customer service and improved cash flow.

Westinghouse's adventure with the computer began seven years ago, when Hague hired James Emery, now teaching production and cost control at M.I.T., to tackle the problem of adjusting inventory supply to demand in the transformer plant at Sharon, Pennsylvania. The job only sounds easy. Inventories of distribution transformers, which are mass produced, had a habit of piling up unless demand was estimated correctly.

Emery and his associates resorted to simulations of demand based on such things as historical buying cycles, abnormal regional growth, and interest-rate levels. They fed the data into an I.B.M. 705, which forecast demand by size, type, and location. Thus simulating demand on a weekly basis, they sharply reduced inventories while giving customers better service. "We replaced a lot of discussion over the conference table with the computer," says Hague. "If we had known years before what we learned in 1958, we would have saved millions."

Don Burnham, the president of Westinghouse and then manufacturing vice president, was enthusiastic about the computer experiment from the start. In 1960, owing to his support, the business-systems department was founded, and plans were made for the Tele-Computer Center. Inventory control is now only part of a large-scale simulation operation that relates factory operation to buying patterns. At the Tele-Computer Center two Sperry Rand Univac 490's link 360 offices, factories, and warehouses in real time. They handle an average of 2,000 orders a day. Not only do they prepare invoices and bookkeep all transactions, they send incoming orders to the nearest warehouse, and pick the next nearest warehouse if (as is unlikely) the nearest is out of the item they are looking for. Because they automatically adjust warehouse stocks to optimum level by sending a reorder to the factory, they have enabled the company to close six of its twenty-six warehouses and to slash inventories by roughly 35 percent as well as to provide better service.

Like many commercial real-time installations, this one uses a standby computer to take over if the on-line machine fails. The standby computer solves engineering problems, turns out payrolls and annual-report figures, pays dividends, and prepares various financial and sales data. This sort of chore, however, can also be done by the on-line computer. Given an urgent query, say one asking if there is a left-handed pink refrigerator in stock, the on-line computer interrupts its routine duties to answer the question or even to make out an order and appropriately adjust inventory. But then it goes right back to the routine job it was doing.

Simulation is a standard procedure at Westinghouse. In scheduling its work, for example, the management of the South Philadelphia turbine plant draws up dozens of alternative plans. Given the plans plus the actual orders on hand and the sequence in which they must be filled, the computer runs through the equivalent of two or three years of operation, and so helps decide on the best schedule. "It often only verifies our hunches," says Hague. "But it can be a real shocker at times." Simulation is also being used to evaluate plant sites and appraise other capital investment, but the most effective use of the technique will occur after more activities or "transactions" have been put on real time.

Westinghouse is now augmenting order and inventory control with production control. In its Elmira, New York, electronic-tube plant and in its South Philadelphia turbine plant the company is installing electronic data-gathering equipment that keeps accurate and timely records of various stages of production; Westinghouse estimates that such systems will pay off at 50 percent.

While all this is going on, the business-systems department keeps its eye on the goal: shrink the management information cycle. To this end it has developed what it claims is a unique technique for retrieving information from a computer's memory. So-called random-access devices, which are standard peripheral equipment, enable a man to retrieve specific facts. But when he wants to find *all* the relevant information on a given subject, random-access devices don't help much. Business systems' solution to the problem, oversimplified considerably, is to instruct the computer to file information under dozens of different headings, and then to use a "list processor" to retrieve the information by scanning appropriate categories serially. Suppose, for example, an official wants to find out how many Westinghouse people working in cryogenics have done graduate work at M.I.T. Working against three variables, the computer would have to labor through the whole random-access file to come up with the answer. But using the processor, it is back with the reply in twelve minutes: two out of 117,000 employees.

Management in the 1980's

Harold J. Leavitt and
Thomas C. Whisler

Harold Leavitt is Professor of Industrial Administration at the Graduate School of Business at Stanford University. Thomas Whisler is Professor of Industrial Relations at the University of Chicago's Graduate School of Business. This paper appeared in the Harvard Business Review, *December 1958.*

Over the last decade a new technology has begun to take hold in American business, one so new that its significance is still difficult to evaluate. While many aspects of this technology are uncertain, it seems clear that it will move into the managerial scene rapidly, with definite and far-reaching impact on managerial organization. We would like to speculate about these effects, especially as they apply to medium-size and large business firms of the future.

The new technology does not yet have a single established name. We shall call it *information technology*. It is composed of several related parts. One includes techniques for processing large amounts of information rapidly, and it is epitomized by the high-speed computer. A second part centers around the application of statistical and mathematical methods to decision-making problems; it is represented by techniques like mathematical programing, and by methodologies like operations research. A third part is in the offing, though its applications have not yet emerged very clearly; it consists of the simulation of higher-order thinking through computer programs.

Information technology is likely to have its greatest impact on middle and top management. In many instances it will lead to opposite conclusions from those dictated by the currently popular philosophy of "participative" management. Broadly, our prognostications are along the following lines:

1. Information technology should move the boundary between planning and performance upward. Just as planning was taken from the hourly worker and given to the industrial engineer, we now expect it to be taken from a number of middle managers and given to as yet largely nonexistent specialists: "operations researchers," perhaps, or "organizational analysts." Jobs at today's middle-management level will become highly structured. Much more of the work will be programed, i.e., covered by sets of operating rules governing the day-to-day decisions that are made.

2. Correlatively, we predict that large industrial organizations will recentralize, that top managers will take on an even larger proportion of the innovating, planning, and other "creative" functions than they have now.

3. A radical reorganization of middle-management levels should occur, with *certain classes* of middle-management jobs moving downward in status and compensation (because they will require less autonomy and skill), while other classes move upward into the top-management group.

4. We suggest, too, that the line separating the top from the middle of the organization will be drawn more clearly and impenetrably than ever, much like the line drawn in the last few decades between hourly workers and first-line supervisors.

THE NEW TECHNOLOGY

Information technology has diverse roots—with contributions from such disparate groups as sociologists and electrical engineers. Working independently, people from many disciplines have been worrying about problems that have turned out to be closely related and cross-fertilizing. Cases in point are the engineers' development of servomechanisms and the related developments of general cybernetics and information theory. These ideas from the "hard" sciences all had a direct bearing on problems of processing information—in particular, the development of techniques for conceptualizing and measuring information.

Related ideas have also emerged from other disciplines. The mathematical economist came along with game theory, a means of ordering and permitting analysis of strategies and tactics in purely competitive "think-" type games. Operations research fits in here, too; OR people made use of evolving mathematical concepts, or devised their own, for solving multivariate problems without necessarily worrying about the particular context of the variables. And from social psychology ideas about communication structures in groups began to emerge, followed by ideas about thinking and general problem-solving processes.

All of these developments, and many others from even more diverse sources, have in common a concern about the systematic manipulation of information in individuals, groups, or machines. The relationships among the ideas are not yet clear, nor has the wheat been adequately separated from the chaff. It is hard to tell who started what, what preceded what, and which is method and which theory. But, characteristically, application has not, and probably will not in the future, wait on completion of basic research.

Distinctive Features · We call information technology "new" because one did not see much use of it until World War II, and it did not become clearly visible in industry until a decade later. It is new, also, in that it can be differentiated from at least two earlier industrial technologies:

1. In the first two decades of this century, Frederick W. Taylor's *scientific management* constituted a new and influential technology—one that took a large part in shaping the design of industrial organizations.
2. Largely after World War II a second distinct technology, *participative management*, seriously overtook—and even partially displaced—scientific management. Notions about decentralization, morale, and human relations modified and sometimes reversed earlier applications of scientific management. Individual incentives, for example, were treated first

as simple applications of Taylorism, but they have more recently been revised in the light of "participative" ideas.

The scientific and participative varieties both survived. One reason is that scientific management concentrated on the hourly worker, while participative management has generally aimed one level higher, at middle managers, so they have not conflicted. But what will happen now? The new information technology has direct implications for middle management as well as top management.

Current Picture · The inroads made by this technology are already apparent, so that our predictions are more extrapolations than derivations.[1] But the significance of the new trends has been obscured by the wave of interest in participative management and decentralization. Information technology seems now to show itself mostly in the periphery of management. Its applications appear to be independent of central organizational issues like communication and creativity. We have tended until now to use little pieces of the new technology to generate information, or to lay down limits for subtasks that can then be used within the old structural framework.

Some of this sparing use of information technology may be due to the fact that those of us with a large commitment to participative management have cause to resist the central implications of the new techniques. But the implications are becoming harder to deny. Many business decisions once made judgmentally now can be made better by following some simple routines devised by a staff man whose company experience is slight, whose position on the organization chart is still unclear, and whose skill (if any) in human relations was picked up on the playground. For example:

> We have heard recently of an electric utility which is considering a move to take away from generating-station managers virtually all responsibility for deciding when to use stand-by generating capacity. A typical decision facing such managers develops on hot summer afternoons. In anticipation of heavy home air-conditioning demand

1. Two examples of current developments are discussed in "Putting Arma Back on Its Feet," *Business Week*, February 1, 1958, p. 84; and "Two-Way Overhaul Rebuilds Raytheon," *Business Week*, February 22, 1958, p. 91.

at the close of working hours, the manager may put on extra capacity in late afternoon. This results in additional costs, such as overtime premiums. In this particular geographical area, rapidly moving cold fronts are frequent. Should such a front arrive after the commitment to added capacity is made, losses are substantial. If the front fails to arrive and capacity has not been added, power must be purchased from an adjacent system at penalty rates—again resulting in losses.

Such decisions may soon be made centrally by individuals whose technical skills are in mathematics and computer programing, with absolutely no experience in generating stations.

Rapid Spread · We believe that information technology will spread rapidly. One important reason for expecting fast changes in current practices is that information technology will make centralization much easier. By permitting more information to be organized more simply and processed more rapidly it will, in effect, extend the thinking range of individuals. It will allow the top level of management intelligently to categorize, digest, and act on a wider range of problems. Moreover, by quantifying more information it will extend top management's control over the decision processes of subordinates.

If centralization becomes easier to implement, managers will probably revert to it. Decentralization has, after all, been largely negatively motivated. Top managers have backed into it because they have been unable to keep up with size and technology. They could not design and maintain the huge and complex communication systems that their large, centralized organizations needed. Information technology should make recentralization possible. It may also obviate other major reasons for decentralization. For example, speed and flexibility will be possible despite large size, and top executives will be less dependent on subordinates because there will be fewer "experience" and "judgment" areas in which the junior men have more working knowledge. In addition, more efficient information-processing techniques can be expected to shorten radically the feedback loop that tests the accuracy of original observations and decisions.

Some of the psychological reasons for decentralization may remain as compelling as ever. For instance, decentralized organizations probably provide a good training ground for the top manager. They make better use of the whole man; they encourage more active cooperation. But though interest in these advantages should be very great indeed, it will be counterbalanced by interest in the possibilities of effective top-management control over the work done by the middle echelons. Here an analogy to Taylorism seems appropriate.

> In perspective, and discounting the counter-trends instigated by participative management, the upshot of Taylorism seems to have been the separating of the hourly worker from the rest of the organization, and the acceptance by both management and the worker of the idea that the worker need not plan and create. Whether it is psychologically or socially justifiable or not, his creativity and ingenuity are left largely to be acted out off the job in his home or his community. One reason, then, that we expect top acceptance of information technology is its implicit promise to allow the top to control the middle just as Taylorism allowed the middle to control the bottom.

There are other reasons for expecting fast changes. Information technology promises to allow fewer people to do more work. The more it can reduce the number of middle managers, the more top managers will be willing to try it.

We have not yet mentioned what may well be the most compelling reason of all: the pressure on management to cope with increasingly complicated engineering, logistics, and marketing problems. The temporal distance between the discovery of new knowledge and its practical application has been shrinking rapidly, perhaps at a geometric rate. The pressure to reorganize in order to deal with the complicating, speeding world should become very great in the next decade. Improvisations and "adjustments" within present organizational frameworks are likely to prove quite inadequate; radical rethinking of organizational ideas is to be expected.

Revolutionary Effects · Speculating a little more, one can imagine some radical effects of an accelerating development of information technology—effects warranting the adjective "revolutionary."

Within the organization, for example, many middle-management jobs may change in a manner reminiscent of (but faster than) the transition from shoemaker to stitcher, from old-time craftsman to today's hourly worker. As we have drawn an organizational class line between the hourly worker and the fore-man, we may expect a new line to be drawn heavily, though jaggedly, between "top management" and "middle management," with some vice presidents and many ambitious suburban junior executives falling on the lower side.

In one respect, the picture we might paint for the 1980's bears a strong resemblance to the organizations of certain other socie-ties—e.g., to the family-dominated organizations of Italy and other parts of Europe, and even to a small number of such firms in our own country. There will be many fewer middle managers, and most of those who remain are likely to be routine technicians rather than thinkers. This similarity will be superficial, of course, for the changes we forecast here will be generated from quite different origins.

What organizational and social problems are likely to come up as by-products of such changes? One can imagine major psychological problems arising from the depersonalization of re-lationships within management and the greater distance between people at different levels. Major resistances should be expected in the process of converting relatively autonomous and unpro-gramed middle-management jobs to highly routinized programs.

These problems may be of the same order as some of those that were influential in the development of American unions and in focusing middle management's interest on techniques for over-coming the hourly workers' resistance to change. This time it will be the top executive who is directly concerned, and the prob-lems of resistance to change will occur among those middle man-agers who are programed out of their autonomy, perhaps out of their current status in the company, and possibly even out of their jobs.

On a broader social scale one can conceive of large problems outside the firm, that affect many institutions ancillary to in-dustry. Thus:

- What about education for management? How do we edu-cate people for routinized middle-management jobs, espe-cially if the path from those jobs up to top management gets much rockier?

- To what extent do business schools stop training specialists and start training generalists to move directly into top management?

- To what extent do schools start training new kinds of specialists?

- What happens to the traditional apprentice system of train⸲ ing within managerial ranks?

- What will happen to American class structure? Do we end up with a new kind of managerial elite? Will technical knowledge be the major criterion for membership?

- Will technical knowledge become obsolete so fast that managers themselves will become obsolete within the time span of their industrial careers?

MIDDLE-MANAGEMENT CHANGES

Some jobs in industrial organizations are more programed than others. The job that has been subjected to micromotion analysis, for instance, has been highly programed; rules about what is to be done, in what order, and by what processes, are all specified.

Characteristically, the jobs of today's hourly workers tend to be highly programed—an effect of Taylorism. Conversely, the jobs shown at the tops of organization charts are often largely unprogramed. They are "think" jobs—hard to define and describe operationally. Jobs that appear in the big middle area of the organization chart tend to be programed in part, with some specific rules to be followed, but with varying amounts of room for judgment and autonomy.[2] One major effect of information technology is likely to be intensive programing of many jobs now held by middle managers and the concomitant "deprograming" of others.

As organizations have proliferated in size and specialization, the problem of control and integration of supervisory and staff levels has become increasingly worrisome. The best answer until now has been participative management. But information technology promises better answers. It promises to eliminate the risk of less than adequate decisions arising from garbled com-

2. See Robert N. McMurry, "The Case for Benevolent Autocracy," HBR January–February 1958, p. 82.

munications, from misconceptions of goals, and from unsatisfactory measurement of partial contributions on the part of dozens of line and staff specialists.

Good illustrations of this programing process are not common in middle management, but they do exist, mostly on the production side of the business. For example, the programmers have had some successes in displacing the judgment and experience of production schedulers (although the scheduler is still likely to be there to act out the routines) and in displacing the weekly scheduling meetings of production, sales, and supply people. Programs are also being worked out in increasing numbers to yield decisions about product mixes, warehousing, capital budgeting, and so forth.[3]

Predicting the Impact · We have noted that not all middle-management jobs will be affected alike by the new technology. What kinds of jobs will become more routinized, and what kinds less? What factors will make the difference?

The impact of change is likely to be determined by three criteria:

1. *Ease of measurement.* It is easier, at this stage, to apply the new techniques to jobs in and around production than in, say, labor relations, one reason being that quantitative measurement is easier in the former realms.
2. *Economic pressure.* Jobs that call for big money decisions will tend to get earlier investments in exploratory programing than others.
3. *The acceptability of programing by the present jobholder.* For some classes of jobs and of people, the advent of impersonal rules may offer protection or relief from frustration. We recently heard, for example, of efforts to program a maintenance foreman's decisions by providing rules for allocating priorities in maintenance and emergency repairs. The foreman supported this fully. He was a harried and much blamed man, and programing promised relief.

Such factors should accelerate the use of programing in certain areas. So should the great interest and activity in the new tech-

3. See the journals, *Operations Research* and *Management Science.*

niques now apparent in academic and research settings. New journals are appearing, and new societies are springing up, like the Operations Research Society of America (established in 1946), and the Institute of Management Sciences (established in 1954), both of which publish journals.

The number of mathematicians and economic analysts who are being taken into industry is impressive, as is the development within industry, often on the personal staffs of top management, of individuals or groups with new labels like "operations researchers," "organization analysts," or simply "special assistants for planning." These new people are a cue to the emergence of information technology. Just as programing the operations of hourly workers created the industrial engineer, so should information technology, as planning is withdrawn from middle levels, create new planners with new names at the top level.

So much for work becoming more routinized. At least two classes of middle jobs should move *upward* toward *de*programedness:

1. The programmers themselves, the new information engineers, should move up. They should appear increasingly in staff roles close to the top.
2. We would also expect jobs in research and development to go in that direction, for innovation and creativity will become increasingly important to top management as the rate of obsolescence of things and of information increases. Application of new techniques to scanning and analyzing the business environment is bound to increase the range and number of possibilities for profitable production. Competition between firms should center more and more around their capacities to innovate.

Thus, in effect, we think that the horizontal slice of the current organization chart that we call middle management will break in two, with the larger portion shrinking and sinking into a more highly programed state and the smaller portion proliferating and rising to a level where more creative thinking is needed. There seem to be signs that such a split is already occurring. The growth of literature on the organization of research activities in industry is one indication.[4] Many social scientists and industrial research managers, as well as some general managers, are worrying more and more about problems of creativity and authority in industrial research organizations. Even some highly conservative company presidents have been forced to break time-honored policies (such as the one relating salary and status to organizational rank) in dealing with their researchers.

Individual Problems · As the programing idea grows, some old human relations problems may be redefined. Redefinition will not necessarily solve the problems, but it may obviate some and give new priorities to others.

Thus, the issue of morale versus productivity that now worries us may pale as programing moves in. The morale of programed personnel may be of less central concern because less (or at least a different sort of) productivity will be demanded of them. The execution of controllable routine acts does not require great enthusiasm by the actors.

Another current issue may also take a new form: the debate about the social advantages or disadvantages of "conformity." The stereotype of the conforming junior executive, more interested in being well liked than in working, should become far less significant in a highly depersonalized, highly programed, and more machine-like middle-management world. Of course, the pressures to conform will in one sense become more intense, for the individual will be required to stay within the limits of the routines that are set for him. But the constant behavioral pressure to be a "good guy," to get along, will have less reason for existence.

As for individualism, our suspicion is that the average middle manager will have to satisfy his personal needs and aspirations off the job, largely as we have forced the hourly worker to do.

---

4. Much of the work in this area is still unpublished. However, for some examples, see Herbert A. Shepard, "Superiors and Subordinates in Research," *Journal of Business of the University of Chicago*, October 1956, p. 261; and also Donald C. Pelz, "Some Social Factors Related to Performance in a Research Organization," *Administrative Science Quarterly*, December 1956, p. 310.

In this case, the Park Forest of the future may be an even more interesting phenomenon than it is now.

CHANGES AT THE TOP

If the new technology tends to split middle management— thin it, simplify it, program it, and separate a large part of it more rigorously from the top—what compensatory changes might one expect within the top group?

This is a much harder question to answer. We can guess that the top will focus even more intensively on "horizon" problems, on problems of innovation and change. We can forecast, too, that in dealing with such problems the top will continue for a while to fly by the seat of its pants, that it will remain largely unprogramed.

But even this is quite uncertain. Current research on the machine simulation of higher mental processes suggests that we will be able to program much of the top job before too many decades have passed. There is good authority for the prediction that within ten years a digital computer will be the world's chess champion, and that another will discover and prove an important new mathematical theorem; and that in the somewhat more distant future "the way is open to deal scientifically with ill-structured problems—to make the computer coextensive with the human mind." [5]

Meanwhile, we expect top management to become more abstract, more search-and-research-oriented and correspondingly less directly involved in the making of routine decisions. Allen Newell recently suggested to one of the authors that the wave of top-management game playing may be one manifestation of such change. Top management of the 1980's may indeed spend a good deal of money and time playing games, trying to simulate its own behavior in hypothetical future environments.

Room for Innovators · As the work of the middle manager is programed, the top manager should be freed more than ever from internal detail. But the top will not only be released to

5. See Herbert A. Simon and Allen Newell, "Heuristic Problem Solving: The Next Advance in Operations Research," *Operations Research*, January–February 1958, p. 9.

think; it will be *forced* to think. We doubt that many large companies in the 1980's will be able to survive for even a decade without major changes in products, methods, or internal organization. The rate of obsolescence and the atmosphere of continuous change which now characterize industries like chemicals and pharmaceuticals should spread rapidly to other industries, pressuring them toward rapid technical and organizational change.

These ideas lead one to expect that researchers, or people like researchers, will sit closer to the top floor of American companies in larger numbers; and that highly creative people will be more sought after and more highly valued than at present. But since researchers may be as interested in technical problems and professional affiliations as in progress up the organizational ladder, we might expect more impersonal, problem-oriented behavior at the top, with less emphasis on loyalty to the firm and more on relatively rational concern with solving difficult problems.

Again, top staff people may follow their problems from firm to firm much more closely than they do now, so that ideas about executive turnover and compensation may change along with ideas about tying people down with pension plans. Higher turnover at this level may prove advantageous to companies, for innovators can burn out fast. We may see more brain picking of the kind which is now supposedly characteristic of Madison Avenue. At this creating and innovating level, all the current work on organization and communication in research groups may find its payoff.

Besides innovators and creators, new top-management bodies will need programmers who will focus on the internal organization itself. These will be the operations researchers, mathematical programmers, computer experts, and the like. It is not clear where these kinds of people are being located on organization charts today, but our guess is that the programmer will find a place close to the top. He will probably remain relatively free to innovate and to carry out his own applied research on what and how to program (although he may eventually settle into using some stable repertory of techniques as has the industrial engineer).

Innovators and programmers will need to be supplemented by "committors." Committors are people who take on the role of approving or vetoing decisions. They will commit the organization's resources to a particular course of action—the course chosen from some alternatives provided by innovators and programmers. The current notion that managers ought to be "coordinators" should flower in the 1980's, but at the top rather than the middle; and the people to be coordinated will be top staff groups.

Tight Little Oligarchy · We surmise that the "groupthink" which is frightening some people today will be a commonplace in top management of the future. For while the innovators and the programmers may maintain or even increase their autonomy, and while the committor may be more independent than ever of lower-line levels, the interdependence of the top-staff oligarchy should increase with the increasing complexity of their tasks. The committor may be forced increasingly to have the top men operate as a committee, which would mean that the precise individual locus of decision may become even more obscure than it is today. The small-group psychologists, the researchers on creativity, the clinicians—all should find a surfeit of work at that level.

Our references to a small oligarchy at the top may be misleading. There is no reason to believe that the absolute numbers of creative research people or programmers will shrink; if anything, the reverse will be true. It is the *head men* in these areas who will probably operate as a little oligarchy, with subgroups and sub-subgroups of researchers and programmers reporting to them. But the optimal structural shape of these unprogramed groups will not necessarily be pyramidal. It is more likely to be shifting and somewhat amorphous, while the operating, programed portions of the structure ought to be more clearly pyramidal than ever.

The organization chart of the future may look something like a football balanced upon the point of a church bell. Within the football (the top staff organization), problems of coordination, individual autonomy, group decision making, and so on should arise more intensely than ever. We expect they will be dealt with quite independently of the bell portion of the company, 'with distinctly different methods of remuneration, control, and communication.

CHANGES IN PRACTICES

With the emergence of information technology, radical changes in certain administrative practices may also be expected. Without attempting to present the logic for the statements, we list a few changes that we foresee:

- With the organization of management into corps (supervisors, programmers, creators, committors), multiple entry points into the organization will become increasingly common.

- Multiple sources of potential managers will develop, with training institutions outside the firm specializing along the lines of the new organizational structure.

- Apprenticeship as a basis for training managers will be used less and less since movement up through the line will become increasingly unlikely.

- Top-management training will be taken over increasingly by universities, with on-the-job training done through jobs like that of assistant to a senior executive.

- Appraisal of higher management performance will be handled through some devices little used at present, such as evaluation by peers.

- Appraisal of the new middle managers will become much more precise than present rating techniques make possible, with the development of new methods attaching specific values to input-output parameters.

- Individual compensation for top staff groups will be more strongly influenced by market forces than ever before, given the increased mobility of all kinds of managers.

- With the new organizational structure new kinds of compensation practices—such as team bonuses—will appear.

Immediate Measures · If the probability seems high that some of our predictions are correct, what can businessmen do to prepare for them? A number of steps are inexpensive and relatively easy. Managers can, for example, explore these areas:

1. They can locate and work up closer liaison with appropriate

research organizations, academic and otherwise, just as many companies have profited from similar relationships in connection with the physical sciences.

2. They can re-examine their own organizations for lost information technologists. Many companies undoubtedly have such people, but not all of the top executives seem to know it.

3. They can make an early study and reassessment of some of the organizationally fuzzy groups in their own companies. Operations research departments, departments of organization, statistical analysis sections, perhaps even personnel departments, and other "odd-ball" staff groups often contain people whose knowledge and ideas in this realm have not been recognized. Such people provide a potential nucleus for serious major efforts to plan for the inroads of information technology.

Perhaps the biggest step managers need to take is an internal, psychological one. In view of the fact that information technology will challenge many long-established practices and doctrines, we will need to rethink some of the attitudes and values which we have taken for granted. In particular, we may have to reappraise our traditional notions about the worth of the individual as opposed to the organization and about the mobility rights of young men on the make. This kind of inquiry may be painfully difficult, but will be increasingly necessary.

Computers and Profit Centers

John Dearden

*John Dearden is Professor of Business Ad-
ministration at the Harvard Business School.
This article was published in* The Impact of
Computers on Management, *which appeared
in 1967*

The purpose of this paper is to consider the potential impact
of computers and related information technology on the profit-
center type of business organization.

In 1958, Leavitt and Whisler published an article describing
what they believed to be the impact of computers and information technology on business organization in the 1980's.[1] This
article predicted that significant changes would occur in business
management. One of these changes would be a movement
toward recentralization made possible by the new information
technology. Specifically, they stated:

> We believe that information technology will spread rapidly. One
> important reason for expecting fast changes in current practices is
> that information technology will make centralization much easier.
> By permitting more information to be organized more simply and
> processed more rapidly it will, in effect, extend the thinking range of
> individuals. It will allow the top level of management intelligently
> to categorize, digest, and act on a wider range of problems. More-

1. Harold J. Leavitt and Thomas L. Whisler, "Management in the 1980's,"
Harvard Business Review, 1958, 36, No. 6. Reprinted in this book, pp. 273–
288.

over, by quantifying more information it will extend top management's control over the decision processes of subordinates.

If centralization becomes easier to implement, managers will probably revert to it. Decentralization has, after all, been largely negatively motivated. Top managers have backed into it because they have been unable to keep up with size and technology. They could not design and maintain the huge and complex communication systems that their large, centralized organizations needed. Information technology should make recentralization possible. It may also obviate other major reasons for decentralization. For example, speed and flexibility will be possible despite large size, and top executives will be less dependent on subordinates because there will be fewer "experience" and "judgment" areas in which the junior men have more working knowledge. In addition, more efficient information-processing techniques can be expected to shorten radically the feedback loop that tests the accuracy of original observations and decisions.[2]

Another, more recent, article was published in *Fortune*.[3] One of the principal themes in this article is that the computer will cause increased centralization of decision-making. Specifically, Burck states:

> The machine's power to help U.S. managers control their operations has generated what appears to be nothing less than a pervasive recentralization or reintegration movement. For twenty-five years or so decentralization has been the word for corporations all over the world and the reason seemed obvious enough. As companies grew larger and more complex or more diversified, one man or a small group was no longer able to run them directly. So top managers broke down their organization functionally, and delegated authority to divisional managers who were often assigned divisional profit goals, and often spurred by profit sharing.[4]

On the following page, Burck states:

> . . . the computer is now radically altering the balance of advantage between centralization and decentralization. It organizes and processes information so swiftly that computerized information systems enable top management to know every thing important that happens as soon as it happens in the largest and most dispersed organizations.[5]

2. *Ibid.*
3. Gilbert Burck, "Management Will Never Be the Same Again," *Fortune*, August 1964, 124–126ff.
4. *Ibid.*, p. 125.
5. *Ibid.*, p. 126.

In this paper, I will first examine the validity of the prediction that computers and the new information technology will cause a recentralization of authority. I will do this by testing this prediction as it applies to the profit-center form of organization, because this form of organization generally represents the greatest degree of decentralization. Secondly, I will examine the potential of the computer to improve the ability of top management to control profit-center activity. Thirdly, I will speculate on the changes that are likely to occur *within* the individual profit centers as a result of developments in computers and related technology.

WILL PROFIT CENTERS BE ELIMINATED?

In order to decide the potential impact of computers on the profit-center form of organization, we must first look at why a profit-center system was established in the first place. Then, we can see whether the computer has made changes that would affect that original reason. If it does, a change in organization may logically result; if it does not, the computer should have no impact on the organization structure. There are two different types of profit-center organization. In this part of the article, I would like to look at each of these types and analyze the changes, if any, that the developments in computer technology might create.

Profit Center: A Natural Organization Unit · One main reason for organizing an activity into profit centers has nothing to do with size or complexity; it is simply that the activity logically divides into a number of more-or-less independent profit-generating responsibilities, and the centralized control of these activities is artificial and inefficient. Take, for example, an automobile dealership. It can logically be divided into new-car business, used-car business, and service business. Many automotive dealers are organized successfully by making each of these a separate profit center. Since all three profit centers are usually located in the same place, there is no problem with information transmittal. Certainly, a typical automobile dealership is not so complex that one man could not control the entire profit responsibility. They are organized into profit centers because it is convenient and effective; thus, this type of organization will not be affected by computer developments.

There are, of course, other types of businesses where the same conclusion also holds. Gasoline service stations are one; venture-capital companies are another. I believe, therefore, that we can conclude that where a business is naturally divided into separate independent, profit-determining units, the computer will cause no change from the profit-center type of organization.

Large, Complex Business · What about the large, complex businesses referred to earlier in the article? Many of these deliberately established profit centers in what was originally a centralized business. General Motors did this in the thirties and General Electric in the forties, to name two out of a great many. It is clear that as a business grows in complexity and size, top management must delegate more responsibility for decisions simply because they do not have the time or the knowledge to make these decisions. Ultimately, management must delegate all but the most vital operating decisions.

Of course, in any business, there is a gradual delegation of authority. Periodically, however, a growing company examines the state of its organization and decides whether it should be changed. Basically, the delegation of authority could take a functional form (manufacturing, marketing, research, finance, and so forth) or a profit-center form. The functional form frequently just evolves, whereas a change to a profit-center system takes a specific decision in those companies not naturally divided into profit centers.

In order for a business organized on a functional basis to change to a profit-center system, it must be possible to separate it into profit-determining units. That is, in order to hold a manager responsible for profit performance, he must have control over the principal determinants of that profit. (Complete autonomy is usually not practicable. It becomes, therefore, a decision in many companies as to whether there is a sufficient degree of autonomy to make it reasonable to hold the manager responsible for profits.) In other words, if a business can be more logically broken down by type of business than by type of activity (manufacturing, marketing, etc.), a profit-center system is appropriate. Under these conditions, a profit-center system will have the following main advantages:

1. Each profit-center manager can become a specialist in a particular type of business.
2. Each manager will be motivated to maximize the return on his investment and thus contribute to the profit goals of the company. In other words, his goals will be consistent with those of the company. (The problem of establishing goal congruence will be discussed later in this paper.)
3. A profit center is a good training ground for future top managers.

To summarize, then, two conditions are necessary before a centralized company will change to a profit-center form of organization: (1) the company must be sufficiently large and complex to require a considerable amount of delegation on the part of top management; and (2) the business must be such that it can logically be divided into profit-responsible units. If computers are going to affect the profit-center system of organization, it must affect one or both of these conditions. Let us look at each.

Delegation of Authority. Will the computer allow management to decrease significantly the degree of delegation? In the quotations given earlier in the article, Leavitt and Whisler as well as Burck obviously believe this to be so. My own investigation of this problem, however, has led me to a different conclusion. It is not lack of *information* that has required delegation; it is two other factors. The first is that management lacks the *time* to make all but the important decisions. As the president of a multi-billion-dollar corporation told me, "My scarcest resource is my time. I have to allocate my time to those activities where my contribution is greatest. In fact, as a rule of thumb, I try to make no decisions that involve less than a million dollars." Secondly, managers have had to delegate authority because they are unable to maintain expertise in all of the different businesses in which their company is engaged. They cannot, therefore, make as good decisions as the expert *even with the same information.* It is not, therefore, lack of information or timeliness of information that has made it necessary to delegate authority; it is the lack of the knowledge necessary to use the information most effectively. As a result, I do not see how the increased use of computers and more sophisticated information technology will have any significant effect on the degree of the delegation of authority in our large, complex, decentralized concerns. It will, of course, have some minor impact. For example, inventory levels will tend to be more closely controlled centrally. In some instances, however, the computer could result in an *increase* in decentralization. If information is available to check more closely on what is happening, it might be practical for top management to delegate certain operating decisions formerly made centrally.

The method usually proposed to overcome the problems of executive time is called the "exception" principle. That is, management will be provided with information only when it exceeds some predetermined norm. The real problem, however, is to determine this norm and to prescribe the conditions where the norm has not been met. If this could be done, a limited delegation of authority would have been possible in the first place. The reason for delegation is that the establishment of satisfactory standards for most aspects of a business *are not now practical.* Further, as will be indicated later in the paper, the computer does not appear to have increased significantly the ability of management to set such standards or determine meaningful deviations from them. Consequently, in most situations, management by exception is *not* an answer to the problem of executive time.

Profit-Center Structure. If the computer will not affect significantly the necessity to delegate authority, will it affect the profit-center system by making a functional breakdown more desirable? As will be explained later, the computer will affect two principal areas of organization: (1) the data-processing activity will tend to become centralized; and (2) there will be much more centralization of the logistics systems (the flow of goods through the company). The impact of these two changes on organization will be considered below. For the present, let us see if they will affect the typical profit-center organization. Will these changes make it less logical to delegate profit responsibility?

Data-Processing. I do not see how the centralization of data-processing can have any effect on the decentralization of profit responsibility. If the same information is available at the same time, the place where it is processed makes no difference. Further, it is not necessary for a profit-center manager to control directly the processing of the information that is reported to him, as long as he can determine what that information will be.

Logistics. The centralization of the logistics systems may, of course, reduce the authority of the profit-center manager. The question is: Will it change it enough to make the delegation of profit responsibility unreasonable? I believe that it will not. It seems to me that it is entirely reasonable for a profit-center manager to participate in a centralized control of material flow and still retain most of his authority over profit determination. As evidence that this can be done, I would like to cite the General Motors Corporation as an example. They have had centralized control over most of their automotive scheduling while enjoying an extremely successful profit-center organization. Note, also, that many companies may only centralize logistics *within* profit centers rather than between profit centers. This is true where each profit center produces and markets more-or-less independent products.

To summarize, I do not see how the centralization of logistics will have any serious impact on profit-center responsibilities. Even when the centralization of logistics is extreme (as in the case of the automotive industry), profit centers can and do operate effectively. About the only exception to this generalization that I can think of would be the case where the logistics function was the *major* responsibility of the profit-center manager. This situation would be most unusual, however, because, if a manager's main responsibility is logistics, it is generally illogical to make him responsible for profit performance.

Conclusion · My conclusion is that we can expect no significant change in the degree of delegation of authority by top management or in the profit-center system of organization as a result of developments in computers and information technology. Profit-center decentralization has been somewhat of a fad in the past few years, and many companies have established profit-center organizations when they should have maintained centralized profit responsibility. Furthermore, many companies have gone to extremes in giving autonomy to profit-center managers. Consequently, we can expect some changes in the new few years away from profit centers and to less autonomy by the profit-center manager. These changes, however, will not be caused by computers, although they may be attributed to them by many.

WILL COMPUTERS HELP PROFIT-CENTER CONTROL?

If, as I believe, computers and information technology will have no significant impact on the profit-center form of organization, to what extent will the computer improve top management's control over the profit-center manager? I shall examine this question by reviewing the critical problems of controlling a group of profit centers and determining if the computer can be of significant help in solving these problems.

Critical Problems of Profit-Center Systems · Top management typically controls profit-center activity by setting a goal (usually an annual profit budget) for each profit center and periodically (usually monthly) by evaluating actual performance against this goal. Presumably, if the division is meeting its budget, top management need take no action. If the budget is missed, top management must decide what, if any, steps it should take to correct the situation. The profit budget is, first, an instrument for coordinating all divisional plans with over-all company plans. After approval, it is a means of evaluating the divisional manager and motivating him to maximize company profits.

Although simple in concept, the proper execution of profit-center control is very difficult, requiring a high degree of managerial judgment. In this part of the paper, I shall examine each of the problems that I have found to cause these difficulties and try to see to what extent computers will be helpful in solving these problems.

Establishing Goals. The evaluation of a profit-budget proposal is frequently a very difficult matter. Does the proposed profit represent an adequate goal? Is it comparable in difficulty to other profit centers? Should more research costs have been budgeted? And so forth. The profit budget is the key to the control system, yet frequently, top management has no real notion as to how much profit potential a division has. Consequently, management settles for a budgeted profit that is somewhat higher than last year's actual profit.

There has been some experimental work done in developing models of profit centers to help to predict their profitability. Also, companies have developed computer models of the budget and, then, have manipulated this model to show the effect of various alternatives proposed by management. (This is called the "what if" game.) This is of help to management in that it allows them to examine more alternatives. It is a little hard to say how much the computer can help management in setting goals. There are frequently intangible factors that are impossible to quantify. Furthermore, even where quantification is possible, the necessary information is not available. My conclusion is that the computer will help management to set better profit goals in some cases and that it will make it practicable for management to look at more alternatives. I believe, however, that the computer is a long way from providing a universal answer to the question, "How much should this division earn this year?" Furthermore, as you go into the details that make up the profitability, the computer tends to become progressively less useful.

Evaluating Performance. Perhaps the most difficult problem in profit-center management is the evaluation of divisional performance. The reason for this is that it is frequently nearly impossible to decide the extent to which unfavorable variances from budget are caused by the inadequacies of the profit-center manager and the extent to which they are beyond his control. Where performance is favorable, the same problem exists in deciding how much of the favorable variance is due to good performance and how much is due to fortuitous circumstance. This condition occurs because many variances are semicontrollable or controllable only under certain conditions. Frequently, one of top management's more difficult tasks is to decide what action is warranted from a report of actual profits compared to budget.

Clearly, much work needs to be done to improve management's ability to evaluate profit performance. To what extent the computer will be necessary to these improvements is a little difficult to say. As in the case of goal setting, I think the computer will be helpful in implementing new methods for analyzing variances. I believe, however, the computer will provide help only in limited situations. The evaluation of performance will still be one of management's principal problems in most instances.

Personnel. Somewhat related to profit-performance evaluation is the entire problem of personnel selection. Whom to hire, promote, discharge, or demote, as well as when these actions should be made, are critical to the successful operation of a decentralized company. Except for some convenience in the retrieval of personnel information, I see no impact on the solution of personnel problems by the computer.

Goal Congruence. In setting up a profit-center control system, one of the principal requirements is that the goals of the profit-center manager should be congruent with the goals of the company. That is, what improves profit-center performance should also improve the company performance by the same amount. The problems of developing a system that does this are quite technical. Even if a system is as technically perfect as we know how to make it, there will be, however, instances where the goals of the manager will not be consistent with the goals of the company. In this part of the paper I shall examine three major goal-congruence problems to see if the computer will help to solve them.

1. *Short-Run Profits.* A profit-center manager tends to be motivated to maximize short-term profits. This results from his belief (often justified) that he will not be around for the long run if his division is not profitable in the short run. This problem is overcome by such things as education, insistence on a certain level of research, and so forth. Consequently, I do not see how the computer and related technology will have any impact on solving this problem.

2. *Cooperation Among Divisions.* A second goal-congruence problem is that it is to a division's advantage *not* to cooperate with those divisions of the company with which it is in competition, even though such cooperation would be to the benefit of the company. (Even where divisions are not in direct competition, there are instances where the best interests of the company will require a profit sacrifice on the part of a division in favor of another.) As in the case of a short-term profitability, I see no

way in which the computer can be used to help solve this problem.

3. *Early Warning of Trouble.* When a divisional manager begins to run into serious problems, it is to the company's interests that this condition be communicated to top management as soon as possible. Frequently, however, the divisional manager is not only reluctant to call for help but may even try to hide the condition. Usually he hopes that he can correct it or that the condition will change for the better before he has to report he is having difficulties.

Top management needs a system to indicate when a division is in trouble as soon as it is in trouble. This problem comes up when conditions degenerate *between* reporting periods to such an extent that management should know about it. (Most serious divisional problems are of a long-run nature and cover several reporting periods.) The problem is usually solved by requiring the profit-center manager to report immediately when certain conditions exist or, more importantly, are expected to exist.

The computer has only limited ability to monitor the happenings within a division. In the first place, it can only monitor historical data, when often the important information is known only to the manager (e.g., a threatened strike). Secondly, it can only monitor on a daily basis certain kinds of data (e.g., profits on a daily basis are not practical). Consequently, I do not see how the computer will improve significantly present methods of early warning.

Conclusions · Computers will reduce the cost of data-processing; they will make it possible to have performance information earlier; they will make it possible to have somewhat more accurate and complex variance analysis; they will be of help in determining profit goals. It is my conclusion, however, that computers and related technology will not have a great impact in the typical company on ability of top management to control divisional operations.

HOW WILL COMPUTERS AFFECT MANAGEMENT?

As indicated above, I believe that the top management of a decentralized company will be relatively unaffected by the computer. The purpose of this part of the article will be to consider what changes might take place at the divisional level.

Logistics and Data-Processing · There are two pronounced trends taking place in industry today that are related to computer developments. The first is the centralization of logistics systems and the second is the centralization of the data-processing activity. I will now describe each of these trends and speculate on their impact on divisional management.

Logistics. Recent developments in time-sharing, cheap random access equipment, and cheap and fast data transmission have made the automation and centralization of logistics systems economically feasible. (Logistics are the flow of material through a company, from the purchase of the raw material and components to the delivery of the finished goods to the customer.) For example, a household-appliance company will have raw-material and work-in-process inventories at the factory and finished-goods inventories at warehouses, at distributors, and at dealers. There is an almost continuous flow from the purchase of the material to the delivery of the appliance to the ultimate consumer. In some instances, it is now economically practicable to keep track of the flow of all of the inventory in a central computer. In the future, I believe that we will find the centralization of logistics systems commonplace. This will, of course, result in marked improvements in inventory control, customer service, and distribution costs, because the computer can help solve the critical logistics problems—knowing quickly the amount and flow of products through the company.

Logistics will tend to be centralized by product. Where a company is divisionalized by product line, logistics will tend to be centralized by division. Where several divisions are involved in the same product line (as in the automobile business), the logistics systems will tend to be centralized at the group or corporate level.

Data-Processing. Data-processing will tend to be centralized, at least at the divisional level, and frequently at the corporate level. This will be true of such activities as accounting, scheduling, and personnel information. The reason for this is purely economic. It is cheaper to maintain a large central computer than to maintain several small computers. Also, where two or more locations use the same data, a common data base may be maintained more efficiently.

Management Changes · Within the division, the main changes that will occur from the automation and centralization of logistics and data-processing will be at the plant or warehouse level. As I see it, the following four changes can be expected:

1. The divisional manager will tend to spend less time co-ordinating and solving logistics problems because these will be handled automatically at a lower level.
2. Anyone at a plant, warehouse, or geographically decentralized office who is principally concerned with the supervision of data-processing personnel may have his job either changed or eliminated. For example, the plant controller who is now concerned mostly with maintaining accounting records will have to become more of an interpreter of data and a financial adviser to the divisional manager.
3. Anyone at the plant or warehouse who is largely engaged in making logistics decisions (i.e., ordering parts or scheduling production) may have his job down-graded or eliminated. For example, the manager of a parts warehouse may well become merely a supervisor of stock handlers, receiving and shipping parts in accordance with a schedule received from the divisional office.
4. Anyone who is partially concerned with making logistics decisions may have that part of his job eliminated. (Because most jobs are becoming more complex, I do not think that generally the elimination of logistics decisions will affect the job status.)

Notice that these changes will have a limited impact on most managers at any level. They will be confined to relatively two types—managers engaged primarily in supervising decentralized data-processing or logistics activities. Further, not all of these managers will be affected. With respect to logistics, they must be engaged in the type of activity that can be logically centralized. In some situations, local conditions are so important that a centralization of these decisions is not practical. With respect to data-processing, the type and extent of this activity must be such that centralization is economic.

CONCLUSIONS

My conclusions are that the computer will have no impact on the organization of top and divisional management, relatively little impact on the ability of the top manager to control profit centers, and limited impact on management levels below the divisional manager. Consequently, I believe that the opinions quoted at the beginning of this paper are incorrect. There will be some centralization of data-processing and logistic systems. I do not see how this limited centralization, however, can have anywhere near the impact envisioned by many writers on the subject.

The Corporation: Will It Be Managed by Machines?

Herbert A. Simon

*Herbert A. Simon is Associate Dean of the
Graduate School of Industrial Administration
at Carnegie Institute of Technology. This
article is taken from his paper in* Management and Corporations, 1985, *published in
1960.*

I don't know whether the title assigned to me was meant seriously or humorously. I shall take it seriously. During the past five years, I have been too close to machines—the kinds of machines known as computers, that is—to treat the question lightly. Perhaps I have lost my sense of humor and perspective about them.

My work on this paper has been somewhat impeded, in recent days, by a fascinating spectacle just outside my office window. Men and machines have been constructing the foundations of a small building. After some preliminary skirmishing by men equipped with surveying instruments and sledges for driving pegs, most of the work has been done by various species of mechanical elephant and their mahouts. Two kinds of elephants dug out the earth (one with its forelegs, the other with its trunk) and loaded it in trucks (pack elephants, I suppose). Then, after an interlude during which another group of men carefully fitted some boards into place as forms, a new kind of elephant appeared, its belly full of concrete which it disgorged into the forms. It was assisted by two men with wheelbarrows —plain old-fashioned man-handled wheelbarrows—and two or three other men who fussily tamped the poured concrete with metal rods. Twice during this whole period a shovel appeared —on one occasion it was used by a man to remove dirt that had been dropped on a sidewalk; on another occasion it was used to clean a trough down which the concrete slid.

Here, before me, was a sample of automated, or semiautomated production. What did it show about the nature of present and future relations of man with machine in the production of goods and services? And what lessons that could be learned from the automation of manufacturing and construction could be transferred to the problems of managerial automation? I concluded that there were two good reasons for beginning my analysis with a careful look at factory and office automation. First, the business organization in 1985 will be a highly automated man-machine system, and the nature of management will surely be conditioned by the character of the system being managed. Second, perhaps there are greater similarities than appear at first blush among the several areas of potential automation— blue-collar, clerical, and managerial. Perhaps the automated executive of the future has a great deal in common with the automated worker or clerk whom we can already observe in many situations today.

First, however, we must establish a framework and a point of view. Our task is to forecast the changes that will take place over the next generation in the job of the manager. It is fair to ask: Which manager? Not everyone nor every job will be affected in the same way; indeed, most persons who will be affected are not even managers at the present time. Moreover, we must distinguish the gross effects of a technological change, occurring at the point of impact of that change, from the net effects, the whole series of secondary ripples spreading from that point of initial impact.

Many of the initial effects are transitory—important enough to those directly involved at the time and place of change, but of no lasting significance to the society. Other effects are neither apparent nor anticipated when the initial change takes place but flow from it over a period of years through the succession of reactions it produces. Examples of both transient and indirect effects of change come to mind readily enough—e.g., the unemployment of blacksmiths and the appearance of suburbia, respectively, as effects of the automobile.

Since our task is to look ahead twenty-five years, I shall say little about the transient effects of the change in the job of the manager. I do not mean to discount the importance of these effects to the people they touch. In our time we are highly conscious of the transient effects, particularly the harmful ones, the displacement of skill and status. We say less of the benefit to those who acquire the new skills or of the exhilaration that many derive from erecting new structures.

Of course, the social management of change does not consist simply in balancing beneficial transient effects against harmful ones. The simplest moral reasoning leads to a general rule for the introduction of change: The general society which stands to benefit from the change should pay the major costs of introducing it and should compensate generously those who would otherwise be harmed by it. A discussion of the transient effects of change would have to center on ways of applying that rule. But that is not the problem we have to deal with here.

Our task is to forecast the long-run effects of change. First of all, we must predict what is likely to happen to the job of the individual manager, and to the activity of management in the individual organization. Changes in these patterns will have secondary effects on the occupational profile in the economy as a whole. Our task is to picture the society after it has made all these secondary adjustments and settled down to its new equilibrium. * * *

PREDICTING LONG-RUN EQUILIBRIUM

To predict long-run equilibrium, one must identify two major aspects of the total situation: (1) the variables that will change autonomously and inexorably—the "first causes"—and (2) the constant, unchanging "givens" in the situation, to which the other variables must adjust themselves. These are the hammer and the anvil that beat out the shape of the future. The accuracy of our predictions will depend less upon forecasting exactly the course of change than upon assessing correctly which factors are the unmoved movers and which the equally unmoved invariants. My entire forecast rests on my identification of this hammer and this anvil.

The Causes of Change · The growth in human knowledge is the primary factor that will give the system its direction—in particular, that will fix the boundaries of the technologically feasible. The growth in real capital is the major secondary factor in change—within the realm of what is technologically feasible, it will determine what is economical.

The crucial area of expansion of knowledge is not hard to predict, for the basic innovations—or at least a large part of them—have already occurred and we are now rapidly exploiting them. The new knowledge consists in a fundamental understanding of the processes of thinking and learning or, to use a more neutral term, of complex information processing. We can now write programs for electronic computers that enable these devices to think and learn. This knowledge is having, and will have, practical impacts in two directions: (1) because we can now simulate in considerable detail an important and increasing part of the processes of the human mind, we have available a technique of tremendous power for psychological research; (2) because we can now write complex information-processing programs for computers, we are acquiring the technical capacity to replace humans with computers in a rapidly widening range of "thinking" and "deciding" tasks.

Closely allied to the development of complex information-processing techniques for general-purpose computers is the rapid advance in the technique of automating all sorts of production and clerical tasks. Putting these two lines of development together, I am led to the following general predictions: Within the very near future—much less than twenty-five years—we shall have the *technical* capability of substituting machines for any and all human functions in organizations. Within the same period, we shall have acquired an extensive and empirically tested theory of human cognitive processes and their interaction with human emotions, attitudes, and values.

To predict that we will have these technical capabilities says nothing of how we shall use them. Before we can forecast that, we must discuss the important invariants in the social system.

The Invariants · The changes that our new technical capability will bring about will be governed, particularly in the production sphere, by two major fixed factors in the society. Both of these have to do with the use of human resources for production.

1. Apart from transient effects of automation, the human resources of the society will be substantially fully employed. *Full employment* does not necessarily mean a forty-hour week, for the allocation of productive capacity between additional goods and services and additional leisure may continue to change as it has in the past. *Full employment* means that the opportunity to work will be available to virtually all adults in the society and that, through wages or other allocative devices, the product of the economy will be distributed widely among families.

2. The distribution of intelligence and ability in the society will be much as it is now, although a substantially larger percentage of adults (perhaps half or more) will have completed college educations.

These assumptions—of capability of automation, accompanied by full employment and constancy in the quality of the human resources—provide us with a basis for characterizing the change. We cannot talk about the technological unemployment it may create, for we have assumed that such unemployment is a transient phenomenon—that there will be none in the long run. But the pattern of occupations, the profile showing the relative distribution of employed persons among occupations, may be greatly changed. It is the change in this profile that will measure the organizational impact of the technological change.

The change in the occupational profile depends on a well-known economic principle, the doctrine of comparative advantage. It may seem paradoxical to think that we can increase the productivity of mechanized techniques in all processes without displacing men somewhere. Won't a point be reached where men are less productive than machines in *all* processes, hence economically unemployable?[1]

1. The difficulty that laymen find with this point underlies the consistent failure of economists to win wide general support for the free trade argu-

The paradox is dissolved by supplying a missing term. Whether man or machines will be employed in a particular process depends not simply on their relative productivity in physical terms but on their cost as well. And cost depends on price. Hence—so goes the traditional argument of economics—as technology changes and machines become more productive, the prices of labor and capital will so adjust themselves as to clear the market of both. As much of each will be employed as offers itself at the market price, and the market price will be proportional to the marginal productivity of that factor. By the operation of the market place, manpower will flow to those processes in which its productivity is comparatively high relative to the productivity of machines; it will leave those processes in which its productivity is comparatively low. The comparison is not with the productivities of the past, but among the productivities in different processes with the currently available technology.

I apologize for dwelling at length on a point that is clearly enough stated in the *Wealth of Nations*. My excuse is that contemporary discussion of technological change and automation still very often falls into error through not applying the doctrine of comparative advantage correctly and consistently.

We conclude that human employment will become smaller relative to the total labor force in those kinds of occupations and activities in which automatic devices have the greatest comparative advantage over humans; human employment will become relatively greater in those occupations and activities in which automatic devices have the least comparative advantage.[2]

---

ment. The central idea—that comparative advantage, not absolute advantage, counts—is exactly the same in the two cases.

2. I am oversimplifying, for there is another term in this equation. With a general rise in productivity and with shifts in relative prices due to uneven technological progress in different spheres, the demands for some kinds of goods and services will rise more rapidly than the demands for others. Hence, other things being equal, the total demand will rise in those occupations (of men and machines) that are largely concerned with producing the former, more rapidly than in occupations concerned largely with producing the latter. I have shown elsewhere how all these mechanisms can be handled formally in analyzing technological change. See "Productivity and the Urban-Rural Population Balance," in *Models of Man* (New York, John Wiley & Sons, Inc., 1957) chapter 12; and "Effects of Technological Change in a Linear Model," in T. Koopmans (ed.), *Activity Analysis of Production and Allocation*, (New York, John Wiley & Sons, Inc., 1951) chapter 15.

Thus, if computers are a thousand times faster than book-keepers in doing arithmetic, but only one hundred times faster than stenographers in taking dictation, we shall expect the number of bookkeepers per thousand employees to decrease but the number of stenographers to increase. Similarly, if computers are a hundred times faster than executives in making investment decisions, but only ten times faster in handling employee grievances (the quality of the decisions being held constant), then computers will be employed in making investment decisions, while executives will be employed in handling grievances.

Part Ten

Economic Analysis in the Public Sector

MODERN ECONOMIC analysis and operations research are coming to play an important role in the public sector of the economy as well as in private business. For example, such techniques have been introduced on a large scale in the Department of Defense. The papers in Part Ten attempt to show how these techniques can be, and are being, applied to problems of public policy and high-level government planning.

In the first article, E. S. Savas shows how some relatively simple analytical techniques were used to help New York City do a better job of coping with snow emergencies. The next article, by Howard, Matheson, and North, describes how decision theory has been used to analyze whether or not the federal government should seed hurricanes. In the next paper, Charles Hitch and Roland N. McKean describe the elements of a military problem of economic choice and show that two frequently-used approaches to these problems suffer from important defects, and that an application of elementary economic principles yields more satisfactory results. In the following article, the editor describes how a standard part of economic theory—the theory of exchange —was used to help solve an important problem facing military planners in the early fifties: How should fissionable material be allocated between strategic and tactical missions?

Next, we discuss benefit-cost analysis, an important tool of applied economics that has been employed frequently to help improve decision-making in the public sector of the economy. Roland McKean describes the nature and limitations of benefit-cost analyses, such analyses being "attempts to estimate certain costs and gains that would result from alternative courses of action." McKean points out the common elements in all such analyses, and cites some pitfalls that may lie in wait for the unwary analyst. In the next article, A. R. Prest and Ralph Turvey provide an extensive discussion of applications of cost-benefit analysis to public policy issues concerning water projects, transport projects, land usage, and health. Finally, Hirshleifer, De-Haven, and Milliman discuss the economic aspects of the utilization of existing water supplies. They show various ways that economic analysis can be useful in formulating public policy in this area.

The Political Properties of Crystalline H₂O: Planning for Snow Emergencies in New York

E. S. SAVAS

E. S. Savas is Professor of Public Systems
Management at Columbia University. This
paper appeared in Management Science in
1973.

It was on Sunday, February 9, 1969, that a malevolent god of weather deposited a goodly amount of snow upon New York City —this in spite of repeated forecasts by the official U.S. weather seers that nothing of the sort was going to happen. By the time the Department of Sanitation realized that the city was in for a real humdinger and called in additional men to augment its skeletal Sunday work force, many men could not reach their work stations because traffic arteries were impassable and public transit was reduced to spasmodic operation. Those who managed to report to work found that their equipment frequently could not cope with the deep drifts that had accumulated, and broke down. Or, they looked back on their freshly plowed swath and watched the wind undo their work. Others could not proceed because abandoned cars blocked their paths. Some succeeded in finishing their plowing assignments, only to discover later that what they had plowed turned out to be an isolated street segment because the abutting, complementary plow routes fore and aft of their stretch, lying within adjacent districts, could not be completed.

Late Sunday the city was a winter wonderland. Families tumbled out of the canyons and frolicked together in the snow, while some skiers were sighted ostentatiously poling along the truly Great White Way. By mid-week however, with only scant progress evident in the mammoth task of clearing away the snow, the brief holiday mood had long since given way to denunciations by assorted politicians, labor leaders, businessmen, and a high United Nations official, complaints from the public, critical editorials, calls for resignations, City Council hearings—and loud, prolonged jeering with pointed, indelicate suggestions during a visit to Queens—all directed at Mayor John V. Lindsay. In particular, many self-professed "little people" living in the "outer boroughs" of Queens, Brooklyn, the Bronx, and Staten Island resented what they felt was an undue concentration on cleaning up the snow in Manhattan, where the sophisticated smart set is reputed to live, while Mayor Lindsay, as usual in their eyes, ignored them and their simple, middle-class needs in favor of the rest of the city. That the mayoral election later in the year would afford a splendid opportunity for retribution did not entirely escape the attention of the mayor's angry critics.

Every special interest group had its own diagnosis of the problem and its own preferred solution. Surprisingly enough, each solution that was offered usually meant more money for the offerer. For example, one proffered solution was to have more sanitation workers on duty around the clock during the winter, at overtime rates. Another was to buy more snow-removal equipment. Yet another was to hire more mechanics to maintain the existing equipment. Still another was to allow sanitation workers to report for snow-removal duty wherever they found it convenient, presumably near their homes. Finally, owners of large bulldozers thought that the problem would be substantially alleviated if the city would merely agree to pay usurious rates to hire their equipment during snow emergencies.

It was in such harried, emotional, and politically charged circumstances, eight days after the storm, that Mayor Lindsay directed the systems analysis unit in his office to undertake a thorough study of the city's snow-fighting capability. The analysts pounced upon the problem like dogs presented with a choice T-bone steak, delighted at the opportunity to gnaw on such a fresh and meaty morsel.

The analysis was not to be an inquisition to find a culprit or a scapegoat. Its objective was to find out what went wrong and to prevent its recurrence. Realistically, the project could not be expected to produce meaningful results soon enough to be useful during the remaining few weeks of the current snow season. In fact, Deputy Mayor Timothy W. Costello, to whom the unit reported, cautioned them against excessive enthusiasm and subsequent disappointment by suggesting that it would be a warm day in New York when the study was finished, with interest in the problem having melted away with the snows of yesteryear.

STRUCTURING THE PROBLEM

A review of the literature and a survey of practices in other cities, together with an examination of the written procedures in New York City, proved generally informative but failed to provide a methodology suitable for the task at hand. Accordingly, it was necessary to create an original approach to the problem and after some initial groping the effort gradually crystallized about four fundamental, strategic questions:

(1) How much snow falls on New York City?
(2) How much work has to be done to clean it up?
(3) What is the city's capacity for performing this work?
(4) What improvements are needed to eliminate any imbalances between work load and work capacity?

How Much Snow Falls on New York? · To answer the first question required a methodical search of U.S. Weather Bureau records back to 1910, which revealed that a storm matching or exceeding the February storm's depth of fifteen inches occurs once in twelve years, on the average. This means that such a storm will occur "at the wrong time"—i.e., when only a minimal (Sunday) force is on duty—once in 84 years, and, if the weather forecasters are credited with merely 50 percent accuracy, such an unfortunate episode will occur "unexpectedly and at the wrong time" no more than once in 168 years, on the average. (To spin this out further, the better part of a millennium is likely to pass before a recurrence in an election year!) When the analysts presented the statistics, with the wry remark that we were fortunate to have observed such a rare event during our lifetimes, Mayor Lindsay, to his credit, mustered a wan smile.

More constructively, inspection of snow records disclosed that:

(a) Snowfall in New York City averages 33 inches annually.

(b) An average season has two storms greater than four inches (see Figure 1).

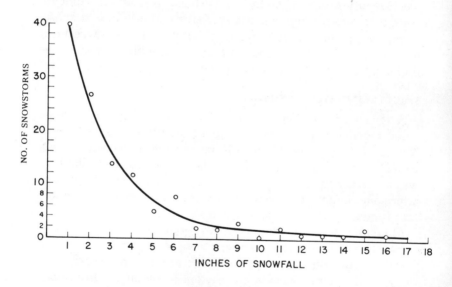

FIGURE 1

FREQUENCY DISTRIBUTION OF SNOWSTORMS, BY DEPTH, 1948–1967
(FOR SNOWFALLS OF AT LEAST ONE INCH)

(c) An average season has six to seven snowstorms of an inch or more (see Figure 2).

(d) The rate of accumulation of snow during a snowstorm was as high as 10.4 inches in eight hours, as shown in Table 1.

How Much Work Has to Be Done? · Coping with a snow-storm in New York involves up to three sequential activities:

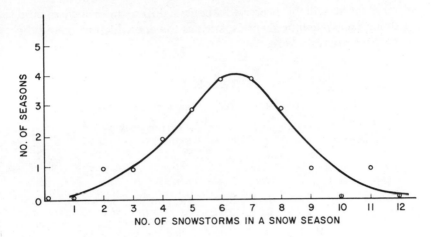

FIGURE 2

FREQUENCY DISTRIBUTION OF SNOW SEASONS BY
NUMBER OF SNOWSTORMS, 1948–1967
(FOR SNOWFALLS OF AT LEAST ONE INCH)

spreading salt, plowing, and hauling away snow. Spreading salt, which is done by special-purpose vehicles, is the routine, first line of defense and is usually done perhaps twelve times a year; that is, not only for the six or seven snowfalls which turn out to be greater than óne inch, but also for others which appear threatening but ultimately deposit less than an inch, and for freezing rain. Plowing is done three or four times an average year, as depths approach four inches or so. (Specific decisions about plowing will depend on such factors as current ground temperature, predicted air temperature, wind, and traffic conditions—because spreading salt is more effective for melting snow when traffic is relatively heavy.) Removal of snow by hauling is relatively rare, being reserved generally for snowfalls greater than six inches when the temperature is expected to remain below freezing for an appreciable period of time. The study addressed all three activities— spreading, plowing, and hauling—but only the first two will be discussed here.

The data on snowfalls, and the work activity dictated in response to snow, confirm that a comprehensive snow plan is necessary, for it will be exercised about a dozen times a year even though incapacitating storms, such as the one which triggered the propect, are quite rare.

TABLE 1

PEAK ACCUMULATION RATES FOR SNOWFALLS[1]

A. *Average accumulation during the peak period of indicated duration* [2]

Final depth	No. of storms	1 hr.	2 hrs.	3 hrs.	4 hrs.	5 hrs.	6 hrs.	7 hrs.	8 hrs.
4"–9"	14	1.0"	1.7"	2.4"	2.9"	3.3"	3.6"	4.0"	4.3"
9"+	9	1.7"	2.9"	3.9"	4.8"	5.6"	6.3"	6.9"	7.4"

B. *Maximum accumulation during the peak period of indicated duration* [3]

Final depth	No. of storms	1 hr.	2 hrs.	3 hrs.	4 hrs.	5 hrs.	6 hrs.	7 hrs.	8 hrs.
4"–9"	1	1.4"	2.6"	3.3"	4.2"	4.7"	5.2"	5.5"	5.6"
9"+	1	2.5"	4.1"	5.4"	6.7"	7.6"	8.6"	9.5"	10.4"

[1] Based on the 23 storms greater than or equal to four inches during the period 1958–1967.

[2] For example, if one looks at the 3-hour period of heaviest snowfall for each of the 14 storms whose final depth was 4"–9", the average accumulation during those 3-hour periods was 2.4".

[3] For example, the greatest 5-hour accumulation for any storm was 7.6"; this occurred for a storm whose final depth was greater than 9".

To determine the amount of cleanup work called for by a snowstorm, it was necessary to analyze the street system. The Department of Sanitation, which is responsible for snow removal, divides the streets into three priority classes, primary, secondary and tertiary, corresponding to the relative importance of the streets. As shown in Table 2A, primary streets comprised 43 percent of the linear street mileage, but 45 percent of the spreader miles, 53 percent of the plow miles in the city. (Depending on the width of the street, a vehicle may have to traverse it more than once in order to salt it or plow it, while spreaders and plows have different effective widths.) Clearly, a ranking system which was so undiscriminating as to assign more than half the total plowing work an equally high priority left something to be desired.

TABLE 2

STREET MILEAGE

A. Existing street network

Class of street	Linear miles		Spreader miles		Plow miles	
	Number	Percent	Number	Percent	Number	Percent
Primary	2530	43	2733	45	6755	53
Secondary	1978	34	1978	33	3500	28
Tertiary	1331	23	1331	22	2444	19
Total	5839	100	6042	100	12,699	100

B. Recommended street network

	Number	Percent	Number	Percent	Number	Percent
Primary						
Emergency	1600	27	1730	28	4272	33
Other	930	16	1003	17	2483	20
Secondary	1978	34	1978	33	3500	28
Tertiary	1331	23	1331	22	2444	19
Total	5839	100	6042	100	12,699	100

There did exist within the primary streets a category labeled Snow Emergency Streets, which totaled only 428 miles, some 7 percent of the total street mileage. However, this distinction was not used in actual operations, and furthermore an inquiry concluded that much of this street network was originally devised as the best way to flee the city in the event of a nuclear holocaust, rather than as a network which, if cleared, would enable the city to function adequately after a major snowfall. Therefore, a new high-priority network was designed during this study; it included all parkways and bus routes, and the streets which connect hospitals, police stations, fire houses, bus garages, and fuel depots to those arteries. It represents 1,600 linear miles, or 33 percent of the city's total plow miles. Clearing these streets represents the minimum work that has to be done to permit the city to function during a snow emergency. Table 2B defines the work load, in terms of the number of miles to be covered, given a policy determination that only primary, or primary and secondary, or all streets are to be cleared.

What Is the Capacity for Performing This Work? · In order to estimate the city's capacity for snow removal work, it was necessary to look at the type, amount, and productivity of equipment. The principal snow fighting equipment consists of spreaders and plows, for which a conservatively high down-time figure of 40 percent was assumed in the analysis; that is, it was assumed that 40 percent of the spreaders and plows would be out of commission, so that only 134 spreaders and 1,050 plows would be available for work. (Actual down time was on the order of 30 to 35 percent.) Productive time was estimated by making allowance for meal time, rest breaks, refueling time, travel time to and from routes, etc., and from this it was concluded that about 12 hours of productive time on the route is available during the two-shift, 22-hour winter work day. Furthermore, it was assumed that

TABLE 3

PLOWING CAPABILITY

	Snow emergency streets	All primary streets	Primary and secondary streets	All streets
Plow miles	4,272	6,755	10,255	12,699
Max. hrs. to plow	2.75	3.65	4.85	5.70
Avg. peak accumulation *	3.7"	4.5"	5.5"	6.1"
Max. peak accumulation *	5.0"	6.3"	7.5"	8.3"

* Derived from Table 1, for storms greater than 9" for the indicated "Max hrs. to plow."

up to 1.25 hours would be needed to start up and reach the beginning of a route. Finally, an extremely conservative figure of only 5 mph was assumed for the vehicles while on their routes. (This is the average auto speed in mid-Manhattan at noon on weekdays; plow speeds at midnight in Staten Island are obviously much higher.)

Putting together all these productivity figures and the street mileages leads to the striking conclusion that there is sufficient equipment available, in the aggregate, to plow *every* mile of *every* street in the city in only six hours, and to plow the high-priority streets in less than two hours! Based on the snow-accumulation rates of Table 1, and the above productivity estimates, Table 3 is derived. Recognizing that plows can work in depths up to about eight inches, it can confidently be concluded that the high-priority network can "always" be kept plowed.

That is, the plowing force can "always" complete plowing those streets well before eight inches of snow would accumulate, and they could keep those streets open during the remainder of "any" snowstorm by repeatedly traversing those routes.

A corresponding analysis shows that the salt-spreading capability was inadequate, for it would take seven hours to spread salt on all primary streets, during which time (see Table 1) 9.5 inches has been observed to accumulate and the spreaders would therefore be unable to complete their work. Additional spreaders are needed in order to assert with confidence that the high-priority streets could "always" be salted before the snow becomes too deep for the spreaders to negotiate.

From the foregoing analysis of work loads and equipment capability, and contrary to some of the touted "solutions," the inexorable conclusion was that aside from additional spreaders, neither more plows nor improved maintenance was necessary; the plowing problem lay elsewhere. Indeed, if the available equipment could, in principle, plow the entire street network so quickly, where was the problem?

What Improvements Are Needed? · The answer was to be found in the geographic deployment of equipment and the rate of mobilization of manpower to man the equipment.

The matter of equipment deployment is an interesting one. Most of the plowing vehicles are simply refuse-collection trucks fitted with plows. The trucks may have been satisfactorily distributed throughout the boroughs for their primary function, collection, but they were not properly distributed for plowing. (See Table 4.) The reason is obvious: a one-mile street segment in a bucolic area of Richmond will generate much less refuse than will a one-mile street segment in densely populated Manhattan, but it will have just as much snow to be plowed. In other words the public, without benefit of systems analysis, perceived the situation quite correctly: Manhattan did indeed receive better snow-cleaning service. But this was a direct, technical consequence of Manhattan's high population density rather than a deliberate decision to withhold services from the other boroughs.

In order to satisfy these widely differing needs, for refuse collection and for plowing, one is faced with the necessity of pro-

TABLE 4

GEOGRAPHICAL DEPLOYMENT OF PLOWS
IN RELATION TO NEED

Area	Plow-miles of primary streets (%)	Distribution of plows (%)
Manhattan West	8.6	9.2
Manhattan East	6.5	10.7
Bronx West	6.6	8.9
Bronx East	9.9	8.4
Brooklyn West	9.6	11.0
Brooklyn North	7.5	11.5
Brooklyn East	6.8	9.8
Queens West	14.7	12.8
Queens East	20.8	13.5
Richmond	9.2	4.0
Total	100.2%	99.8%

viding two widely differing truck allocation patterns. This dilemma was ultimately resolved by taking advantage of vehicles
such as flushers, on which plows can be mounted. During the
winter, when these see little use for flushing, they are to be re-
located in such a way that, together with its normal complement
of refuse-collection trucks, each borough will have a plowing
capability proportional to the number of plow miles of high-
priority streets in that borough. The few remaining disparities
can be eliminated by directing certain truck-rich areas to send
the desired number of trucks to certain truck-poor areas at the
start of a snowstorm. This final distribution is designed to equalize the time it takes for each borough to clean its high-priority
streets.

In a completely analogous way, the spreaders were shown to be
distributed inappropriately, leading to disparities between areas
of up to 3:1 in the amount of time needed to spread salt on their
primary streets. Because spreaders are single-purpose vehicles,
unlike plows, it was possible to deploy them in such a way as to
equalize spreading time for all areas of the city. (It should be
noted that reported productivity differences between different
parts of the city were used to "fine tune" the recommended deployment of plows and spreaders; however, because of reporting
uncertainties, the allocation ultimately was made based on the
distribution of plow-miles and spreader-miles among areas.)

Another finding worth noting concerns the distance between garages and the plow routes. In deriving Table 3, a startup delay of 1.25 hours was allowed as a conservative city-wide average. Again, however, looking at geographic variations proved useful, for in eastern Queens the travel time from the garage to the routes was as much as two or three hours during a snowstorm. This study confirmed the previously perceived need for a new garage in that area, and it was eventually acquired and put into operation.

Given sufficient equipment properly allocated throughout the city, with a rational set of priorities for work assignments, the only remaining need is for a good mobilization plan, i.e., a plan which provides the right number of workers at the right place and at the right time.

Ordinarily, the more than 9,000 uniformed members of the department's work force are easily sufficient to man all the snow equipment. However, manpower mobilization was a problem on Sunday, when for a 24-hour period the field force was insufficient to man even the full complement of spreaders, let alone any plows. Now this staffing problem can easily be solved with money. More men could be assigned routinely to Sunday duty or called up on short notice and at premium rates. In fact, two weeks after this famous storm, when another storm threatened and no one was taking any chances, the city spent one-third of a million dollars mobilizing and not a flake fell. The issue was how to provide, in effect, low-cost insurance against a serious snow emergency. The solution was to devise operating procedures which would increase the rate of mobilization and thereby decrease the elapsed time needed to have an adequate number of men and machines out on the streets.

This was accomplished by mounting plows on one-fifth of the trucks just before winter weekends. By doing this in advance, a critical time advantage is gained, for it takes almost two man-hours to prepare a truck in this way. In addition, some of the spreaders are loaded with salt just prior to winter weekends, even though unused salt will have to be unloaded on Monday to prevent caking and flat tires. Finally, in cooperation with the union, a special Sunday roster was developed, a snow emergency force which had agreed to respond to a telephone callup and to report

promptly to their assigned posts. This agreement was encouraged
by making more attractive arrangements for compensatory time
off.

Implementation · The analysis was completed in June and then
presented to Mayor Lindsay. By that time the mayoral campaign was in full swing and it was clear that the snow of February was gone but not forgotten; it had become a very lively
campaign issue, with many candidates emphasizing it in speeches
and in their TV advertisements.

In this environment, implementing the recommendations
proved relatively easy; for once, a management science unit was
in the right place at the right time with the right answers to an
important problem—and without even a written report in hand.

The word went forth to put the findings into practice promptly,
viz., before election day in November.

Week-long work sessions and regular reviews with the commis-
sioner and the mayor's assistant gradually generated modifications, improvements, unanimous acceptance, budget alterations—
and visible changes. Finally, the effort culminated in the preparation of a detailed briefing report, for issuance at a major press
conference. The process of writing this press release was itself
salutary, for it served to crystallize some hitherto unresolved
areas, and clear up some lingering ambiguities. The final document described quite specifically the changes and improvements
made in the city's snow-fighting tactics since the disastrous snowstorm, as evidence that the administration had learned from its
experiences and that the problems would not recur. This candor
was in keeping with the dominant motif of the mayoral campaign, the theme of chastened wisdom gained from experience in
the second toughest job in America.

Near the start of the next snow season, just a few weeks before
election day, a major press conference was held—at the famous
corner in Queens where there was much ado nine months earlier.
Mayor Lindsay announced the various changes and improvements made since then and was able to state with confidence that
the problem would not recur.

Because the news photographers and TV cameramen would
have found nothing very photogenic about allocation charts

and tables, and lists of names, some of the city's new snow-fighting equipment was put on display for the occasion. In other words, for the results of urban systems analysis to be published in the right journals—*The New York Times* and the *Post*—the skills of a public relations expert in the City Hall Press Office were indispensable.

The city's new Snow Emergency Plan went into effect. Mayor Lindsay was re-elected. (No causal relationship is implied.) A report documenting the work was finally written and issued.

In the ensuing four years only one storm represented any sort of practical test of the system, an eight-inch storm on a holiday, January 1, 1971. Everything went smoothly and the city was cleaned up within a few hours, with credit properly going to the Mayor, the Department of Sanitation, and the new plan.

The Decision to Seed
Hurricanes

R. A. HOWARD, J. E. MATHESON,
AND D. W. NORTH

R. A. *Howard is Professor of Engineering–
Economic Systems at Stanford University,
and J. E. Matheson and D. W. North are
staff members of the Stanford Research Institute. This piece has been condensed from
their article in* Science *in 1972 by eliminating some of the substantiating technical
analyses. Their original article includes extensive discussion of the evaluation of additional seedings such as those carried out on
Hurricane Debbie in 1969.*

The possibility of mitigating the destructive force of hurricanes by seeding them with silver iodide was suggested by R. H. Simpson in 1961. Early experiments on hurricanes Esther (1961) and Beulah (1963) were encouraging, but strong evidence for the effectiveness of seeding was not obtained until the 1969 experiments on Hurricane Debbie. Debbie was seeded with massive amounts of silver iodide on 18 and 20 August 1969. Reductions of 31 and 15 percent in peak wind speed were observed after the seedings.

Over the last ten years property damage caused by hurricanes has averaged $440 million annually. Hurricane Betsy (1965) and Hurricane Camille (1969) each caused property damage of approximately $1.5 billion. Any means of reducing the destructive force of hurricanes would therefore have great economic implications.

DECISION TO PERMIT OPERATIONAL SEEDING

In the spring of 1970 Stanford Research Institute began a small study for the Environmental Science Service Administration (ESSA) to explore areas in which decision analysis might make significant contributions to ESSA, both in its technical operations and in its management and planning function. At the suggestion of Myron Tribus, Assistant Secretary of Commerce for Science and Technology, we decided to focus the study on the decision problems inherent in hurricane modification.[1]

The objective of the present U.S. government program in hurricane modification, Project Stormfury, is strictly scientific: to add to man's knowledge about hurricanes. Any seeding of hurricanes that threaten inhabited coastal areas is prohibited. According to the policy currently in force, seeding will be carried out only if there is less than a 10 percent chance of the hurricane center coming within fifty miles of a populated land area within eighteen hours after seeding.

If the seeding of hurricanes threatening inhabited coastal areas is to be undertaken, it will be necessary to modify the existing policies. The purpose of our analysis is to examine the circumstances that bear on the decision to change or not to change these existing policies.

The decision to seed a hurricane threatening a coastal area should therefore be viewed as a two-stage process: (i) a decision is taken to lift the present prohibition against seeding threatening hurricanes, and (ii) a decision is taken to seed a particular hurricane a few hours before that hurricane is expected to strike the coast. Our study is concentrated on the policy decision rather than on the tactical decision to seed a particular hurricane at a particular time. It is also addressed to the experimental question:

1. A detailed discussion of the research is to be found in the project's final report (D. W. Boyd, R. A. Howard, J. E. Matheson, D. W. North, Decision Analysis of Hurricane Modification [Project 8503, Stanford Research Institute, Menlo Park, California, 1971]). This report is available through the National Technical Information Service, U.S. Department of Commerce, Washington, D.C., accession number COM-71-00784.

What would be the value of expanding research in hurricane modification, and, specifically, what would be the value of conducting additional field experiments such as the seedings of Hurricane Debbie in 1969?

Our approach was to consider a representative severe hurricane bearing down on a coastal area and to analyze the decision to seed or not to seed this "nominal" hurricane. The level of the analysis was relatively coarse, because for the policy decision we did not have to consider many geographical and meteorological details that might influence the tactical decision to seed. We described the hurricane by a single measure of intensity, its maximum sustained surface wind speed, since it is this characteristic that seeding is expected to influence. The surface winds, directly and indirectly (through the storm tide), are the primary cause of the destruction wrought by most hurricanes. The direct consequence of a decision for or against seeding a hurricane is considered to be the property damage caused by that hurricane. (Injuries and loss of life are often dependent on the issuance and effectiveness of storm warnings; they were not explicitly included in our analysis.)

However, property damage alone is not sufficient to describe the consequence of the decision. There are indirect legal and social effects that arise from the fact that the hurricane is known to have been seeded. For example, the government might have some legal responsibility for the damage caused by a seeded hurricane. Even if legal action against the government were not possible, a strong public outcry might result if a seeded hurricane caused an unusual amount of damage. Nearly all the government hurricane meteorologists that we questioned said they would seed a hurricane threatening their homes and families—if they could be freed from professional liability.

The importance of the indirect effects stems in large part from uncertainty about the consequences of taking either decision. A hurricane is complex and highly variable, and at present meteorologists cannot predict accurately how the behavior of a hurricane will evolve over time. The effect of seeding is uncertain also; consequently, the behavior of a hurricane that is seeded will be a combination of two uncertain effects: natural changes and the changes induced by seeding.

*   *   *

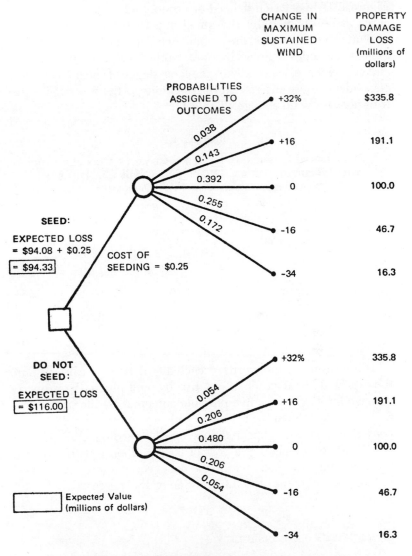

FIGURE 1

THE SEEDING DECISION FOR THE NOMINAL HURRICANE

The decision to seed is shown in the form of a decision tree in Figure 1. The decision to seed or not to seed is shown at the decision node denoted by the small square box; the consequent resolution of the uncertainty about wind change is indicated at the chance nodes denoted by open circles. For expository clarity and convenience, especially in the later stages of the analysis, it is convenient to use discrete approximations to the probability distributions for wind change (Table 1).

TABLE 1

PROBABILITIES ASSIGNED TO WIND CHANGES OCCURRING IN
THE 12 HOURS BEFORE HURRICANE LANDFALL. DISCRETE
APPROXIMATION FOR FIVE OUTCOMES.

Interval of changes in maximum sustained wind	Representative value in discrete approximation (%)	Probability that wind change will be within interval	
		If seeded	If not seeded
Increase of 25% or more	+32	.038	.054
Increase of 10 to 25%	+16	.143	.206
Little change, +10 to −10%	0	.392	.480
Reduction of 10 to 25%	−16	.255	.206
Reduction of 25% or more	−34	.172	.054

As a measure of the worth of each alternative we can compute the expected loss for each alternative by multiplying the property damage for each of the five possible outcomes by the probability that the outcome will be achieved and summing over the possible consequences. The expected loss for the seeding alternative is $94.33 million (including a cost of $0.25 million to carry out the seeding); the expected loss for the not-seeding alternative is $116 million; the difference is $21.67 million or 18.7 percent.

*   *   *

GOVERNMENT RESPONSIBILITY

The analysis in the section above indicates that, if minimizing the expected loss in terms of property damage (and the cost of seeding) is the only criterion, then seeding is preferred. However, an important aspect of the decision—the matter of government responsibility—has not yet been included in the analysis. We have calculated a probability of .36 that a seeded hurricane will intensify between seeding and landfall and a probability of .18 that this intensification will be at least 10 percent. This high probability is largely the result of the great natural variability in hurricane intensity. It is advisable to consider both the legal and the social consequences that might occur if a seeded hurricane intensified.

The crucial issue in the decision to seed a hurricane threatening a coastal area is the relative desirability of reducing the expected property damage and assuming the responsibility for a dangerous and erratic natural phenomenon. This is difficult to assess, and to have a simple way of regarding it we use the concept of a government responsibility cost, defined as follows. The government is faced with a choice between assuming the responsibility for a hurricane and accepting higher probabilities of property damage. This situation is comparable to one of haggling over price: What increment of property-damage reduction justifies the assumption of responsibility entailed by seeding a hurricane? This increment of property damage is defined as the government responsibility cost. The government responsibility cost is a means of quantifying the indirect social, legal, and political factors related to seeding a hurricane. It is distinguished from the direct measure—property damage—that is assumed to be the same for both modified and natural hurricanes with the same maximum sustained wind speed.

We define the government responsibility cost so that it is incurred only if the hurricane is seeded. It is conceivable that the public may hold the government responsible for not seeding a severe hurricane, which implies that a responsibility cost should also be attached to the alternative of not seeding. Such a cost would strengthen the implication of the analysis in favor of permitting seeding.

The assessment of government responsibility cost is made by considering the seeding decision in a hypothetical situation in which no uncertainty is present. Suppose the government must choose between two outcomes:

(1) A seeded hurricane that intensifies 16 percent between the time of seeding and landfall.

(2) An unseeded hurricane that intensifies more than 16 percent between the time of seeding and landfall. The property damage from outcome 2 is x percent more than the property damage from outcome 1.

If x is near zero, the government will choose outcome 2. If x is large, the government will prefer outcome 1. We then adjust x until the choice becomes very difficult; that is, the government is indifferent to which outcome it receives. For example, the indifference point might occur when x is 30 percent. An increase of 16 percent in the intensity of the nominal hurricane corresponds to property damage of $191 million, so that the corresponding responsibility cost defined by the indifference point at 30 percent is (.30) ($191 million), or $57.3 million. The responsibility cost is then assessed for other possible changes in hurricane intensity.

The assessment of government responsibility costs entails considerable introspective effort on the part of the decision-maker who represents the government. The difficulty of determining the numbers does not provide an excuse to avoid the issue. Any decision or policy prohibiting seeding implicitly determines a set of government responsibility costs. As shown in the last section, seeding is the preferred decision unless the government responsibility costs are high.

Let us consider an illustrative set of responsibility costs. The government is indifferent, if the choice is between:

(1) A seeded hurricane that intensifies 32 percent and an unseeded hurricane that intensifies even more, causing 50 percent more property damage.

(2) A seeded hurricane that intensifies 16 percent and an unseeded hurricane that causes 30 percent more property damage.

(3) A seeded hurricane that neither intensifies nor diminishes (0 percent change in the maximum sustained wind speed after the seeding) and an unseeded hurricane that intensifies slightly, causing 5 percent more property damage.

(4) A seeded hurricane that diminishes by more than 10 percent and an unseeded hurricane that diminishes by the same amount. (If the hurricane diminishes after seeding, everyone agrees that the government acted wisely; thus, responsibility costs are set at zero.)

The analysis of the seeding decision with these government responsibility costs included is diagramed in Figure 2. Even with these large responsibility costs, the preferred decision is still to seed.

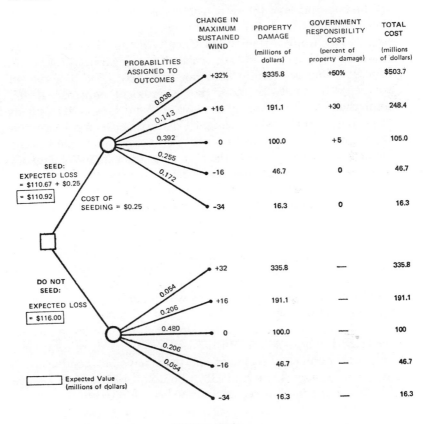

FIGURE 2

THE SEEDING DECISION FOR THE NOMINAL HURRICANE
(GOVERNMENT RESPONSIBILITY COST INCLUDED)

The responsibility costs needed to change the decision are a substantial fraction of the property damage caused by the hurricane. For the $100-million hurricane chosen as the example for this section, the average responsibility cost must be about $22 million to change the decision. If the hurricane were in the $1-billion class, as Camille (1969) and Betsy (1965) were, an average responsibility cost of $200 million would be needed. In other words, an expected reduction of $200 million in property damage would be foregone if the government decided not to accept the responsibility of seeding the hurricane.

The importance of the responsibility issue led us to investigate the legal basis for hurricane seeding in some detail. These investigations were carried out by Gary Widman, Hastings College of the Law, University of California. A firm legal basis for operational seeding apparently does not now exist. The doctrine of sovereign immunity provides the government only partial and unpredictable protection against lawsuits, and substantial grounds for bringing such lawsuits might exist. A better legal basis for government seeding activities is needed before hurricane seeding could be considered other than as an extraordinary emergency action. Specific congressional legislation may be the best means of investing a government agency with the authority to seed hurricanes threatening the coast of the United States.

❊   ❊   ❊

EXPERIMENTAL CAPABILITY DECISION

The occurrence of hurricanes is a random phenomenon. Therefore, it is uncertain whether there will be an opportunity for an experimental seeding before the arrival of a threatening storm that might be operationally seeded. Opportunities for experimental seeding have been scarce. In the last few years there have been only six experimental seedings, and these have ben conducted on three hurricanes, Esther (1961), Beulah (1963), and Debbie (1969). Experimental seedings have been limited to a small region of the Atlantic Ocean accessible to aircraft bases in Puerto Rico, and few hurricanes have passed through this region.

There are many other regions of the ocean where hurricanes might be found that satisfy the present criterion for experimental seeding—that is, the hurricane will be seeded only if the probability is less than .10 that it will come within 50 miles of a populated land area within 18 hours after seeding. However, a decision to expand the present experimental capability of Project Stormfury would need to be made well before the experiment itself. Whereas the seeding itself requires only that an aircraft be fitted with silver iodide pyrotechnic generators, the monitoring of the subsequent development of the hurricane requires other aircraft fitted with the appropriate instrumentation. The requirements in equipment, crew training, and communications and support facilities are substantial. In addition, permission may be needed from nations whose shores might be threatened by the seeded hurricane. The experimental decision, then, involves an investment in the capability to perform an experimental seeding. Whether an experiment is performed depends on the uncertain occurrences of hurricanes in the experimental areas.

The expected time before another experimental opportunity for Project Stormfury's present capability is about one full hurricane season. There was no opportunity during 1970. Preliminary estimates of the cost of a capability to seed hurricanes in the Pacific are about $1 million. The incidence of experimentally seedable hurricanes in the Pacific appears to be more than twice that in the Atlantic. Therefore, it appears advisable to develop a capability to conduct experimental hurricane seeding in the Pacific Ocean since the benefits expected from this capability outweigh the costs by a factor of at least 5.

CONCLUSIONS FROM THE ANALYSIS

The decision to seed a hurricane imposes a great responsibility on public officials. This decision cannot be avoided because inaction is equivalent to a decision not to permit seeding. Either the government must accept the responsibility of a seeding that may be perceived by the public as deleterious, or it must accept the responsibility for not seeding and thereby exposing the public to higher probabilities of severe storm damage.

Our report to the National Oceanic and Atmospheric Administration recommended that seeding be permitted on an emergency basis. We hope that further experimental results and a formal analysis of the tactical decision to seed a particular hurricane will precede the emergency. However, a decision may be required before additional experimental or analytical results are available. A hurricane with the intensity of Camille threatening a populous coastal area of the United States would confront public officials with an agonizing but unavoidable choice.

The decision to seed hurricanes can not be resolved on strictly scientific grounds. It is a complex decision whose uncertain consequences affect many people. Appropriate legal and political institutions should be designated for making the hurricane-seeding decision, and further analysis should be conducted to support these institutions in carrying out their work.

❉   ❉   ❉

Economic Choice in Military Planning

Charles J. Hitch and Ronald N. McKean

Charles Hitch was Assistant Secretary of Defense until 1965, when he became Vice President of the University of California. Roland McKean is Professor of Economics at the University of California at Los Angeles. This paper comes from their book, The Economics of Defense in the Nuclear Age, *published in 1960.*

THE ELEMENTS OF AN ECONOMIC ANALYSIS

The essence of economic choice in military planning is not quantitative analysis: calculation may or may not be necessary or useful, depending upon the problem and what is known about it. The essential thing is the comparison of all the relevant alternatives from the point of view of the objectives each can accomplish and the costs which it involves; and the selection of the best (or a "good") alternative through the use of appropriate economic criteria.

The elements of a military problem of economic choice, whether its solution requires advanced mathematics, high speed computing equipment, or just straight hard thinking, are therefore the following:

1. An objective or objectives. What military (or other national) aim or aims are we trying to accomplish with the forces, equipments, projects, or tactics that the analysis is designed to compare? Choice of objectives is fundamental: if it is wrongly made, the whole analysis is addressed to the wrong question.

2. Alternatives. By what alternative forces, equipments, projects, tactics, and so on, may the objective be accomplished? The alternatives are frequently referred to as *systems*[1] because each combines all the elements—men, machines, and the tactics of their employment—needed to accomplish the objective. System A may differ from System B in only one respect (for example, in number of bombs per bomber), or in several (number of bombs per bomber, number of strikes, and so on), but both are complete systems, however many elements they have in common. The great problem in choosing alternatives to compare is to be sure that all the good alternatives have been included. Frequently we lack the imagination to do this at the beginning of an analysis; we think of better alternatives (that is, invent new systems) as the analysis proceeds and we learn more about the problem. The invention of new and better systems in this fashion is indeed one of the principal payoffs from this kind of analysis.

3. Costs or resources used. Each alternative method of accomplishing the objective, or in other words each system, involves the incurring of certain costs or the using up of certain resources (these are different phrases to describe the same phenomena). Costs are the negative values in the analysis (as the objectives are positive values). The resources required may be general (as is commonly the case in problems of long-range planning), or highly specific (as in most tactical problems), or mixed.

4. A model or models. Models are abstract representations of reality which help us to perceive significant relations in the real world, to manipulate them, and thereby predict others. They may take any of numerous forms. Some are small-scale physical representations of reality, like model aircraft in a wind tunnel. Many are simply representations on paper—like mathematical models. Or, finally, they may be simple sets of relationships that are sketched out in the mind and not formally put down on paper.

1. Hence "systems analysis," a term frequently applied to complex quantitative analyses.

In no case are models photographic reproductions of reality; if they were, they would be so complicated that they would be of no use to us. They have to abstract from a great deal of the real world—focusing upon what is relevant for the problem at hand, ignoring what is irrelevant. Whether or not one model is better than another depends not on its complexity, or its appearance of reality, but solely on whether it gives better predictions (and thereby helps us to make better decisions).[2] In systems analyses models of one type or another are required to trace the relations between inputs and outputs, resources and objectives, for each of the systems to be compared, so that we can predict the relevant consequences of choosing any system.

5. A criterion. By "criterion" we mean the test by which we choose one alternative or system rather than another. The choice of an appropriate economic criterion is frequently the central problem in designing a systems analysis. In principle, the criterion we want is clear enough: the optimal system is the one which yields the greatest excess of positive values (objectives) over negative values (resources used up, or costs). But as we have already seen, this clear-cut ideal solution is seldom a practical possibility in military problems.[3] Objectives and costs usually have no common measure: there is no generally acceptable way to subtract dollars spent or aircraft lost from enemy targets destroyed. Moreover, there may be multiple objectives or multiple costs that are incommensurable. So in most military analyses we have to be satisfied with some approximation to the ideal criterion that will enable us to say, not that some system A is optimal, but that it is better than some other proposed systems B, C, and so on. In many cases we will have to be content with calculating efficient rather than optimal systems, relying on the intuitive judgment of well-informed people (of whom the analyst may be one) to

2. Bombardiers once bombed visually, using simple models in their heads to estimate the bomb's trajectory in relation to the target. Modern bomb-sights use mathematical models, requiring high speed computers for solution, to make the same estimate. The model used by the modern bombsight is better only if its predictions are more accurate—a question of fact which has to be tested by experiment.

3. In private industry this "ideal" criterion is the familiar one of profit maximization.

select one of the efficient systems in the neighborhood of the optimum.

It cannot be stated too frequently or emphasized enough that economic choice is *a way of looking at problems* and does not necessarily depend upon the use of any analytic aids or computational devices. Some analytic aids (mathematical models) and computing machinery are quite likely to be useful in analyzing complex military problems, but there are many military problems in which they have not proved particularly useful where, nevertheless, it is rewarding to array the alternatives and think through their implications in terms of objectives and costs. Where mathematical models and computations are useful, they are in no sense alternatives to or rivals of good intuitive judgment; they supplement and complement it. Judgment is always of critical importance in designing the analysis, choosing the alternatives to be compared, and selecting the criterion. Except where there is a completely satisfactory one-dimensional measurable objective (a rare circumstance), judgment must supplement the quantitative analysis before a choice can be recommended.

THE REQUIREMENTS APPROACH

In the absence of systematic analysis in terms of objectives and costs, a procedure that might be called the "requirements approach" is commonly used in the military departments and throughout much of the government. Staff officers inspect a problem, say, the defense of the continental United States or the design of the next generation of heavy bomber, draft a plan which seems to solve the problem, and determine requirements from the plan. Then feasibility is checked: Can the "required" performance characteristics, such as some designated speed and range, be achieved? Can the necessary budget be obtained? Does the nation have the necessary resources in total? If the program passes the feasibility tests, it is adopted; if it fails, some adjustments have to be made. But the question: What are the payoffs *and the costs* of alternative programs? may not be explicitly asked during the process of setting the requirement or deciding upon the budget. In fact, officials have on occasion boasted that their stated "requirements" have been based on need alone.

This, of course, is an illusion. Some notion of cost (money, resources, time), however imprecise, is implicit in the recognition of any limitation. Military departments frequently determine "requirements" which are from 10 to 25 percent higher than the available budget, but never ten times as high, and seldom twice as high. But this notion of cost merely rules out grossly infeasible programs. It does not help in making optimal or efficient choices.

For that purpose it is essential that alternative ways of achieving military objectives be costed, and that choices be made on the basis of payoff and cost. How *are* choices made by military planners prior to any costing of alternatives? We have never heard any satisfying explanation. The derivation of requirements by any process that fails to cost alternatives can result in good solutions only by accident. Probably military planners sometimes weigh relative costs in some crude manner, at least subconsciously, even when they deny they do; or they make choices on the basis of considerations which ought to be secondary or tertiary, such as the preservation of an existing command structure, or the matching of a reported foreign accomplishment.

The defects of the requirements approach can be seen clearly if we think of applying it to our problems as a consumer. Suppose the consumer mulls over his transportation problem and decides, "on the basis of need alone," that he requires a new Cadillac. It is "the best" car he knows, and besides Jones drives one. So he buys a Cadillac, ignoring cost and ignoring therefore the sacrifices he is making in other directions by buying "the best." There are numerous alternative ways of solving the consumer's transportation problem (as there are always numerous ways of solving a military problem), and a little costing of alternatives prior to purchase might have revealed that the purchase of "the best" instrument is not *necessarily* an optimal choice. Perhaps if the consumer had purchased a Pontiac or a secondhand Cadillac he would have saved enough to maintain and operate it and take an occasional trip.[4] Or if he had purchased a Chevrolet he could have afforded to keep his old car and become head of a two-car family. One of these alternatives, properly costed and compared,

---

4. Costing in our sense is never simply the cost of a unit of equipment; it is always the cost of a complete system including everything that must be purchased with the equipment and the cost of maintaining and operating it.

might have promised a far greater amount of utility for the consumer than the purchase of a new Cadillac "on the basis of need alone." Or the exercise might have reassured the consumer that the new Cadillac was indeed optimal. While expensive unit equipment is not necessarily optimal, in some cases it can be proved to be.

THE PRIORITIES APPROACH

Another procedure that seems to have a great deal of appeal, in both military planning and other government activities, is the "priorities approach." To facilitate a decision about how to spend a specified budget, the desirable items are ranked according to the urgency with which they are needed. The result is a list of things that might be bought, the ones that are more important being near the top and the ones that are less important being near the bottom. Lists that rank several hundred weapons and items have sometimes been generated in the military services.

At first blush, this appears to be a commendable and systematic way to tackle the problem. When one reflects a bit, however, the usefulness and significance of such a list begins to evaporate. Consider the following items ranked according to their (hypothetical) priorities: (1) Missile X, (2) Radar device Y, (3) Cargo aircraft Z. How do you use such a ranking? Does it mean that the entire budget should be spent on the first item? Probably not, for it is usually foolish to allocate all of a budget to a single weapon or object. Besides, if a budget is to be so allocated, the ranking of the items below the first one has no significance.

Does the ranking mean that the money should go to the first item until no additional amount is needed, then to the second item until no further amount is needed, and so on? Hardly, because there could be some need for more of Missile X almost without limit. Even if only a limited amount of Missile X was available, to keep buying right out to this limit would usually be a foolish rule. After quite a few Missile X's were purchased, the next dollar could better be spent on some other item. Even using lifeboats for women and children first is foolish if a sailor or doctor on each lifeboat can save many lives.

Perhaps a priority list means that we should spend more money on the higher-priority items than on those having a lower priority.

But this makes little sense, since some of the items high on the list, for example, the radar device, may cost little per unit and call at most for a relatively small amount of money; while some lower-ranking purchases, such as the cargo aircraft, may call for comparatively large sums if they are to be purchased at all. In any event, the priorities reveal nothing about how much more should be spent on particular items.

Just how anyone can use such a list is not clear. Suppose a consumer lists possible items for his monthly budget in the order of their priority and he feels that in some sense they rank as follows: (1) groceries, (2) gas and oil, (3) cigarettes, (4) repairs to house, (5) liquor, and (6) steam baths. This does not mean that he will spend all of his funds on groceries, nor does it mean that he will spend nothing on liquor or steam baths. His problem is really to allocate his budget among these different objects. He would like to choose the allocation such that an extra dollar on cigarettes is just as important to him as an extra dollar on groceries. At the margin, therefore, the objects of expenditure would be equally important (except for those that are not purchased at all).

The notion of priority stems from the very sensible proposition that one should do "first things first." It makes sense, or at least the top priority does, when one considers the use of a small increment of resources or time. If one thinks about the use of an extra dollar or of the next half-hour of his time, it is sensible to ask, "What is the most urgent—the first-priority—item?" If one is deciding what to do with a budget or with the next eight hours, however, he ordinarily faces a problem of *allocation*, not of setting priorities. A list of priorities does not face the problem or help solve it.

Thus in formulating defense policy and choosing weapon systems, we have to decide how much effort or how many resources should go to each item. The "priorities approach" does not solve the allocation problem and can even trap us into adopting foolish policies.[5]

5. For a revealing discussion of priority lists, see *Military Construction Appropriations for 1958,* Hearings before the Subcommittee of the Committee on Appropriations, House of Representatives, 85th Congress, 1st Session, U.S. Government Printing Office, Washington, D.C., 1957, pp. 420-427.

The Allocation of Fissionable Materials and the Theory of Exchange

Edwin Mansfield

Edwin Mansfield is Professor of Economics at the University of Pennsylvania. This article is from his book Microeconomics: Theory and Applications, *published by Norton in 1970.*

1. INTRODUCTION

Economic analysis has proved useful in many aspects of decision-making concerning military problems. The purpose of this paper is to describe how a standard part of economic theory —the theory of exchange—was used to solve an important problem facing military planners in the early fifties. In the following section, we present the relevant aspects of the theory of exchange. In the next section, we describe the nature of the problem that faced the military planners. In the final section, we indicate how the theory of exchange was used to help solve the problem.

2. EXCHANGE BETWEEN CONSUMERS

Let's begin by analyzing the exchange that can fruitfully take place between consumers. The essential elements of our theory can be presented if we assume that there are only two consumers, Bill and Joe, and only two commodities, good X and good Y.

We assume that Bill has a certain amount of each of the goods and that Joe has a certain amount of each of the goods. Moreover, we assume that they meet and discuss the possibility of trading. The question is: what sort of trading or exchange will occur?

To answer this question, we construct a special diagram, called an *Edgeworth box diagram*. This diagram is shown in Figure 1.

FIGURE 1

THE EDGEWORTH BOX DIAGRAM

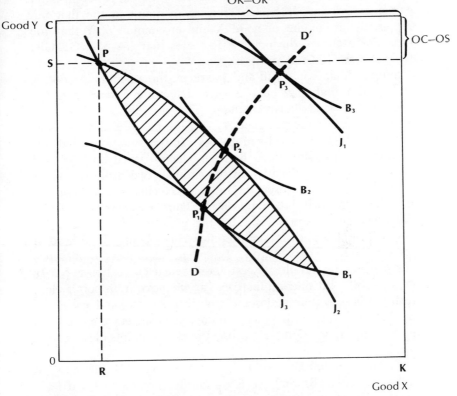

It is constructed in the following way: The width of the box, which is equal to OK, is the total amount of good X that Bill and Joe together have. The height of the box, which is equal to OC, is the total amount of good Y that Bill and Joe together have. The amount of good X that Bill has is measured horizontally from the origin at O. The amount of good Y that Bill has is measured vertically from the origin at O. Thus any point in the box diagram indicated a certain amount of good X and a certain amount of good Y that Bill has. For example, the point, P, indicates that Bill has OR units of good X and OS units of good Y.

The amount of good X that Joe has is measured by the horizontal distance to the left of the upper-right-hand corner of the box diagram. And the amount of good Y that Joe has is measured by the vertical distance downward from the upper-right-hand corner of the box diagram. Thus, every point in the diagram represents an amount of good X and an amount of Y that Joe has. For example, the point P indicates that Joe has (OK-OR) units of X and (OC-OS) units of good Y.

Suppose that, when Bill and Joe meet, the amounts of good X and good Y that they have is such that point P represents the allocation of goods between them. That is, Bill has OR units of good X and OS units of good Y, and Joe has (OK-OR) units of good X and (OC-OS) units of good Y. In this situation, what sort of trading will take place between them? What can be said about the optimal allocation of the goods between the two men? To find out, we must insert the indifference curves of Bill and Joe into the Edgeworth box diagram in Figure 1. Three of Bill's indifference curves are B_1, B_2, B_3, the highest indifference curve being B_3 and the lowest indifference curve being B_1. Three of Joe's indifference curves are J_1, J_2, and J_3, the highest indifference curve being J_3 and the lowest indifference curve being J_1. In general, Bill's satisfaction increases as we move from points close to the origin to points closer to the upper-right-hand corner of the box. Conversely, Joe's satisfaction increases as we move from points close to the upper-right-hand corner to points closer to the origin.

Given the initial allocation of good X and good Y, Bill is on indifference curve B_1, and Joe is on indifference curve J_2. If both men are free to trade it would obviously be in the interest of both parties for Bill to trade some good Y in exchange for some good X. Unless there is coercion, the point at which they will finally end up is somewhere in the shaded area in Figure 1; this area includes all points at which both men are no worse off than at P. The exact point to which they will move cannot be predicted, however. If Joe is the more astute bargainer, he may get Bill to accept the allocation at Point P_1, where Bill is no better off than before (since he is still on indifference curve B_1) but Joe is much better off (since he moves to indifference curve J_3). If Bill is the more astute bargainer, he may get Joe to accept the allocation at P_2, where Joe is no better off than before (since he is still on indifference curve J_2) but Bill is much better off (since he moves to indifference curve B_2). The ultimate outcome is likely to be a point between P_1 and P_2.

If after some exchange occurs a point is reached at which Bill's indifference curve is tangent to Joe's indifference curve, then there is no opportunity for further mutually advantageous exchange. One man can be made better off only by making the other man worse off—and surely such a situation would not result in further exchange. The locus of points where such a tangency occurs is called the *contract curve*. Some points on the contract curve are points P_1, P_2, and P_3 in Figure 1. Because of obstinacy or ineptness, exchange may cease at a point off the contract curve, but this would not be optimal in the following sense: If the consumers are at a point off the contract curve, it is always preferable for them to move to a point on the contract curve, since one or both can gain from the move while neither incurs a loss. Clearly, such a move results in a net gain. In this sense, the contract curve is an optimal set of points.

3. FISSIONABLE MATERIALS: AN APPLICATION OF THE THEORY OF EXCHANGE

Back around 1950, one of the key problems in the defense establishment was the allocation of fissionable material—U258 and Pu 239. In particular, how much of our supply of fissionable material should be used for strategic purposes, and how much should be used for tactical purposes? The strategic forces, principally long-range bombers at that time, were the foundation of our capability to strike back at an enemy's cities and bases. The tactical forces were concerned with more limited engagements with enemy forces. At that time, the strategic mission had exclusive claim on the national stockpile of fissionable materials, and an urgent question was whether some tactical air squadrons should be equipped with small-yield atomic weapons. As you can imagine, this was a very, very important question— one which occupied and concerned the minds of some of the nation's highest officials.

Both for the strategic and tactical mission, the two most important determinants of the effectiveness of the mission were (1) the amount of fissionable material used, and (2) the number of aircraft used. Within limits, it was possible to substitute airplanes for fissionable material and vice versa. For example, if the object of an Air Force operation was the expected destruction of a certain number of targets, fewer aircraft would be required to destroy these targets if atomic weapons, rather than conventional weapons, were used. Also, one way of increasing the probability that a bomb would get to the target was to have several empty decoy bombers accompanying each aircraft with an atomic bomb—which clearly was a way of substituting aircraft for fissionable materials.

In the very short run, it was sensible to view the total number of aircraft available for either strategic or tactical missions as fixed. It was also sensible to view the total amount of fissionable material available for either strategic or tactical missions as fixed. However, this was appropriate only in analyzing the problem in the short run; in the long run, it was possible to add to our supplies of aircraft and fissionable materials. Also, it is important to note that there was no way to establish the relative importance of strategic and tactical targets. For example, no one was willing to say that the destruction of a strategic target was worth the destruction of two tactical targets. Instead, strategic and tactical targets were regarded as incommensurable.

4. SOLUTION TO THE PROBLEM

The reader can be forgiven if he asks in a somewhat bewildered tone: "What in the world has this problem got to do with the theory of exchange we discussed in section 1?" The answer is that, strange as it may seem, economists used the theory of exchange described in section 1 to help solve this question. The way in which they solved the problem is instructive in many respects, one being that it illustrates how simple models can be adapted to throw light on very complicated problems.

In effect, the economists said: "Let's view the strategic mission as one consumer and the tactical mission as another consumer. Let's regard airplanes and fissionable material as two goods to be allocated between these two consumers, the total amount of these two goods being fixed in the very short run. Let's use as indifference curves for the strategic mission the combinations of aircraft and fissionable material that will result in the expected destruction of a particular number of strategic targets. Let's use as indifference curves for the tactical mission the combinations of aircraft and fissionable material that will result in the expected destruction of a particular number of tactical targets. Then let's use the Edgeworth box diagram to indicate which allocations of aircraft and fissionable materials between strategic and tactical missions are on the contract curve. This will tell us whether the existing allocation is on the contract curve. If it isn't, the allocation can be improved."

To actually attack the problem in this way, the first step was, of course, to construct the appropriate Edgeworth box diagram. Figure 2 shows what the resulting box diagram looked like. As in Figure 1, any point in the diagram represented a possible allocation of the two goods, airplanes and fissionable material, between the two "consumers," the strategic mission and the tactical mission. For example, point P in Figure 2 represents a case where the strategic mission gets OU units of aircraft and OV units of fissionable material, and the tactical mission gets (OA-OU) units of aircraft and (OM-OV) units of fissionable material.

The two "consumers" are not ordinary consumers. They are military missions. What do indifference curves mean in such a situation? Consider the tactical mission's indifference curve, T_1. Each point on T_1 represents a combination of aircraft and fissionable material that results in the same number of *tactical* targets expected to be destroyed. The fictitious consumer, "the tactical mission," is viewed as being interested in maximizing the expected number of tactical targets that can be destroyed. In other words, the expected number of tactical targets that can be destroyed is a measure of this consumer's "utility." Thus, he is indifferent among all of the points on T_1. And he clearly prefers indifference curve T_2 to indifference curve T_1. Similarly, consider the strategic mission's indifference curve, S_1. Each point on S_1

FIGURE 2

ALLOCATION OF FISSIONABLE MATERIALS AND AIRPLANES BETWEEN STRATEGIC AND TACTICAL MISSIONS

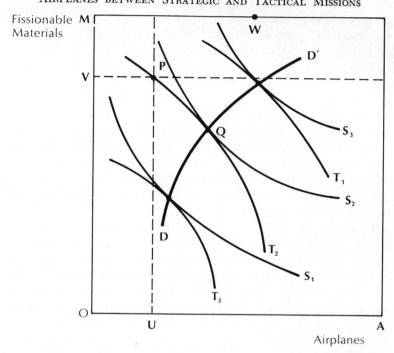

represents a combination of aircraft and fissionable material that results in the same number of *strategic* targets expected to be destroyed. The fictitious consumer, "the strategic mission," is viewed as being interested in maximizing the expected number of strategic targets that can be destroyed. In other words, the expected number of strategic targets that can be destroyed is a measure of the consumer's utility. Thus, he is indifferent among all of the points of S_1, and he prefers S_2 to S_1.

From the discussion in section 1, we know that any allocation of aircraft and fissionable materials that is represented by a point that is not a point of tangency between an indifference curve of the tactical mission and an indifference curve of the strategic mission is not an optimal allocation. For example, P in Figure 2 is not an optimal allocation since it is not a point of tangency between an indifference curve of the tactical mission and an indifference curve of the strategic mission. Why isn't P an optimal allocation? Because if we hold constant the expected number of tactical targets that can be destroyed (the "utility" of the tactical mission), we can increase the expected number of strategic targets that can be destroyed (the "utility" of the strategic mission) by moving to point Q. The locus of optimal points—the contract curve—is shown by DD' in Figure 2.

Having constructed the contract curve, what did the economists conclude? Recall that the existing allocation assigned all of the nation's stockpile of fissionable material to the strategic mission and none to the tactical mission. Thus, the existing allocation was at point W in Figure 2. However, according to the economist's calculations, this point was not on the contract curve, DD'. Consequently, the existing allocation was shown to be sub-optimal, a movement to the contract curve being called for. Specifically, the stockpile of fissionable material needed to be reallocated, some atomic weapons being reserved for the tactical mission. However, this analysis could not indicate which particular point on the contract curve should be chosen, since this decision hinged on whether we wanted to increase our strategic capability at the expense of our tactical capability, or vice versa. On the basis of the information given here, no judgment on this score could be made.

This was an important example of the application of the theory described in previous sections. For that reason, it is interesting. In addition, it is interesting because it illustrates the fact that most aspects of microeconomics are concerned with means to achieve specified ends, not with the choice of ends. Thus, economists in the case discussed here were able to increase the destructive power of given supplies of aircraft and fissionable material. But they took as given the hypothesis that it was a good thing to increase their destructive power. In other words, they took as given the fact that the "utility" of the "consumers" should be increased. In certain circumstances, this hypothesis could be quite wrong. For example, there might be circumstances where an increase in destructive power might increase the chances of war. Of course, this does not mean that it is not valuable to have techniques like those discussed here: they obviously are of great value. What it does mean is that one cannot expect them to do more than they are designed to do.[1]

1. For further discussion, see S. Enke, "Using Costs to Select Weapons," *American Economic Review*, May 1965; and "Some Economic Aspects of Fissionable Materials," *Quarterly Journal of Economics*, May 1954.

Cost-Benefit Analysis

ROLAND N. McKEAN

This selection by Roland N. McKean of the University of California (Los Angeles) appears in his book Public Spending, *published in 1968.*

"Cost-benefit analyses" are attempts to estimate certain costs and gains that would result from alternative courses of action. For different applications, other names are often used: "cost-effectiveness analysis" when courses of action in defense planning are compared; "systems analysis" when the alternatives are relatively complex collections of interrelated parts; "operations research" when the alternatives are modes of operation with more or less given equipment and resources; or "economic analysis" when the alternatives are rival price-support or other economic policies. The term "cost-benefit analysis" was originally associated with natural-resource projects but has gradually come to be used for numerous other applications. The basic idea is not new: individuals have presumably been weighing the pros and cons of alternative actions ever since man appeared on earth; and in the early part of the nineteenth century, Albert Gallatin and others put together remarkably sophisticated studies of proposed U.S. government canals and turnpikes. But techniques have improved, and interest has been growing. All these studies might well be called economic analyses. This does not mean that the economist's skills are the only ones needed in making such analyses or, indeed, that economists are very good at making them. It merely means that this analytical tool is aimed at helping decision makers—consumers, businessmen, or government officials—economize.

In recent years, the Bureau of the Budget, the National Bureau of Standards, many other U.S. agencies, and governments and agencies in other nations have been exploring possible uses of cost-benefit analysis. Sometimes the analyses are essentially simple arithmetic. Sometimes high-speed computers are used— as they were, for instance, in the search by a Harvard group for the best way to use water in the Indus River basin in Pakistan. One of the major applications of cost-benefit analysis will continue to be the comparison of alternative natural-resources policies—proposals to reduce air and water pollution, to divert water from the Yukon to regions further south, to do something about the rapidly declining water level in the Great Lakes, and so on. But other applications are appearing with growing frequency— comparisons of such things as alternative health measures, personnel policies, airport facilities, education practices, transportation systems, choices about the management of governmental properties, and antipoverty proposals.

All such analyses involve working with certain common elements: (1) objectives, or the beneficial things to be achieved; (2) alternatives, or the possible systems or arrangements for achieving the objectives; (3) costs, or the benefits that have to be foregone if one of the alternatives is adopted; (4) models, or the sets of relationships that help one trace out the impacts of each alternative on achievements (in other words, on benefits) and costs; and (5) a criterion, involving both costs and benefits, to identify the preferred alternative. In connection with each of these elements there are major difficulties. Consider a personal problem of choice that an individual might try to analyze— selecting the best arrangements for his family's transportation. Spelling out the relevant objectives, that is, the kind of achievements that would yield significant benefits, is no simple task. The objectives may include commuting to work, getting the children to school, travel in connection with shopping, cross-country trips, and so on. Part of this travel may be across deserts, along mountain roads, in rainy or icy or foggy conditions. The family may attach a high value to the prestige of traveling in style (or of being austere, or of simply being different from most other people). Another objective that is neglected all too often is a hard-to-specify degree of flexibility to deal with uncertainties. Adaptability and flexibility are particularly important objectives if one is examining alternative educational programs, exploratory research projects, or R&D policies. Overlooking any of the relevant objectives could lead to poor choices.

The second element, the alternative ways of achieving the benefits, also deserves careful thought, for selecting the best of an unnecessarily bad lot is a poor procedure. In choosing a family's transportation system, the alternatives might include various combinations of a compact automobile, a luxury automobile, a pickup truck, a jeep, a motor scooter, an airplane, a bicycle, the use of a bus system, and the use of taxicabs.

In many problems of choice, the alternatives are called "systems," and the analyses are called "systems analyses." This terminology is quite appropriate, because the word "system" means a set of interrelated parts, and the alternative ways of achieving objectives usually are sets of interrelated parts. At the same time, the word "system" is so general that this usage is often confusing. In defense planning, for example, the term "system" can be used to refer to such sets of interrelated parts as the following:

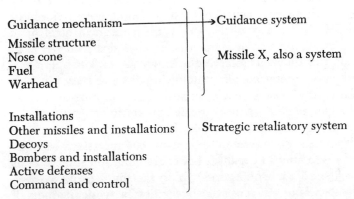

All three of these systems are collections of interrelated parts. How large should systems be for their comparison to be called a "systems analysis" or for their comparison to be a useful aid?

There are no correct answers; one must exercise judgment in deciding how large the systems should be to provide worthwhile assistance in tracing out the costs and benefits. (In effect, one must weigh the costs against the benefits of preparing alternative cost-benefit analyses.) Where interrelationships are relatively important, one is usually driven to consider large systems. Thus to choose between two engines for a supersonic airliner, one can hardly compare thrusts alone and make an intelligent selection, for weight, reliability, cost, noise, etc., may have diverse effects on overall desirability. The power plants must be fitted (at least on paper) into rival aircraft designs, and thence into airline and airport systems to see their net impact on the real objectives and the full costs. Moreover, other components of the projected systems may have to be modified so as not to use either engine stupidly. Suppose one engine would make possible the use of relatively short runways. To use an aircraft with this power plant in an intelligent way, one might have to modify many parts of the proposed airports, traffic patterns, ground installations for instrument-landing systems, and even proposed airline schedules. Hence one would end up comparing rather broad systems having many common components but also having several components that differed.

So much for the alternative systems to be compared. The third element of cost-benefit analysis, cost, is crucial because it really reflects the alternative benefits that one might obtain from the resources. It is just as foolish to measure costs incorrectly or to neglect part of them as it is to measure benefits incorrectly or neglect part of them. If selecting a luxury car entails building a new garage or paying higher insurance premiums, these are part of the costs of choosing that alternative. If one already has an adequate garage, the value foregone by using it (but *not* the cost of building a garage) is the relevant cost.

"Models," the fourth element of cost-benefit analysis, are simply crude representations of reality that enable one to estimate costs and benefits. If a person figures, "With the bus I could average ten miles per hour, traverse the five miles to work in one-half hour, spend five hours per week commuting to work, and would stand up 50 percent of the distance on 50 percent of the trips," he is using a model. If he says, "With Automobile X, I would get a motor tune-up every 5,000 miles and would therefore spend $50 per year on that item," he visualizes these events and uses a set of relationships, that is, a model, to estimate this cost. When one tries to perceive how something would work, it has become convenient and fashionable to say, "Let's build a model," though one could simply say, "Let's devise a way to predict what would happen (or a new way to estimate costs and benefits)."

The fifth element of cost-benefit analysis is the criterion or test of preferredness by means of which one points to the best choice. People tend to make a variety of criterion errors. One error, the use of the ratio of benefits to costs, is such a perennial favorite that it merits a brief discussion. Suppose at first that both benefits and costs can be measured *fully and correctly* in monetary terms and that one must choose among the following three discrete (and not mutually exclusive) alternatives:

	A	B	C
Cost	$100	$100	$200
Benefit one year later	$150	$105	$220
Ratio of benefits to costs	1.5	1.05	1.10

Suppose further that the constraint is that funds can be borrowed at 6 percent. Which projects should be undertaken, and what is the criterion? A and C, both of which yield more than 6 percent, should be undertaken, and the proper criterion is to maximize the present value of net worth or, its surrogate, to undertake projects wherever the marginal benefit exceeds the marginal cost. Note that the criterion is *not* to maximize the ratio of benefits to costs, which would restrict one to Project A. If the constraint is a fixed budget of $200, Projects A and B should be selected. Again, maximizing the ratio of benefits to costs would limit one to Project A.

Or consider two discrete and mutually exclusive alternatives (for example, two sizes of a dam):

	A	B
Cost	$100	$200
Benefit one year later	$150	$260
Ratio of benefits to costs	1.50	1.30

If funds can be borrowed at 6 percent, Project B should be undertaken. One should not choose A simply because the benefit-cost ratio is larger. Ratios are not irrelevant—every marginal productivity is a ratio—for one often seeks to *equalize* certain ratios as a condition for achieving a desired maximum. But the ratio itself is not the thing to be maximized.

The issue takes on a good deal of importance when the benefits can only be suggested by physical products or capabilities. In these circumstances, presumably in desperation, people frequently adopt as a criterion the maximization of some such ratio as satellite payload per dollar, hours of student instruction per dollar, or target-destruction capability per dollar. But the benefit-cost ratios of rival proposals simply cover up the relevant information. Take another example from the choices that confront the individual. If one is selecting a hose with which to sprinkle his lawn, one may have the following options:

	⅝-IN DIAMETER	1-IN. DIAMETER
Cost	$3	$5
Benefit (water put on lawn per hour)	108 gallons	150 gallons
Ratio of benefits to costs	36/1	30/1

The ratios are irrelevant. The pertinent question is whether or not the extra capability is worth the extra $2. Less misleading than showing the ratio would be showing the physical capabilities and the costs à la consumers' research. Or, where it makes sense to do so, one can adjust the scale of the alternatives so that each costs the same or achieves the same objectives. Then one can see which system achieves a specified objective at minimum cost, or achieves the greatest benefit for a specified budget. This is not a perfect criterion, for someone has to decide if the specified budget (or objective) is appropriate. But at least this sort of test is less misleading than a benefit-cost ratio.

With regard to this fifth element of cost-benefit analysis, discussing the correct way to design criteria may seem like discussing the correct way to find the Holy Grail. In a world of uncertainty and individual utility functions, judgments must help shape choices, and no operational test of preferredness can be above suspicion. Moreover, analyses vary in their quality, which is hard to appraise, and in their applicability to different decisions. For these reasons, responsible decision makers must treat cost-benefit analyses as "consumers' research" and introduce heroic judgments in reaching final decisions. In a sense, then, it may be both presumptuous and erroneous to discuss having a test of preferredness in these quantitative analyses.

Criteria should be considered, nonetheless, in connection with such analysis. First, cost-benefit analysts do apply criteria, especially in designing and redesigning the alternatives to be compared. They delete features that appear to be inefficient, add features that appear to be improvements, and probe for alternative combinations that are worth considering. This screening of possibilities and redesign of alternative systems entails the use of criteria, and these should be explicitly considered and exhibited. Second, whether or not they ought to, analysts often present the final comparisons in terms of a criterion. Thus while it may be wrong to talk as if a definitive criterion is an element of every analysis, these warnings about criterion selection should be emphasized.

Needless to say, in reaching decisions, one should attempt to take into account *all* gains and *all* costs. Some people feel that there are two types of gain or cost, economic and noneconomic, and that economic analysis has nothing to do with the latter. This distinction is neither very sound nor very useful. People pay for—that is, they value—music as well as food, beauty or quiet as well as aluminum pans, a lower probability of death as well as garbage disposal. The significant categories are not economic and noneconomic items but (1) gains and costs that can be measured in monetary units (for example, the use of items like typewriters that have market prices reflecting the marginal evaluations of all users); (2) other commensurable effects (impacts of higher teacher salaries, on the one hand, and of teaching machines, on the other hand, on students' test scores); (3) incommensurable effects that can be quantified but not in terms of a common denominator (capability of improving science test scores and capability of reducing the incidence of ulcers among students); and (4) nonquantifiable effects. Examples of the last category are impacts of alternative policies on the morale and

happiness of students, on the probability of racial conflicts, and
on the probability of protecting individual rights. In taking a
position on an issue, each of us implicitly quantifies such considerations. But there is no way to make quantifications that
would necessarily be valid for other persons. This sort of distinction between types of effects does serve a useful purpose, especially in warning us of the limitations of cost-benefit analysis.

One should recognize, too, that cost-benefit analysis necessarily
involves groping and the making of subjective judgments, not
just briskly proceeding with dispassionate scientific measurements. Consider the preparation of such analyses to aid educational choices. No one says, "This is the educational objective,
and here are the three alternative systems to be compared. Now
trace out the impacts of each on cost and on achievement of the
objective, and indicate the preferred system." What happens is
that those making the analysis spend much time groping for an
operational statement of the objective, such as a designated improvement in specific test scores without an increase in the
number of dropouts or nervous breakdowns. A first attempt is
made at designing the alternative ways of realizing this objective.
Preliminary costs are estimated. Members of the research team
perceive that the systems have differential impacts on other objectives, such as flexibility, or student performance on tests two
years later, or student interest in literature. Or the rival arrangements may elicit different reactions from teachers, parents, and
school boards, affecting the achievement of other objectives.
The analysts redesign the alternatives in the light of these impacts, perhaps so that each alternative performs at least "acceptably" with respect to each objective. Next it appears that certain
additional features such as extra English-composition courses
might add greatly to capability but not much to cost. Or the
research team's cost group reports that certain facilities are extremely expensive and that eliminating them might reduce costs
greatly with little impairment of effectiveness. In both cases
the systems have to be modified again. This cut-and-try procedure is essential. Indeed, this process of redesigning the alternatives is probably a more important contribution than the
final cost-effectiveness exhibits. In any event, the preparation of
such an analysis is a process of probing—and not at all a methodical scientific comparison following prescribed procedures.

An appreciation of cost-benefit analysis also requires an awareness that incommensurables and uncertainties are pervasive. Consider the impacts of alternative educational policies that were mentioned above. These effects can perhaps be described, but not expressed in terms of a common denominator. Judgments about the extent of these effects and their worth have to be made. Some costs, such as the monetary measures of foregone benefits, perhaps additional sacrifices in terms of personality adjustment and ultimate effectiveness, or undesirable political repercussions that yield costs, cannot validly be put in terms of a common denominator. Furthermore, because of uncertainties, whatever estimates can be prepared should in principle be probability distributions rather than unique figures for costs and gains. The system that performs best in one contingency may perform worst in another contingency. Finally, costs and gains occur over a period of time, not at a single point in time, and there is no fully acceptable means of handling these streams of costs and gains in analyzing many options.

These difficulties are present because life is complex, and there is no unique correct choice. The difficulties are not created by cost-benefit analysis. Moreover, they do not render quantitative economic analysis useless. They simply mean that one has to be discriminating about when and how to use various tools. In general, the broader choices made by higher-level officials pose relatively great difficulties regarding what value judgments to make and what the physical and social consequences of alternative actions would be. Consider, for example, the allocation of the U.S. budget among various departments or the allocation of funds among such functions as the improvement of health, education, or postal service. Cost-benefit analysis gives relatively little guidance in making these choices, for in the end the decision maker's task is dominated by difficult personal judgments. Cost-benefit analysis may help somewhat, for it is the appropriate framework in terms of which to *think* about these broad choices, and it can usually provide *some* improved information. When personal judgments must play such a huge role, however, the improved information may not be worth much.

Consider another example of such broad choices: the government's allocation of its R&D effort between basic research and applied development. To choose between these two alternatives, officials must rely heavily on personal judgments about the consequences and judgments concerning the value of those consequences. Values cannot be taken as agreed upon, and physical-sociological effects cannot be predicted with confidence. Quantitative analysis can probably contribute only a little toward the sharpening of intuition here. Or consider the allocation of effort between improving medical care for the aged and improving it for the young. Suppose one could make extremely good predictions of the effects, which would of course aid decision makers. The final choice would be dominated in this instance by value judgments about the worth of prolonging the lives of elderly persons, the worth of lengthening the lives of persons in great pain, the worth of saving the lives of weakened or physically handicapped children, the relief of different kinds of distress, and so on.

Another broad or high-level choice that brings out these difficulties is the allocation of funds to, or for that matter within, the State Department. In the tasks of diplomacy it is hard to visualize taking a set of value tags as being clearly stated, let alone agreed upon. And disagreement is quite understandable in predicting the effects of alternative courses of action on the probabilities of stable alliances, provocations, little wars, nuclear wars, and so on. Positive science has provided few tested hypotheses about these relationships.

As one proceeds to narrower or lower-level problems of choice, these difficulties frequently, though not always, become less severe. (Actual decisions, of course, vary continuously in the extent to which they present these difficulties, but it is often economical to think in terms of such categories as broad and narrow or high-level and low-level choices). Within such tasks as education and health improvement, there are lower-level choices for which quantitative analysis may be very helpful, but there are also many middle-level choices that are fraught with difficulties. Should more effort be placed on the improvement of mental health even if it means less emphasis on the treatment of conventional ailments? Should effort be reallocated from higher education toward the improvement of elementary-school training, or vice versa? Or, as an alternative policy, should government leave such allocative decisions more than at present to the uninfluenced choices of individuals families? Cost-benefit analysis cannot do much to resolve the uncertainties about the consequences of such decisions, about their relative worths to individual citizens, or about whose value judgments should be given what weights.

Within applied research and development, a choice between specific projects might appear to be a low-level choice that economic analysis could greatly assist. In such instances, it is true that values can sometimes be taken as agreed upon. In selecting research and development projects for new fuels, for instance, the values to be attached to various outcomes are not obvious, yet they are probably not major sources of divergent views. Perhaps the principal difficulty is the inability to predict the physical consequences, including "side effects," of alternative proposals. Here too, cost-benefit analysis may be destined to play a comparatively small role.

One can list many problems of choice that seem to fall somewhere in this middle ground—that is, where cost-benefit analysis can be helpful but not enormously so. It would appear, for instance, that the selection of antipoverty and welfare programs depends heavily on consequences that one cannot predict with confidence and on value judgments about which there is much disagreement. Similar statements apply also to the selection of foreign-aid programs, urban-development proposals, or law-enforcement programs—the comparison of different methods of curbing the use of narcotics, say, or of different penal institutions and procedures. In education, many decisions that may appear to be low-level or relatively simple—for example, the selection among alternative curricula or teaching methods or disciplinary rules—are inevitably dominated by judgments about the consequences of these policies and about the value tags to be attached to those consequences.

It is in connection with comparatively narrow problems of choice that cost-benefit analysis can sometimes play a more significant role. In these instances, as might be expected, the alternatives are usually rather close substitutes. Science can often predict the consequences of govenmental natural-resource investments or choices affecting the utilization of water or land, and people can often agree on the values at stake—at least to a sufficient extent to render analyses highly useful. Competing irrigation plans, flood-control projects, swamp drainage and land reclamation ventures, and water-pollution control measures are examples of narrow problems of choice in which cost-benefit analysis can help.

Cost-benefit analysis also promises to be helpful in comparing certain transportation arrangements. The interdependencies of transportation networks with other aspects of life are formidable, yet with ingenuity extremely useful studies of some transportation alternatives can be produced. Numerous transportation alternatives have been the subject of such studies: highways, urban systems, inland waterways, modified railway networks, the utilization of a given amount of sea transport, air transport fleets, and of course many lower-level choices, such as alternative road materials, construction practices, airport facilities, and loading arrangements. In some instances, of course, the interdependencies may be too complex for analyses to be very valuable; transportation alternatives that affect a large region and its development yield chains of consequences that are extremely difficult to trace out.

At best, the difficulties of providing *valuable* information are awesome. There can always be legitimate disagreement about any of these policy decisions, and analyses must be regarded as inputs to decisions, not as oracular touchstones. Nonetheless, to think systematically about the costs and gains from alternative policies is surely more sensible than to rely on haphazard thought or intuition. Such analyses can bring out the areas of disagreement so that people can see where their differences lie. Even with considerable divergence in judgments, they can screen out the absurdly inferior alternatives, focusing the debate on subsets of relatively good alternatives. For some choices, cost-benefit analysis provides information that can help officials agree upon a course of action that is preferred or accepted by most citizens. And for all choices, it is the right framework to use in organizing the evidence and one's thoughts and intuitions regarding alternatives. Even in deciding which research project to undertake, or how much time to spend on it, a researcher consults rough cost-benefit T-accounts. In deciding anything, a person should weigh costs and gains. Preliminary weighing may suggest that the use of a tentative rule of thumb or "requirement" is preferable to further or repeated analyses, but he should not initially pull some mythical requirement out of the air.

Applications of Cost-Benefit Analysis

ALAN R. PREST AND RALPH TURVEY

Alan R. Prest and Ralph Turvey are well-known British economists. This piece is from their article in the Economic Journal, *1965.*

We [present here] illustrations of the ways in which the principles previously set out have been employed in cost-benefit studies. We shall first look at some water projects and then turn to transport—these being the two areas where cost-benefit studies have been common. Subsequently, we shall survey the application and applicability of these techniques in land-usage schemes (urban renewal, recreation, and land reclamation), health, education, research and development, and defense. Throughout, we shall be illustrative rather than comprehensive—both in the sense that we are concerned only with the main features of, say, irrigation schemes rather than detailed case studies, and in that we shall emphasize the differences in treatment rather than the similarities. This means that we examine general techniques for enumerating and evaluating costs and benefits rather than "standard" items, such as the choice of appropriate discount rates, the exclusion of superogatory secondary benefits, etc. We are not reproducing any examples in full detail, but good ones can be found in Krutilla and Eckstein on water-resource projects, Foster and Beesley on transport, and Borus on labor retraining.

1. WATER PROJECTS

Water projects take many different forms. They may differ enormously in respect of their engineering characteristics, *e.g.*, an estuarine barrage or a dam in the hills. Similarly, the purposes of water investment are many—provision of more water for an industrial area, provision of irrigation water, prevention of flood damage, and so on. In some cases there may be only one such purpose in a particular scheme; in others it may be a case of multi-purpose development. The details of cost-benefit analysis inevitably differ from project to project, and we can only cover a sample. We shall look at irrigation, flood control, and hydro-electric schemes in turn, and in this way hope to catch the smell even if not the flavor of the ingredients. Finally, we shall have a few words to add on the particular characteristics of multi-purpose schemes.

(a) *Irrigation* · Since it is seldom possible to ascertain directly the price at which water could be sold upon the completion of a proposed irrigation project, and since this price would in any case give no indication of consumers' surplus, the *direct* benefits of a project have to be estimated by:

    (i) forecasting the change in the output of each agricultural project, leaving out those outputs which, like the cattle feed, are also inputs;

    (ii) valuing and summing these changes;

    (iii) deducting the opportunity cost of the change in all farming inputs other than the irrigation water;

in order to get, as a result, the value of the net change in agricultural output consequent upon the irrigation of the area.

We now discuss each step in turn.

(i) Forecasts of additional output, whether sold in the market or consumed on the farm, can be made in countries with well-developed agricultural advisory services. But this is only the beginning of the story. Even if there were no delay in the response of farmers to new conditions, it will often be the case that the full effects of irrigation will take some years to be felt. Since, in addition, farmers will take time to adapt, it is clear that what is required here is not just a simple list of outputs but a schedule showing the development of production over time. Yet this is too complicated in practice, and usually the best that can be done is to make estimates for one or two benchmark dates and extrapolate or, alternatively, postulate a discrete lag in the response of farmers.

The forecast is difficult as well as complicated (in principle), because it is the behavior of a group of people that is involved, behavior which may depend upon peasant conservatism, superstition, political tensions, and so on, just as much or more than it depends upon any nice agronomic calculus. Thus, an Indian study (Sovani and Rath) reports that the peasants in an area irrigated by the Hirakud dam erroneously believed that planting a second crop on the valley-bottom land would lead to to waterlogging and salinization. The authors explicitly assumed that in the first ten years after irrigation began the area would settle down to irrigated agriculture with the least possible change in techniques and capital investment.

The probability that farmers will not follow an income-maximizing course of action is one reason why a farm-management or programming approach may be of little use—except in setting an outside limit to outputs. Another is that the requisite information may be lacking. Thus, it is frequently necessary either to substitute or supplement the projections based upon the assumption of maximizing behavior with projections based upon the assumption that behavior of other farmers elsewhere constitutes a useful precedent. The effect of irrigation in A is then forecast by comparing an irrigated area B either with B before irrigation or with an unirrigated area, C. There is obviously scope for judgment (and bias) here.

(ii) The amount the farmer gets for his crops may differ markedly from their value to the community where agriculture is protected or subsidized, as in the United States or the United Kingdom (Eckstein, Renshaw). In fact, some United States calculations have allowed for this by making an arbitrary 20-percent deduction in the prices of major commodities in surplus or receiving federal support. This is one example of the point that when the conditions for optimal resource allocation are not fulfilled in the rest of the economy market prices may prove a poor guide to project costs and benefits. Another general problem on which we have already touched arises when the increment in the output of any crop is large enough to affect its price, so that there is no unique price for valuation purposes. There is the further point that output should be valued at a given price-level, consistent with the valuations of other benefits and of costs, but that future changes in price relativities need to be taken into account. Thus, price projections are required, and once again there is scope for judgment, as anything from simple extrapolation to highly sophisticated supply and demand studies may be utilized. Finally, there is the old problem, much aired in social accounting literature (*e.g.*, Prest and Stewart) about the appropriate valuation of subsistence output.

(ii) The principles for valuing farm inputs are the same as those for valuing outputs, while the forecast of input quantities is clearly related to the forecast of output quantities. In an elaborate income-maximizing analysis inputs and outputs would be simultaneously determined, while in a simpler approach inputs per acre of irrigated land or per unit of output will be taken as being the same as on comparable irrigated land elsewhere. In either case, costs include the opportunity earnings, if any, of any additional farmers who come to work in the irrigated area.

The *secondary* benefits which have sometimes been regarded as appropriately included in irrigation benefit calculations reflect the impact of the project on the rest of the economy, both via its increased sales to farmers and via its increased purchases from them. We have already discussed the appropriateness of including these benefits. More important is the technological interdependence which is likely to be found in many irrigation schemes, such as when the effects on the height of the water-table in one area spill over to another district.

Any irrigation project will have a number of *minor* effects not obviously covered in the categories so far discussed. As these will vary from case to case, and no general list is possible, some examples may be of use. They are taken from an *ex-post* study of the Sarda Canal in India:

> Canal water is also used for washing, bathing, watering cattle. Silt is deposited at the outlet heads, which necessitates constant and laborious cleaning of the channels.

Some plots of land have been made untillable by unwanted water.

The canal divides the area (and sometimes individual fields) into two parts, but has few bridges, so that much time is wasted in circumnavigating it.

Many such effects will be unquantifiable, but must nevertheless be remembered in any analysis.

(b) *Flood Control* · Ever since the River and Harbor Act of 1927 the United States Army Corps of Engineers has had the responsibility of preparing plans for improving major rivers for flood control purposes—as well as irrigation, hydro-electric power and navigation. On the flood control side, the major benefits which have been categorized in this—and other—work have been the losses averted. Losses of this sort can refer to different types of assets—property, furnishings, crops, etc.; or to different types of owners—individuals, business firms, government, and so on. In all these cases the general principle is to estimate the mathematical expectation of annual damage (on the basis of the likely frequency of flood levels of different heights) and then regard such sums as the maximum annual amounts people would be willing to pay for flood control measures.

Other benefits which must be taken into account are as follows:

(i) Avoidance of deaths by drowning. We shall deal with the general principles relevant in such cases in connection with health improvements.

(ii) Avoidance of temporary costs, *e.g.*, evacuation of flood victims, emergency sand-bag work, etc., risks of sanitation breakdowns, epidemics, etc.

(iii) Possibilities of putting flood land to higher uses if the risk of inundation is eliminated.

The costs involved in flood control calculations are relatively straightforward. Obviously, the initial costs of the flood-control works and their repair and maintenance charges must be included. The most difficult point in any such compilation is likely to be the cost of land acquisition for reservoirs, etc. In the absence of anything remotely approaching a free land market in a country such as the United Kingdom there is bound to be an arbitrary element in such items.

There are some obvious reasons why private investment principles are insufficient in the case of flood-control measures. Protection for one inhabitant in a district implies protection for another, and so one immediately runs into the collective goods problem; protection for one district may worsen flood threats to another, and so this inevitably brings up technological externalities; finally, flood works often have to be on a large scale and of a complex nature, and so this brings up non-marginal and imperfect competition problems. So one simply has to try to estimate willingness to pay for flood protection by the roundabout devices described above. There is no simple-cut appeal to market principles.

(c) *Hydro-electric Power Schemes* · The standard way of measuring the value of the extra electricity generated by a public hydro-electric scheme is to estimate the savings realized by not having to buy from an alternative source. This sounds simple, but in fact raises all sorts of complicated issues: we shall look at these by, first, considering the simple alternative of a single hydro-electric source versus a single private steam plant, and secondly, by considering the implications of adding another source to a whole supply system.

In the first case the general point is to say that benefits can be measured by the costs of the most economical private alternative. As Eckstein shows at some length, this raises a number of issues, *e.g.*, a private sector station will not be working under competitive conditions, and so its charges may not coincide with opportunity costs; private sector charges will not be directly relevant to public sector circumstances in that they will reflect taxes, private sector interest rates, etc.; as we need the pattern of future, as well as current, benefits, we have to allow for the effects of future technological changes in reducing alternative costs, and hence benefits, through time. A further point arises when a new hydro-electric station provides a proportionately large net addition to the supply in a region. In this case the alternative-cost principle would produce an over-estimate of benefits, and we are forced back to a measure of what the extra output would sell for plus the increased consumers' surplus of its purchasers. Presumably a survey of the potential market for the power will provide some of the needed information, but the difficulties of making reliable estimates are clearly enormous.

We now turn to the case where a new hydro-electric station has to be fitted into a whole system.

The amount of power produced by a new hydro-electric station and the times of year at which it will be produced depend not only upon the physical characteristics of the river providing the power but also upon the cost characteristics of the whole electricity supply system and upon the behavior of the electricity consumers. The supply system constitutes a unity which is operated so as to minimize the operating costs of meeting consumption whatever its time pattern happens to be. Hence the way in which the hydro-electric station is operated may be affected by alterations in the peakiness of consumption, the bringing into service of new thermal stations, and so on.

If we now try to apply the principle of measuring benefits by the cost savings of not building an alternative station it follows from the system interdependence just described that the only meaningful way of measuring this cost saving is to ascertain the difference in the present value of total system operating costs in the two cases and deduct the capital cost of the alternatives. A simple comparison of the two capital costs and the two running costs, that is to say, will only give the right answer if the level and time pattern of the output of each would be exactly the same. In general, therefore, a very complicated exercise involving the simulation of the operation of the whole system is required (Turvey), as, for that matter, may be the case for other water-resource analysis (Maass).

Finally, there is another point, emphasized by Krutilla and Eckstein. Even if two or more hydro-electric stations are not linked in the same distribution and consumption network, there may be production interdependence. The clearest example is that when upstream stations in a river basin have reservoirs for water storage, this is highly likely to affect water flows downstream, and hence the generating pattern of stations in that area. If technological interdependence of this type is not internalized by having both types of station under the same authority it will be necessary to have some system of compensatory arrangement if we want to cut down resource misallocation.

(d) *Multi-purpose Schemes* · In practice, many river developments have a number of purposes in mind—not only those we have dealt with above but also transport improvements, etc., as well. Obviously, the range of choice now becomes much wider. Not only does one have to look at the cost-benefit data for, say, different sized hydro-electric stations, but one also has to take different combinations of, say, irrigation and navigation improvements. The calculations will also be more complicated, in that the possibilities of interdependence are clearly multiplied, and so the warnings we have already uttered about the feasibility of some calculations will be even more applicable. We shall have no more to say at this stage on multi-stage projects, but simply make the final point that these reflections are highly apposite in the case of projects such as the Morecambe Bay and Solway Firth barrage schemes (providing for industrial and domestic water supplies, transport improvements, land reclamation, improved recreation facilities, etc.), which are receiving a good deal of attention at the time of writing (in 1965).

2. TRANSPORT PROJECTS

(a) *Roads* · A great deal of work has now accumulated on the principles and methods of application of cost-benefit techniques in this field, ever since the first experiments in the State of Oregon in 1938. We shall illustrate the arguments by references to the work done on the M1 in the United Kingdom (Coburn, Beesley and Reynolds, Reynolds, Foster), this being a typical example of what one finds in this field.

The calculation of net annual savings was classified under four heads: (i) those relating to diverted traffic; (ii) those to generated traffic; (iii) savings in non-business time; and (iv) the effects of the growth of G.N.P. Under (i) (diverted traffic) estimates were made of the likely net savings of the traffic diverted from other routes to the M1, *i.e.*, positive items, such as working time savings of drivers, vehicle-usage economies, gasoline savings, accident reduction, etc., together with negative items in respect of additional mileages traveled on faster roads and maintenance costs of the motorway.

In respect of generated traffic the argument is that the opening of the motorway would in effect reduce the "price" (in terms of congestion and inconvenience of motoring) and enable demand which had hitherto been frustrated to express itself in motorway usage. As it must be assumed that benefits per vehicle-mile to frustrated consumers are of less consequence than those to actual consumers (if not, they would not remain frustrated), they were rated as half as great as the latter in the M1 calculations.

Savings in non-business time were the third main ingredient. This calculation involves many complications, to which we shall return in a moment. The fourth component was the introduction of a trend factor, to allow for the long-term growth of G.N.P. and the effects on the demand for road travel—an obvious ingredient of any calculation, whether relating to private or public investment. The upshot of the combined calculations was that the rate of return was of the order of 10 to 15 percent.

A number of comments can be made on these calculations. First, there are the obvious statistical shortcomings which are recognized by everyone, including the authors. Second, there are a number of minor omissions, such as allowances for police and administrative costs, the benefits accruing to pedestrians and cyclists, etc., the advantages of more reliable goods deliveries (Foster). Thirdly, there are some inconsistencies in these particular calculations, in that on some occasions a long-period view seems to be taken (*e.g.*, when calculating the savings resulting from reductions in road vehicle fleets) and on others a short-period one (*e.g.*, in assessing the benefits of diversion of traffic from the railways). Much more important than these points are the savings due to accident reduction and to economies in travel time, where important logical and practical issues arise. On the first of these, the economic benefits of a fall in the amount of damage to vehicles and to real property, the work done by insurance companies, the work of the police and the courts are simple enough. It is the loss of production due to death or, temporarily, to accident or illness which raises complications. However, these complications are exactly the same as those raised in cost-benefit studies of health programs, and so it will be convenient to leave discussion of this general topic until we reach that heading.

This leaves us with the problem of valuing time savings; as these savings often form a very high proportion of total estimated benefits of road improvements, they are extremely important. Unfortunately, these calculations have not so far been very satisfactory.

Whatever the valuation procedure followed, it is necessary to assume that one time saving of sixty minutes is worth the same as sixty savings each lasting one minute, since estimates of the value of time savings of different lengths are unobtainable. On the one hand, it is clear that some short-time savings are valueless, since nothing can be done in the time saved. On the other hand, however, there are cases where the extra time makes possible some activity which would otherwise be precluded, as, for instance, when arriving a little earlier at a theater means that one does not have to wait until the interval to gain one's seat. Similarly, the value of an hour gained may depend partly upon when it is gained. *Faute de mieux*, such variations have to be ignored and an average treated as meaningful.

It is customary to distinguish between working time saved and leisure time saved, valuing the former at the relevant wage-rate, *e.g.*, drivers' wages in the case of buses and lorries. The argument is simply that this is what the worker's time is worth to his employer. As Winch has pointed out, this raises certain difficulties: if the driver does the same work as before, the gain is a matter of his having more leisure, while if he works the same hours as before and does more work, the value of his marginal net product may fall. The first point matters only if leisure time is valued differently from working time, as Winch points out, but the second is awkward, if only in principle.

The various methods that have been proposed for valuing leisure time all rest upon the observation of choices which involve the substitution of leisure for some other good which, in contrast to leisure, does have a market price. Leisure can be substituted:

(i) for wages, net of tax, by workers;
(ii) for transport expenditure, by those who travel in their own time and are able to choose between alternative speeds of travel either directly (as drivers) or indirectly (*e.g.*, train versus bus);
(iii) for housing and transport expenditure, by people who

can choose the location of their dwelling in relation to that of their place of work, and hence determine the length of the journey to work.

Each of these approaches has its difficulties. One difficulty which is common to all of them is that the substitution rarely involves just leisure and money; for example:

(i) A man may refuse to work an extra hour for an extra $1, yet value leisure at less than $1 because extra work involves missing a bus.

(ii) The driver who pays a toll alters the running cost he incurs in order to get to his destination faster by using a toll road is buying not only a time-saving but also the pleasure of driving along a restricted access highway. (A separate and trickier problem is that he may not know the true effect of the change in route and speed upon his car's running costs.)

(iii) A house nearer work may be in a less or more attractive environment.

These problems are surveyed in Winch; Mohring presents the theory underlying the approach via land values and shows how difficult it is to apply in practice; and Moses and Williamson discuss the related problem of passengers' choice between alternative modes of transport and list American applications of the approach via toll-road utilization. A recent piece of research in the United Kingdom (Beesley) produces valuations of time savings on journeys by public transport on the basis of comparing different combinations of cash and time outlays for given journeys; by substituting this result into the comparison of public and private transport opportunities, an estimate of the valuation of time savings by private transport is obtained. It might be noted that those investigations yield markedly lower estimates than those quoted on previous occasions in the United Kingdom (*e.g.*, Foster and Beesley, *Report of Panel on Road Pricing*). So, at the very least, one can say that there are major unknowns which may or may not prove tractable to further analysis.

So far we have made no mention of the many American studies

of the impact of road improvements on bypassed shopping centers, on the value of adjacent property, and on the pattern of land use. This is because, as Mohring and Harwitz explain, these "studies suffer from either or both of two shortcomings: (1) they have concentrated on measuring benefits to specific population groups, and have done so in such a way that *net* benefits to society as a whole cannot be estimated from their results; and/or (2) they have concentrated on measuring highway-related changes in the nature and locus of economic activity and have not isolated those aspects of change that reflect net benefits."

We have concentrated on the application of cost-benefit analysis to a major motorway construction. The same general principles apply in other types of road investment, ranging from the "simple" kind of case such as the Channel Tunnel or the Forth Bridge to the far more complex network problems such as the whole transport system of a metropolitan area. If one wishes to include the *Buchanan Report* notion of "environment" in the calculus for urban road improvements the estimation process is likely to become very complex and laborious, if indeed it is feasible at all. The Report's own attempt to give an empirical filling to the idea is perfunctory in the extreme, but Beesley and Kain have proposed the principle of "environmental compensation" as an operational way of taking some account of environmental benefits and disbenefits in allocating budgeted expenditure on urban roads.

Finally, one might take note of the work of Bos and Koyck. They construct a complete general equilibrium model of a simple economy with three geographical areas and four goods. This involves a series of demand equations, technical equations, supply equations, and definitional equations. They show that a reduction in transport costs between two of these areas will raise national income by much more than the customary estimate of benefits, *i.e.*, the saving of transport costs of existing traffic between these areas plus half the cost of saving for the generated traffic. The essential point is that there is a much fuller allowance for ramifications, *e.g.*, they not only allow for the effects on goods transported but also on goods not transported. This system, of course, requires knowledge of all the demand and supply equations in the economy, so is scarcely capable of application by road engineers. It does, however, serve to remind us of the limitations of partial analysis.

(b) *Railways* · Railways have received a great deal less attention than roads from cost-benefit analysis, perhaps because they have, relatively if not absolutely, been a contracting sector of the transport industry in many countries. However, there have been two railway projects which have attracted attention in the United Kingdom in the last few years, and brief reference to them may be sufficient to illustrate the general principles.

In their well-known study of the new Victoria underground line in London, Foster and Beesley followed much the same principles as those employed in cost-benefit studies on the roads. The main benefits were time savings, cost savings (*e.g.*, private vehicle operating costs), extra comfort and convenience, and a variety of gains to Central London resulting from an effective widening of the catchment area. These benefits were distributed among the traffic diverted to the Victoria line, the traffic not so diverted and generated traffic. But by and large, gains by generated traffic were unimportant compared with the other two categories; and of the various categories of savings, time savings amounted to almost half the total. When compared with the totality of costs involved in constructing and maintaining the line over a fifty year period it was found that there was a "social surplus rate of return" of something of the order of 11 percent, the precise figure depending on the rate of interest chosen. The reasons why this rate of return is much greater than any financial or accounting return were said to be two-fold: first, that London Transport's policy of averaging fares over different modes of traveling from one place to another meant that potential money receipts would underestimate benefits, and second, that potential revenue was reduced by the fact that road users are not charged the full social cost of the resources they absorb.

Although the proposals in the Beeching Report for closing down sections of the United Kingdom main-line railway system were not couched in cost-benefit terms, various commentators (*e.g.*, Ray and Crum) have looked at these aspects. The financial savings of the measures in view can be classified under four heads:

improved methods of working, increased charges to some particular users (*e.g.*, National Coal Board), the savings from closing
commuter lines, and the savings from rural closures. The first of
these clearly represents a social as well as a financial saving, and
need not detain us further. The second is more debatable; raising
charges does not as such save any real resources, but it is
possible that it would stimulate some savings of cost, and so to
that extent would involve a social gain. In so far as the closure
of commuter lines leads to further road congestion in large cities,
the social saving is likely to be very small indeed, if anything
at all. Finally, the closure of rural lines involves questions such
as redundancies of specialist labor in out-of-the-way areas, extra
road maintenance, more road accidents, lengthier journeys, etc.
We are not concerned with the details of such calculations, but
it might be noted that the overall result of Beeching would seem
to be a substantial saving in real terms, even if not quite as large
as the financial one. This does, however, leave out many intangibles, such as the more indirect and longer-term effects on
particular regions, *e.g.*, the North of Scotland; and no one, to our
knowledge, has suggested any unique and convincing way of
quantifying and incorporating such repercussions in the analysis.

To summarize, the principles developed in the analysis of road
improvements can fairly readily be applied to railway investment
and in the assessment of the overall consequences of railway
closures. As before, time savings are an important item in many
cases, and to the extent that we are still very ignorant of how to
crack this hardest of nuts, we are still in a position of intellectual
discomfort.

(c) *Inland Waterways* · A good deal of work has been done in
the United States on the estimation of benefits from new canals
or from rendering an existing river channel navigable. It has been
discussed especially by Eckstein and Renshaw. This is of interest
both for its own sake and for the light it throws on other transport
fields.

Let us start with some points first made by Dupuit and raised
diagrammatically by Renshaw. Let DD in Figure 1 be the
demand curve for transport of a given commodity along a
specified route and OF_r be the present rail freight rate. Then
F_rR will be the existing volume of traffic. If a canal were buil

FIGURE 1

INLAND WATERWAYS

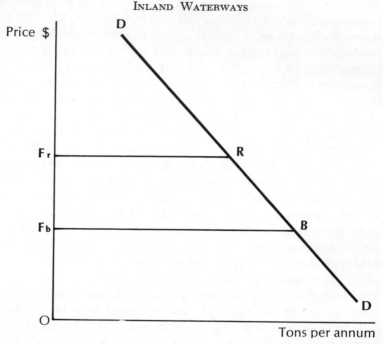

and the barge freight rate were OF_b traffic would expand to F_bB and the gain to shippers would be F_rRBF_b. This can be approximated by multiplying the existing volume of traffic F_rR by the unit freight saving F_rF_b, and this is the procedure followed in practice, *e.g.*, by the United States Corps of Engineers.

We now bring in complications.

1. The gain to shippers will not measure social gain unless freight rates adequately reflect marginal social costs. The main reason why this may not be so is that railways are frequently subject to regulation. Thus, if the freight receipts of the railway from the traffic in question exceed its avoidable costs, part of the gain to shippers is merely a transfer from the railway's owners, and must be deducted to obtain a measure of the social benefit from the canal.

2. The single demand curve of the diagram is a legitimate

construction only when neither canal nor railway are part of a network and only when they both link exactly the same points. If neither of these conditions is fulfilled a more complicated construction is required, since total system rail traffic and total system barge traffic are both functions of both rail and barge freight rates (including shippers' terminal costs). The net gain to shippers who direct traffic from rail to a canal joining points A and B will differ from the simple product of the freight rate differential between A and B and the number of tons of freight diverted to the canal because:

(i) There may be a saving or gain in transport costs beyond A and B. Consider, for example, traffic from A to C; this may previously have gone by rail all the way without going through B.

(ii) There may be a saving or gain in costs other than freight. Thus, if canal is slower than rail more working capital will be required.

(iii) The railway may cut its freight rate in response to competition from the canal, so reducing the amount of traffic diverted. This is discussed by Eckstein with examples.

Taking these three complications into account we find that the social benefit from the canal (gross of its costs) equals:

The saving in railway system costs
Less barge costs
Less increase in shippers' other costs
Plus the value to shippers of generated traffic on the canal.

This amount will be less than the product of the diverted traffic volume and the rail-canal freight rate differential unless the consumers' surplus on generated canal traffic outweighs any excess of railway rates over avoidable costs, any deficit between canal freight rates and barge costs and any increase in shippers' other costs. Thus, except where traffic generation is expected to be large, multiplying the rate differential by traffic diversion may exaggerate benefits.

An example of the application of these techniques in a particular case relates to a cross-Florida barge canal. The following figures were produced:

$000 per annum

Item	Corps of Engineers	Consultants' evaluation
Amortisation, interest, maintenance	5,960	8,235
Transportation savings	6,980	1,102
Commercial fishing boats' benefits	70	0
Contractor's floating equipment benefits	30	0
New vessel delivery benefits	110	0
Recreational boating benefits	110	0
Flood control benefits	240	0
Enhancement of waterfront land values	590	0
Benefit-cost ratio	1.20	0.13

To what extent the divergence is due to the facts that the Corps likes to build canals and that the consultants were retained by the railroads, and to what extent it is due to the intrinsic impossibility of making accurate estimates is left entirely to the reader to decide!

3. LAND USAGE

(a) *Urban Renewal* · The application of cost-benefit analysis to proposals for redevelopment projects in towns has been discussed by Rothenberg and by Lichfield, both of whom have provided partial examples. The problem is complicated by the large number of types of people or institutions involved in urban development. Thus, the public acquisition of all private property in a slum area which is then redeveloped may involve more than one public agency, the dispossessed property owners, dispossessed tenants, owners, and tenants of property adjacent to the redevelopment area, owners and tenants in other areas affected by the search for alternative accommodation on the part of the dispossessed tenants, potential developers and tenants of the cleared area, and finally, the population of the town at large, both as taxpayers who meet some of the cost and (more indirectly) in so far as they suffer any adverse consequence from the slum.

Lichfield is primarily concerned to show how all the costs and benefits to all affected parties can be systematically recorded in a set of accounts. The arguments in favor of proceeding this way instead of by simply listing and evaluating the net amount of each type of cost or benefit are threefold. First, starting on an all-inclusive gross basis and then cancelling out to obtain net social benefits and costs insures against omissions. Second, the financial consequences of any project are sometimes important, and it may need to be redesigned in the light of the distribution of benefits and costs so as to compensate parties who would other- wise stand to lose from it, securing their support for it. The notion of compensation is familiar enough in welfare economics; here is a case where it can be important in practice. Third, whether or not financial transfers are used to affect the final distribution of net gains, that distribution will often be relevant to choice. In practice, that is to say, for good or bad reasons, the attitude of a county council or similar body towards a scheme will depend upon who gains as well as upon how much they gain. As the client of the cost-benefit analyst, it will therefore want to know more than just the total net figures.

Rothenberg discusses those types of benefits from urban development projects which involve slum clearance (mentioning other, aesthetic, considerations in a footnote). The first is the "internalization of market externalities," which we discuss in a moment, the second is the effect on real income distribution, and the third consists of the reduction in fire risks, crime, and other social consequences of slum living.

By internalizing market externalities, Rothenberg is thinking of the improvement of efficiency in resource allocation which can be achieved when a neighborhood is regarded as a unit where previously each of the separate owners in it had paid no regard to the adverse effects upon other owners' property of the inadequate maintenance of his own. Leaving aside a property tax complication which arises in the United States, Rothenberg's basic suggestion is that the social gain is measured by the increase in the total site value of the redevelopment area ("the value of the increased productivity of the land on the redevelopment site") corrected for any change in locational advantages brought about by redevelopment plus any increase in the value of properties adjacent to the redevelopment area resulting from its physical improvement (*i.e.*, technological externalities). The nature of the locational advantages is not very clear, and the convenient assumption that the sum of locational effects in the town as a whole is zero requires a good deal of justification.

Another difficulty relates to the increment of site values. The relevance of site values after slum clearance is obvious enough, since these values are the capitalized values of the rents to be had from the new buildings which are most appropriate, less the present value of the costs of erecting and maintaining those buildings. But the relevance of site values in the absence of a redevelopment scheme is not so clear.

A second difficulty with Rothenberg's expositions is that the illustrative example of his technique is an *ex-post* one. This introduces problems which are irrelevant to the *ex-ante* calculations that are required if the technique is ever to be of use. How different an actual past change in land value would have been if things had been different, that is to say, is no concern of the man making forward-looking estimates. His problem is to estimate how much the site would sell for if not only it but also all the surrounding sites were to be redeveloped. The way to answer this question is surely to start with an estimate of the rental or selling value of new accommodation in the improved area and then deduct for building costs. But does this not require the art of the valuer as much as the science of the economist or econometrician?

(b) *Recreation* · The problem of estimating and valuing recreational gains or losses due to projects has received a good deal of attention in the United States, where much of the discussion has been usefully surveyed by Clawson. An example of the problem is provided by the conflict between the provision of hydroelectric power and the preservation of the salmon runs in the Pacific Northwest (though this involves commercial fishing as well as sports fishing), while the gain to pleasure-boating from harbor improvements constitutes another case.

The principle is clear enough: what is needed in any particular case, on the benefit side, is measurement of the demand curve for access to the recreational facility in question. In practice, however, the choice has often lain between getting a figure by the wrong method and not getting one by the right method. Thus,

Crutchfield lists four invalid techniques that have been used in the case of sports fishing.

(a) The argument that recreational facilities should not, in principle, be measured in money terms and that some level of provision should thus be arbitrarily set regardless of competing demands.

(b) Expenditure on providing and using the fishery. This merely measures the size of the sport fishing industry, but provides no indication of the loss that would be sustained if it disappeared.

(c) Imputing to sport fishing the market value of the fish caught, which implies that the angler is simply out to get some food.

(d) Valuing anglers' fishing time at the earnings the anglers could have acquired by working. This implies, among other things, that every hour spent in any kind of recreation is equally valuable.

The method proposed by Clawson and Trice and Wood, though statistically dubious, in practice does at least attempt to get at an imputed demand curve. The basic idea is to deduce the amount of usage at different "prices" from data of differential travel (and other) costs actually incurred in utilizing recreational facilities. If visitors to a recreation area come from a series of concentric zones one can reasonably postulate that anyone coming from the nearest zone enjoys a consumer's surplus which can be measured by the difference between his travel costs and those incurred by a man coming from the farthest zone. (There is an implicit assumption that the inner-zone resident derives as much satisfaction from a visit as the outer-zone man, but in a situation where approximations have to be made this does not seem too wild a one.) It is understood that this notion is due basically to Hotelling, and that use has been made of it in an Upper Feather River basin study. Unfortunately, it ignores the point that part of the consumers' surplus derived from proximity may be swallowed up in residential rent.

(c) *Land Reclamation* · A Dutch paper describes the use of cost-benefit analysis for evaluating land-reclamation schemes.

The particular points singled out are the insistence that one must not overlook related investment expenditure (*e.g.*, for the manufacture of raw materials for use on reclaimed land or for processing) and the corresponding returns, the use of foreign exchange shadow prices for such calculations as the expected saving in imports, allowances for harm done to fisheries and for benefits to road traffic and a general recognition of the widespread nature and importance of intangibles ("indeterminables" in Dutch-English). This is in no sense a complete listing of the relevant variables, but may be sufficient to savor the flavor of the dish.

4. HEALTH

The major purpose of health programs is to save lives and reduce illness, and on this score there is some overlap with flood-prevention and road-improvement measures. There are no special problems which relate to the estimate of the costs of such programs, and the special problem of quantifying their effects is a matter for engineers and doctors rather than for economists. The interest of the latter is thus concentrated on the problem of valuing the benefits per life saved or per illness avoided, and this is all we shall consider here. And even within this limited area, we shall devote most of our time to the former. Our task is aided by the work of Weisbrod, and the useful surveys of Mushkin and Klarman. It might be further noted that this subject is a well-established one, having attracted the attention of Irving Fisher many years ago.

Before exploring the conceptual problems, it should be noted that some of the differences between authors in the way they estimate benefits stem from differences in the availability of statistics rather than from differences in what the authors would like to measure if they could. Thus, some of the simplifications in Reynolds' classic paper on the cost of road accidents were surely dictated by statistical exigencies rather than by considerations of high principle. This paper at least has the merit that after calculating the average costs in 1952 of various consequences of accidents (death, injury, property damage, insurance, administrative costs) the author went on, in an appendix, to show how his results could be used to estimate the purely economic benefits that would have accrued from new pedestrian crossing regulations and from adequate rear lighting on all vehicles and cycles. A death avoided means that a loss of production may be avoided. Thus the present value of this is an economic benefit to be credited to the measure responsible for saving life. The first step in estimating it is to ascertain what the average person whose life is made safer will earn over the rest of his life. This depends upon age at death, the probability of survival to each higher age, the proportion of people at each age who will both be in the labor force and employed, and their contribution to production at each age.

(a) Age at death of those whose lives would be saved can be assumed to equal the average age of all those who die from whatever it is, unless the proposed life-saving expenditure obviously discriminates between age groups.

(b) The probability of survival to each age can be calculated from a life table for the group at risk, which should be amended to take account of any projected changes in its age-specific death-rates.

(c) Participation rates have to be forecast. It is generally agreed that the appropriate unemployment percentage to assume is that corresponding to "full employment."

(d) The earnings of a person are usually taken as a measure of the value of his marginal product, average product being obviously too high. Since it is future earnings which are relevant, the trend of growth in earnings should be allowed for if the analysis starts with figures of current earnings.

In practice, Weisbrod was able to construct estimates only for all men and all women and not for any particular group at risk, on account of data limitations. He and Reynolds both took earnings in a recent year without making any addition for future productivity increases.

The question whether housewives' services should be included as lost production has produced some discussion. Since there can be no question but that the loss of these services does impose a cost upon the survivors, it would sometimes bias choice to disregard the services of housewives in calculating production loss.

As Klarman points out, the distribution of diseases between the sexes is not uniform, so that the relative economic benefits of different health programs will be affected by the weight given to housewives' services. What is really at issue, therefore, is how to measure their value, not whether to measure it. One possibility is to estimate their opportunity cost, *i.e.*, what housewives could earn in paid jobs (net of taxes and extra expenses), since this provides a minimum estimate of what the services are worth to the family. Alternatively, replacement cost, *i.e.*, the cost of a housekeeper, could be used. Weisbrod develops a very ingenious measure along these lines, where the value of a housewife's services is an increasing function of the number of other persons in her family. Neither measure can be accurately estimated in practice.

An even larger question is that of consumption. If society loses the production of the decedent, does it not also gain by not having to supply his own consumption? The answer is a matter of definition. If society is defined to exclude the decedent, the loss is confined to the wealth he would have accumulated and the taxes he would have paid less the transfers he would have received, and would be borne partly by his heirs and partly by the Government on behalf of all other taxpayers. It thus constitutes the amount which society so defined would find it worthwhile to pay to save his life (leaving aside all non-materialistic considerations for later discussion). Now the society whose representatives decide whether or not to undertake a measure which would save lives includes those people who may lose their lives if the proposed measure is not undertaken. Hence, so the argument might run, society is relevantly defined as including the prospective decedent, and his consumption is part of the social loss contingent upon his death.

Those, like Weisbrod, who take the line that consumption should be deducted have to face the problem of estimating it, and Weisbrod does so with commendable ingenuity. He argues that marginal rather than average consumption is relevant, and measures this as the change in family consumption with a change in family size, given income. Using family budget data, he calculates for each age bracket a weighted mean of the marginal consumption of persons in mean-income families of all sizes. It is only fair to add that he is far from dogmatic about the virtues of this approach.

Whether or not consumption is deducted, the economic value of a life saved varies according to a variety of factors, including age (it rises during childhood and falls after a certain age because of the twin influences of life earning patterns and discounting). Other things being equal, therefore, these calculations are worth undertaking only if we believe that more resources should be devoted to saving a more "productive" life than a less "productive" life—*e.g.*, the average man in preference to the average woman of the same age, a white Protestant American in preference to a colored one, the average Englishman rather than the average Scot, a young worker rather than a baby.

To put the question this way outrages many people's feelings who do not see that the "other things" which are here assumed "equal" include one's estimate of the moral worth and human value of the different people and of the sorrow caused by their death. Without taking any position, therefore, we pass on to consider the non-economic value of a human life. By this we mean merely the amount which it is worth sacrificing in economic terms to save a life. It is less than infinity (since there are avoidable deaths), it exceeds zero (since money is spent to save lives) and it is worth ascertaining (in so far as consistent decision-making implies such a value).

The problem has been discussed by two French authors (Thedié and Abraham) with a certain Gallic elegance which does not entirely conceal the (necessary) arbitrariness of their procedure. They speak of "affective" loss and distinguish: affective injury to the family, affective injury to the rest of the nation, *pretium doloris*, and *pretium vivendi*, the last two corresponding to the prospective decedent's aversion to suffering and death respectively. Court judgments, they consider, "should . . . make it possible in each country to obtain an average opinion as regards the sums to be spent to avoid the various affective losses."

Estimates of the benefits to be had from reducing illness, relating to particular diseases, offer no new problems of principle but involve great statistical difficulties. Mushkin discusses some of the principles, making the useful distinction between the effects of disability (*e.g.*, loss of working time) and debility (*e.g.*, loss of capacity while at work). Weisbrod and Klarman also raise valuable pointers. But the fundamental difficulty—and this affects the loss through deaths arguments too—is that of the multiplicity of variables—when there are manifold influences at work on life-expectancy, productivity, and the like, how can one hope to sort out the unambiguous influence of a particular health program or any other single causative factor?

Finally, mention should be made of a different approach to all those problems, even though, as far as we are aware, it is not one which has been pursued. This stresses that the problem is essentially the *ex-ante* one of deciding how much to spend in reducing various kinds of risk. Since people in their private capacities do incur costs to reduce risks to which they and their children are exposed, it is conceivable that their valuation of diminutions in risk could be inferred from their behavior.

The Utilization of Existing Water Supplies

JACK HIRSHLEIFER, JAMES DE HAVEN, AND JEROME MILLIMAN

Jack Hirshleifer is Professor of Economics at the University of California at Los Angeles; James De Haven is at the RAND Corporation; and Jerome Milliman is at Indiana University. This piece is from their book, Water Supply, published in 1960.

1. EFFICIENCY EFFECTS AND DISTRIBUTION EFFECTS

The economic effects of any proposed policy can be divided under two headings: the effects on *efficiency* and the effects on *distribution*. Efficiency questions relate to the size of the pie available; distribution questions, to who gets what share. More formally, we can think of the pie as representing the national income or community income. Someone may propose reducing income taxes in the upper brackets on the ground that the high rates now effective there seriously deter initiative and enterprise and so reduce national income; he is making an efficiency argument that the present taxes reduce the size of the national pie. Someone else may point out that such a change will help large taxpayers as against small—a distributional consideration. In the field of water supply it is possible to find examples in the West where a certain amount of water could produce goods and services more highly valued in the market place if it were shifted from agricultural to industrial uses—this is an efficiency argument. On the other hand, this shift may hurt the interests of farmers or of their customers, employees, or suppliers while helping industrial interests—all distributional considerations.

Now economics can say something of the distributional consequences of alternative possible policies, but what it says stops short of any assertion that any man's interests or well-being can be preferred to another's. The fact that economics has nothing to say on such matters does not mean, of course, that nothing important can be said. Ethics as a branch of philosophy and the entire structure of law (which to some extent embodies or applies ethical thought) are devoted to the consideration of the rights and duties of man against man, and many propositions arising out of such thought may well command almost unanimous consent in our society. Ethics may say that no one should be permitted to starve, and law that no one should be deprived of property without due process, but these are propositions outside economics.

Most of what the existing body of economic thought has to say concerns the *efficiency* effects—the effects on size of the pie—of alternative possible policies or institutional arrangements. There is, of course, a sense in which enlarging the size of the pie may be said to be good for the eaters as a group irrespective of the distribution of shares. This sense turns upon the *possibility* of dividing the enlarged pie in such a way that everybody benefits. If such a distribution of the gain is not adopted, there may or may not be good reason for the failure to do so, but the reason is presumed to be legal or ethical and so outside the sphere of economic analysis. Economics alone cannot give us answers to policy problems; it can show us how to attain efficiency and what the distributional consequences are of attaining efficiency in alternative possible ways, but it does not tell us how to distribute the gain from increased efficiency.

It is true that it is often the case that the efficiency and distributional consequences of a proposed change cannot be so neatly separated. Any particular change in the direction of efficiency will involve a certain intrinsic distribution of gains and losses, and in practice it may be unfeasible to effect a redistribution such that everyone gains. Nevertheless, we feel that a presumption in favor of changes increasing the national income is justified, while conceding that this presumption can be defeated if there are irreparable distributive consequences that are sufficiently offensive on ethical or legal grounds.

Nothing is more common in public discussions of economic affairs, however, than a consideration of distributive effects of any change to the utter exclusion of the efficiency question. The agricultural price-support policy, for example, is usually and fruitlessly discussed pro and con in terms of the interests of farmers versus the interests of consumers and taxpayers. But a policy of expensive storage of perishing commodities to hold them out of human consumption is, obviously, inefficient. Concentration upon the efficiency question might readily suggest solutions that would increase the national income and would help consumers and taxpayers a great deal while hurting farmers relatively little or not at all.

2. THE PRINCIPLE OF EQUIMARGINAL VALUE IN USE

Suppose for simplicity we first assume that the stock or the annual flow of a resource like water becomes available without cost, the only problem being to allocate the supply among the competing uses and users who desire it. Economic theory asserts one almost universal principle which characterizes a good or efficient allocation—the principle we shall here call "equimarginal value in use." The *value in use* of any unit of water, whether purchased by an ultimate or an intermediate consumer, is essentially measured by the *maximum* amount of resources (dollars) which the consumer would be willing to pay for that unit. *Marginal* value in use is the value in use of the last unit consumed, and for any consumer marginal value in use will ordinarily decline as the quantity of water consumed in any period increases. The principle, then, is that the resource should be so allocated that all consumers or users derive equal value in use from the marginal unit consumed or used.

An example of the process of equating marginal values in use may be more illuminating than an abstract proof that this principle characterizes efficient allocations. Suppose that my neighbor and I are both given rights (ration coupons, perhaps) to certain volumes of water, and we wish to consider whether it might be in our mutual interest to trade these water rights between us for other resources—we might as well say for dollars, which we can think of as a generalized claim on other resources like clam chowders, baby-sitting services, acres of land, or yachts. My neighbor might be a farmer and I an industrialist, or we might both be just retired homeowners; to make the quantities interesting, we will assume that both individuals are rather big operators. Now suppose that the last acre-foot of my periodic entitlement is worth $10 at most to me, but my neighbor would be willing to pay anything up to $50 for that right—a disparity of $40 between our marginal values in use. Evidently, if I transfer the right to him for any compensation between $10 and $50, we will both be better off in terms of our own preferences; in other words, the size of the pie measured in terms of the satisfactions yielded to both of us has increased. (Note, however, that the question of whether the compensation should be $11 or $49 is purely distributional.)

But this is not yet the end. Having given up one acre-foot, I will not be inclined to give up another on such easy terms—water has become scarcer for me, so that an additional amount given up means foregoing a somewhat more urgent use. Conversely, my neighbor is no longer quite so anxious to buy as he was before, since his most urgent need for one more acre-foot has been satisfied, and an additional unit must be applied to less urgent uses. That is, for both of us marginal values in use decline with increases of consumption (or, equivalently, marginal value in use rises if consumption is cut back). Suppose he is now willing to pay up to $45, while I am willing to sell for anything over $15. Evidently, we should trade again. Obviously, the stopping point is where the last (or marginal) unit of water is valued equally (in terms of the greatest amount of dollars we would be willing to pay) by the two of us, based on the use we can make of or the benefit we can derive from the last or marginal unit. At this point no more mutually advantageous trades are available—efficiency has been attained.

Generalizing from the illustration just given, we may say that the principle of equimarginal value in use asserts that an efficient allocation of water has been attained when no mutually advantageous exchanges are possible between any pair of claimants, which can only mean that each claimant values his last or marginal unit of water equally with the others, measured in terms of the quantity of other resources (or dollars) that he is willing to trade for an additional unit of water.

What institutional arrangements are available for achieving water allocations that meet the principle of equimarginal value in use? Our example suggests that rationing out rights to the available supply will tend to lead to an efficient result if trading of the ration coupons is freely permitted; this is true so long as it can be assumed that third parties are unaffected by the trades. More generally, any such vesting of property rights, whether originally administrative, inherited, or purchased, will tend to an efficient solution if trading is permitted. (The question of the basis underlying the original vesting of rights is a serious and important one, but it is a distributional question.) A rather important practical result is derived from this conclusion if we put the argument another way: however rights are vested, we are effectively *preventing* efficiency from being attained if the law forbids free trading of those rights. Thus, if our ration coupons are not transferable, efficiency can be achieved only if the original distribution of rights was so nicely calculated that equimarginal value in use prevailed to begin with and that thenceforth no forces operated to change these values in use. As a practical matter, these conditions could never be satisfied. Nevertheless, legal limitations on the owner's ability to sell or otherwise transfer vested water rights are very common. While at times valid justification at least in part may exist for such limitations (one example is where third parties are injured by such transfers), it seems often to be the case that these prohibitions simply inflict a loss upon all for no justifiable reason. We shall examine some instances of limitations on freedom of transfer in a later section.

It is important to note here that the market price of water rights or ration coupons, if these can be freely traded, will tend to settle at (and so to measure) the marginal value in use of the consumers in the market. Any consumer who found himself with so many coupons that the marginal value in use to him was less than market price would be trying to sell some of his rights, while anyone with marginal value in use greater than market price which can only mean that each claimant values his last or marginal unit of water equally with the others, measured in terms of the quantity of other resources (or dollars) that he is willing to trade for an additional unit of water.

What institutional arrangements are available for achieving water allocations that meet the principle of equimarginal value in use? Our example suggests that rationing out rights to the available supply will tend to lead to an efficient result if trading of the ration coupons is freely permitted; this is true so long as it can be assumed that third parties are unaffected by the trades. More generally, any such vesting of property rights, whether originally administrative, inherited, or purchased, will tend to an efficient solution if trading is permitted. (The question of the basis underlying the original vesting of rights is a serious and important one, but it is a distributional question.) A rather important practical result is derived from this conclusion if we put the argument another way: however rights are vested, we are effectively *preventing* efficiency from being attained if the law forbids free trading of those rights. Thus, if our ration coupons are not transferable, efficiency can be achieved only if the original distribution of rights was so nicely calculated that equimarginal value in use prevailed to begin with and that thenceforth no forces operated to change these values in use. As a practical matter, these conditions could never be satisfied. Nevertheless, legal limitations on the owner's ability to sell or otherwise transfer vested water rights are very common. While at times valid justification at least in part may exist for such limitations (one example is where third parties are injured by such transfers), it seems often to be the case that these prohibitions simply inflict a loss upon all for no justifiable reason. We shall examine some instances of limitations on freedom of transfer in a later section.

It is important to note here that the market price of water rights or ration coupons, if these can be freely traded, will tend to settle at (and so to measure) the marginal value in use of the consumers in the market. Any consumer who found himself with so many coupons that the marginal value in use to him was less than market price would be trying to sell some of his rights, while anyone with marginal value in use greater than market price former holder of the privilege will lose as compared with all others. The attainment of efficiency in the new situation means that it is *possible* to insure that everyone is better off. But whether it is or is not desirable to provide the compensation required to balance the loss of the formerly preferred customers is a distributional question.

Our discussion of the principle of equimarginal value in use has led to two rules of behavior necessary if efficiency is to be achieved in different institutional contexts: (1) If rights to water are vested as property, there should be no restrictions on the purchase and sale of such rights, so long as third parties are unaffected. (2) If water is being sold, the price should be equal to all customers. This second rule was derived, however, under a special assumption that the water became available without cost. More generally, there will be costs incurred in the acquisition and transport of water supplies to customers; taking costs into account requires a second principle for pricing of water in addition to the principle of equimarginal value in use.

3. THE PRINCIPLE OF MARGINAL-COST PRICING

In our previous discussion we assumed that a certain volume or flow of water became available without cost, the problem being to distribute just that amount among the potential customers. Normally, there will not be such a definite fixed amount but rather a situation in which another unit could always be made available by expending more resources to acquire and transport it, that is, at a certain additional or marginal cost. The question of where to stop in increasing the supplies made available is then added to the question just discussed of how to arrange for the allocation of the supplies in hand at any moment of time.

From the argument developed earlier about the allocation of a certain given supply, we can infer that, whatever the price may be, it should be equal to all users (since otherwise employments with higher marginal values in use are being foregone in favor of employments with lower values). Suppose that at a certain moment of time this price is $30 per unit. Then, if the community as a whole can acquire and transport another unit of water for, say, $20, it would clearly be desirable to do so;

in fact, any of the individual customers to whom the unit of water is worth $30 would be happy to pay the $20 cost, and none of the other members of the community is made worse off thereby. We may say that, on efficiency grounds, additional units should be made available so long as any members of the community are willing to pay the additional or marginal costs incurred. To meet the criterion of equimarginal value in use, however, the price should be made equal for all customers. So the combined rule is to make the price equal to the marginal cost and equal for all customers.

One important practical consideration is that, because of differing locations, use patterns, types of services, etc., the marginal costs of serving different customers will vary. It is of some interest to know in principle how this problem should be handled. The correct solution is to arrange matters so that for each class of customers (where the classes are so grouped that all customers *within* any single class can be served under identical cost conditions) the prices should be the same and equal to marginal cost. *Between* classes, however, prices should differ, and the difference should be precisely the difference in marginal costs involved in serving the two.

Consider, for example, a situation in which there are two customers, identical in all respects except that one can be served at a marginal cost of $10 per unit and the other at $40—perhaps because the latter has a hilltop location and requires pumped rather than gravity service. If they are both charged $10, the community will be expending $40 in resources to supply a marginal unit which the latter customer values at $10; if they both are charged $40, the former customer would be happy to lay out the $10 it costs to bring him another unit. The principle of equimarginal value in use which dictates equal prices was based on the assumption that costless transfers could take place between customers, but in this case any transfer from the gravity to the pumped customer involves a cost of $30. Another way to look at the matter is to say that the commodity provided is not the same: the customer who requires pumped water is demanding a more costly commodity than the gravity customer.

Where water is sold to customers, therefore, the principles we have developed indicate that customers served under identical cost conditions should be charged equal prices and that the commodity should be supplied and priced in such a way that the price for each class of service should equal the marginal cost of serving that class. Where marginal costs differ, therefore, prices should differ similarly.

4. LIMITATIONS ON VOLUNTARY EXCHANGE OF WATER RIGHTS

In our theoretical discussion we saw that, given any particular vesting of water rights an efficient allocation will tend to come about if free exchange of these rights between users is permitted. There is in practice, however, a wide variety of limitations upon the free exchange of water rights. Water rights are sometimes attached to particular tracts of land (i.e., the water cannot be transferred except as a package deal with the land), especially under the "riparian" principle; transfers of water rights or of uses within water rights also often must in a number of jurisdictions meet approval of some administrative agency. Some legal codes grant certain "higher" users priority or preference over other, "lower" users, transfers from "higher" to "lower" uses being hindered thereby. As a related point, "higher" uses sometimes have a right of seizure. While voluntary transfers can usually be presumed to make both parties better off, and so be in the direction of increased efficiency, no such presumption applies for compelled transfers through seizure.

The above are all instances of violation of a general proposition about property rights. If property is to be put to its most efficient use, there should be no uncertainty of tenure and no restrictions upon the use to which it may be put. When this is the case, voluntary exchange tends to make the property find the use where it is valued the highest, since this use can outbid all others on the market. Uncertainty of tenure interferes with this process, because people will be unwilling to pay much for property, however valuable, if a perfect right cannot be conveyed, and the existing holder will be wary about making those investments necessary to exploit the full value of the property if there is a risk of seizure. All restrictions upon free choice of use, whether the restriction is upon place, purpose, or transfers to other persons, obviously interfere with the market processes which tend to shift the resource to its most productive use.

The reasons underlying adoption of restrictions like those mentioned above are probably mixed, but at least one of them may have some validity: changes in water use may conceivably affect adversely the interests of third parties, such as complementary users downstream, for whom some protection seems needed. This protection should not, as it usually does, go beyond what is necessary to insure preservation of the rights of the third parties. Under California law, for example, a riparian user might attempt to sell water to a non-riparian user who can use the water more productively, none of the other riparian users being harmed thereby. However, the nonriparian purchaser gains no rights against the other riparian users, who can simply increase their diversions, leaving none for the would-be purchaser. Again, a holder of certain appropriate rights might attempt to sell his rights to another. This transfer in some cases requires approval of an administrative board which protects the rights of third parties but whose latitude goes beyond this and permits disapproval on essentially arbitrary grounds as well.

We may comment here that the growing trend to limitation of water rights to "reasonable use" is by no means a wholly obvious or desirable restriction. We might reflect on the desirability of legislation depriving people of their automobiles or their houses when it is determined in some administrative or judicial process that their use was "unreasonable." The purpose of such legislation is the prevention of certain wastes which, if only free voluntary exchange of water rights without unnecessary restrictions were permitted, would tend naturally to be eliminated by market processes (since efficient users can afford to pay more for water than it is worth to wasteful users).

The question of "higher" and "lower" uses has an interesting history. The California Water Code declares that the use of water for domestic purposes is the highest use of water and that the next highest use is for irrigation. Essentially the same statement has been attributed to the emperor Hammurabi (2250 B.C.), a remarkable demonstration of the persistence of error.

The correct idea underlying this thought seems to be that, if we had to do almost entirely without water, we would use the first little bit available for human consumption directly, and then, as more became available, the next use we would want to consider is providing food through irrigation. Where this argument goes wrong is in failing to appreciate that what we want to achieve is to make the *marginal* values in use (the values of the last units applied to any purpose) equal. It would obviously be mistaken to starve to death for lack of irrigation water applied to crops while using water domestically for elaborate baths and air conditioning; the domestic marginal value in use in such a case would be lower. Similar imbalances can make the marginal value in use in industry higher than it is in either domestic or irrigation uses. Actually, the principle of higher and lower uses is so defective that no one would for a moment consider using it consistently (first saturating domestic uses before using any water for other uses, then saturating irrigation uses, etc.). Rather, the principle enters erratically or capriciously in limiting the perfection of property rights in water applied to "lower" uses, however productive such uses may be.

5. EXISTING PRICING PRACTICES IN WATER SUPPLY

Our analysis of the principles of efficient allocation among competitive users led to the conclusion that prices should be equal for all customers served under equivalent cost conditions and that the price should be set at the marginal cost or the cost of delivering the last unit. Alternatively, we may say that the amount supplied should be such that the marginal cost equals the amount the customer is willing to pay for the marginal unit. There are considerable theoretical and practical complications in this connection which we are reserving for discussion in later chapters, but a general survey of the existing situation will be useful here for contrasting practice with the theoretical principles.

Examination of the allocation arrangements of local systems for domestic, commercial, and industrial water supply (primarily municipally owned) reveals that the great majority allocate water by charging a price for its use. The leading exceptions are in unmetered municipalities where, since water bills are not a function of consumption, water *deliveries* may be considered free to the consumer. While a certain amount is ordinarily charged as a water bill in such cities, this is a fixed sum (or "flat rate") and does not operate as a price does in leading consumers to balance the value of use against the cost of use. According to a report published by the *American City Magazine*, a survey made in 1949 of seventy-two cities discovered that 97.7 percent of the services in those cities were metered. The survey excluded, however, several of the largest cities which were partially under flat rates—New York, Chicago, Philadelphia, Buffalo, and others. Since that time, according to the report, Philadelphia has abandoned the fixed-bill system, and generally it may be said that in the United States a condition of universal metering has been approached. As of 1954, the report estimates that metering covered from 90 to 95 percent of all services. Since unmetered services usually represent the smaller domestic users, the proportion of *use* that is metered is even greater than the proportion of *services*.

In those cases, such as New York City, where some users (primarily domestic) are unmetered while others users are charged a price per unit of water used, our rule of prices equal to marginal cost is violated. An unmetered consumer will proceed to use water until its marginal value in use to him is nil to correspond to its zero price to him. This is of course wasteful, because the water system cannot provide the commodity costlessly, and hence society will lose (setting distributional considerations aside) by the excess of the cost of delivery over the value in use for such units of consumption.

It might be thought that the domestic consumers, who are the unmetered customers almost always (the only other substantial classes of use frequently unmetered are public agencies, such as park, sanitation and especially fire departments), somehow deserve a priority or preference as compared with "intermediate" economic customers like industrial or commercial services. But an intermediate consumer is essentially a final consumer once removed. If consumers are required to pay more for water used in the production of food, clothing, and other items of value than they pay for water for direct consumption, an inefficient disparity in marginal values in use between the different uses will be created. Conversely, on efficiency grounds consumers should not be required to pay *more* for domestic water and for water used in industry than for water used to grow crops, such being the effect of existing policies which commonly grant the irrigation use of water a subsidy over all other uses.

A situation in which different prices are charged to different users, or to the same user for varying quantities of the same commodity, is called one of "price discrimination." While discrimination may under certain conditions be justified on one ground or another, it has the defect of preventing the marginal values in use from being made equal between the favored and the penalized uses or users. The only exception to this statement is where discrimination is applied within the purchases of a single individual—by, for example, a declining block rate. If there are no restrictions on use, the individual concerned will continue to equate all his marginal values in the various uses to the *marginal* price (the price for the last unit or for an additional unit) he must pay for the commodity purchased. So far as his own purchases are concerned, therefore, he will still equalize his marginal values in use for all his different uses. If such a block system is used for a number of individuals, however, marginal values in use will not in general be equated between individuals; some will tend to consume an amount such that they end up in the higher-priced block, and others will end up in the lower.

All price differences for the "same" commodity are not, however, evidence of price discrimination. In fact, there should be some difference of price where an extra delivery cost or processing cost must be incurred in serving certain users. These users can be considered as buying two commodities together—the basic commodity and the special delivery or processing. If the basic commodity is to be equally priced to all users, uses requiring such additional services must be charged more.

Turning to the practical side, we should mention at once that our earlier metering discussion neglected one important consideration: the cost of metering and the associated increase in billing costs. It is clear that the additional cost of meters (especially for a great many small users) may well exceed the possible gains from the rationalization of use which would follow metering. (There would, in general, be an aggregate reduction of use as well.) While this question bears further investigation, the dominant opinion in the field of municipal water supply seems to be that universal metering produces gains that are worth the cost. By way of contrast, it appears that in Great Britain domestic use is never metered.

Even if we turn, however, to a consideration of that part of water supply that is metered, or to systems that are completely metered, we find that some non-uniform pattern of prices typically exists. There are some exceptions. In Chicago, for example, all metered users pay the same price per unit of water delivered. A more typical rate system is that of Los Angeles, where rates vary by type of use and also by amount of use (a declining or "promotional" block rate), with a service charge independent of use but based on size of connection. A rate distinction is also made in Los Angeles between firm service and service that the water department may at its convenience provide or refuse, and in some cases between gravity and pumped services.

Some of these rate differences may not be inconsistent with our theoretical discussion. The rate differential may reflect an extra cost or difficulty of delivering to the customer (or customer class, where it is not worthwhile distinguishing between individual customers) charged the higher price.

Where customers' demands vary in the degree to which they impose a peak load on the system, some differential service or demand charge can be justified. In a sense, the commodity delivered off-peak is not the same as that delivered on-peak. The common system of basing a fixed-sum demand charge on the size of service connection is, however, very crude; it provides no deterrent to the customer's contributing to the peak load. Charging a lower rate for interruptible service is somewhat more reasonable. Ideally, the situation might be handled by having differing on-peak and off-peak prices. In water enterprises storage in the distribution system usually smoothes out diurnal and weekly peaks. The seasonal peak in the summer is important, however. The Metropolitan Water District of Southern California has at times charged a premium price for summer deliveries.

Other differentiations can be justified by increased delivery costs necessary to reach certain classes of customers. A difference in rate between pumped and gravity service, for example, is eminently reasonable. We have not gone into the question of just how great the differences should be, but for the present we shall not consider such differences as violations of the principle of a common per-unit price to all.

Certain frequently encountered differences, which we may now properly call "price discrimination," are not based on any special cost of providing the service in question. In Los Angeles, for example, there is an exceptionally low rate for irrigation use. Domestic, commercial, and industrial services are not distinguished as such, but they are differentially affected by the promotional volume rates. More serious, because much more common, is the system of block rates, with reductions for larger quantities used. There is typically some saving in piping costs to large customers, since a main can be run directly to the service connection, whereas the same volume sold to many small customers would require a distribution network of pipes. Ideally, the cost of laying down the pipes to connect customers to the system should be assessed as one-time charge against the outlet served—or the lump sum could be converted into an annual charge independent of the amount of water consumed, to represent the interest and depreciation on the capital invested by the water system to serve the customer. The point is that, once the pipes are in, the unit marginal cost of serving customers is almost independent of the volume taken. A lower block rate leads therefore to wasteful use of water by large users, since small users would value the same marginal unit of water more highly if delivered to them. We may say that the promotional or block-rate system in the case of water leads to a discrimination in favor of users of water that happen to find it convenient to use a great deal of the commodity and against users that do not need as much water. The customer paying the lower price will on the margin be utilizing water for less valuable purposes than it could serve if transferred to the customer paying the higher price.

Because of the enormous fraction of water being used for irrigational purposes unusual interest attaches to the method by which water supplies of such projects are allocated to individual users. Not all irrigation water, of course, is distributed through an irrigation district or enterprise, a great deal being simply pumped or diverted by individual users. Such individual users can be considered to pay a price for water in the form of the costs actually incurred in its acquisition for irrigation purposes.

Reliable information is not available on the cost of water to irrigators, partly because of the differing methods of charging for water. The 1950 Census presented an over-all national average of $1.66 per acre-foot in 1949. This figure is not very meaningful, since it is the result of dividing water charges *per acre* by an estimate of average deliveries of water per acre. But the water charges per acre depend, for farmers served by an irrigation district or other supply enterprise, upon the terms of the "payment complex," which may include taxes and assessments, acreage charge, and service fees in addition to the water price.

Unfortunately, there do not seem to be any nationally compiled data on the methods used by irrigation enterprises to charge for water supplied. A tabulation by the Irrigation Districts Association of California indicates considerable variation in practice: some districts make no charge except by assessment of property; others charge a flat rate, either (1) a fixed amount per acre or (2), depending upon the crop, a variable amount per acre; still others charge a price per unit of water, either on a fixed or on a declining block (promotional) basis; still others have a mixture of pricing methods. Where no charge or only a flat-rate charge is made for water, the marginal price of water to the user would be zero if in fact the user can take unlimited quantities as a domestic consumer normally can (subject only to the limited size of his connection). But it seems to be fairly common practice in irrigation districts that the water is more or less rationed to the user; any "price" set is a fiscal measure to cover the operating and maintenance costs of the district and not a market price in the ordinary sense. We have seen that, with rationing of rights, efficiency can be achieved when trading is permitted. Purchase of water rights in irrigation districts normally takes place through purchase of land, which is usually freely possible (except for the so-called 160-acre limitation in Bureau of Reclamation projects), or through purchase of stock in mutual water companies. It may be remarked that a flat rate per acre varying by the type of crop grown is a kind of crude price, the higher flat rate generally corresponding to the more water-intensive crop. Irrigation districts may achieve reasonably efficient water allocations, but perhaps more often through the purchase of rights rather than the correct pricing of water itself. Where the water right cannot be detached from the land, this limitation on sale will create some inefficiency.

DATE DUE

DISPLAY			
8:00	Nov 13		
NOV 13 '78			
OCT 11 1983			
DEC 13 1983			
MAY 22 84			
MAY 15 1984			
GAYLORD			PRINTED IN U.S.A.